"*A TREASURE* . . . impeccably researched and packed with information never before revealed . . ."
—Ann Rule, author of *The Stranger Beside Me*

"*COMPELLING . . . UNFLINCHING* . . . non-fiction written like a novel, composed with a rare combination of fleshy detail and metaphors usually found only in *The New York Review Of Books*."
—*Los Angeles Herald-Examiner*

"The first cohesive, thoroughly researched book about the murders and the love-hate relationship between the two cousins . . . dramatic and chilling."
—*Rochester Times-Union*

"Certain to be a major hit with true-crime readers."
—*ALA Booklist*

"A deeply disturbing book—cool, ironical and ferocious."
—Thomas Flanagan, author of *The Year of the French*

"*ENTHRALLING* . . . this vivid book holds us minute by minute with the acts of two men who elected wickedness."
—Hugh Kenner, writer and critic

D0448735

TWO OF A KIND
The Hillside Stranglers

Darcy O'Brien

A SIGNET BOOK

NEW AMERICAN LIBRARY

A DIVISION OF PENGUIN BOOKS USA INC., NEW YORK
PUBLISHED IN CANADA BY
PENGUIN BOOKS CANADA LIMITED, MARKHAM, ONTARIO

A hardcover edition of *Two of a Kind* was published
simultaneously by New American Library and, in Canada,
by The New American Library of Canada Limited (now Penguin
Books Canada Limited)

 SIGNET TRADEMARK REG. U.S. PAT. OFF. AND FOREIGN COUNTRIES
REGISTERED TRADEMARK—MARCA REGISTRADA
HECHO EN DRESDEN, TN.

SIGNET, SIGNET CLASSIC, MENTOR, ONYX, PLUME, MERIDIAN
and NAL BOOKS are published by New American Library, a division of
Penguin Books USA Inc., 1633 Broadway, New York, New York 10019

First Signet Printing, March, 1987

. 6 7 8 9 10 11 12

PRINTED IN THE UNITED STATES OF AMERICA

To
Benedict Kiely,
cher maître,

and

Patrick MacEntee,
senior counsel

Lex non favet delicatorum votis, neque liber meus.

—after a legal maxim

[The law does not favor the wishes of the delicate. Neither does my book.]

CONTENTS

PREFACE

In the urban America of today, murder has become so commonplace that it often goes almost unnoticed. Occasionally, however, even in a society numbed by violence, analysis, and explanation, certain murders gain publicity by virtue of their peculiar horrors. Ordinary citizens recognize for the moment that they and the civilized life their democracy is supposed to protect are under threat. The routines of daily life are interrupted by a mass anxiety. We grow afraid.

Such was the atmosphere of Los Angeles in recent years, when the term "Hillside Strangler" entered the city's and, given the efficiency of modern communications, even the nation's vocabulary. Actually there were two Hillside Stranglers, but the singular cropped up first and tended to stick. They were cousins, aged forty-four and twenty-six at the time they began killing women in Los Angeles in 1977. Between October of that year and February 1978, they raped, tortured, and strangled to death ten young women and girls, dumping the bruised and stripped bodies mostly on hillsides northeast of downtown. During Thanksgiving week alone five bodies turned up, the victims ranging in age from twelve to twenty-eight.

That was when the panic set in. These five were linked to at least three other killings. In December another body was found nude and spread-eagled on a hillside facing City Hall, as though the killers were making an obscene and defiant gesture toward the city itself. After the New Year, it appeared that the killers had had their fill. They were at large, but by the end of January the city began to breathe a little easier, and stories about the Hillside murders dwindled in the newspapers and on television. But then in February another body: this an eighteen-year-old girl stuffed into the trunk of her new car, which had been pushed over a cliff high on Angeles Crest. The panic renewed itself. Public anger turned on the police, who despite a task force numbering nearly a hundred officers seemed baffled.

Women, if they had to go out at all at night, hurried from their cars to what they hoped was the safety of their houses. Yet one victim, a student at the Pasadena Art Center of Design, appeared to have been abducted from her own apartment; another had apparently been dragged from her car parked just across the street from her parents' house. The victims seemed to have been picked at random and from various parts of the sprawling city: Hollywood, Glendale, the San Fernando Valley. No neighborhood felt safe. The killer or killers might strike anywhere. One victim had been waiting for a bus in Hollywood; another had last been seen leaving her Glendale apartment in her car to go to work.

Nor were the victims alike in appearance or occupation. One was black, one Hispanic, the others Caucasians ranging from dark to fair. The first two and the eighth victims had been prostitutes, the others students and working women. The killers appeared indifferent only to the old; otherwise their tastes were catholic.

Then abruptly the killings stopped. Had the

Strangler or Stranglers simply had enough, or were they afraid of getting caught? Would they resume their spree, once they thought the heat was off? The police had made a couple of arrests, but these suspects proved innocent of the Hillside murders. The first anniversary of the first killing passed with no important, nerve-flaying questions answered. Not even the actual site of the murders, if there was one site, was known. Psychiatrists offered psychological profiles of the killer or killers, but their opinions were contradictory, linked only by the theme of hatred of women.

In January 1979, the case broke. The younger of the Stranglers, Kenneth Bianchi, had moved to far-northern Washington State, where on his own he had strangled to death two more young women, college students. He had left several clues and was arrested immediately by local police. His driver's license showed a Los Angeles address, and when the local police telephoned the Los Angeles County Sheriff's Office for a background check, a primary investigator on the Hillside case happened to take the call. He knew immediately from Bianchi's L.A. address, which was identical to that of one of the Hillside victims, that at least one of the Stranglers had been caught. From there it was easy to find the other, Angelo Buono, a Glendale auto upholsterer who was Bianchi's cousin and only close male friend.

But the ordeal for the police and for the city, apparently over, had only just begun. Bianchi, an articulate young man, at first denied everything and then, supposedly under hypnosis, displayed the classic manifestations of a multiple personality. He apparently revealed that an alter ego, whom he called Steve, had committed the murders, of which Kenneth knew nothing. A third personality, called Billy, later emerged, and possibly a fourth and a fifth. Bianchi implicated his cousin Buono, who he said had collaborated with Steve in the Hillside murders; Steve alone had killed the two girls in Washington. Bianchi's lawyer entered a plea of not guilty by reason of insanity, supported by a psychologist and a psychiatrist. Buono, meanwhile, was under surveillance by Los Angeles police, but he remained free, denying any connection to the Hillside killings. If Bianchi's insanity defense proved successful, he would hardly make a believable witness against his cousin.

Bianchi's insanity plea was challenged, however, by two other psychiatrists, and discoveries made by two Los Angeles homicide detectives further weakened his credibility. After several months of conflicting diagnoses in Washington, Bianchi made a deal with the Los Angeles County District Attorney's Office and the Washington authorities. He would plead guilty to the Washington murders and to five of the Hillside murders, and he would come to L.A. to testify against Buono. In return he would get life with the possibility of parole, and he would be permitted to serve his sentence in California, where the prisons were more comfortable than in Washington. Had he not made the deal, he would have faced the death penalty in Washington and possibly in California.

In October 1979, police arrested Angelo Buono in Los Angeles, and he was charged with ten counts of premeditated murder. A ten-month-long preliminary hearing, lasting until March 1981, resulted in an order for Buono to stand trial on all ten counts. Because he was accused of multiple murders, he faced the death penalty.

As soon as Kenneth Bianchi was brought to Los Angeles, he began violating his agreement to testify against his cousin. His testimony became a morass of contradictions. At times he asserted that he knew nothing of the Hillside killings and that he had no idea whether his cousin Buono had been involved or not. Meanwhile a mysterious Los Angeles woman, an actress and playwright named Veronica Compton, who had visited Bianchi in jail, traveled up to Washington and there attempted to strangle to death a woman she had picked up in a bar. She was arrested, tried, and convicted of premeditated attempted murder, and she was sentenced to life. She became known as the Copycat Strangler. Apparently she had acted out of some strange affection for Bianchi, trying to exonerate him from the Washington murders.

With Bianchi continuing to contradict himself, Buono's trial was scheduled to begin before Superior

Court Judge Ronald M. George in September 1981. In July, the District Attorney's Office suddenly moved to dismiss all ten murder counts against Buono. Bianchi's contradictions, the deputy D.A. argued in his motion, made prosecution of Buono impossible. Without Bianchi's cooperation there would not be enough evidence to convict Buono.

Judge George adjourned court for a week, but no one doubted that he would grant the prosecution's motion to dismiss charges, as judges routinely do. When the judge did just the opposite, denying the motion, ordering prosecution, and saying that if the D.A.'s Office could not pursue the case, he would bring in the attorney general or a special prosecutor, the legal community was stunned, and the city rejoiced. Legal opinions differed on the propriety of the judge's action and the stern language in which he couched it, but the typical citizen, frustrated by years of terror and a seemingly paralyzed system of criminal justice, was delighted and relieved.

The D.A.'s Office withdrew from the case, and two deputy attorneys general were assigned to prosecute. They knew that this would be a long and difficult court battle, lasting perhaps a year, but they did not know how long and how difficult the case of *People* v. *Buono* would actually prove to be. Before the jury would finally reach its verdict on Buono, more than two years would pass, making this the longest criminal trial in the history of the United States.

The foregoing has been as brief a summary as I have been able to make of an acutely horrible series of crimes, their effect on a city that prides itself on being a place of easy and good living, and the extraordinarily complex and lengthy process of bringing the Hillside Stranglers to justice. But these are merely the facts, and only the principal facts at that. No summary can convey the personalities, backgrounds, and motives of the Stranglers, nor the sense of being there as they commit their crimes, nor the pervasive effects and implications of their savagery, nor the frustrations, mistakes, and triumphs of the police, nor the controversial role of psychiatric analysis, nor the emotional and intellectual drama of the trial of Angelo Buono. And no summary can evoke and explore and dramatize the disturbing issues raised by the case. For all this, I decided some years ago, a book was required; and for various reasons, I knew that I should write that book.

In the autumn of 1977 I knew no more about the Hillside Stranglers than any other daily reader of the *Los Angeles Times* and faithful watcher of the evening news. I was a professor at Pomona College then, teaching English and nervously awaiting publication of my fourth book and first novel, a semiautobiographical account of growing up in L.A. as the son of a once-prominent cowboy star and a Broadway actress who retired before my time. I had lived most of my life in Los Angeles and I loved my hometown, as I still do; but mine had been a rather sheltered existence. My friends were middle-class or rich. From my parents I knew something of the down side of show business; from my sister, who by then was a member of the New York Philharmonic, I knew something of the anxious life of the professional musician. But my only contact with a true cross section of the citizens of Los Angeles came when I visited Dodger Stadium or the Coliseum or, earlier in my life, the boxing matches at the Olympic Auditorium. I knew little of the underside of L.A., nothing of the many who make their way through life by brute force. Everything I knew about violent crime and criminals I had read in books.

As I read that autumn about the Hillside Stranglings in the newspaper, I sensed the city's growing panic. When I noticed that one of the murdered girls had apparently been abducted from a street only a mile or two from where my eleven-year-old daughter was living with her mother, I worried, but only briefly, because I knew that Molly did not wander around alone in the city. Had I known then what I know now about the methods of the Stranglers in luring their victims, I would have worried more. No girl or woman was safe.

In January 1978, a month before the final Hillside murder, I took a job at the University of Tulsa that offered me most of the year free to write and, equally important as it turned out, to travel as I wished when I was not teaching. In Oklahoma I became aware by chance of the details of an unsolved murder case, and I immersed myself in police files, court documents, and the opinions of those who had been involved, including a colorful private detective who was new to my gallery of human types. I also spent a great deal of time in honky-tonks, picking up dialogue and approaches to life different from my own. Out of this spontaneous fascination evolved a novel, although in writing the story I removed the murder in favor of a suicide and invented characters and motives. At the time I could not know it, but as I look back I see that somehow I was sharpening my skills for a book about the Hillside Stranglers.

Late in 1981, when I learned that my old friend and Princeton roommate Judge Ronald M. George had been assigned the Hillside Stranglers case and had refused to permit the D.A. to drop murder charges against Angelo Buono, my writer's pulse quickened.

On a visit to Los Angeles I called on the judge and began to ask him about the Stranglers. He cut me off, refusing on ethical grounds to discuss the case while it was in progress. Though surrounded by his family, he looked more solitary than I had ever seen him during the twenty-five years of our friendship. When I said that what little I knew about the Stranglers suggested that they would be a natural subject for a book, he agreed but warned me that I had no idea what I might be getting myself into. He said that there was already enough on the public record to form the basis of a book, one that might have significant social and moral resonances. If I probed beyond and behind the public record, there was no telling what I might discover, but that would be up to me. I did not press him further, but I knew then what I would be doing for the next two or three years.

At first I thought that I would turn the Hillside Stranglers material into fiction, but once I had plunged into the research I saw that the true story had to be told and presented as true. Otherwise no one would believe it; the novelist would be dismissed as having a sick and fantastical imagination. Nor would the social and moral issues stirred by the case have sufficient impact if presented in the guise of an imagined story. Buono's trial itself, I began to see, was drama ready-made for narrative distillation, although at the time I of course had no idea how dramatic and dicey its final act would turn out to be. I would have to write in a hybrid form, telling the story with the techniques of the novelist but denying myself the privilege of inventing characters and events.

The trial of Angelo Buono was not yet a year old when I began my full-time research. I took an apartment in Los Angeles and quickly became obsessed with the Stranglers. I discovered an L.A. I had never known firsthand, yet my familiarity with the city helped immeasurably as places and people came to life for me—and a morbid life it was. Eighteen places in the city, the locations of the abductions and the body dumpings, will in my mind be associated with death as long as I live. Only the other day, on a visit to Warner Brothers studio, I stopped my car at the place on Forest Lawn Drive where the first body was found and got out to look again. I grew apprehensive staring at the spot, photographs of the corpse mingling in my mind with the actual scene. Compulsively I drove to five of the other body sites, as though on a ghostly pilgrimage.

Countless details and encounters have contributed to this book. My work on it, before the actual writing, consisted equally of reading court documents and talking to people involved with the case. Bianchi's interviews with psychiatrists alone ran to over five thousand pages, the videotapes of those sessions some fifty hours, his confessions to police over twenty hours and two thousand pages, the transcript of Buono's trial over fifty thousand pages. I played the tapes of Bianchi's confessions, of which I managed to obtain copies, over and over in my car as I drove around and at night when I was writing, before I went to sleep, so that I could get to know his sounds intimately and dream about him—a ghastly experience but one that always got me writing the instant I woke up in a cold sweat. But in the end none of the reading and watching and listening and poking around I did helped me as much as meeting one particular policeman. He was Sergeant Bob Grogan of LAPD Homicide, and he has become a friend for life.

I first met Sergeant Grogan in March 1983. It had taken me several weeks to make contact with him. I gathered that he did not much care for writers, who he thought were inclined to admire criminals and to give cops a bum rap. So I had stressed my academic credentials, in the hope that he might consider a professor from the University of Tulsa relatively harmless. My message to the sergeant said merely that I wanted to try to understand a homicide detective's point of view on the law as it applied to murderers. What observations did he have on the Hillside Stranglers case? How strong did he consider the evidence, much of which he had gathered, in this trial that had already run on for over a year and threatened to become the longest criminal trial in the history of the United States? Finally Sergeant Grogan returned my call and agreed to have lunch.

For months I had been examining the transcript, by then nearing thirty thousand pages, and the evidence—thousands of things, photographs of the murdered young women, the love poems of Kenneth Bianchi, an empty wallet—in the trial of Angelo Buono. I worked in a little office on the thirteenth floor of the Criminal Courts Building in downtown L.A., checking in every morning at nine and leaving at five, as if I were on salary. Just down the hall in Judge George's courtroom, Angelo Buono sat slumped and contemplative. When something of note was happening in court, I would go in to observe, scrutinizing Buono from various angles and distances, lowering my gaze when I caught his eye. He scared me to death. Even his hands, disproportionately long and sinewy, frightened me.

My subject came to possess me. Each night I found myself jittery and depressed, and my dreams were numerous, but I awoke eager to begin again, like a boozer curing his anxiety with a fresh drink. Mine was a modern sensibility, trained to strive for nuance and irony, conditioned to question absolutes, shaped to be suspicious of words like "good" and "evil." But the more I studied the Stranglers, their acts, their backgrounds, the theater of their lives, the more my early Roman Catholic beliefs intruded on my skepticism and detachment. I was face to face with evil, and try as I would, I could find neither theory nor language to ameliorate the unredeemable nature of these men. Conrad's well-worn phrase "The horror! The horror!" came into my mind every day.

The material, its vastness and its bloodiness, was beginning to overwhelm me. My notebooks filled up; I gave myself daily quizzes on the hundreds of names and places; but I felt that I was losing my bearings. I was getting to know the lives, minds, and acts of two men I once would have thought not human or at least crazy, but now I had to accept both their humanity and their sanity. And, though cousins, the two of them were in their outward personalities wholly unalike, the one silent and watchful, the other all synthetic blabber. Inwardly also they were opposite, the one sober and practical, the other a dreamer, even a romantic. Yet in their brutal acts together they had become two of a kind. How could I continue to try to comprehend them without losing whatever beliefs in life and in the human race I had managed to preserve from my youth?

And so it was that I was increasingly anxious to talk to Sergeant Grogan. He was apparently something of a legend in the LAPD. Whenever his name came up, I noticed that people either smiled or shuddered. He had been a principal investigator on the case from the beginning, or almost, and the story was that catching and convicting the Hillside Stranglers had become the ruling passion of his life. I hoped that talking to him might give me a perspective and perhaps a principle of organization. He was said to be a man of powerful opinions who was not reluctant to express them.

In my experience the best way to get a man to talk is to give him a good meal and many drinks, but Sergeant Grogan was having none of that. He arranged to pick me up on the corner of Temple and

Spring in his unmarked Plymouth, and he drove me at catastrophic speed over to the Los Angeles Police Academy in Elysian Park, near Dodger Stadium. Short of being locked into a room at headquarters, I could not have been more on his turf.

At the entrance to the academy's restaurant I noticed a kind of shrine to Jack Webb, the creator and star of the old *Dragnet* television series, which as a kid in L.A. I had watched loyally. Badge 714 shone there in a glass case. "This is the city. Los Angeles, California. I work here. I'm a cop." I quoted aloud the famous opening lines of the show, and Sergeant Grogan laughed mildly. He told me that the academy's restaurant, swimming pool, and other amenities had been built with money Jack Webb had donated to the LAPD out of profits from *Dragnet*. This familiar sort of link between show business and the city pleased me. We found a booth and ordered pastrami sandwiches and iced tea.

The next several minutes were difficult. I did not know where to begin, the sergeant was obviously unenthusiastic about talking to me, and I immediately noticed that I had forgotten to bring a pen, so that if he did tell me something important, I might forget it anyway. Of course I was too embarrassed to ask to borrow his pen, imagining what he would think of a penless author. I later found out that the sergeant considered my not taking notes a good sign. He never took notes himself when working on a case, having discovered that they could be turned against him in court by some clever defense attorney. But at the time my penlessness added to my unease, as did the sergeant's size. I am six feet tall, but sitting opposite him, I felt diminished.

He was not only three or four inches taller than I but far broader, and he boiled with energy. His face was red, his eyes bright blue points, and his big bald head, fringed with red hair, seemed to watch me like a third eye. In a harsh Boston accent that, especially there in slumbrous Southern California, made his every utterance sound accusatory, he did a background check on me.

I told all. I confessed that I wanted to write a

book encompassing everything that I could about the Hillside Stranglers, their effect on Los Angeles, the city's effect on them, and their minds and motivations, telling the truth. I wanted to find out what was not known by the newspapers or could not or would not be printed in them.

Grogan stared through me. Eagerly I let drop that my grandfather, Dan O'Brien, had been chief of police in San Francisco during the 1920s.

"Oh yeah? Dan O'Brien, huh?" I sensed that Grogan was noting the name so that he could check it out later. "Well your grandfather would probably be turning in his grave if he could see San Francisco today."

I agreed, thinking of photographs of my grandfather on parade with his rearing horse, strong, fearless, jovial, tough, his jaw a bulwark, a darker Irish type than Grogan but just as intimidating. I had the feeling that a bond had been established between Grogan and me through Dan O'Brien's ghost. As if making one last check, Grogan asked me what I thought of a couple of famous books about murder. Spontaneously I expressed negative opinions, citing what I considered sentimental approaches to evil.

"Okay, O'Brien," Grogan said, "I'll talk to you." He settled back and drew a deep breath into his big chest. "I'll tell you one thing right off. I've been a cop all my life and I never saw two sons of bitches as cold as Buono and Bianchi. If I could get away with it I'd kill them myself. And if Buono gets off . . ." He left the sentence unfinished.

I expressed surprise that Grogan thought Angelo Buono might get off.

"Are you kidding?" Grogan said. "In this crazy state? In this town? With the law like it is and a jury? Don't you know he already almost got off? Don't you know they wanted to let the bastard go? Jesus, you got a lot to learn, professor. Okay, I'll teach you. I'll teach you about life in the big city. But you'd better write it straight, pal. Somebody's got to."

I had no need of notes to remember what Sergeant Grogan told me during the next hour. It formed the basis for many of the key insights and incidents in this book. He told me about the killers and their victims and the families of the victims, about how close he had become to two of those families, about how his own family life had been consumed and wrecked:

"I lost my wife from this case, not her fault, and maybe my sanity."

He told me about his fellow detectives and the frustrations and breakthroughs of the investigations. The episodes he recounted and the savage indignation with which he punctuated his stories were unforgettable. We would have many more conversations, in more relaxed surroundings, over the next two years. He would even come to visit me in Tulsa to play golf, talk through the night, and read what I was writing, urging me on, correcting details, adding Groganesque touches. Sometimes we would disagree about this or that person or motivation, and once, I recall, we got into a shouting match about an aspect of Kenneth Bianchi's background, with Grogan reminding me that he ought to know more about murderers than I did. He sometimes changed my mind. Whether I ever changed his I cannot say, but the debates sharpened my perceptions, I am sure. Often as I wrote his image would float before me, his blue eyes ice-hot and his big red-haired fist banging the table. His rage against Buono and Bianchi never lapsed, and he brought the dead to life.

A writer feels a sense of purpose only when his subject matter so consumes him that he can take on the role of a shaping spirit, disappearing other than in the service of the story. So it is that I have banished myself from the narrative after this point, confident that the characters and events that made up the Hillside Stranglers case will enthrall the reader as they have me.

To some readers portions of the first third of the book may appear unduly shocking, for here I have reconstructed several of the stranglings and their accompanying brutalities in precise detail. These scenes function, however, as necessary groundwork for the psychiatric and legal drama that follows. Without them one can have no good grasp of what Buono and

Bianchi actually did, how they did it, and, most important of all, why they acted as they did, progressing from victim to victim with their own diabolical logic. The reader may act as a member of a jury as numerous as humankind, taking on the responsibility of the trier of fact and of motivations more elusive than fact.

I have come to view the story of the Hillside Stranglers as a parable, although it is of no matter whether others see it differently. There are villains here and victims. There are those who chose passivity as safe passage and those who, whether out of ignorance or self-interest or both, aided the villains in their schemes and scams. But there are heroes, too, people who gave of themselves for no price, never doubting the necessity of doing so, weighing lightly what they gave, knowing what they did was right. Without them the story would not have been worth the telling.

D. O'B.

I

"Mi numi!"

Hail, holy Queen, Mother of mercy; our life, our sweetness and our hope; to thee do we cry, poor banished children of Eve; to thee do we send up our sighs, mourning and weeping in this valley of tears. Turn then, most gracious Advocate, thine eyes of mercy toward us, and after this, our exile, show unto us the blessed fruit of thy womb, Jesus. O clement, O loving, O sweet Virgin Mary.

> —*Salve Regina*, prayer to the patroness of the City of Our Lady Queen of the Angels, Los Angeles

ONE

Nude and violated, she lay on her back in the flower-bed like a discarded doll. Her head was turned toward the northern hills. Eyes shut, legs akimbo, fingers trapped beneath her buttocks, she proclaimed sacrifice. Ants crawled across her belly, leaving red bites. She was murdered and nameless.

Sergeant Frank Salerno, genuflecting to look, could feel the squeeze of the rope at her neck, which was encircled by a line of dark, purplish bruise. Rope or twine or cord, she had been strangled. Strangulation by ligature was the phrase that occurred to him. He would use it in his report.

It was now just after eight on the morning of Halloween, 1977, a gray day, the air about fifty-five degrees. Salerno, a detective with the Homicide Bureau of the Los Angeles County Sheriff's Department, had been called from his bed to examine the body. It had been discovered at six o'clock where it now lay, about two and a half feet from the curb at 2844 Alta Terrace

Drive in La Crescenta, a middle-class town in the foothills just north of Glendale. Charles Koehn, who had the curious habit of leaving his house at four each morning to go to work at his electrical shop and returning home at six to eat breakfast and check on his family, had noticed the body as he parked in front of his house in the early light. Forgetting what he had learned from hundreds of television cop shows about not disturbing evidence, Koehn had covered the body with a tarp. He had not wanted his or other neighborhood children to go off to school having seen a corpse.

Other detectives, who had arrived before Salerno, had not touched the tarp. Salerno removed it carefully, hoping that nothing important had been lost.

She was pale, small and thin, maybe ninety pounds, neither pretty nor not, her straight, reddish-brown hair neither long nor short. She could not have lived more than fifteen or sixteen years. Scrutinizing her, Salerno reflected that in a decade as a sheriff's deputy and in more than two years with homicide, he had never seen a body like this. He noted ligature marks at five points: neck, wrists, and ankles. The wrist and ankle bruises were fainter and more irregular than the line on her neck. She must have been tied or handcuffed or both. Her open mouth revealed blood along the upper gumline. Her body bore no other signs.

But as he stared at her face, leaning in closer, Salerno noticed something on the right eyelid. A speck, a white tuft of something. A wispy bit of fluff. He picked it off and held it up to the overcast sky. It looked like angel's hair, the stuff you put on Christmas trees. It would have to be analyzed. It might be all they had, and it might be nothing. He hoped it had not come from the tarp.

He rolled her over. Nothing. He assumed that she had been raped, but the coroner would determine that.

He stepped back to take in the scene. The body, lying so close and parallel to the street, could not have been missed as the people of the neighborhood began their Monday. It must have been placed there deliberately, Salerno reasoned, not tossed or dropped. On the north side of the street a chain-link fence, covered with oleander bushes, bordered a big storm basin. Had the killer or killers wished to conceal the body, he or they could have forced it up over the fence, where it would not have been noticed until the smell got bad. The way it lay there, knees out, meant that they had wanted it to be noticed and had wanted it to shock the neighborhood. The more Salerno looked at the position of the body, the more it seemed to him to have been placed there by two men, or more than two. They had probably removed it from a car, carried it over the curb, and put it down. There were no drag marks, neither on the body nor on the ice plant that, still wet with dew, covered the curb. One man could have carried her, but it was unlikely.

Salerno knew that he had no proof that there had been two, nor even that they were men, but he assumed it. He was confident of his instincts: they would not be enough in court but they were enough for him now.

It was a quiet neighborhood, heavily planted, high up in the hills above Foothill Boulevard, old Route 66, remote enough to make Salerno wonder from the start why, having traveled this far up, someone would pick this street to dump a body. Alta Terrace Drive was accessible only from La Crescenta Boulevard—at its other end it dead-ended—but someone this far up could have gone on only a little farther and hidden the body where it would not have been found so quickly. Relatively prosperous working people lived here. They were not rich, but they were well-off and respectable. They would notify the police immediately of anything unusual, as Charles Koehn had. The houses, one-story, ranch-style, had wonderful views of the city to the south at night or when there was enough wind to dissipate the smog. You could see Forest Lawn from Alta Terrace and, to the west, the San Fernando Valley.

Then Salerno noticed something that confirmed or at least supported his hypothesis that there had been two men. A portion of the ice plant next to the curb, almost directly opposite the girl's feet, had been pushed out of place, tufted up eighteen inches or more

5

and folded back from the curb. He bent down. Under the disarranged ice plant, the dirt had been freshly disturbed. Kicked? Or had a car jumped the curb and done this?

The scene materialized in Salerno's imagination. Two men had removed the body from a car. One had carried her by the head or had gripped her under the arms; the other had held her feet or had gripped her under the knees. The man carrying the upper part of her body had stepped across the curb first, and his momentum had caused the other man to trip on the curb or to stumble, catching the toe of his shoe under the ice plant.

Then they had put the body down. Had she been placed facedown at first? Then unhandcuffed or untied? Then rolled over onto her back, hands still behind her? Salerno speculated. He guessed at last that she had already been unhandcuffed or untied. Her hands, dangling, had caught beneath her.

Salerno went into Charles Koehn's house to talk to him and his wife. They had heard nothing during the night. "I sleep like a log," Koehn said. Had he noticed anything when he had left for work at four in the morning?

"It was pitch-black."

What about the ice plant? Had it been tufted up like that yesterday? It had not, Koehn said. He would have noticed something like that. He took care of his property. He had just put in that fountain in the patio.

Salerno asked about the tarp. Koehn had taken it from the backyard, where it had been used to cover some toys.

"What kind of toys?"

"Stuffed animals and things. See for yourself."

In the backyard, Salerno was sorry to see the stuffed animals, some of which had fuzz that might be the wispy stuff he had plucked from the girl's eyelid. For the same reason, Salerno regretted the Koehns' white poodle. He called in the man from the Sheriff's crime laboratory and had him cut samples from the dog and the toys. Then he set about interviewing everyone on Alta Terrace. It was a peaceful street, he found. People worked hard to live there for the view.

TWO

Angelo Buono, inaptly named, looked like a gargoyle, but the resemblance was only skin-deep. Great roots of hands, with thumbs on them the size of zucchinis, hung down from his long, sinewed arms. The hands swung backward as he walked. He was wiry, about five foot ten. He had Sicilian coloring. He was kind to animals and had a way with the ladies.

That Sunday evening in the autumn of his forty-fourth year, Angelo was lying on his king-sized water bed, dressed in his customary blue workpants and short-sleeved shirt, bored. There was nothing on TV. He got up to straighten one of the framed family photographs on the wall: his son Peter, in full Marine dress uniform, posed before an American flag. Below Peter, Angelo Buono, Sr., deceased, looked content in his dark security guard's uniform, grinning. Farther along the wall hung a small Italian flag. And next to it, a print of an anonymous early Italian Renaissance Madonna, eternally serene, gazed at the room with ancient eyes.

Angelo wandered through his house, straightening, checking for dust. In the den he tidied shelves of knickknacks: his Zippo lighter collection, antique model cars, a plastic sphinx, a miniature barber's pole, poker chips and playing cards, against which was propped a little wooden sign, reading, "Candy Is Dandy but Sex Won't Rot Your Teeth." He made sure his files of *Penthouse* and *Playboy* magazines, two neat piles on a bottom shelf, were in order. He opened the glassed door of his gun case and dusted his five rifles, two .45 pistols, and Thompson submachine gun. Everything was shipshape.

Angelo was house-proud. He had tired of sharing apartments, putting up with other people's habits and tastes, having others' eyes on him. Angelo trusted no one. He had found this place at 703 East Colorado Street in Glendale in 1975, one of a very few inhabited one-story frame residences left on a street that was now four lanes and franchise restaurants, small businesses and the general offices of Bob's Big Boy hamburgers. It was ideal for him because he could live in the house and have his auto upholstery shop in a converted garage at the back. His girlfriends or children could come to stay, but he could kick them out when he chose. He had worked hard on the house, painting the outside a homey yellow with brown trim. Inside he selected an eggshell white for the walls and put down Mexican tile in the kitchen and dining area. He covered the spare bedroom's floor with wear-resistant auto carpeting. He hung his pictures, mingling family sentiment with aesthetic preference, a romantic seascape with Italian fisherman, for instance, next to a photograph of his daughter and another of a girl called Peaches. He did no cooking, but other than that Angelo was a domestic sort of fellow.

In the living room he lowered himself into the brown vinyl easy chair, rested his feet on the beanbag hassock, and stared at the lighted fish tank, listening to the hum of its electric pump, its air bubbles. Angelo liked angelfish. The little castle the fish swam through had fallen over. He got up, put the castle right, and

8

sprinkled fish food on the water. The fish rose to the food, and he remembered the rabbits. He walked back through the kitchen and out the side door around to where the hutches were, between the house and the shop. Across the garage door "Angelo's Trim Shop" was spray-painted in black graffiti script.

Out back his yellow mutt, Sparky, greeted him and rolled over. Angelo scratched Sparky's belly and made guttural sounds. Then he opened the hutches and gave food pellets to the rabbits, stroking them with his big hands, mumbling at them.

He heard a car pull into the driveway. He could tell from the sound of the motor that it was Kenneth Bianchi's Cadillac. My crazy cousin, Angelo thought. Maybe we'll get some action.

They went into the house together. Kenneth Bianchi was twenty-six and more fashion-conscious than his cousin. This evening he wore a three-quarter-length brown leather coat, jeans, and earth shoes. His dark hair was freshly permed, not naturally curly like Angelo's. Bianchi was just under six feet, a fairly well-knit hundred and eighty pounds. With his mustache, he looked like one of the many thousands of young men in Southern California who aspired to stardom but had not landed a role. Something in his manner suggested that he thought he was being photographed. He was Burt Reynolds without a contract but not so tan. The acne scars on his neck lent some character to a bland though not unhandsome face. Lately he had been working for a land title company, where he always wore a dark three-piece suit and carried an attaché case, the eager young executive look. He was called a title officer, though he was but a clerk. Bianchi was a man of many parts. From time to time he lost conviction in his mustache and shaved it off. The perm, too, was a matter of whim from month to month. He was a man easy not to recognize.

"Great party last night," Bianchi said, pacing about. "Really terrific. Kelli and I and her brother and two other guys. We all hit the Circus Maximus. You wouldn't have believed it, you know?" They had celebrated Halloween two days early.

Angelo made a low noise.

"Guess what. We went dressed as—you're not going to believe this—slugs!" Angelo did not react. "Can you believe it? You know, like a snail or something. Really creepy. Kelli made the costumes. It was so very cool. We painted our faces green and put on these green garbage bags and green leotards and, get this, we had Saran Wrap kind of trailing off us, like *slime*, you know? It was so great. Fuck it! Halloween in Hollywood! Un-fucking-believable!"

"It ain't even Halloween yet. Halloween's tomorrow, dumbbell."

"What's the difference?"

"Nothing on TV," Angelo said. Sunday was a bad night for cop shows, Angelo's favorites. (He rarely missed an episode of *Kojak* or *Baretta;* he identified with their tough-guy heroes.) "What you want to do?"

Angelo's speech was rough—a grunt, a grumble, a rasp, the snarl of the underdog. If you had not known that he had been born in Rochester and raised in Los Angeles, you would have guessed Brooklyn or maybe Hoboken. A slight speech impediment, trouble with r's and l's, made him slide from syllable to syllable as though his tongue had been greased. Articulation was not Angelo's strong suit, but he always got his point across.

In the kitchen, he opened a can of clams, ate a spoonful of them, and followed that with a spoonful of olive oil. When he took this mixture, his ulcer never bothered him. With the back of his hand he wiped a smear of oil from his mustache, moving aside his long, arched nose.

"What'll we do?" Angelo said. "Gotta get out of the house. Need some action."

"It's super chilly out," Bianchi said. Though he had lived on the Coast for less than two years, Bianchi already spoke like a New Age Californian, inflectionless, smooth, a mellowed-out beach boy, not a trace remaining of the aggressive East in his sounds. "Hey. I wore my coat." He gave his ingratiating grin and half-twirled, like a fashion model.

"Yeah. That ain't what I asked. You want to do something?"

"You got something in mind?"

Angelo stared up at his cousin. Angelo's eyes were dark under bony brow ridges, his forehead prehistoric. He said nothing. Talking was not something he did much of. He had found that a few words usually got him what he wanted. One of the things he hated about his cousin was that Kenny never seemed to shut up. But Kenny could be useful. He was not stupid, and if you just stared at him long enough, he would get the picture. He would sense what Angelo wanted and then perform as if by remote control. Kenny was a willing slave, Angelo had figured out. A pain in the ass much of the time, but very cooperative when you wanted to make use of him. He was better than most bitches that way. And Angelo knew that he could do and say certain things with Kenny that he could not with anyone else. They had the understanding of an old married couple or two cellmates. Kenny was almost, but not quite, Angelo's punk.

"We could go scamming," Bianchi said. "We could go scamming in Hollywood." He sounded boyishly eager. A Beaver Cleaver. His voice lacked the resonance of manhood.

Angelo grunted.

"We could do that," Bianchi said.

Another grunt.

"Like last time. It worked."

"Better, *mi numi*. Got to be better."

"We go cruising. We pick up a girl. Same scam. Super."

"This time we need more time. Got to have time. Last time was rushed, man."

"Sure. Listen, I can tell you, it isn't super great in a backseat, either. I mean, what's that, you know? Strictly for kids. Backseat screwing is strictly overrated."

"You forget, asshole. I didn't get nothing."

"Sure, Tony." Angelo was sometimes called Tony by family and friends. They also called him the Buzzard. "It happened too fast. We just winged it. If you'd said something, you know. Anything I—"

"We got to plan this shit. We need more time, like I said." Angelo grunted out his words. His voice

11

was a faulty pump spewing silt. "Scam's okay. We need a place. Need some place. Fucking pad someplace. Need a place to nail her, man, you see?"

"Hey, how about right here?"

Angelo sat down in the brown vinyl easy chair and pulled on his right earlobe with his right hand. He let half a minute pass. When Bianchi started to speak again, Angelo said, "Shut up." Finally Angelo said: "Yeah. Here would be good. Real good thinking. Nobody can't see nothing here, can't hear nothing. Perfect. You ain't so dumb."

"Well, I've got a master's from Columbia University, don't I?"

"Yeah, I seen it, asshole. You are some bullshitter. You oughta be rich. How come you ain't got a dime?"

"I'm getting there."

"How much money you owe me?"

"Give me some time, Angelo. Kelli's pregnant, you know."

"Dumb bitches," Angelo said. "Goddam bitches. That goddam Becky and that fucking Sabra. Tits. Okay, bullshitter. So we bring the cunt back here. So there's no question afterwards, we got to . . ." He drew a line across his throat. "No problem?"

"Nah. No problem at all, Tony. We can do it right."

"They don't fuck me over and live. They're gonna know that."

"They'll know it, Angelo, they'll know it."

A vein in Bianchi's neck began to pulse. He paced around, rubbing his hands on his jeans. They went over the details. The governing concept was rolling a prostitute. It had been on their minds for weeks, having sex with a prostitute and not paying and then doing what they agreed they had to do. They had had some success, but perfection had eluded them. Tonight had to be better.

"Let me get my jacket," Angelo said. "Want to change my shirt."

Bianchi shadowed Buono. He trailed him to the bathroom, which was decorated with *Penthouse* centerfolds. Through the open door he watched him pee, apply Arrid Extra-Dry deodorant from a spray can, and splash on Brut after-shave. In the bedroom Angelo put on a clean shirt and a beige windbreaker and picked his wallet off the top of the dresser. He opened the wallet and flashed the police badge that was pinned inside, grinning, showing crooked teeth. He reached into his closet and brought out a Roi Tan cigar box, extracting from it a pair of shiny handcuffs. "Let's get going," he said, like a lieutenant in a war movie or a kid playing war, shoving the handcuffs down into a back pocket.

On the way out, prudent householder that he was, Angelo switched off lights, leaving one burning in the bathroom and another in the fish tank. No sense encouraging burglars. And there was one other light which he never turned off at night: the spotlight on the Italian flag which flew from a pole atop his house. Angelo's place was easy to find at night. He secured the deadbolts on the front door and, from the outside, on the laundry-room door. Bianchi opened the black iron gate and followed Angelo to the Cadillac. Angelo got behind the wheel.

From Glendale Angelo drove west on Los Feliz Boulevard past Griffith Park toward Hollywood. He knew the way blind, had driven to Hollywood to look for girls ever since high school, just like everyone else. Cruising Hollywood Boulevard and the Sunset Strip was something to do, was one of the main reasons to get your driver's license at sixteen. And since the sixties it had become the sex-for-sale center of Southern California. The streets were hooker-crowded, the bars and discos and coffee shops the easiest places in L.A. to score whores or boys or drugs.

In the fifties, when Angelo had been in junior high school, Hollywood Boulevard and the Strip had been lined with jazz clubs, beatnik cafés, nightclubs like Ciro's and the Crescendo, where Peggy Lee sang, Mort Sahl shocked an audience by actually insulting Eisenhower, and, later, Lenny Bruce told jokes about Hitler and described what it was like to screw a chicken. In those days you might stop girls on the street, find out they were tourists from Salt Lake City, buy them cherry Cokes, and call it a successful night.

Now Hollywood was home only to the lost ones. The movie palaces—the Chinese, with its stars' footprints in concrete, the Egyptian, the Pantages—were old bitches gone in the teeth. Off the boulevards, people crowded the apartment buildings, shooting up, getting down, freaking out. The only living remnant of the past was the annual Santa Claus Parade, which looked okay on television and offered local-channel exposure to minor celebrities. Runaways headed for Hollywood now. You could live on nothing there, sell your butt for a bed and die young.

That night, October 30, 1977, Buono and Bianchi cruised slowly west on Hollywood Boulevard in the '72 four-door Cadillac, white vinyl top over metallic dark blue body. A sticker bearing the official seal of the County of Los Angeles was displayed on the lower left-hand corner of the windshield. They were enjoying that presumptive arrogance peculiar to Los Angeles, that if you are driving around in a good car in L.A. you are somehow luckier and freer and more privileged and more with-it than the poor slobs in the rest of the country. You pity the people in Michigan or Iowa who can't cruise Hollywood. Buono drove as he had since high school, slumped down, his right wrist controlling the wheel. Bianchi fiddled with the radio dial, searching out the soft rock he liked. He stopped at James Taylor.

"Turn that shit off," Angelo said.

There did not seem to be much action.

"Sunday," Bianchi said. "Dead."

"They ain't in church," Buono said. "We'll find something. Probably won't get her on a main street. Better on a side street."

He turned left on Highland. Nothing.

Angelo discoursed on strategy. He reminded Bianchi that most of the girls had pimps who watched out for unmarked police cars. He suggested that they not use the police ruse right away. They would spot a girl. One of them would get out and wait somewhere while the other picked up the girl, acting like a regular john. Buono was driving, he would get the girl. Then he would pick up Bianchi, and Bianchi would show the badge and tell her she was under arrest: get her

14

into the back seat and handcuff her so she wouldn't make trouble. Angelo handed Bianchi the wallet and handcuffs.

"I'll hang a right," Angelo said, turning west on Sunset. "The Strip is always full of ass. Any day of the week."

The Strip began just past Fairfax Avenue at Schwab's Pharmacy, where Lana Turner was supposed to have been discovered in her sweater, and the old Garden of Allah hotel, once home to Eastern literary refugees like Scott Fitzgerald, its Moorish bungalows now replaced by a travertine monolith called Great Western Savings. Beyond this point, Sunset Boulevard curved in and out among giant billboards announcing a new album or a Las Vegas act, motels with adult movies, the Body Shop, offering "Burlesque, Amateur Contests Mondays and Wednesdays," and various bars and restaurants, until the boulevard straightened out and entered the heavily policed hush of Beverly Hills. About halfway along the Strip, Buono and Bianchi noticed a small girl standing alone on the sidewalk.

She stood in a driveway next to Carney's Express Limited, a diner converted from an old Union Pacific railroad car. Buono drove well past her, pulled over, and stopped. "I'll go around the block and get her," Buono said. "You wait over there across the street."

Bianchi got out, crossed Sunset, and sat down on a bus bench to wait. He was at the corner of Sunset and Sweetzer, just down from the Golden Crest Hotel, its marquee proclaiming: "Retirement Living at Its Finest. Most Luxurious Residence in L.A." He could see the girl across the street still standing in the driveway of the railroad diner, obviously hooking.

A minute later he caught sight of the Cadillac coming up Sunset again. Angelo drove slowly past the girl and turned left, heading around the block once more. He was making it look, Bianchi figured, as though he had just spotted her. He would have made eye contact with her, continuing on as if he had not yet decided. Then he would return.

This time Buono pulled into Carney's driveway. The girl came up to his window, and they talked. Then the girl went around to the passenger side and got in next to Angelo. They sat chatting for a bit until the traffic thinned. Angelo backed out onto Sunset, made a U-turn, passed the bench where Bianchi waited, and turned right on Sweetzer, rolling slowly down the side street. Bianchi, sensing that Angelo did not want to work the scam where there was so much traffic, followed on foot.

Sweetzer ran down a steep hill, the lights of the city glimmering to the south. At the next corner Angelo turned right and pulled over.

In seconds Bianchi was there. He opened the front door on the girl's side, leaned in, and said, "You're under arrest," showing the badge.

"Oh, no, not again," the girl said.

"Could you please step out of the car?"

She did.

"Just get in the back, please," Bianchi said, taking her arm. He opened the rear door. "Okay, now you're going to have to go for a ride." He guided her into the seat and climbed in after her. Angelo reached over and closed the right front door, Bianchi closed the rear door, and Angelo pushed a button that locked all the doors: a safety device for children. "All right," Bianchi said, "I've got to put handcuffs on you. Would you lean forward, please?" He handcuffed her, palms outward. She had to sit on her fingers.

As Angelo drove off, he said: "There was a guy standing in that parking lot. You got a pimp?"

"No," the girl said.

"There was a guy," Angelo said. "Might be a problem." He headed back up to Sunset and glanced into the parking lot of the railroad diner. Nobody there. He headed east, not rushing, obeying the traffic laws.

"Are we going to the Hollywood Division?" the girl asked.

"No," Angelo said, looking at her through the rearview mirror. "We're going to a special unit."

The girl was silent as they drove back through Hollywood, turning east on Franklin to Western, north on Western to Los Feliz, east on their way to

Glendale. Finally she asked why she was being arrested.

"I haven't done nothing wrong."

"You're being arrested for soliciting," Bianchi said. "Have you ever been arrested before?"

"No. Picked up for questioning is all. I never done nothing."

Bianchi studied her. She was tiny. She was wearing a light blouse and slacks and a dirty suede jacket. Her small leather purse sat in her lap. The handcuffs made her lean forward, her straight brown hair obscuring her face. She looked fourteen, sixteen at the outside. She wouldn't give much trouble.

She said nothing more until Angelo pulled all the way into his driveway, under the metal awning that joined the house and the shop. The Orange Grove Apartments overlooked the shop and the house from the rear, but peering down from a second- or third-floor apartment, Angelo knew, no one could see anything except the roofs and the metal awning. There was no way for anyone to get curious. And on the east side of the house and shop was a car wash, on the west side a glass-repair shop, both closed at night. Angelo liked privacy.

"Wait here," Angelo said. He got out and walked over to the laundry-room door at the side of the house, unlocking it. Sparky was waiting on the steps but knew not to enter the house.

"What is this place?" the girl said to Bianchi.

"This is a satellite police station."

Bianchi looked around at Angelo, who was holding the screen door and motioning for him to come ahead. "Slide over," he said to the girl. He grabbed her purse, took her elbow, helped her out of the car, and walked her into the house. Angelo secured the deadbolt again, as Bianchi guided the girl into the living room and sat her down in the brown vinyl easy chair. He put her purse on the dining-room table. Angelo switched on some lights and approached the girl.

"Now you just sit there and don't move. We'll be right back."

In the kitchen with Bianchi, Angelo said: "How do you want to do this? Everything's perfect so far.

17

We want to do this right. No screw-ups." He reached under the sink and brought out a roll of masking tape about three inches wide. "We should blindfold her. That way, if she tries to run, she won't know where to go. Wait a minute. I got an idea. Go back in there and watch her. I got stuff in my shop."

Bianchi stood over the girl. She stared at the fish tank, avoiding his eyes.

"How old are you?"

"Fifteen."

"That's pretty young to be whoring, isn't it?"

"I'm not. I didn't do nothing wrong. What is this? This isn't a police station. Aquarium in a police station?"

"Shut up," Bianchi said. "Do what you're told." He wondered what Angelo would bring in from the shop. Angelo would know what to do next. "Sit there and shut up. You move, you'll be sorry."

When Angelo returned, he called Bianchi into the kitchen again. From his shop Angelo had retrieved an orange work rag and a brick-sized piece of white, foamy polyester material he used in stuffing car seats. He cut the foamy stuff in half with a pair of scissors and explained that they would put the material over each eye, secure it with tape, stuff the rag into her mouth, and secure that with the tape. It would be a good idea to make sure the masking tape went all the way around her head. "Do you want to do it or do you want me to do it?"

"You better do it," Bianchi said.

"Okay. The best thing to do is, I'll walk in front of her and you get behind her and put your hands on her shoulders just in case she starts to kick up a fuss, you know, you'll be ready."

They returned to the living room, Angelo holding the materials behind his back. They walked slowly up to her, and Bianchi moved behind her, resting his hands on her shoulders.

"What's going on?" the girl said. She tried to rise. Bianchi pressed down. She started to scream.

"Shut up!" Buono said. "Don't you say nothing!"

"Keep quiet," Bianchi said. She was easy to hold down.

Angelo produced the orange rag, rolled it into a ball, stuffed it into her mouth, unreeled a length of tape, sealed it over her mouth, and wrapped the tape around her head three times, snipping it off with the scissors and rubbing it flat on the side of her face. Then he brought out the two pieces of foamy stuff and approached her eyes.

She lowered her head, trying to avoid him. Bianchi shoved her down as she squirmed and tried to rise again.

"Grab ahold of her forehead!" Angelo said. "Pull her head up!" Bianchi pulled back on her forehead with one hand and yanked back on her hair with the other. Buono pressed the foam onto her eyes and wrapped it with tape, around her head three times. The girl slumped.

Angelo took the tape back into the kitchen, replaced it under the sink, and put the scissors away in a drawer. He called to Bianchi.

"You just stay right there," Bianchi said to the girl.

"How do you want to do this?" Angelo said. "How do you want to get her clothes off?"

"I don't know. I really have no idea. The handcuffs."

"Well, the best thing is, if I take the handcuffs off of her. You stand behind her, just in case she decides to fight or take off or whatever."

They returned to the girl.

"Okay, now stand up," Bianchi said. She tried to obey but lost her balance and fell back into the chair. They each took an elbow and helped her up and away from the chair.

On a wall opposite her, a plaque, the kind sold in souvenir stores, spelled out in Gay Nineties red lettering: "Please Remove Your Clothes."

"All right," Angelo said. "Now we're gonna take the handcuffs off of you, and we don't want you to start nothing. You do, you're gonna get hurt." He found the handcuffs key on his keyring and removed them. He pulled off her jacket, walked with it over to the dining area, and dropped it to the floor. A gold-smoked mirrored wall behind the dining-room table reflected the scene. Angelo stared into the mirrored wall and liked what he saw. Everything was working. It was going to be great. In the smoky mirror he watched Bianchi remove her blouse. "Bring that over here," Angelo said. "Keep everything together."

Angelo unhooked her bra as Bianchi placed her blouse on her jacket. "Not much tits," Angelo said. He rolled up the bra and tossed it to Bianchi. Then he put the handcuffs back on her. "Hey. Tits look better now."

Bianchi stood behind her again, holding her upper arms to steady her while Angelo unzipped her pants.

"Okay now," Angelo said. "We've got you. We're balancing you. Just back up and sit down and have a seat." They eased her back into the chair. Angelo removed her shoes and socks, told her to stand up again, and slid off her pants, telling her to lift one leg at a time. The girl complied. He let her stand there for a moment, nude except for her underpants. Then he pulled off her underpants, smiled up at Bianchi, and gave the okay sign. He put her pants and underpants with the rest of her clothes, returned, and grabbed an arm.

"Just come with me," he said. "Don't worry, honey. I won't let you run into nothing. I got you so you won't fall. Don't worry about nothing." He led her into the spare bedroom.

The spare bedroom, on the east side of the house between Angelo's bedroom and the bathroom, had nothing in it except a single bed. No other furniture, nothing on the walls. The spare bedroom had a simple function. He sat the girl on the bed and told her to lie down on her back, helping her get her legs up. She lay there nude, gagged, blindfolded, handcuffed. "You wait there. Don't move."

Angelo passed through the beading that hung down in place of a door between the spare bedroom and his bedroom. He turned on a light in his room and checked to see if it shone enough into the spare bedroom. Satisfied, he returned to Bianchi.

"How do we decide who goes first?" Angelo said.

"I don't care," Bianchi said.

"Okay, we'll flip a coin." Angelo dug into his pocket and pulled out a quarter. "Call it."

"Tails."

Angelo flipped. "It's heads," he said. "You got sloppy seconds. You get all her shit together while I'm in there. Put it all on the table. I'll take care of it when I get done. Take her purse and empty it and leave the stuff on the table. See if there's any money in there. Go through her pockets."

"She's fifteen. She told me."

"Good age." Angelo grinned. "Real good age." He disappeared into the spare bedroom.

Bianchi followed Angelo's instructions. In her purse he found two dollars and some change in a wallet with nothing else in it except a snapshot of two little boys, one about eight, the other maybe four. He went through her jacket pockets but found nothing. He heard noises: Angelo's voice, indistinct but harsh, commanding, and female squeals. He must have taken the gag off. What was Angelo doing to her? Bianchi felt he knew. The squeals turned him on. He wanted to see what Angelo was doing, imagined Angelo's heavy dick up there now. Bianchi waited until it was quiet. I don't want to miss this, he thought. Angelo wouldn't mind.

Bianchi entered the spare bedroom through Angelo's room, parting the hanging beads. Angelo had left his socks on. He was lying atop the girl, who was on her back now, unmoving, knees up. The tape across her mouth had been partly ripped off, and the orange rag lay on the bed next to the wall. Bianchi figured Angelo had gotten one or both of the things he liked best.

"She good? I put everything on the table, just like you said."

"Go and get my camera. I got to have a picture of this."

Bianchi fetched Buono's Polaroid camera from his bedroom closet. It had film in it and a flash attached.

"Where do you want me to take it from?"

"Just stand there by the bed. Hurry up. I can't stay in here all night."

Bianchi took the picture and tore off the film. Buono got off the girl and told her to put her legs down. "Just relax, honey," he said. He took the camera and film from Bianchi. "Your turn."

"I want to see how it came out," Bianchi said.

They waited a minute in the dim light. Buono peeled back the photograph. "Not bad. Not bad at all. Okay, your turn. I'll get her things together."

Bianchi took off his clothes and climbed onto the girl. After a few strokes he breathed at her, "Did he fuck you in the ass? Did he? Did he? Well, turn over, bitch. Turn over. Get ready for it."

When Bianchi emerged from the spare bedroom, Angelo had arranged her clothes in a neat pile on the dining-room table. The two dollars and change was gone, and the purse sat atop the pile.

"We better gag her again," Angelo said, handing Bianchi the roll of tape. "You know where the rag is." Bianchi found the rag on the bed, told the girl to open her mouth, stuffed the rag back in, and sealed her mouth with a few strips of tape. He returned to Angelo and watched him put the clothes and purse into a large green garbage bag. Angelo ripped up the photograph and the negative and dropped them into the bag.

"Well," Angelo said, "how're we gonna do this?"

"What do you mean?"

"You know. How're we gonna strangle her? We got to strangle her. It's the only way to do this, unless you got some other ideas."

"Me? No, sounds fine to me."

They had already agreed on strangulation. Angelo had been eloquent on the subject. He always liked talking about the best way to do someone in. Shooting was too dangerous, he said; gunshot wounds told too much of a story, they were messy, and bullets could be traced. Other methods—bludgeoning her to death, chopping her up, poisoning—introduced too many complications. They had never worked out the details, but strangulation was definitely the way to go. Be-

22

sides, the thought of watching a girl gasping for breath was appealing in itself, they agreed.

"I got some stuff out in my shop would be good to use. It's strong. We'll decide how we'll do it. Be right back. Watch her. Just stand by and watch her."

Bianchi kept an eye on the girl through the doorway. She did not move. She was breathing heavily. Angelo appeared lugging a large wooden spool wound with white nylon cord. Ordinarily he used it for edging seat covers. "Probably the best way to do this," he said, "is take off lengths of it." He unreeled some of the cord and measured it efficiently around his elbow and fist, two, three, four arm lengths. He got the scissors from the kitchen drawer, cut the cord, and tied a large knot into each end.

"When I put this around her neck—I'll do it," Angelo volunteered. "You watch how I do it. When I put this around her neck, she's going to kick and she's going to fuss and she's really going to squirm. So probably the best way is, you kneel on her legs. Or you can sit on her legs. Just sit on her legs, you know, facing her. Like you was going to kiss her. No, wait." He snipped off another length of cord. "First, tie up her ankles with this. That will cut down on her moving around and she won't kick you in the nuts."

"Got it."

"Okay. Let's go. I'll give you the sign when to sit on her."

"Jesus," Bianchi said. "My hands are sweating."

"Wipe 'em on your ass, motherfucker."

In the spare bedroom, the girl lay still, but she had begun to shake.

"Wait a minute," Angelo said. He handed Bianchi the cord. "Hold this a minute. Be right back."

He brought in her slacks and underpants. "We'll put these on her," he whispered into Bianchi's ear, " 'cause when she kicks off, she's going to pee or crap and I don't want her to mess my rug."

Angelo approached the bed. "Here now, honey. Sit up now, honey." He pulled her up and pushed her legs over the side of the bed. "We're going to put your clothes on now. That's right." He eased on her underpants and slacks. He zipped up the slacks. "Now, just stand up. Come on, stand up, that's it. Now, just sit down." He motioned to Bianchi that he was going to put her on the floor. Bianchi prepared to catch her. "Just sit down, don't worry, you're not going to fall. I got you." Angelo lowered her to the floor. "Now, just lay there a minute. I'll be right back." And he whispered to Bianchi: "I thought of something else. This'll be perfect, and it'll save time."

Bianchi bound her ankles as tightly as he could. Her shaking had become violent. Angelo came back holding a plastic vegetable bag, the kind dispensed free at supermarkets. "We'll put this on her head," he whispered. He seemed delighted with his ingenuity. "That way, she can't get any air, it's cutting off her air, she can't get any new air. When I put the bag on her head, that's when you sit on her legs." He took the long cord from Bianchi and slung it around his neck. Angelo was ready. He flexed his fingers and stood there looking as efficient as a professional hangman.

The girl lay on her back on the floor. Angelo knelt behind her head. He looked up at Bianchi, nodded vigorously at him, and Bianchi lowered himself quickly onto the girl's legs, facing her, sitting on her knees. She groaned behind her gag, tried to roll to the side, tried to rise up at the waist. Angelo pressed his knees down onto her shoulders. He opened the plastic bag with both hands, jammed it over her head, pulled the cord from around his neck, and wrapped it quickly once around her neck, sealing the bag. She wriggled. Bianchi raised his legs, letting his full weight press down through his butt on her knees. Buono started to pull on the two ends of the cord, then shifted around and put one of the ends under his right foot, catching the knot against the side of the sole of his shoe, putting all his weight on that foot. Then he pulled on the other end of the cord with both hands and rose up, pulling, yanking. She was trying to buck and flex now. Her bagged, roped head hit Buono's foot, and he lost his balance, falling over backward, shouting, "Fuck it! Hold her!" He regained his position, one foot on one end of the cord, both hands on the other end. He yanked with all his strength, pulling upward and backward, letting out grunts of effort which mingled with the gargling of the girl, who arched her back, jerking for her life. The vegetable bag puffed frantically in and out with her breathing, then less frantically, then barely, and then it stopped puffing, she stopped flexing, she stopped breathing, it was over.

"Hard work," Buono said, letting the cord fall loose, rubbing his face on his shirtsleeve. He stood and caught his breath and lit up a Kool.

"Can I bum one?" Bianchi asked. "I'm out of smokes."

Angelo knelt down and put his ear to her left breast. "She's croaked," he said. "Can't be too sure, though. Sometimes when things like this happen, people start breathing again. Really hard to tell. Let's put everything away. Then if she's still not breathing, she's definitely croaked. When you take off her pants, make sure you don't get nothing on the carpet."

In the stillness after death, Buono busied himself. He brought in the green garbage bag with her purse, shoes, socks, bra, and blouse in it. He unhandcuffed her and replaced the cuffs in the cigar box. Bianchi removed the vegetable bag from her head and the tape and foam from her eyes, the tape and rag from her mouth. A little blood trickled from her lips.

"Only women bleed," Angelo said. It was a favorite phrase of his. He had picked it up from a current Alice Cooper song. With greater originality he added, "Girls like that deserve to die." He said that one often, too.

The cord, the tape, everything went into the green garbage bag, which Angelo took outside to the dumpster in his driveway. He tossed the bag into the dumpster and moved other trash on top of it. It would be picked up tomorrow and taken to a vast dump of a landfill with millions of tons of what no one wanted. Gradually it would become methane gas.

"What do we do with the body?" Bianchi asked.

"We'll find a place. I got something in mind. First off, we got to get it into the car. Here's what we do. We take it as far as the washing machine there. Put it down by the back door. I go out, see if the coast is clear, I get your trunk open. We put it in the trunk and we get the hell out of here."

Bianchi took her under the knees, Buono under the arms. They carried her through the kitchen. Her dangling arms flopped about, hit the floor hard. One hand clonked against the washing machine.

"Put her down here," Buono said. "Give me your keys." He went out the side door, opened the trunk of the Cadillac, came back in. "Coast is clear. Now, fast. Fast as we can."

Hefting her again, they shuffled hurriedly through the door, over to the car, her skin glowing dully in the night. The trunk was plenty big enough for her.

"Come on back inside," Buono said. "Make sure we didn't leave nothing."

They checked all the rooms.

"Let's go," Buono said. "I'll drive."

He headed the Cadillac northward through the night. Glendale Avenue to Verdugo Road, La Cañada Boulevard, and up La Crescenta Avenue, straight up into the hills.

"Where are we?" Bianchi asked.

"You'll see. I know where I'm headed."

Far up into the hills, Buono turned left onto Alta Terrace Drive. He cut the headlights and rolled slowly along the street.

"How did you know this place?"

In the darkness Buono pointed to a two-story white house halfway down the street. "That's where that cunt Melinda Hooper lives. I picked her up there a couple times. Had dinner there. Wait till she wakes up tomorrow. She'll get some surprise." He slowed to a stop on the left side of the street in front of 2844. "Real quiet now. And quick. Get that trunk open." Bianchi reached into the glove compartment and pushed a button that released the trunk lid. "Open your door real quiet. And don't close it, get me? All right. We'll get her and dump her over there."

"People could see her."

"You got it. Maybe Hooper will find her. Like to see that."

Quietly and quickly they picked up the girl, Buono carrying her under the arms, Bianchi under the knees. Buono stepped first over the curb, and as Bianchi followed, his foot caught under the ice plant. He stumbled, almost fell, got his foot loose, and they dropped the body parallel to the curb, heaving her slightly, as you would throwing someone into a swimming pool.

"Don't close your door yet," Buono whispered, getting behind the wheel. He had left the motor running. He turned around in the street, headed back the same way, made a right down La Crescenta, switching his headlights back on and telling Bianchi it was all right to close his door. They were safely away, speeding toward the city lights.

"Shall we do something?" Bianchi asked as they crossed Foothill.

"I'm heading home."

The Italian flag hung spotlit above Buono's house. When Angelo stopped in the driveway, Bianchi started to get out.

"Let's call it a night," Angelo said. "I'm beat."

"Okay." Bianchi held out his hand across the Cadillac. "We did it, Buzzard. We really did it this time. Wait till they find her. It'll make the papers. It'll be on every channel. Listen, I'll talk to you. I'll be in touch."

Angelo took his hand and looked into his eyes.

"*Mi numi!*" Angelo said.

The words, emitted more than articulated, were a benediction. Bianchi did not understand them, although it was not the first time that Angelo had addressed him so. Bianchi took the phrase as some Italian form of affection and endearment. A bastard, he did not have the syllables in his blood. He thought that Angelo was saying "my friend," or "my companion," or "my beloved cousin," or maybe something silly, like "Dumbo," or maybe nothing more than "Here's looking at you, kid." It was all of that, but it was more. Had Bianchi understood it, it would have made no impact on his contemporary sensibility. It was a term that had migrated all the way from Sicily, and it came to Angelo's lips with no more deliberate consciousness than the howling of a dog at the moon, a phrase typical of southern Italians, whose speech and customs still reflect the survival of ancient ways, even in the new world, even in Glendale.

Literally it meant "my gods." More deeply, it invoked a pre-Christian pagan world ruled by the religion of the Numa: a time when the gods determined every man's and woman's fate or destiny, when the presence of divine will and inspiration was palpable in every human act; a time when a spark from the hearth was a living sign of the divine presence—Romulus had been born from such a spark, Deity was in this place —*Numen Inest!* And it was a time when the gods demanded that most perfect of all sacrifices, a young, newly ripe human life.

"*Mi numi!*" was how one tragic lover would address another, a spontaneous, pagan religious ejaculation evoking the fateful bonds of blood and death. The lover addressed would symbolize the destiny of the other. The use of *mi* rather than the grammatically orthodox *miei* indicated the southern Italian dialect. When Angelo spoke these words to Bianchi, they conveyed: "You are my fate, my destiny. You and I are bound together. Forever. In blood and in death."

"*Mi numi!*" Angelo said, calling it a night.

THREE

Neither the press nor television paid much attention to Buono and Bianchi's Halloween prank, and on radio there was not a word of it. Murder was so common in Los Angeles: there was one committed every three or four hours in the county, not counting the whores routinely overdosed by their pimps. It took something special to titillate the media, an eviscerated actress or a child stuffed down a sewer. But the girl remained unidentified for two days, and so, at the request of Sergeant Salerno, the *Times* ran this bulletin on the fourth page of the Metro section:

PUBLIC'S AID SOUGHT

Los Angeles County Sheriff's homicide detectives were seeking public assistance Tuesday in trying to identify a young woman whose nude body was found in the bushes in front of a La Crescenta residence. Investigators said the victim, described as between 16 and 22, five feet two inches tall, weighing 90 pounds, with reddish brown hair, appeared to have been sexually molested before she was strangled.

Her body was found Monday in front of a home at 2844 Alta Terrace Drive, La Crescenta.

The article was illustrated with two vivid drawings of the girl's face as it might have looked in life, one in profile. The *Herald-Examiner* also ran the story, and local television news programs gave it a few seconds.

When her parents or relatives or friends still failed to appear to identify her, Frank Salerno started haunting Hollywood Boulevard every night until three or four in the morning. Salerno was acting on an educated hunch. Since no one had come forth to identify the girl, the chances were that she had been living for some time as a runaway. Either her parents did not know that she was missing, or they did not care, or she had no parents, all equal possibilities. Although her body had been found miles from Hollywood, runaways in Southern California gravitated toward the Boulevard. Some of the street people might recognize her from the drawings, might have noticed her missing, might even have seen her on the night of the murder.

It was not much, but Salerno had nothing else. The coroner had concluded only that she had been vaginally and anally raped and that she had been strangled to death by ligature within two hours of midnight, before or after. The time frame had been established by the temperature of her liver, which had cooled off quickly in the brisk air. It had been forty-five degrees or lower that night in the hills.

Not knowing the murder scene, Salerno was at a great disadvantage. Ordinarily he would take an investigation outward from there, but Alta Terrace had not been the murder scene. None of the residents aroused the least suspicion, nor had any of them heard anything unusual during the night. Charles Koehn's peculiar work schedule checked out. One man, a truck driver, had gone to a party with his wife but had returned home before midnight, noticing nothing. The others had been home all night and asleep early. Tests on the fiber Salerno had taken from the girl's eyelid had been inconclusive, except that it had not come from the Koehns' toys or from their poodle.

And so Salerno began walking Hollywood Boulevard through the nights, questioning its floating citizens, showing them the drawings and asking whether they knew this girl. These were the dropouts: addicts and pushers, bikers, whores, socially and sexually displaced persons, entrepreneurs of the transitory, a new American class. They had the morals of the Fortyniners but were not prospecting for gold. Most of them had given over their lives to the next fix. They often knew one another, or were aware of one another, by sight and by name, and they knew, vaguely, when somebody overdosed or simply disappeared, wasted. Their hearts entwined by sadomasochism, they outwardly resembled refugees from the Haight-Ashbury culture of the sixties, favoring leather and denim and lots of hair, an acid-rock Paleolithic look, except for the whores, many of whom looked like whores, and the male prostitutes, who were typecast for an Andy Warhol movie. They had street names like Stinkyfoot, Sunshine Sally, Eggnog, Youngblood, Cowboy Dave, Pigvalve, Flakey, Skateboard, Lobo, Green Irene, Funny Bunny; and since they were all either selling or taking drugs, or both, Salerno could not trust their answers to his questions. But night after night, he kept asking. Through them all Miss Miller, an old lady carrying a tote bag and wearing a lampshade hat decorated with paper leaves, who had consecrated her life to sitting in the front row of Merv Griffin's television studio audience every night, threaded her way.

The street people depressed Frank Salerno. They sometimes made him indignant. You could not be a homicide detective and have a weak stomach, but these nights tested him. He was a conservative man. He liked evenings at home with his wife and two teenage sons in their San Fernando Valley house. His pleasures were fishing trips or reading in silence or, after mass, Sunday dinner with the relatives, cooked by his grandmothers, both of whom had been born in Italy.

31

Moving among the street people made him feel contaminated. It was like bathing in raw sewage.

Salerno could not have been mistaken for one of the street people. He might have been a college professor who had gotten off at the wrong stop. He wore a soft tweed jacket, a muted tie, and light wool slacks. His shoes were thin-soled and expensive. He kept his straight, graying hair neatly trimmed and combed. His wire-rimmed aviator-style glasses accentuated an air of mannerly inquisitiveness. Meeting him, you would not have guessed that he carried a little .38 pistol in the small of his back.

Salerno kept his weight down and had the fluid moves of a centerfielder: if he resembled an Italian physical type, it was DiMaggio. He moved among the street people like an anthropologist, questioning, hypothesizing, inwardly calculating, outwardly impassive. "Excuse me," he would say to a knot of bikers, appearing to grant them, for the moment, membership in civilization, showing his badge, "do you recognize this girl?" "Sure," one would say, "I know the chick. She was here last week." Or: "She's from Denver. Name of Debby. Maybe Donna." When he got what he could out of them, he would thank them and go on. He was almost courtly. They were his antithesis, but he disguised his moral indignation. That he saved for quiet talks with his wife and sons or more animated talks over many drinks with friends. Then he would use words like "scumbag" and "evil."

Salerno made notes of everything the street people told him, but he filtered everything through his experience with liars. It was only when several of the boulevardiers gave the girl in the drawing the same name, Judy Miller, that he knew he was getting closer. The name came out among coffee drinkers at the Howard Johnson's on Vine and again at the Fish and Chips shop, a favorite hangout of the damned that stood between the old Hollywood Theater (then showing *Deep Throat*) and a tattoo parlor.

At the Fish and Chips, two people volunteered the name Judy Miller. One was a whore approaching retirement age; the other described himself as an unemployed disc jockey and bounty hunter. They both

32

claimed to know her, and both described her as a teen-age runaway, a green kid who sometimes turned a trick for a bed or a hot dog. The bounty hunter, a meaty, nervous guy wearing a leather vest, said that he had seen this Judy Miller leave the Fish and Chips on Sunday evening no later than nine or ten. Salerno noted that the timing was about right. But the mature whore claimed that she had seen Judy Miller getting into a car with a light-skinned Negro as late as two or three on Monday morning, near the International Hot Dog stand. Remembering the coroner's calculations, Salerno figured the whore was lying or hallucinating or simply mistaken, but her description of the girl did jibe with the bounty hunter's. Salerno took their names and addresses. He would interview Markust Camden and Pam Pelletier again. If a witness knew something, you never got it all on the first interview. Sometimes you didn't get it until the tenth. He gave them his card and asked them to phone him if they remembered anything else or heard anything.

And then everything changed.

On Sunday morning, November 6, a woman jog-ging near the Chevy Chase Country Club in Glendale came upon the nude body of another strangled girl, crumpled up beside a road that ran past the golf course. The case was being handled by the Glendale police, but when Salerno talked to them, he immedi-ately saw connections with the girl he was beginning to believe was called Judy Miller. Like the first girl, this one had been found nude and, the Glendale police said, had been strangled by ligature. Checking a map, Salerno calculated the distance between the sites of the two bodies as six or seven miles. In Los Angeles, that was close.

More links established themselves the next day, when the girl's mother identified her as Lissa Kastin, a twenty-one-year-old waitress at the Healthfaire Res-taurant near Hollywood and Vine, who had been liv-ing in an apartment on Argyle, just off Hollywood Boulevard. Her parents were divorced, and the night previous to her disappearance she had spent with her mother, complaining of how little money she was making and saying that she was considering becoming a prostitute. But she was a hardworking, ambitious girl, her mother said, and very health-conscious. She did not like red meat and had her heart set on show business. She had performed with the L.A. Knockers, an all-girl rock dance group.

It was the association with Hollywood, not the girl's dreams or dietary preferences, that struck Salerno. Lissa Kastin had last been seen leaving the Healthfaire at about nine-fifteen the night she had been murdered. If she had told her mother about considering becoming a prostitute, she might already have been one. It was possible that both girls had been picked up in Hollywood by the same trick or tricks, and had then been killed and dumped in the same general area, a twenty- or thirty-minute drive from the pickup spots. Her car, a Volkswagen convertible, was found unlocked half a block from her apartment. In her apartment, Glendale officers found a key to the car's locking hood but not the ignition key, and the apartment had been locked. Salerno reasoned that she had been either walking the street or walking from her car to her apartment when she had been picked up. But it was odd for a girl living in Hollywood not to have locked her car.

Salerno decided to have a look at Lissa Kastin's body. He wanted to compare it with that of the first girl. He called the coroner's office and asked to have the two bodies displayed side by side at the morgue. The first had been kept on ice for nine days.

One glance at the two bodies, lying next to each other on gurneys, face up, made Salerno think: Xerox copy. Their necks, wrists, and ankles were encircled with nearly identical lines of bruises. "Five point ligature," Salerno wrote in his notebook. Physically they were very different—about the same height, but the new girl was heavier, stocky, with large breasts and thick, unshaven legs. It was the bruised lines that made Salerno think of a Xerox copy. And Lissa Kastin, like the first girl, had been raped, although with Lissa there was no evidence of sodomy. Her vagina was severely bruised. There was now no question in

Salerno's mind that the girls had been killed by the same men.

And he was more certain than ever that there had been two men. Neither body showed any signs of having been dragged. They seemed certain to have been lifted cleanly from a car and placed or dropped where they were found. Of course, more than two men could have been involved, but that seemed less likely to Salerno. He conferred with the Glendale police, and they agreed with him. He also examined the place near the golf course where Lissa Kastin had been found and noticed a three-foot guard rail between the road and the body site: surely it had taken two men to get the body over that rail cleanly. Salerno then drove at a steady thirty-five miles an hour directly to 2844 Alta Terrace. The distance between the two body sites was 6.8 miles, and the drive had taken him a mere fifteen minutes. The two murders were now inextricably linked to him.

But if there were two, there would likely be another. How much should he or the Glendale officers tell the media? Salerno felt that he had made some progress, but all he had really established, to his own satisfaction, was that two murders had been committed by the same two men, with the crime beginning in Hollywood and ending in the foothills of La Crescenta and Glendale, neighboring communities. The more the killers knew about how those deductions had been made, the more likely they would be to change their modus operandi and throw the investigation off track. Their m.o. was the only solid lead Salerno had. And so it was decided, among the agencies now involved, to reveal a little but not very much. "TWO GLENDALE SLAYINGS MAY BE LINKED," read the *Times*' headline on a small story buried in Part I, page twenty-seven on November 10. There were no details except that the two girls "were strangled in the same fashion": nothing about the five-point ligature marks nor about any of the evidence suggesting two killers. Salerno would have preferred that not even that much be disclosed, but you always had to tell the reporters something. Otherwise they would try harder to find out more on their own. Lissa Kastin was identified, but Judy Miller remained anonymous—and unburied. It was not until the evening of November 10 that Salerno finally ran down her family, such as it was.

More tips from the street people had led him late that Thursday afternoon to the Hollywood Vine Motel, an establishment of no pretentions that offered bargain weekly rates. There in a room sour with old food and old diapers he came upon what was left of the Miller family: Judy's mother and father and her two little brothers, the younger of whom resided in a cardboard box shoved into a corner. Mr. Miller was an unemployed security guard. He nodded and identified his daughter from the drawings Salerno showed him.

"Do you know where your daughter is?" Salerno asked.

Neither the father nor the mother knew. Salerno did not bother asking the older boy, who was absorbed in a cartoon on the television.

"Was she a runaway? Did she run away from home?" Salerno could not think of another word than "home," though there was none. Obviously Judy had run away from nothing.

"She run away from home sometimes," Mrs. Miller said. "Then she come back. I seen her last month."

"When last month?"

"Don't know. Middle of the month, maybe. We had the apartment in Pasadena."

"Mr. and Mrs. Miller," Salerno said, "I'm very sorry to tell you this, but we believe your daughter may be dead. Would you mind looking at some photographs and telling me if this is Judy?"

He showed them the coroner's pictures. They both agreed that the body was Judy's. The boy watched the cartoon.

"I'm very sorry," Salerno said. He started to say more, to try to comfort them. That was a part of his job, maybe the hardest part, one of the many roles he had to play along with the sleuth, the tough guy, the buddy to a witness, the giver of precise court testimony, and, at home, the husband and father. Sometimes he saw himself as an actor, and it was then that he liked to say that after all, this was Hollywood, wasn't it, and wasn't Hollywood all bullshit anyway? Sometimes he thought the real Frank Salerno emerged only in a boat on a lake in the Sierras, holding a fishing pole, silent. But comforting victims, that was the most difficult of all. If you weren't careful, you could get so emotionally involved with these martyrs to the indifference and improvisational violence of a screwed-up society that you could go to pieces yourself, identify with the victims so much that you forgot who you were and what your primary responsibilities were, to your wife and children.

But Salerno looked at the Miller family and knew that there was little chance he would be able to identify with them. They were already done for. They were holed up in this motel room like people waiting for the end of the world, hoping it would come quickly. They had not needed the murder of their daughter to finish them off. They just sat there, bloodless, unmoving, expecting the worst, maybe even, Salerno thought, relieved that at least one burden had been taken from them. If so, it would not be the first time that he had encountered parents who, either beaten by life or from what was to him an incomprehensible indifference, apparently did not react to what happened to their children. It seemed a kind of emotional paralysis. Himself, he probably worried more about his son's getting a driver's license than about his homicide cases, but maternal and paternal love were more natural to animals than to human beings, Salerno had come to believe.

The Millers received in silence his questions about funeral arrangements. He tried to inquire about Judy's friends. Was she dating anyone? The question mocked itself. They did not know where or how she had been living. He gave them his card and left.

Salerno felt like getting drunk. But it was just eight o'clock. He decided to try the Fish and Chips, which was nearby. The bounty hunter and the whore might be there.

Markust Camden was shoveling in his evening meal. He did not look pleased to see the sergeant, but Salerno went right up to him.

"How you doing, Markust? Everything going all right?"

"Oh, yeah. I just wish people would stop messing with my mind. I told you everything."

Salerno did not think so. Gently, he probed Camden again about the events of the night before Halloween. What time had he seen Judy Miller? In what direction had she been heading when she left? Camden stuck to his previous answers. Salerno tried softening him up by asking him about his activities during the day, previous to his seeing Judy Miller.

"Let's see. It was just a day, man. I don't know."

"Well, did you work?"

"I ain't been working. Somebody needs me, I work. They don't, I don't work."

"What do you work at? You told me you were a disc jockey and a bounty hunter. Did you work at that lately?" Salerno's voice was middle-register, calculated to reassure rather than to threaten.

"I do a lot of things, man." He held up his big hands. From two fingers on the left hand, tips were missing. "These are lethal weapons. I go after you, it's assault with a deadly weapon. I been a martial arts instructor. I can take care of myself and anybody else. I been a personal bodyguard."

"You must be pretty tough."

"Listen. You want something done? I'll take care of it. I'll do anything necessary for you for two hundred and fifty bucks a day."

"That's pretty reasonable. Do you own a car?"

"A car? No. I ain't got wheels at the present time. Wheels come extra."

Salerno had not considered Markust Camden much of a suspect anyway: there was something too frantic about him for a crime like this. He might have killed people in fights, but Salerno could not imagine him doing something as deliberate as these two murders seemed to have been. And if he was telling the truth about not having a car, that would make him still less suspect. The killers must have had a car. But Camden undoubtedly believed himself a suspect, and if he had seen more of Judy Miller that night, he might be afraid to reveal it.

"They tell me you're called Youngblood on the street," Salerno said.

"Yeah. That's me. I'm Youngblood."

"Well, Youngblood, try to remember what you were doing on that day. It could help us. It was Sunday, remember? The day before Halloween?"

"Yeah, okay. It's coming back. It was like this. Okay? I got up late, right? I went out and crushed somebody's elbow that owed me some money and then I went and kicked the door in and took care of some other people. Then I took and went back to the hotel—"

"The hotel where you live, right? The Gilbert Hotel?"

"Right. I took and went back to the hotel, took a shower, went out and talked to a police officer—"

"A police officer. Sheriff's deputy? LAPD? What's his name?"

"Can't recall. Jim. Charlie, could be."

"What did you talk to him about?"

"Nothing in particular. I seen the guy. I talked to him. I seen him around. He's all right. And after I left him I went down and made a big scene at the hot dog stand and I came back to the Gilbert Hotel and like to put a man in the hospital because he was getting a little bit too upset and after that, that was it. That was my daytime story."

"This guy was getting too upset?"

"He was blocking the stairs, man. I helped him along. I helped him downstairs. That was it."

"And later that night, you saw Judy Miller here?"

"That's right. That's the last I seen of her."

"You're sure that's the last you saw of her?"

"That's it. She just split."

"You have no idea where she went?"

"She could of went anywheres, right? Looks like she went out and bought it, what you tell me."

FOUR

"It finally made the papers," Bianchi said. He was on the phone to Buono. "Little dipshit story way back where nobody will read it."

"You at work?"

"Hell no. I took off. They think I have cancer." Bianchi enjoyed telling people he had to go for a chemotherapy treatment when he didn't feel like working. He was lounging in his Hollywood apartment, which he shared with his girlfriend. "I'm at Tamarind. Kelli's out."

"I don't want you calling me about this shit from work."

"Angelo, Angelo," Bianchi said in his unmodulated, boyish way, "I know that much. Anyway, it's in the paper. Might be on the news tonight. They still don't know who she is. Was."

"The cunt don't have no name?"

"Sheriff's asking for public assistance, can you beat that? Maybe we should help them out. They might offer a reward. Boy, that would be something. We ought to figure out how to make money from this deal. How many times do you think we could work this thing?"

"The scam's a winner. The scam's foolproof. We can do what we goddam like. Just so we're careful."

"The Buzzard strikes again."

"Got to be another," Angelo said. "We do another, we put every bitch on notice. One other anyways."

"You know you're right? I mean, nobody's going to notice this, looks like."

"Got to be done. Some girls deserve to die. Dead people tell no tales."

"Yeah. Tonight?"

"I got too much work piled up here. I'm gonna be beat tonight. I got this Bentley, the guy is pissed it ain't ready. Maybe Saturday."

"Saturday's not too good for me. You know, Kelli likes to go out Saturday nights."

"I always said you was pussy-whipped."

"Okay, okay, don't get me wrong. Saturday's okay."

"I got a customer." Angelo hung up.

Bianchi reread the newspaper article a few times and spent the afternoon watching soap operas and browsing through the latest addition to his library of texts on psychology, *Psychoanalysis and Behavior Therapy*. The walls of his apartment were decorated with framed degrees and certificates, including a Master of Science from Columbia University and a diploma conferring on him the title of "Certified Sex Therapist, in recognition of his attaining the required standards of competency, awarded by the American Association of Sex Educators, Counselors and Therapists, Washington, D.C." He kept other bogus degrees at the office he had rented in North Hollywood at a nominal rate from a bona fide psychologist, Dr. Charles Weingarten, who had been most impressed by the spiel Bianchi had spun for him about Gestalt therapy and transactional analysis. Dr. Weingarten had thought the young Dr. Bianchi so pleasant and so sincere that he had been moved to give a struggling colleague a break.

At this office, in a tower on Lankershim Boulevard in the San Fernando Valley, Dr. Bianchi offered weight-reduction counseling to young women. Some had responded to a flyer Bianchi had distributed which bore the salutation "Hi, Neighbor!" and asked why anyone would want to pay exorbitant fees for counseling when Dr. Bianchi from Columbia University would answer any five questions for ten dollars. Bianchi's office walls displayed an Honorary Doctorate in Psychiatry from the National Psychiatric Association of America and a Certificate of Achievement Award of Merit as Intern in Residence, Strong Memorial Hospital, New York City. His practice, however, cannot be said to have flourished. He was leading such a varied, busy life, he had not been able to devote his full intellectual resources to counseling; but there was the future.

In the meanwhile he had another scam cooking. One day, looking respectable in his three-piece suit and carrying his attaché case, he wandered into some offices at Universal Studios, having conned his way past the guarded gates, and hung around as though he had an appointment, waiting for a receptionist to leave her desk. When she did, he grabbed some stationery and left. He knew it would be of use in carrying out his new idea. He would pose as a movie scout. Every other girl he met in Los Angeles aspired to stardom. Why not encourage their hopes and pick up some cash? He was especially short of money now that a prostitution scheme he and Angelo had shared was defunct.

The wind from the east, thirty and forty miles an hour, was whipping the Italian flag Saturday night, November 5, when Bianchi arrived at Angelo's house. He had been telephoning all week, anxious to make thorough preparations, but Angelo had been close-mouthed, as usual, saying he would take care of everything, all Kenny had to do was follow orders. Angelo had suggested, however, that it would be a good idea for Kenny to obtain a police badge, too, and had tipped him off to a swap meet where you could get anything you wanted—badges, guns, uniforms. Bianchi found Angelo watching television in the den and proudly showed him the new badge. It was the star of the California Highway Patrol.

"Great," Angelo said, "you dumb shit. You think we're giving traffic tickets?" Angelo's badge was an LAPD shield. "Well, it don't probably matter. Cunts don't know the difference. You get away all right? You get permission to go out like a good boy?"

"Come on," Bianchi said. "She understands. I come and go as I please."

"Sure."

But Kelli and Kenny had fought over his going out on a Saturday night. He had said he needed to be alone. She had accused him of neglecting her because she was pregnant. By the time he had left, he had told her that no man wanted to spend time with a pregnant bitch who was sick all the time, and he reminded her that he had said all along that she should get an abortion. Driving over to Glendale, he was already planning how to mollify her the next day. He would write her a poem and bring her flowers. The poem would be about sadness and loneliness and their child growing within her. She would go for it.

"I'm ready when you are," Bianchi said.

Angelo looked up at him and stared. Angelo was wearing a T-shirt. Through the hair on his strong, long arms his tattoos showed: on the left forearm, a capital B in Old English lettering, a black panther on the left upper arm; on the right upper arm the head of a panther, on the right forearm a rose with a banner proclaiming "Mother." He continued staring at Bianchi.

"What are you staring at me, Angelo? Makes me nervous. Hey, Tony, why are you staring at me like that?"

Angelo let a smile form: "You know, *mi numi* . . . you know."

Bianchi followed Angelo into the kitchen. On the counter he had laid everything out: tape, foam, rag, cord. So prudent, he had already cut everything into the right lengths. He had even stuck the foam onto a long piece of tape, so that all they would have to do

43

was apply it to her eyes and wrap her head. Whoever she would be.

"No sense running back and forth from the shop," Angelo said. "I'll get a shirt and my jacket."

Outside at the car, the wind blowing, the night smogless and starry, Angelo had another idea and stepped into his shop. He produced a flashlight, bright metal with a red plastic rim around the glass. "This'll be a good touch," he said.

Bianchi drove this time. At the corner of San Fernando and Los Feliz, just a couple of blocks from Forest Lawn, Angelo pointed to a Mexican fast-food restaurant and said, "Pull over there. I got to eat something." Bianchi waited in the car until Buono came out, bearing a big beef burrito. As they pulled out of the restaurant, Buono mumbled through a mouthful of tortilla, "Hey, look over there. Beep your horn."

Across the street at a gas station, Angelo had spotted one of his ex-wives, Candy, and their daughter, Grace. Bianchi beeped, everyone waved, and Bianchi headed the Cadillac for Hollywood.

They turned down Western and out Sunset to the Strip, passing Carney's, the railroad diner, glancing at each other to acknowledge a now-hallowed spot. The Strip was alive, the traffic thick, the sidewalks crowded, too crowded for a pickup. At La Cienega Boulevard, Buono told Bianchi to head back toward Hollywood. They would try the side streets, the dimly lit ones. "We could check out the parking lots," Buono said. "I was thinking, she don't even have to be a hooker, you know?"

"What do you mean?"

"Why she have to be a hooker? With this scam, we could stop anybody. We could stop a fucking nun, see what I mean? We got our pick of the city, *mi numi*. We got it all. You got to think big. We could find us a virgin."

"You're really on tonight, Angelo."

Angelo outlined the possibilities. Why, he wondered, couldn't they carry their police ruse one step further? They could stop a girl, any girl. Say they're taking her in. Once she's in the car, it's all over. The

44

girl wouldn't even have to be walking. She could be driving. They could spot some girl driving alone and just follow her. She would stop somewhere. She would be driving home. She would lead them to some side street with nobody on it and they could make their move. Bianchi agreed that it could work. It was worth a try. With this scam, there was no telling what they could do.

"I can taste it," Bianchi said. "I can taste it now."

"Just keep your pecker in your pants till we get home."

At Highland they turned left, northward toward the Hollywood Hills.

"I'll try around my place," Bianchi said.

"Not too close."

And then they spotted her. A dark-headed girl driving a lime-green Beetle convertible.

"Follow that," Buono said. "Get close enough we can look her over. Follow her."

The Beetle turned right onto Franklin with the Cadillac in pursuit, crossed Cahuenga and Vine, passed under the Hollywood Freeway, and turned left on Argyle Avenue, a street of apartment houses.

"Slow down," Buono said. "She's going to park."

Near the corner of Argyle and Dix Street, the girl stopped against the curb and switched off her lights.

"Just double-park behind her," Buono said. "Get your badge ready. Be cool. Be real cool. Looks good. No one else around."

As the girl got out of her car and started to lock the door, Buono and Bianchi were on her. Buono had his flashlight.

"Police officers," Bianchi said, quickly showing her his CHP star, which he had pinned to his wallet, and just as quickly slipping it back into the pocket of his leather coat. "May we see some identification?" The girl fumbled in her purse and brought out her driver's license. Bianchi glanced at the license and handed it to Buono, who shined his flashlight on it.

"Why am I being stopped?" Lissa Kastin asked. "Did I run a light or something?"

"There's been some trouble, Miss, ah . . ." Buono tried to puzzle out the syllables of her name on the license. Bianchi looked at it under the flashlight.

"There's been a robbery, Miss Kastin," Bianchi said. "Your car was pointed out by a witness as leaving the scene."

"That's ridiculous," Lissa Kastin said. "I just got off work."

"Where do you work?" Bianchi asked.

"Healthfaire Restaurant. I'm a waitress."

"A waitress. And what is the location of the Healthfaire Restaurant?"

"Vine Street."

"That's very near where the alleged robbery took place."

"You have to go along with us," Buono said.

"We'll have to take you in for questioning."

"But this is a complete mistake," she said. "I haven't done anything. There must be hundreds of cars like mine around. There's been a mistake."

"It's a very distinctive color," Bianchi said. "You'll have to come with us. Just step over to our car there."

"You have no reason at all to question me," Lissa Kastin said. Her voice was beginning to sound angry, and she made a step backward toward her car.

"You don't want to make a scene here," Angelo said, approaching her.

"You have no right," she said, her voice rising.

"You don't want to start something here on the street, do you?" Bianchi said. "So you'd better just come along with us, and if everything checks out, we'll bring you back again. If you haven't done anything, everything will check out. That's what we have our systems for. You'd better step over to our car now."

Lissa Kastin hesitated, then walked slowly over to the Cadillac. Buono opened the right rear door and ushered her in, sitting down beside her. As they started up, Bianchi clicked the automatic door locks. He made a U-turn, headed east on Franklin, and passed Tamarind Avenue, his own street. At Western, he turned left, and Angelo said:

"I'm going to have to put handcuffs on you."

"You must be kidding! What is this? Why do you guys have to play cops and robbers? You don't have to handcuff me! I'm telling you, I haven't done anything!"

"It's procedure," Angelo said. "It's police procedure."

"Wait a minute. There's no need for you to put handcuffs on me." She lowered her voice. "Look, I'm not going anyplace. You've got me. I can't go anywhere. I'm not going anywhere."

"We really wish we didn't have to, Miss Kastin," Bianchi said soothingly from the driver's seat. "Believe me, if it were up to us, we wouldn't do it. But you have to understand, some suspects aren't nearly as cooperative as we know you'll be. We've had some pretty ugly incidents, if you understand me. Officers have been hurt, you know, just doing their duty. So we've evolved these procedures. Because if you make one exception, then the whole system breaks down. We hope you understand."

"Fine," she said, sighing. She leaned forward, and Buono handcuffed her behind her back.

"I'm double-locking," he said. "That way they don't hurt."

"This is a bunch of baloney," she said. "You guys are wasting your time. When you check me out, you're going to find out you wasted your time. This is a false arrest."

"We have probable cause," Bianchi said. "I'm sure everything will check out. Then we can take you back."

"I am completely innocent," she said. "I've never done anything in my life. I'm nothing but a lousy waitress. Why don't you pick on a real crook?"

"We have to follow up leads," Bianchi said. "If you're innocent, you have nothing to worry about."

From time to time as they drove toward Glendale, Lissa Kastin continued to protest, and when at last Bianchi pulled into Angelo's driveway and cut the motor, she refused to get out of the car. But Bianchi coaxed her into the house, suggesting that she had no choice, which she did not.

From that point on the procedure was the same as with Judy Miller, except that Angelo worried that this girl might fight, so he kept her handcuffed and cut off her clothes with a big pair of upholstery scissors. Naked, she appealed to neither cousin. Angelo especially was put off by her unshaven legs and derided her as "some kind of a health nut." He decided to pass up the sex this time, not even bothering to flip a coin, growing sullen and resentful at this affront to his intentions. Watching Kenny trying to work up some enthusiasm for rape in the spare bedroom, Angelo handed him a root-beer bottle. Kenny applied the bottle with such eagerness and animation that he made her bleed, much to Angelo's irritation. To make sure she did not bleed on the carpet when she was strangled, Angelo spread a piece of her coat on the floor.

The murder itself went as before, except that Angelo added one new twist, tightening and then slackening the cord, bringing her to the brink of death and back again several times over, delighting in the absolute power of it. At Kenny's request, the cousins traded places, with Bianchi doing the final killing while Buono, sitting on her knees and showing real passion for the first time that night, shouted, "Die, cunt! Die!"

Her belongings safely in the dumpster, her body in the trunk, Angelo headed the Cadillac north toward the hills. About two miles from his house he pointed out an apartment building on Chevy Chase where he had once lived. He knew the area well, he said.

"Nobody knows the city like the Buzzard," Kenny said.

After a very few minutes they were in the hills, but not high up this time. It was the beginning of a canyon dotted with expensive, rather new houses and then, on the left, the golf course of the Chevy Chase Country Club. At a bend in the road there were no houses on the right, and the golf course, fenced and bordered by big eucalyptus trees, was on the left. Angelo drove ahead until he could make a U-turn, came back down to the relatively secluded spot beside the golf course, stopped the car, and cut the headlights but left the motor running. Bianchi reached into the glove compartment and pushed the trunk button.

"Make it quick," Angelo said. "Nobody's coming."

The wind blew hard. With all the trees, it was very dark. Between the golf-course fence and the road lay a deep drainage ditch, then a steep embankment, then a metal guard rail about three feet high. They swung the body over the guard rail, trying to heave it into the ditch. But she landed heavily and rolled with a rustling of leaves down the embankment about fifteen feet and came to rest against an invisible guy wire. Up the road, Angelo spotted headlights.

"Let's go," he said. "You drive."

As Angelo nipped around the back of the Cadillac, he grabbed from the trunk a remnant of Lissa Kastin's coat, which he had used to keep the body from bleeding onto the car, and slammed the lid. The other car passed them as they drove off.

"You think that guy noticed anything?" Angelo asked.

"Nah. What're you going to do with the coat?"

"Pull over at the next corner."

Angelo stuffed the bloody remnant down a curbside storm drain.

"It was a bust, you know that?" Angelo said as they approached Colorado Street. "It wasn't worth it. She was a dog. If I'd've knowed it would turn out like this, I'd've watched TV."

Kenny had to agree, although he said that the slow strangulation had been good. It offered all kinds of possibilities.

Disappointment burdened them during the next couple of days. On the phone, they agreed that the foul-up could be traced to the process of selection. They had been overeager, picking out Lissa Kastin because she was easy prey. They had ignored aesthetics. There ought to be some way of signaling approval to each other before a girl was finally chosen. Following her onto a poorly lit street had been an error, since neither of them had gotten a good look at her. With all the girls in L.A., why should they settle for anything but the tops? It had been like casting an unknown actress without a screen test.

"We couldn't really tell how bad she was until we got her clothes off," Bianchi said.

"Bullshit," Angelo said. "You can tell, you can tell. We moved too fast, that's all. What's the rush? We could take all night finding the right one. We could take all week."

"Yeah. We could really look one over. We could find something totally choice."

"You got it. There are thousands, *mi numi,* thousands."

It was a mere four nights later that they decided to go for it again. There had been no public notice as yet of Lissa Kastin's death, the city knew nothing of the act, and to Buono and Bianchi it had become an irritating nonevent, a draw in a bout that cried out for a rematch. On Wednesday evening, November 9, Bianchi dropped in to see Angelo. They were going to discuss strategy, merely. Bianchi found Angelo out back stroking his rabbits in the darkness, with Sparky barking jealously at his feet.

Inside, they rehearsed again the inadequacies of Lissa Kastin. Sheltered by the house that had now concealed two successful murders, they grew agitated. Angelo floated about, straightening, dusting, checking the fish, as Bianchi talked. They had the perfect setup. It would be a crime not to take better advantage of it. How many other guys had a chance like this? There had never been such a scam. As long as they were careful, it could work again. And again.

"Yeah, there's got to be a limit," Angelo said. "We go too far, we're gonna slip up. We can't do every girl in town. Keep your lid on, Kenny."

"Right," Bianchi said, "but I tell you, we got it made. I can taste it, Tony, I can taste it."

"Let me get my jacket," Angelo said.

"We going now? Tonight?"

"You got it. But calm down, will you, asshole? This time, it's perfect, understand me? And one other thing. We don't find the right one, we don't go for just anything, see what I mean? We forget it this time. We come back here and we figure this just wasn't the night. Right?"

"I got a feeling this is going to be it."

50

"That's real nice. But if I say it's no go, it's no go. Understand? I say it's no good, we scrub the mission. I ain't even gonna lay out the stuff this time. Maybe that was bad luck. Sometimes you plan everything, it puts a jinx. Sometimes you just gotta see how it goes down, follow me?"

"I follow you. You're the boss, Angelo. You're the captain."

"Don't forget it."

Bianchi drove his Cadillac. In Hollywood, they cruised slowly, down the Boulevard, along the Strip. There were plenty of whores. None appealed.

"I feel like some fresh pussy," Angelo said.

"Maybe we should try another area. Maybe we should try Westwood. We could get some UCLA cheerleader. A blonde."

"Too far."

"Let's try around my place again. It's after ten. There's girls around there, always are. We could get somebody coming out of a movie."

"Go ahead."

Back in his own neighborhood, Bianchi checked the parking area of his apartment building on Tamarind to make sure Kelli's Mazda was there. It was. He didn't want her going out at night without his knowing it, even if she was pregnant. She was into her sixth month.

On Franklin they passed two young girls walking together, considered them, passed them up. And then, in front of the Mayfair Market at the corner of Franklin and Bronson, they observed a girl standing alone next to a bus bench. She was slim and blond, wearing tight jeans rolled at the bottoms. Bianchi slowed. They took a good look, cruising past.

"Do you see what I see?" Buono asked.

"You bet I do."

"What do you want to do?"

Bianchi headed around the block. They agreed that this one looked prime, at first glance anyway. But Angelo wanted another look. He told Bianchi to approach the bus bench on Franklin again. A block or so east of the bus stop, they pulled up to the curb, stopped, and looked.

She was sitting on the bench now, apparently waiting for the bus. She had her long legs out in front of her, crossed at the ankles.

"Super shoes," Bianchi said. "High heels."

"She ain't no slob, I can see that much. What do you want to do? She won't go with two guys. Right out there in the open, we got to get her easy. She's got to want to go. Tell you what. I'll go talk to her. Then you come back. I'll think of something. Sit here a minute. See if she's getting a ride."

"Let me rap with her," Bianchi said.

"Yeah. Okay. What're you gonna use?"

"You know me," Bianchi said. "I can bullshit anyone."

"Look at her. She's choice. Look at that."

"I'll go talk to her. You drive around for a few minutes. Give me some time. Then you come back. And . . . I know. You offer me a ride. We know each other, okay? You offer me a ride and I offer her a ride, and if I do this right, she'll come along."

"It might work. No badges?"

"I might work that in. I'll get that in somehow. Leave it to me. I'll get the chick to go along. Let me off in the supermarket parking lot there. It's like I just came out of the market."

They switched places, and Angelo let Bianchi out in the parking lot and took off. Bianchi approached the bus bench. He sat down next to the girl and looked her over unobtrusively. She was beautiful. Blonde and angular. A model type. Her high-heeled shoes were silver below her rolled, tight jeans.

"Hi," he said. "Excuse me. Do you know when the bus is coming?"

"We just missed one. There might be another soon. It might be half an hour. You know how they are."

"I know, I know. My car, I can't believe it, my car's in the shop, and gosh, it's terrible. Public transportation in Los Angeles is really terrible. I can't wait till I get my car back."

"You're not from L.A.?"

"Back East originally," Bianchi said. "Rochester, New York. You know, Kodak? Where all the film gets made. I've been out here awhile, though. I'm getting my feet on the ground, anyway. You meet some nice people. People are friendly out here, I'll say that. Everybody's got a smile on their face. It's not like back East. Back East, you know, you talk to somebody at a bus stop, they think you're crazy. It's not like that out here. I like that. I really, really do. You just get off work or something?''

His voice, his manner, so unaggressive, rather epicene, reassured her.

"No. I just came from acting class, over there.'' She pointed to an ornate, castlelike building across the street. Bianchi noticed that her hand was long and tapered and graceful. He looked down at her silver shoes again.

"What's that building? Is that a studio or something?''

"It's one of the Scientology buildings. Scientology Manor. That's where they have the acting workshop.''

"Oh. That's interesting. An acting workshop. Is that, I mean is it just acting, or does it have something to do with Scientology? Like, is it part of the religion, or what?''

She gave a little laugh. "Well, in a way, everything is connected to Scientology. It's a little of both. What I mean is, the acting is based on principles of Scientology. If you understand the principles, you can do anything, really.''

"You must be into Scientology. I don't know much about it. I've heard about it. It's not weird or anything, is it? I'm more into psychology, myself. Gestalt and behavioristic theory. You don't look like a weird person yourself. You look pretty normal and healthy to me.''

"There's nothing weird about it,'' she said. "Some people are jealous, that's all. They try to give it a bad name. The other religions, they're afraid if everyone knew how wonderful it is, they'd lose people, that's all. It's human nature.''

"I'm sure that's true. But I mean, do you go to church, or what?''

"Yes. There's so much to it.''

"Tell me something about it. I'm really interested. I mean, if so many people are in it, it must have something."

Bianchi feigned an eager interest as she discoursed on Scientology. She explained at length that she had her reality, just as he had his.

"Hey," Bianchi said, "there's my friend! Can you beat that? Hey!" He waved as though signaling Angelo, who brought the Cadillac to a stop in front of the bus bench. Angelo gave the horn a friendly toot-toot and lowered the window. "Hey, Tony. How about a lift? Can you take me home?"

"Sure. Where you been? Where you been hiding?"

Bianchi approached the car window and, leaning in, whispered to Buono that he was going to ask the girl if she wanted a ride. Angelo nodded.

"Say," Bianchi said to the girl. "My friend Tony says if you're not going too far, he'll give you a ride, too. We really lucked out tonight."

"I don't think so," she said. "I think I'll just wait for the bus. It's okay."

"You don't have to worry," Bianchi said. "That's my cousin. Don't worry, we're both in the L.A. Police Reserve." He flashed his badge at her. "I'll tell you, you're a lot safer with us than sitting here alone on this corner. I hope you don't live too far, though, that's the only thing. I don't want to put him out. I hope you understand."

"I don't live far. Straight down Franklin."

"Great. Hop in." He opened the front door for her.

"Okay."

Bianchi got in the front seat after her. They headed west on Franklin.

"This is my cousin Tony Buono. And Tony, this is . . . I'm sorry. I forgot to ask your name."

"Jane King."

"Tony, this is Jane. I'm Kenny. Kenny Bianchi."

"Hi, Kenny. This is awfully nice of you guys."

"It's nothing," Bianchi said. "Glad to help out. I don't like to see a nice girl in Hollywood alone anyway. You don't have a car?"

"My roommate sometimes picks me up."

"That's a better idea. Say, Tony, pull into that market over there, would you? I need some cigarettes."

"Yeah, I do too." He drove into the Hughes Market at the corner of Highland.

"Do you mind waiting in the car for a minute?" Bianchi asked. "We'll be right out. Do you need anything, cigarettes or gum or anything, Jane?"

"No. I'll be fine. Take your time."

In the market Bianchi asked Buono what he thought. Buono gave his hearty approval. He thought that Jane King was one of the best-looking chicks he had seen in a long time. How had Bianchi conned her?

"Never mind. She's one of those Scientology crazies. The thing is, we've got her so she trusts us. We could handcuff her now, or better if we could just get her to ride with us all the way home. She won't fall for a party or something, though. She's pretty cautious."

"Tell her I got to go home first. Tell her you'll take her home after."

"I'll try it."

In the car: "Listen, Jane, would you mind something? The thing is, my cousin here, he's such a nice guy, he didn't want to tell us, but he really has to go home right away. He's got some things to do and he'll really be messed up if he doesn't get home right away, and the thing is, he could go home, and then I could drop you off, if that's all right."

"It's too much trouble for you guys."

"No, no. Really. I mean, we can't offer you a ride and then say no, can we? It's no trouble. No trouble for me at all."

"Okay. I really appreciate it."

Bianchi switched on some music, and Jane King did not even seem to notice how far they were going, up over the Hollywood Hills, down along Forest Lawn Drive and on to Glendale. It was after eleven at night, traffic was light. Jane King stared ahead, nestled between the samaritans, content with her good luck, listening to the music and rhythmically chewing on the gum Bianchi had given her. She hummed the

tunes she recognized. Bianchi commented on her ring.
It was called a mood ring, she said. It changed colors
with her mood. She said she was in a good mood now.
Bianchi kept expecting her to ask how far they were
going, and when she did not, he wondered whether
she was spaced out on something. He wished he had
a joint on him. He would have offered her a toke. This
was so easy, and he was proud of his negotiating
skills. In the big car distances rolled by like clouds.

In the driveway Angelo switched off the motor.
Sparky ran up. For a moment the three of them sat
there, Jane King waiting for Angelo to get out and
Bianchi to drive her home.

Bianchi looked at Buono behind Jane King's head
and saw him give a slight nod. Angelo grabbed her left
arm, Bianchi her right. She started squirming.

"What are you doing? What's going on?"

Angelo pulled out the handcuffs with his free
hand.

"Don't hurt me! Let me go!"

They pushed her forward and forced her hands
together behind her back, and Angelo snapped on the
cuffs. Bianchi grabbed her purse.

"Keep your mouth shut," Angelo said, "and
nothing's gonna happen to you." She began to shake.
She let out a sound. "Just button that lip."

Inside, they sat her down in the easy chair.

"Don't be nervous, honey," Angelo said. "Nothing's gonna happen to you. Keep calm and keep your
mouth closed." *Sotto voce* he told Bianchi to watch
her while he went to the shop to get the materials.
This time he brought some sponge rubber, a white rag,
and coarse brown twine. With the tape and scissors
from the kitchen, he was ready. He worked quickly.
Jane King, trembling violently, was gagged and blindfolded in seconds. He stood her up and removed the
handcuffs, saying that she wasn't going to be any trouble, but as soon as he had removed her light jacket,
she began flailing her arms, so he clapped on the cuffs
again and cut her blouse and bra free with the scissors.
Her skin was pale; her frail ribcage heaved. Angelo
unzipped the fly of her jeans and with great effort
began to drag them down. "She's sewn into these

things," he said. "Tight to show her ass. Cunts love to show their ass if they've got one. Nice ass." He smoothed his hand across the round buttock. "Lift your leg." He removed a shoe. "Silver. Silver fucking shoes. Class. Lift the other leg, honey." Now she stood in green pantyhose. Angelo pulled them down.

Then he stood back, pointing, grinning, doing a little hop from foot to foot like Geppetto gleeful at a new puppet. Wordlessly pointing, he motioned Bianchi to come around from behind her for a look.

She stood there, a moon-tinted offering, slender, bound, a silvery undine, her narrow thighs pressed together and quivering, tapering upward to an absence. She had no pubic hair.

"Bald pussy!" Angelo whispered reverently. He gripped his hands together and lowered his head. "Shaved pussy, can you believe it? We must be living right. Hurry up, man. I can't wait for this. Stash her stuff over there by the mirror."

Angelo permitted himself a long appreciative gaze at her. So helpless, her hands linked behind her back, her sex bare as a girl-child's, blindfolded and gagged, her narrow feet self-consciously pressed together, she was everything Angelo Buono could desire, a tender virgin vessel, soft-hued as ivory, immaculate, enslaved.

He led Jane King into the spare bedroom, put her on her back on the bed, and told her in a low, paternal voice that nothing was going to happen to her. He returned to the living room and found Bianchi already putting her belongings into a garbage bag. "Don't put the purse in yet. We want to go through it. How are we gonna do this? Shit." He rubbed his crotch. "I need to go first. I want to real bad, man. But I'll show you what kind of a guy I am. We'll flip a coin, just like before."

Angelo won the toss. He shook Kenny's hand and disappeared into the spare bedroom. Kenny decided that he wanted to see this one from the beginning. Quietly he stepped into Angelo's bedroom and took up a position behind the hanging beads in the doorway. He watched as Jane King did everything she could to deny Angelo, protesting that only her boyfriend was allowed to see her naked and to have sex with her, then questioning whether her boyfriend had set this scene up as a sick joke. She gave in to Angelo's stabs when he threatened to beat her if she continued to resist.

When he was done, Angelo pronounced her "choice," but with Kenny she was equally resisting, saying that she might not be able to do anything about what was happening to her but she was not going to pretend to like it. Hearing this, Angelo got an idea.

He brought in the twine and worked quickly. "She needs a lesson," he said. He wrapped the twine around her ankles, turned her over, forced her legs backward toward her arms, and wrapped the twine around her handcuffed wrists, hog-tying her. Bianchi, picking up his cue, mounted her from behind as Angelo watched, pulling out his penis, feeling himself, ejaculating as Bianchi reached his own climax.

"Stay in her," Angelo said. From the kitchen he brought a vegetable bag, and, Bianchi still in her from behind, forced the bag over her head and wrapped the twine around her throat.

"See if you can get off again," Angelo said. He pulled, Bianchi pumped. Jane King screamed within the bag, tried vainly to suck air. Building on his technique with Lissa Kastin, Angelo let the twine slacken, reviving her, then pulled again. He repeated the pulling and slackening several times as Bianchi rutted, but finally Jane King had no more breath. Bianchi finished after she was dead.

"I could have gone on longer," Kenny said. "I could have gone on all night. She's still hot."

Searching her purse, they were surprised to learn from her driver's license that she had been born in 1949. "Well-preserved," Kenny called her. "She's the kind of chick would have looked good at forty."

"We let her die gorgeous," Angelo said. "We did her a favor."

Angelo drove. As usual, he said nothing of his destination. This time he headed back toward Griffith Park. It was now after one in the morning and the cars were few. "We'll head up there," he said, pointing vaguely in the direction of Dodger Stadium, holding a steady fifty-five on the Golden State Freeway, but he slowed as he approached the Los Feliz offramp.

On the offramp, curved and dark with trees and heavy shrubbery, he suddenly pulled over to the side, saying, "Quick. Let's dump her here. Move fast."

They threw Jane King well into some bushes.

"No one will see her there," Angelo said as he drove off. "She could be there till somebody gets out to take a piss. She could be there for days."

"Somebody'll get a shock." Bianchi laughed. "What'll you think of next?"

"You never know."

During the next few days they talked about what a great success the Jane King murder had been. Angelo recapitulated the pleasures of her shaved pubis. The weekend arrived without any press or television coverage of their latest act. *Impunitas semper ad deteriora invitat*, goes the Latin legal maxim: Impunity always invites to greater crimes. They were beginning to feel invincible. There was no telling what they might be able to get away with. Angelo, still praising Jane King, began suggesting the next logical step: to abduct a very young girl, a schoolgirl, unspoiled, inviolate, barely ripe and helpless; a girl, Angelo emphasized, who did not have anything to shave or only the first fuzzy hints of womanhood. Bianchi said that he had never been with so young a girl but had often fantasized about it, the buttery baby skin, the thin little voice, the hairless smallness. Angelo assured him that there was nothing comparable to very young girls, their helplessness, their fear, their crying out. To make a sacrifice of one—that would be something to make life worth living. If they could find one and "break her in" and then kill her, she would have lived just for them, they would be her beginning and her end. That would be the ultimate snuff.

On Sunday, November 13, four days after Jane King, Buono and Bianchi drove over to the Eagle Rock Plaza in search of their vestal virgin.

FIVE

Jane King lay moldering beside that Golden State off-ramp during that week and the next. Her roommate and her boyfriend reported her missing. The room-mate, a young man she had met through an apartment-sharing service, who lived with her only to share rent and to enjoy safety in numbers, had seen her near six o'clock that Wednesday evening. They had eaten TV dinners, before she had gone off to her Scientology class. Her boyfriend had not been with her since the previous Friday, when she had spent the night with him. They had quarreled a couple of days later because he had not wished to spend another night with her, but he had telephoned Wednesday evening and had been told she was at a Scientology class.

Her fellow students at Scientology Manor de-scribed her as a quiet girl, introverted, fond of exer-cise and salads. One of her friends there, a girl who had roomed with her that past summer, said that she had offered Jane a ride home after class at eleven, but

Jane had preferred to take the bus. On other nights Jane had complained that she was wary of sitting alone at bus stops and often preferred to hitchhike. That way you could select the person to hitch a ride from, Jane had said. You could tell by looking at a person whether he was all right. Jane had not been known for logic. Her friends liked to call her Jupiter Jane.

Frank Salerno was then aware of none of this. Other officers were handling Jane King as a missing person; until and if she turned up dead, there was no call for the Homicide Bureau. Salerno was spending his days and nights pursuing the Judy Miller case and keeping an eye on the Lissa Kastin investigation. His partner, an older detective, was helping out but was due to retire soon, so Salerno felt that this was really his own case for now, unless another body showed up. He spoke to the bounty hunter, Markust Camden, again, getting nothing more out of him but still sensing that he had more to tell. Salerno decided to check out Pam Pelletier, the prostitute. Maybe she had more to tell about seeing Judy Miller leave the International Hot Dog stand early Halloween morning.

Pam Pelletier turned out to be one of those many tantalizing but false leads which take up most of a detective's time. When she seemed to be unable to recall much of anything, Salerno asked her to undergo hypnosis, and she revealed that she had worked in her spare time as the subject for a professional hypnotist, who she said had hypnotized her thousands of times before audiences. She was so used to this man's techniques, she doubted that she could be put under by anyone else. Salerno acquiesced and permitted her hypnotist to work on her in an office in Hollywood, where for hours she recalled the sad story of her life —constant moving around, changing men, attending the Woodstock Festival, three times giving birth, ending up in Hollywood drugging and hustling, drifting.

It was a familiar story to Salerno and not helpful. When the hypnotist at last got around to asking her about Halloween and Judy Miller, Pam Pelletier spun out a tale Salerno believed was imagined about seeing Judy Miller take off with "a light-skinned Negro in a maroon pimp hat" who had "eyes like a Doberman."

The hypnotist obligingly drew Salerno a sketch of this improbable suspect, complete with mirrors and buckles on his hat and a Teddy Roosevelt mustache. This was one instance, Salerno felt, in which hypnosis had stimulated the imagination rather than the memory of a subject. He had to keep himself from snickering when the hypnotist awakened Pam Pelletier by shouting at her:

"You will not feel anything but great! You will feel as though you just had a steam bath! A cold shower or a complete body massage! One! You're waking up! Two-completely-relaxed-Three-light-elevated-exceptionally-clear-headed-Four-look-at-you-Five-you're-wide-awake! And now you will be able to resume whatever *miserable* life to which you are accustomed!"

Listening to Pam Pelletier's ramblings made Salerno think that he had better check out Markust Camden again, unless he wanted to waste days looking for the guy in the pimp hat. He would file his report on Pam Pelletier, but he did not think anything she had said would end up meaning much.

This time Salerno cornered Markust Camden at the Fish and Chips and let him know that since it appeared that he was the last person to have seen Judy Miller alive, he would have to be considered a suspect. Blood tests would have to be run on him. They would have to take samples of his hair, stuff like that. Without threatening him, Salerno let Camden know that this was serious. If he knew anything else, he had better come across with it now. Camden understood. He suggested they take a walk.

Out on the Boulevard, Camden had a lot more to tell. He admitted that he had seen more of Judy Miller than he had let on, but he hoped Salerno understood his point of view, too. He had not done anything, yet he didn't want to say anything to incriminate himself. Salerno assured him that he had nothing to worry about. The more he helped the police, the better off he would be.

"I'm a law enforcement kind of guy myself," Camden said.

"Fine. Go ahead. What happened?"

Camden talked. He had not let Judy Miller walk off from the Fish and Chips that night. After he had chatted with her for a while, he had invited her back to his room at the Gilbert Hotel.

"You had sex with her?"

"Yeah. You see now, I didn't want to say nothing."

"You had sex with her. Anything unusual?"

"Just a straight lay, man. I mean, it was nothing."

"Then what happened?"

"Then, let's see. We took a shower. She said she was hungry. She was broke, man, and thin, real thin. I didn't have nothing to give her. I give her a bra."

"You keep a lot of bras around?"

"No. Don't get me wrong. It was just some bra one of my girlfriends left behind. I give it to Judy Miller. She didn't have nothing. Then I said, okay, so let's get something to eat or a cup of coffee or something."

The Gilbert Hotel was on Wilcox just above Sunset. Camden said that he and Judy Miller had walked down to Sunset and turned west. They had walked for a long time. She was looking for a trick. She had said that she needed a trick, but because she was walking with Camden, nobody stopped. Eventually they ended up at a place that looked like a railroad car.

"Carney's?" Salerno asked. "Carney's railroad diner?"

"That's it. Anyways, we went into this place and got coffee. Then she left to find a trick."

"Did you see her pick up a trick?"

"I'm getting to that."

Camden said that Judy Miller had gone outside. He had watched her through the window of the railroad diner for a while.

"Where was she standing?"

"Right in the driveway, between the diner and some store. It was a kitchen place. Sold pots and pans or something. I was a little worried about the chick, I don't know why. So I took and went outside and waited."

"You waited with her?"

63

"Not with her. I sort of stood back, you know. So after a while, this car pulls in and she starts talking to the guy. You know, making arrangements."

"Wait a minute," Salerno said. "What kind of a car was it?"

"Big car. A limo."

"A limousine. You sure of that?"

"It was a limo. Dark blue limousine, yeah."

"How close were you? Did you get a look at the guy driving? Was he alone?"

"He was alone. Yeah, I saw him. I kind of moved closer. I got a good look. I'd say he looked like a Puerto Rican."

Salerno wanted to know why the man looked like a Puerto Rican. Camden said that the man was dark, with curly dark hair. Latin-looking. And he had a big nose. He remembered that now. The man had definitely had a big nose. Salerno questioned Camden several times about this description, but he stuck to it.

"Do you think you would recognize this guy again if you saw him?"

"I would," Camden said.

Salerno asked Camden whether he would mind driving over to the railroad diner so that he could demonstrate exactly what had happened. Camden said he would be happy to do that. As they approached the diner on Sunset, Salerno did not slow down until Camden pointed it out. Next door to the diner was a kitchen design and equipment store called, appropriately, Kitchens.

Camden repeated his story exactly and added that after Judy Miller had gotten into the limousine, it had pulled out onto Sunset, had turned east, and had then turned south at the next corner, which was Sweetzer. He had watched the limousine disappear down the hill.

After checking Camden into Cedars-Sinai Hospital for tests, which Salerno doubted would show anything, he drove downtown to file his reports. The Sheriff's Homicide Bureau was in room 832 of the old Hall of Justice Building at Temple and Spring, just across the street from the Criminal Courts Building. Room 832 had been converted from a courtroom—the

64

Manson case had been tried there—and now consisted of about thirty metal desks, each with a telephone, lined up side by side in rows. The floor above its high ceiling was still a jail, holding cells for prisoners awaiting trial across the street, and when the prisoners got bored they would amuse themselves by stopping up the toilets with paper and rags. You could tell when the prisoners were playing this game because the toilets would overflow and urine would drip down through the old ceiling and form little puddles on the detectives' desks. It was not an ideal place for a detective to work, puzzling out leads and making the endless phone calls that made up a good portion of his job, but morale in the bureau was excellent. Sheriff's Homicide had the best record of obtaining convictions in the region, 71.6 percent versus 49.3 percent for the Los Angeles Police Department. Partisans of the LAPD would explain the discrepancy on the basis of a disparity in case loads, but prosecutors and judges tended to rate the Sheriff's higher, saying that it was more inclined to stick with a case as it progressed through the tangled court system, while the LAPD seemed to lose interest once an arrest was made. They also praised the Sheriff's practice of preparing a detailed "murder book" for prosecutors, a meticulously arranged file of all material relevant to the case, with suggestions concerning the strongest and weakest points. The LAPD, it was said, presented only a miscellaneous file, which made the prosecutors' job more difficult and increased the chance that important elements of evidence might be overlooked or misconstrued. Again, people who were pro-LAPD had their own versions of the relative merits of the two departments, arguing that all that time spent shepherding cases through the courts could be better spent arresting more murderers. If the LAPD conviction rate was lower, it was the fault of sloppy, lazy prosecutors and muddle-headed judges: that was where reform was needed. Why should the police do the courts' job? The Sheriff's, the LAPD would argue, was overly concerned with its public image.

What no one would deny was that the rivalry between the two agencies was intense and of long historical standing. Officers of either department were always ready to cast aspersions on the other, usually in the form of dark allusions to "the way they do things over there." The rivalry was much the same as that among the Army, Navy, and Air Force, and it had similar consequences: intensified esprit-de-corps within each department and a tendency to secrecy and self-interest when cooperation between them was needed. They worked better alone than together, and when a case called for their combined efforts, as with a crime affecting both county and city jurisdictions, they too often worked at cross purposes.

Salerno himself cared little about the rivalry. He had friends in the LAPD and would not hesitate to call on them even though his loyalties were to the Sheriff's. After he had written up his reports on Camden and Pelletier, he walked over to the Code 7 bar, a favorite police hangout a couple of blocks from his office, where he knew he would find members of both departments and deputy D.A.s and a newspaper reporter or two. As he ordered his Scotch and water at the bar, a big LAPD homicide sergeant named Bob Grogan came over, threw his arm around Salerno, and told the bartender to put Salerno's drink on his tab. For himself, Grogan ordered a double straight shooter of John Jameson's Irish.

"Hey, Frank," Grogan said in his booming Boston-Irish voice, "what's happening? Goddammit, you wouldn't believe what they laid on me today. A 1968 suicide, so now it's supposed to be a murder. Jesus Christ, I love those. Can you believe it? Why do they do this to me? Holy shit, nine years too late and they want me to make a case. I guess they want to make me prove what a genius I am."

Bob Grogan was six-three and well over two hundred pounds, but his brash Boston voice and his wild gestures made him seem even bigger. His buddies called him Cro-Magnon. He had been known to kick in a door, rumble past a cowering suspect, grab two beers from the refrigerator, slam the cans down on the table, and read the poor bastard his rights. Grogan had a fringe of red hair left on his bald head and a red mustache under his little nose on a broad, red face that looked as though it had been airmailed over in a bottle from County Kerry. He had just turned forty. He asked Salerno what he was working on.

"This strangling," Salerno said. "Runaway girl. I've been living on Hollywood Boulevard."

"Scum of the earth," Grogan said. "Worst collection of assholes in America. You find the parents?"

"Took me ten days. They didn't care, I guess. I don't know."

"That's it. Sure. Makes you feel terrific, doesn't it? You're trying to find who killed their kid and they don't give a shit? I'm telling you, Frank, this town is the ends of the earth. I had one like that last month. You know what I did? Listen to this, will you listen to this? I find the parents' house, right? The family abode. A shithole. A fucking rat pit. So I knock on the door and this cretin, you know, the guy looks like he was strained through a sheet, remember that one? This guy opens the door to the family abode and he tells me to get the hell out of there. I wanted to kill him right there. It's her father, right? So I tell him, look, *sir,* I say, I'm a homicide detective, show him the badge, I'm here to find out who killed your daughter. I *care* who killed your daughter, for Christ's sake. He tells me get the fuck out, we don't want no cops here. The fucking illiterate turd doesn't want cops here!

"Listen, Frank, I got so pissed off, you know what I did? I lifted the son of a bitch up by the neck, like this, right off the ground his legs are dangling and he's gurgling and trying to spit in my face, and I threw him into the street and I handcuffed the asshole to a telephone pole. I said, don't go anywhere, motherfucker, and shut up or I'll kick the shit out of you.

"So I go inside, and you know, what a lovely group. *What a beautiful collection of human beings!* I wouldn't want my dog living in there. And they all just glared at me, like, get out of here, cop, we don't want you. We don't care who killed her. Fuck it. I left. Write it off.

"Listen, Frank, it's a great job we got, isn't it?

It's great to be appreciated. Have another. Have an Irish, Frank. It's okay, Salerno, listen, Italians can drink Irish. You got special dispensation from me, Frank. Have one. It's the pure stuff."

Salerno acquiesced. He did not know Grogan very well, but he enjoyed him. Grogan seemed to be in a perpetual state of moral outrage, an unusual condition for homicide detectives, most of whom kept their outrage buried, if they had any left. Grogan had been a cop for his entire adult life, yet he continued to act and feel as though he had only recently discovered that people often cheat, lie, and murder one another. The lawyers who defended killers, Grogan liked to skewer with what was for him the most withering of all epithets, "unethical." His blue eyes shot bolts of anger, judgment, humor, and disgust.

"Frank," Grogan continued, his voice improper Bostonian, a shout, an order, a commandment, "you want to keep your sanity—of course I lost mine years ago—you want to keep your sanity, you got to get a boat."

"A boat."

"Yeah. I just bought a cabin cruiser. Greatest thing in the world."

Grogan explained that he had picked up a small bundle of cash working as a technical adviser to a new television series called *T. J. Hooker*. It was about an L.A. cop, and Grogan had dreamed up situations and characters. The production company had hired him at twelve hundred a week for advice. They had fired him, however, when he told them flat out that they were ruining his ideas and turning the show into just another piece of Hollywood horseshit. But he had earned enough to buy himself a new car and to put a down payment on the cabin cruiser.

"I keep it down at Long Beach. Took my kids out last weekend. Greatest therapy in the world, Frank. I get out there and do a little fishing and a little drinking, go over to Catalina. I tell you, you could be anywhere, you could be in Tahiti. Just sitting out there peaceful and quiet. I'm working on some fucking case, I don't care how bad it is, now I know I've got that boat. I can get out there and there's nothing but ocean, you feel like a human being again. Come on out with me, Frank. Bring the wife and kids. You got to get away from all this shit."

SIX

Even before he had begun murdering women, Angelo Buono had not been living the humdrum life of any ordinary upholsterer. If not glamorous, neither were his days dull. There were fast cars and frequent women. Fortunately for his wives, his marriages ended in divorce, but from youth he was a ladies' man and a lady-killer in spirit long before flesh. Although he was more goat than horse, when in the mid-seventies he chose "Italian Stallion" as his Citizens Band radio handle, inspired by the title of a pornographic movie, no one who knew him denied that he had earned it.

Italian Stallion was by Angelo Buono, Sr., out of Jenny Sciolino. He claimed Sicilian breeding, and there is no reason to doubt the purity of line, but he was born in Rochester, New York, on October 5, 1934, the child of native-born parents and immigrant grandparents. His parents divorced, and he arrived in Los Angeles in the year of *Gone with the Wind*, 1939, accompanied by his mother and his ten-year-old sister, Cecilia. They settled in that section of the City of Angels then known as Dogtown, so christened for its nearness to the municipal animal pound, northeast of downtown and Union Station. Only an old-timer would have called it Dogtown after World War II: it was Highland Park, the south edge of Glendale, and also, according to signs and maps but never in the common tongue, the Elysian Valley, one of those places in Southern California, like El Contento Drive and La Placentia and Happy Valley, named by way of some real estate developer's calculation of nirvana. Its most prominent feature was the Southern Pacific freight yard. With its freeways and broad streets and railroad tracks, the Elysian Valley had by the 1960s become nearly all steel and concrete, and except for rare days of wet or breezy weather, its air was so polluted that it would turn the windmill in a Dutch painting. In the seventies it was still favored by newcomers to the city. The Chinese, descendants of railroad workers, had stayed on; but the Irish, originally railroad workers also, had scattered westward, supplanted mostly by Mexicans. The dog pound had yielded its place as touchstone to Dodger Stadium, that blue monument to an Easterner's vision and gall that overlooked Angelo's theater of operations to the north and downtown Los Angeles to the south.

For forty years the Elysian Valley remained not the abode assigned by the Greeks to the blessed after death but Angelo's stomping grounds: he rarely strayed farther from it than Hollywood, and although he often moved and married, his mother's house at 3113 LaClede Avenue, just off Glendale Boulevard, was the omphalos of his life until her death in 1978. It must have been difficult for Jenny Sciolino Buono to maintain that house in the early years, though it was small, a frame bungalow. Her salary as a piece worker in a shoe factory, where she did top-stitching, was minimal. Angelo Sr. later remarried and moved to Los Angeles to work as a security guard, but he was a remote, silent figure, and he had acquired another family to support. After her children were grown,

Jenny would marry George White, an American Indian, but she raised the children on her own.

Although Jenny's family were practicing Roman Catholics, Angelo had no formal religious instruction, and what spiritual inspiration he obtained from attending mass did not impart with it a sense of sin. Nor did his education in the Los Angeles public school system have much effect on him, since he went into the world without learning reading, writing, or arithmetic. Junior Buono, as his mother, much to his annoyance, called him, had his mind on other things, and only the indifference or liberality of teachers enabled him to pass through elementary school and Washington Irving Junior High on to John Marshall High School. It cannot be said of him that he grew up too hopeful and trusting. He believed he could figure out life for himself, without the aid of education or authority. By the time he enrolled at Marshall High, he thought he had figured out something about his mother, and he began referring to her as "that cunt."

It was an appellation that rang so true to him that he continued to use it in reference to his mother and, later, to all other women, for the rest of his life. Though he had no evidence for it other than that Jenny did have boyfriends, he considered his mother loose, a whore. Throughout his manhood he told intimates, and there were not many, of being taken along by Jenny as a child on visits to men. He would be kept waiting outside, he said, while she would go with a man. He said he knew what she had been up to, and in this she was no different from all women. He found that he could break Jenny down by calling her a whore and accusing her of sleeping with repairmen, shop owners, and delivery boys in return for favors, a reduced bill or a free radio or refrigerator. Jenny would deny his accusations, but he could get at her that way. And in other ways. One of his favorites was to bring home a black girl and announce his engagement, knowing that his so much as dating a black would infuriate Jenny. As to women, Angelo was no racist. They were all the same to him, and it gave him satisfaction to observe his mother's anxiety at his black date.

Indeed, Angelo had formed in his mind his concept of the proper function of women by the time he was fourteen. Though he was still too young to have a driver's license, he enjoyed stealing a Buick or a Cadillac, driving around with his pals, and bragging about what he planned to do with girls. He wanted to pick up one who was hitchhiking, he said, and take her to some secluded place and rape her and "fuck her in the ass," as he phrased it, showing a precocious awareness of sodomy. It was just talk, then, but one of his friends, Stillman Sorrentino, was confused by Angelo's boasts. Sorrentino was fairly sure he knew what rape was, but he had no idea why Angelo or anyone would want to have sex with a girl "in the ass." Maybe Angelo meant something else. Sorrentino was so puzzled that he asked his parents what Angelo meant. They forbade him ever to see or speak to Angelo again.

Angelo quit high school at sixteen, and by that time he was getting himself into a lot of trouble, picking fights and running with gangs, stealing and earning a reputation as a tough, bad character. When he was first arrested for "grand theft auto" and committed to the California Youth Authority, he managed to escape, but when he was rearrested in December 1951, the juvenile authorities decided that he needed to cool off for a spell at the Paso Robles School for Boys, in central California, where he celebrated his seventeenth Christmas. The reformatory did not reform him.

Out on parole, he would drive around with his buddies looking for girls or, in the parlance of the day, for some guy to "choose off." Marshall High was always a good place to spot a victim: it was common for those who had left school to hang around and taunt the students. One afternoon Angelo and his pals cruised by as school was letting out and noticed a boy standing alone with his books, waiting for a ride. The boy was wearing a maroon satin jacket with the name "Aristocrats" spelled out across its back.

"Hold it," Angelo said. "I want that jacket."

Angelo got out of the car while his three buddies waited. He walked up to the solitary boy.

73

"Hey, I like your jacket," Angelo said with the gruff brusqueness that was already his characteristic speech. "How about letting me try it on?"

The boy, younger and smaller than Angelo, hesitated, but when Angelo, long thumbs in pockets, feet apart, pelvis forward, stepped closer, the boy slipped off the jacket and handed it over. Angelo's friends lounged against the car, watching.

"Looks good," Angelo said, and he shouted to his pals, "Not bad, huh?" They gave their approval.

"Hey," Angelo said to the boy, "I think I'll keep it." He started to walk off.

The boy came after him and jumped on his back. Angelo threw him off, turned, and slapped his face, and his three buddies came running up to help. The boy panicked and ran away.

In the next days Angelo worked at removing the word "Aristocrats" from the back of the jacket. He had gotten only as far as the first two letters, but was wearing the jacket when one afternoon the boy and four older kids spotted Angelo at a gas station and surrounded him. Angelo gave the jacket back.

But the next day the boy appeared at Angelo's house, again accompanied by his four older friends. He pointed to the missing letters. He did not want a jacket that said "istocrats." He wanted money from Angelo to repair the jacket.

Angelo ran out onto his front porch, pulled out his pocket knife, and offered to cut the face of anybody who tried to get money from him. He scared them off.

The boy reported the entire incident to the police. Angelo was called in and warned that he was facing jail if he continued getting into trouble. Angelo said it had all been a misunderstanding. The boy had given him the jacket, willingly, and when he had asked for it back, Angelo had returned it. But he would be glad to give the boy money for repairs, he said.

By this time Angelo had a hero. His hero was not the usual sports figure, although he enjoyed seeing Golden Boy Art Aragon, then the most prominent of Los Angeles boxers, perform at the Olympic Auditorium. And occasionally Angelo went to see the Los

Angeles Angels, a Chicago Cubs farm team, play at Wrigley Field. But neither boxing nor baseball produced Angelo's real hero. His hero played in a different league.

He was Caryl Chessman, known as the red-light bandit, who had been arrested and convicted in 1948 on charges of kidnapping with infliction of bodily harm, a crime then punishable by death in California, and sexual assault. Chessman's crimes and mode of operation, his scam, made an indelible mark on Angelo's mind, for Chessman had demonstrated the possibilities of a police ruse. The red light he had attached to his car enabled him to con lovers parked in the hills of Los Angeles into opening their car windows and doors to him. They took him for a policeman telling them to move on. Showing a .45, Chessman would force the girl into his car, drive her to another secluded spot, and, usually, make her perform oral sex.

Unfortunately, from Angelo's point of view, Chessman failed to kill his victims, so their testimony assured conviction. But Angelo admired Chessman for more than the scam. By 1951 Chessman was acting as his own attorney on appeal, and his manipulation of the law enabled him to fend off his own execution for twelve years. He became the most notable, if that is the word, jailhouse lawyer in California history. To Angelo he was a heroic combination of guts and brains, no everyday rapist, a man who could stand up to the system and, if not beat it, foul it up beautifully.

Angelo always worked on some job or other. He started as a plasterer and builder of brick fireplaces, and he quickly displayed his manual skills. Then, working in garages, he caught on to the auto upholstering trade. He had some money in his pocket, and he dated a lot of girls. At twenty he cut a dashing figure, in a raffish sort of way, favoring suits, dark shirts, and bright ties in imitation of movie gangsters, and somehow he drove Cadillacs. He hung around the old Van de Kamp's Drive-in at the corner of Fletcher and San Fernando Road. It was a good place to meet girls.

But his favorite place to take girls parking was Landa Street, an obscure little road up in the hills on the western side of the Elysian Valley, just beyond Elysian Park. It was, and it remained, very hard to find, paved but more of a track than a road, heavily wooded, with owls and bats and coyotes that wandered over from Griffith Park. At night you could see the lights of the city from Landa, but the street itself was dark, a Halloween sort of place, ghostly enough to make a girl want to cling, a place that might have been imported with its running ivy and morning-glory vines from some less arid clime than Southern California's. Hardly anyone traveled it except lovers, people who got lost, and people looking for an obscure spot to dump trash. And there was enough trash dumped on Landa's slopes to make it stink. Angelo liked to call it the "cow patch," by which he meant that it stank like a cow pie. But still, the cow patch was the best place to take a girl. You could get away with anything there.

It may have been at the cow patch that Angelo got Geraldine Yvonne Vinal pregnant in April 1955. She was seventeen, from Marshall High. He did what any gentleman would do. He made Geraldine a June bride.

A Protestant minister performed the ceremony, and this upset Jenny, but within a week Angelo had left, never to return to his first wife. Their son, Michael Lee Buono, who in the 1970s moved to North Carolina and toured with a band called the Sidewinders, was born on January 10, 1956, and shortly afterward Geraldine filed for divorce, on grounds of desertion, and child support. The court awarded her twenty dollars a month, but she never saw a penny from Angelo. Michael knew his father, but Angelo would not permit his son to call him Dad, and in the Buono family, whose holiday celebrations she sometimes attended, Geraldine became known as Aunt Gerry.

Angelo had not been around to celebrate Michael's birth. Two months before the event he had been sentenced to sixty days in the county jail for petty theft. He had been arrested on suspected auto theft.

But once released, Angelo lost no time with the ladies. By the end of 1956 he had fathered another son,

Angelo Anthony Buono III, and on April 15, 1957, he married Angelo III's mother, Mary Catherine Castillo, in time for her to give birth later that year to his third son, Peter Buono. His fourth, Danny, was born in 1958, and his fifth, Louis, in 1960, and a daughter, Grace, in 1962.

It was a Roman Catholic ceremony this time, performed by the Reverend K. R. O'Brien, who was able to sanctify the nuptials because Angelo could claim the Pauline Privilege, which then denied the validity of a non-Catholic marriage for a Catholic. In the eyes of the church, this was Angelo's first marriage, and it can be said of it that it lasted longer, though it was no happier, than the Protestant one.

Mary Catherine, called Candy, was seventeen when she married Angelo. They had courted at the cow patch. At first, when they married, they lived in a cottage behind Jenny's house. Then they moved to Huntington Drive, then to Coolidge, to Highland Park Boulevard, to York, to Casitas, finally to Glover, where in 1964 they divorced. All of the houses were within a two-.or three-mile radius of Jenny's, but there were seven moves in seven years, and Candy bore Angelo a child in every year but two. She found him a difficult husband.

Yet it was not so much the serial childbearing: Candy's Latin background had conditioned her for that. Nor did Angelo fail to support his multiplying family while it lasted. He was becoming skilled at auto upholstery now and could always find a job. And when the family needed something they could not afford, he could always steal it. He had become more adept at avoiding the law and was not arrested frequently during the marriage: in 1962 he served five days and in 1964 sixty and another five days for petty theft associated with automobiles. No, it was Angelo's violence and sexual behavior which finally drove Candy to divorce.

She did not like Angelo's calling her a cunt, and she was disgusted when he referred to Jenny by the same word. And he made her feel like one. One night during their first year together, he appeared in their bedroom with rope in his hands, tied her spread-eagled to the bedposts, and raped her so violently that she feared for her life. More and more as the years passed, her pain seemed to give him his greatest pleasure, and when she failed to respond to his pinches and slaps and pile-driver poundings, he would tell her she was "a dead piece of ass." Nor did she share his passion for anal intercourse. But Angelo was not a man to be denied. Although he never drank, he beat and kicked her when she failed to please him, and far from caring whether the children witnessed the beatings, he seemed to want them to watch.

One afternoon in 1963, when the children ranged in age from one to seven, she refused him what he considered his prerogative and he decided to teach her a lesson. He dragged her into the living room, threw her down on the floor in front of the children, and forced himself up her backside.

It was about this time that Angelo accused Candy of having an affair with his cousin Joe. She at last decided that no matter what she would be facing trying to raise the children alone, she had to get rid of him. In her divorce complaint of May 1964, she cited extreme cruelty as cause, mentioning the beatings, and the court responded by awarding her a hundred and fifty dollars a month in support—not per child but in total. She did not ask for alimony. But to avoid paying anything at all, Angelo started spelling his name Bono instead of Buono, and Candy was forced to draw on the county for assistance as an abandoned mother whose husband had disappeared.

She stayed in the house on Glover, and he moved to an apartment in Glendale. But not long after they had separated, Candy's fears for her children's survival got the better of her and she went to visit Angelo to see about a reconciliation. He responded by handcuffing her, forcing her into his car, and driving into the hills, where he ordered her out and up against a tree. There he shoved a pistol into her stomach and announced that he was about to kill her.

He did not, but Candy gave up the idea of reconciliation.

Angelo was not long without a mate. In 1965 he began living with Nanette Campina, a twenty-five-year-old from New York whom he had met on a blind date. Although this union was never made official by church or state, it lasted as long as his marriage to Candy and resembled it in many ways. Nanette already had two children, Annette and Danny, but Angelo's paternal urge was still unspent, and he sired Tony in 1967 and Sam in 1969. By his thirty-fifth year he had multiplied himself eight times, with enough sons to ensure that the Buono/Bono line would not vanish with him.

He beat Nanette as he had Candy, but this time he told his woman that if she ever so much as considered leaving him, he would kill her or have her killed. He had friends, he said, powerful people he called "the boys," and they would hunt her down no matter where she went. She stayed.

In March 1968, Angelo had his most serious brush with the law up to that time. Trying to stop a rash of auto thefts, the police had staked out a parking lot at the corner of Vermont and Marathon in Hollywood, from which several cars had disappeared. They observed Angelo as he and a friend, Ralph Harper, worked a wire coat hanger into the window of a Thunderbird, sprang the lock, and started to remove the hardtop. The police closed in, and, searching him, they found handcuffs in Angelo's pocket.

The judge, noting that Mr. Bono (sic) was a family man with children to support, sentenced him to three years' probation, with fifteen weekends to be served in the county jail. In September 1968, however, the courts recognized Bono as Buono, and Angelo was ordered to serve a year in the county jail for failure to provide support for his five children by Candy. This sentence was suspended on condition that he pay Candy no less than a hundred and ninety dollars a month and obey all laws. He did neither. By 1971, in consideration of his faithful weekend attendance at jail, and because he had managed to elude the scrutiny of probation officers, his auto theft conviction was reduced from a felony to a misdemeanor.

In that year Nanette finally got up the courage to leave him. She decided that she would rather risk death than remain with Angelo, and she suspected, or hoped, that his threats were empty. Her daughter Annette, by then fourteen, had begun complaining that Angelo was fondling her too intensely and making obscene suggestions to her, and Nanette feared that Angelo had achieved more than that with the girl. "She needs breaking in," Angelo had been saying. "I'll break her in." Without telling him, one day Nanette put herself and the four children on a plane to Florida and never came back.

A year later Angelo married a girl named Deborah Taylor at the Silver Bell Wedding Chapel in Las Vegas, but this was a mere lark; they never lived together, and they never bothered to get divorced. Angelo was learning not to take women too seriously. He changed apartments often, moving from Glendale over to the Oakwood Apartments above Forest Lawn Drive, then back to Glendale on Chevy Chase, and for a time he shared a place in the Silver Lake District, known locally as the Swish Alps, with Ralph Harper. Harper was an aspiring actor who joined Angelo in auto theft only when between roles. He appeared in productions of *Hello, Dolly* and *Gaily, Gaily* but lost out to Archie Moore, the light heavyweight champ, for the part of Nigger Jim in the movie of *Huckleberry Finn*. Harper's stage name was Artie Ford, and he was proud to be buddies with Jay Silverheels, who had played Tonto in the *Lone Ranger* television series. Through Artie Ford, Angelo met a lot of Hollywood people and began building his reputation as one of the few auto upholsterers who could work with classic and antique cars. He did not yet have his own shop, but it was during this period that he fixed up a sports car belonging to Frank Sinatra and a limousine that was said to be Joe Bonnano's. Angelo had a fine Italian hand with cars.

Life in the Swish Alps suited Angelo for a time, but Artie Ford found him a difficult apartmentmate. He was obsessively neat, Ford thought. He would complain when anything, even a telephone receiver, was not put back properly, and he was constantly dusting and cleaning. And he had some peculiar habits. Their apartment overlooked a high school, and sometimes Artie Ford would catch Angelo looking through binoculars at the students and playing with himself. Normal enough, Artie thought, but he did not know what to think of Angelo's boast that he had "banged" his stepdaughter, Annette Campino, who he said was just the right age, because young girls' "pussies smell real good, like cheese." Angelo also claimed with pride that he had turned Annette over to his sons, so that they could have a go at her, and that they had. Everyone had banged Annette, Angelo said. And when Angelo's son Peter told Artie Ford that Angelo had had sex with *him,* too, Artie thought that Angelo was probably a little strange. But when Angelo told Artie that he was so angry with Candy that he had snuck into her house and turned the gas on when she was out, hoping that she would light a cigarette when she got home and blow herself up, Artie was alarmed.

"My God," Artie said, "what about the kids?"

"Fuck the kids," Angelo said.

Still, Angelo and Artie were good friends and remained so after Angelo moved out.

In 1975, Angelo finally got what he had been thinking about for some time, his own shop, when he found the place at 703 East Colorado Street. Now that he had resolved his financial responsibilities to his wives and children, he had been able to save enough money for a down payment on the property, and he was handy enough to do most of the painting and plumbing and carpentry himself. By the middle of that year, he was moved in and open for business, and he began living the kind of life that he knew was right for him, a bachelor's life filled with women who could be dismissed when they had fulfilled their function, and an independent businessman's life, with no one to call boss. Now he could set his own hours, and when an opportunity presented itself, he could seize it. He worked alone. When he needed someone to clean up or run an errand, he hired Frankie Anderson, a local kid whose nickname was Goofy. Angelo had no use for an employee with an inquiring mind.

For Angelo, the set-up on Colorado was perfect.

With his shop behind his house, he hardly needed a car, and when he did need one he would drive one of his customers'. The location between the car wash and the glass shop gave his business exposure during the day and gave him privacy at night, and the metal awning he put up between the shop and his house shielded his activities from the view from the Orange Grove apartments behind. He already knew the neighborhood well. It took him no time at all to establish himself and settle into his diurnal-nocturnal routine and its variations.

His work habits were generously punctuated by women. He would arise early and go to breakfast with a friend, Dave Stuart, who ran a gas station, at one of the local restaurants, Henry's or the Copper Penny, both within walking distance. Soon Bob Brinkman, who owned Henry's, brought his gull-wing Mercedes coupe to Angelo for repair, and the waitresses brought themselves. Angelo liked to kid the waitresses. His favorite line was a mild insult, something like "You ought to get your teeth fixed, honey. Then I might take a second look." Said in the right way, with his rough voice and the hint of a grin, a remark like that would usually get them going:

"How would you know? My boyfriend don't complain. I bet you'd like to see more."

"Nah, you're too ugly for me," Angelo would say, eyes fixed on her chest.

"You'd be surprised."

"Yeah? Well, surprise me. I like surprises."

It was easy. Women were drawn to Angelo. They liked his swagger and his big hands and the way he looked straight into them. He let them know right away what was on his mind, and he followed through. They would take him up on his invitation to visit his shop. He might offer to make them floor mats or sew up a torn car seat for nothing.

One of the Henry's waitresses, Tonya Dockery, a little brunette teenager, got to like Angelo so much that she gave him a dog, Sparky, and later a couple of rabbits. She was living with a man, but Angelo said she could drop by anytime, and she did. When she would complain about her lover, Angelo would tell her not to act like a cunt, and she liked that: it made her feel that her lover couldn't get her down, and it gave her the illusion that Angelo believed that she was capable of acting like something other than a cunt. Sometimes she would come by Angelo's late at night with a bottle of wine.

"I don't drink," Angelo would say. "It eats your brain cells."

So Tonya would drink the wine and spend the night with Angelo on his big water-bed.

Tonya introduced Angelo to her friend Twyla Hill, and soon Angelo was servicing Twyla, too. But when Angelo would put his penis down Twyla's throat until she gagged and then refuse to take it out, telling her that she should like it that way and that if she passed out sucking on him she would get "a terrific head-rush," Twyla would get angry and pound on him with her fists. "Go ahead," Angelo would say. "Go ahead and fight. It makes my dick hard." And one night when Tonya and Twyla were at Angelo's together and Tonya suggested that it might be fun if all three of them got into bed, Angelo was all for it, but Twyla backed out once she had her clothes off. Angelo said she was a bitch and told her to get into bed. When she refused, Angelo grabbed her and said he was going to put her ass outside.

"I'll scream!" Twyla said.

"Go ahead," Angelo said. "Nobody will hear you." And to prove it, he did put her outside naked for a minute, but he let her back in when she promised to behave. She called Angelo a motherfucker, but she behaved.

Soon Angelo was known throughout the neighborhood as an excellent upholsterer and a stud. The girls came around so often and in such numbers that Angelo did not get a great deal of work done. You can't fuck that much and become a millionaire, as someone said, but the situation suited Angelo just fine. He would chat up the girls everywhere he found them, in restaurants, on the street, in local businesses. He liked them young, the younger the better. Cristoforo Guglielmo Salvaggio, who owned a gutter shop and was Angelo's partner in a Christmas-tree lot at the corner of Glendale and Chevy Chase every year, was amazed at the number and the youth of Angelo's girls.

"Hey, Angelo," Cristoforo said, "some of these broads you got, they're so young, they don't even know how to wash their pussies yet."

"I show them how," Angelo said.

Melinda Hooper was one. Angelo had broken her in when she had been only thirteen, in 1973. She was the girl who lived with her parents way up on Alta Terrace. Angelo was her mentor, as it were, and she kept returning to him even after she had other boyfriends, including one she had gotten herself put in jail for when she had gone all the way to Oklahoma to help him break out of the state prison there. She liked Angelo so much that she introduced him to her parents and invited him to dinner at her house, but when the parents saw that Angelo was forty years old, they objected, so Angelo would usually drop Melinda off at the corner of Alta Terrace and La Crescenta after seeing her.

Angelo's sons' girlfriends provided another source. Not only could they introduce him to other young girls, sometimes they offered themselves. Peter Buono for a while was dating Dawn Vaiarelli, who was sixteen, and Angelo managed to sleep with her on several occasions and with her friend Julie Villaseñor, who was dating another of his sons, Danny. It was a close family situation.

There were so many young girls that Angelo stuffed his wallet with their school pictures, arranging them in the plastic windows next to his police badge, little colored squares of bright-eyed California teenagers, who inscribed them:

> To the *stud* of the year!
> It's been really fun
> knowing you.
> See ya around.
>
> Love ya,
> Dawn

For her picture, blond Dawn wore a pink angora sweater and a tiny gold cross. Another blond girl, large-featured and wholesome-looking, wrote in careful, rounded script:

> Tony,
>
> Someday when I get mad and walk out
> on you you'll have a picture of me.
> But that day will probably never come.
> We've come this far, let's go all the way.
>
> Love, Missy

Another snap showed Angelo kissing a brunette in a long Laura Ashley dress. A Glendale romance.

One lovely young girl posed wearing very short red cutoffs and a white, lacy blouse tied up in front to display her caramel midriff. She was bent slightly to one side, brushing out her tawny hair. She had inscribed the picture:

> Dear Tony (Dad)
>
> Here's a small picture for your wallet,
> to keep just in case you can't picture
> me and you can remember it and what I
> looked like.
>
> Love you,

So that the picture could fit into the plastic window, Angelo had snipped off the signature, but it had read "Annette"—Nanette Campino's daughter, who was far away in Florida with her mother and brothers. She had come to visit Angelo in his new house. Ever resourceful, Angelo had conned yet another of his girlfriends into paying Annette's air fare.

He kept the payee's picture in his wallet, too. Of all the little wallet-girls, this one was the plainest, a frizzy-headed, dark girl who looked out of her photograph with eyes so innocent that they might have come from a different time and place, Italy a hundred years ago or Ellis Island. She was Antoinette Lombardo, sixteen, the daughter of the couple who owned Tony's Hardware in Glendale. Antoinette worked in her parents' store after school and on Saturdays, and Angelo often saw her there. He was so friendly and warm and strong-looking that Antoinette got a crush on him. To her, Angelo was mature and self-confident, not like the high school boys. They were children, compared to Angelo. When Angelo gave her his card and said that she should come by his shop, she started riding her bicycle over to see him, on her way to and from work or after her tennis lessons. She was trying out for the high school tennis team, and when Angelo presented her with a tennis racquet, he won her heart. He was her first love, old enough to be her father yet, she thought, with a softness and tenderness beneath his tough exterior that she longed to cradle in her arms and make her very own. The sight of him, the thought of him, began to quicken her teenage pulse. She longed for him to embrace her gently, like a real man, crushing her little body to his big one, and love her, his very own Antoinette, for herself alone. Marriage was on her mind.

Angelo broke Antoinette in slowly. There were so many other girls, he was in no rush, and he was too clever and skillful to want to frighten a girl who was more naive than most. When he first kissed her he left it at that and sent her away on her bicycle atingle with romantic passion. Then he took her into his bedroom and lay with her on the water bed, lightly touching her, sliding his big hand beneath her bra. He spent weeks at the foreplay, touching her adolescent heart with his artful, thoughtful tenderness. Only after a couple of months did he begin initiating her into some of the deeper mysteries of love, but once seduced, she believed everything he told her and accepted everything he did to her, even when it hurt, though she did tell him that she preferred not to have him put a cucumber into her. When he would put his penis down her throat and tell her that it would feel better if she passed out, she thought this was another of the mysteries, although she found this one painful and frightening and preferred not to lose consciousness. And when Angelo told her that he would marry her after she finished high school, she knew that this was no passing fancy but life's most profound commitment.

She believed that Angelo would marry her, even though he sometimes did things that upset her. When a lively, creamy-coffee-colored girl called Peaches began living at Angelo's from time to time, Antoinette accepted his assurances that Peaches was just a girl out of a job who sometimes needed a place to stay. When one day Antoinette walked into the house to find Angelo with his penis in Twyla Hill's mouth, Antoinette went away and came back later. She wept, but she understood that Angelo was a man of enormous passion; that once they were married, everything would be sacred and it would be just the two of them, faithful till death; but that until she could be with him every day and share his bed all night long, she could not expect him to be perfect. He was a real man.

When Angelo asked her to loan him three hundred dollars so that he could fly Annette out for a visit—he would pay it back as soon as this year's profits from the Christmas-tree lot began to roll in; at the moment he needed his capital to buy trees—she dug into her savings and gave him the money, happy to be of use. When Antoinette got pregnant, she was frightened and confused: was it a disaster or only the beginning of their real life together? But Angelo comforted her and told her not to tell her parents, and he arranged an abortion for her at a local clinic, assuring her that it would be better to start the family after she graduated. After the abortion, he said that they should probably not have any children together, but that she did not have to worry about getting pregnant again. He was getting a vasectomy.

Her trust was absolute; they resumed their romance; six months later, she was pregnant again. This time she suffered a miscarriage. But she was certain he would marry her before too long. They had gone through so much together.

With all the young things in his life, Angelo had to think about his image. He began dyeing his gray hair black. He added a gold chain, a big turquoise ring, and red silk underwear to his wardrobe. With his swagger and his cocky, if monosyllabic, joshing, he made a plausible Glendale Don Giovanni. When, in January 1976, Kenneth Bianchi arrived from the East, he found his cousin Angelo living in what could have passed for a harem. Cousin Kenny did his best to fit in to Angelo's ménage and to adjust to a new life in the metropolis of make-believe.

SEVEN

Back in Rochester in 1972, Kenneth Bianchi, then twenty-one years old, wrote a letter to his girlfriend telling her that he had killed a man. He was not too worried about being caught, because he had made the death look like a heart attack, but at the same time he was sure he was a suspect in three other murders, killings of little girls, one aged ten and two aged eleven. These were being called the Alphabet Murders, because each of the girls had first and last initials which were the same. He told his girlfriend that he knew that the police were looking for a young man driving a small blue car.

The girlfriend, Janice Duchong, did not take the letter seriously. She knew that it was just another one of Kenny's crazy stories. She understood him as the kind of guy who would make things up just to impress a girl and to gain her sympathy, and she could see through the stories. They were so far out. Kenny was really a nice guy, and he could be so sweet. He was always writing her poems and sending her flowers, and not many guys did that these days. There was something old-fashioned about Kenny Bianchi; he was so courteous, thoughtful, almost courtly, but sometimes she wondered if he knew what century he was living in or who and where he was. He had such an imagination—there was a touch of the artist about Kenny. That stuff about the police looking for a guy in a small blue car, for instance. Kenny didn't even own a car. She had a small blue car, it was true, which Kenny sometimes drove, but that was hardly something to make him a murder suspect. She wished Kenny could be more practical, have more common sense. He wasted a lot of time. He must have spent hours constructing a collage of pictures of little girls cut out of magazines and pasted up on a big piece of cardboard. He was artistic, he said, and he loved children, but still . . .

Yes, he was smart and nice and fun to be with; he was always entertaining; but she wished he'd get his feet on the ground. A young man like that might fritter away his life on dreams.

But young Kenny was no practical, workaday sort of a guy. Kenny had the imagination of a visionary or a deadbeat. If Angelo Buono believed that in acquiring his own upholstery shop and house and the freedom to carry on with women as he liked he had accomplished most of what he wanted out of life, Kenneth Bianchi would never be satisfied with such banalities.

He sensed a future of ill-defined greatness. Following his father into the American Brake-Shoe foundry was not for him. Bianchi was temperamentally an aristocrat, inherently convinced that ordinary work and certainly manual labor were beneath him. Yet, not being an aristocrat in fact, he sensed that he would rise, as effortlessly and inevitably as hot air. In the street sense of the word, he had class. His favorite comic book character had been Prince Valiant; he could imagine himself sipping mead with the other knights at the Round Table and attracting maidens by means of words and hair. He knew that anyone could be President. He considered becoming a statesman, an artist, a doctor. He had a confidence in his opinions comparable to that of an evangelist. He had the egocentricity of a method actor. Had he turned out harmless, he might have been just another Walter Mitty.

Kenneth Alessio Bianchi was born May 22, 1951, the child of a Rochester prostitute. He never met his mother but knew vaguely who she was, a woman whom he associated with bars and working-class nightclubs. She gave him up at birth, and at the age of three months he was adopted from a foster home by Jenny Buono's sister, Frances Sciolino Bianchi, and her husband, a foundry worker fond of following the horses. The unfortunate Bianchis—they were no luckier at picking a child than at the ponies.

Kenny appears to have arisen from the cradle dissembling. By the time he could talk, Frances knew she was coping with a compulsive liar, and his childhood unfolded as one of idleness and goldbricking. When he was five and a half, Frances became worried by his frequent lapses into trancelike states of daydreaming; she knew that this would not do when he went to school, and she consulted a physician. The doctor, hearing that little Kenny's eyeballs would roll back into his head during these trances, reached a diagnosis of petit mal seizures. But they were nothing to worry about. He would grow out of them.

By the age of eleven, Kenny's inattention to schoolwork and his angry outbursts at home had become major worries to his adoptive mother, who, as a first-generation Italian-American, wondered whether her boy had been struck by the evil eye. His IQ tested out at 116, considered "bright-normal," but of course neither his nor any intelligence could be measured by a number, and his laziness affected his attention to the test. His teachers said that he was working at well below his capacity; his grades ranged from average to below. He had verbal and artistic abilities, but even in his best subjects his performance was erratic, and whenever he could get away with it he would plead some illness to avoid going to school. Frances's anger at his sloth provoked temper tantrums. She took him to a clinic, where a psychologist prescribed an extensive course of therapy, finding Kenny a hostile child overly dependent on his mother and suggesting counseling for the mother as well. Frances declined. She hoped that Kenny would find himself. Maybe religion would take hold.

He spent six years at Holy Family elementary school, where even the minimal tuition was a sacrifice for the Bianchis. Although he learned to read and write with superior facility, showing particular adeptness at what would now be termed "creative writing," daily indoctrination in the precepts of Christianity and the Roman Catholic Church failed in their intended effect. He took communion and made his confession weekly; he was taught about sin, its occasions and its consequences. He was told about the four sins crying to heaven for vengeance: willful murder, the sin of Sodom, oppression of the poor, and defrauding laborers of their wages. A person committing any of these would have to make a perfect act of contrition to avoid eternal damnation.

None of this made any serious impression on Bianchi. He heard the words, but they were mere words to him, of no obvious and immediate use, and in language as in life, he did not separate the wheat from the chaff. In Christian terms he remained unregenerate, a soul lost to God, rudderless on the voyage of life, a creature who caused weeping in heaven. In secular terms he was the sort of child any experienced teacher could see was headed for trouble. But no one could have foreseen how much trouble he would be in and how much misery he would cause.

When he was thirteen, his adoptive father died, and Frances went to work to support herself and her son. At Gates-Chili High School, Kenny dated frequently, approaching all the girls as he did Janice Duchong, with Prince Valiant courtliness. Considering the period in American life, 1966–70, he was remarkably clean-cut in high school, avoiding long hair and sloppy clothing, giving every appearance of a boy respectful, even emulative, of his elders. He joined a motorcycle club, but they were no Hell's Angels. He had his right arm tattooed with the image of a motorcycle and the letters "Satan's Own M.C.," but was regretful and remained embarrassed and apologetic for the rest of his life, though he took some pleasure in the hint of waywardness in the emblem.

At eighteen he married Brenda Beck, whom he had known since childhood. The marriage lasted only a few months, soured in part by his belief that Brenda had been intimate before the union with another young man. Her being a nurse also made him nervous, for he thought nursing an occupation dangerous for a married woman, because it provided too many opportunities for illicit relationships and even encouraged them.

Bianchi set high standards for his women, which they repeatedly failed to meet. His Catholic education served him here in a twisted way. He was able to confuse ordinary women with the Virgin and could be moved to bitter disappointment, even anger and fury, at their human frailties. The import of the idea of the Virgin, that she was unique, he chose to ignore. Denying female sexuality even as he was attracted to it, he objected to V-neck sweaters and tight jeans and asked of women absolute fidelity in return for his outwardly absolute devotion. Yet he always dated several girls at once and did not require of himself comparable standards of purity. With Catholicism as with other systems or bodies of belief, he was self-pleasingly selective.

After his divorce, which he liked to term an "annulment," he went on as before, wounded but persistent. He proposed to another girl, Susan Moore, but she told him that she could not consider him seriously until he learned to stay out of trouble and hold on to a job.

Neither was Susan Moore happy about Bianchi's chronic lying and his skill at it. She suspected that he was simultaneously seeing another woman, Donna Duranzo, and herself, although he assured Susan that his only interest in Donna was concern for her two children, especially her little boy, for whom he professed acute fondness. "The poor little kid," Kenny would say, "he needs a father. I know how he feels. My daddy died when I was thirteen, you know, and I never knew my real father." But twice Susan caught Kenny and Donna alone together, once in her apartment and once in his. "I didn't know how to tell you, Sue," Kenny said, looking miserable.

His demands for both women's fidelity in the face of his duplicity created some heated confrontations. One night, on the outs with Donna, he came to her apartment and she refused to open the door to him. He shouted at her in the hallway, then went outside to peer at her through a window. He demanded that she open the window and speak to him, and when she turned her back, he smashed the glass and started to climb into the apartment. Donna fled out the front door and called the police.

But she dropped charges when, at the police station, Kenny seemed so contrite, so pitiful and polite, assuring everyone that he had not meant to break the window, only to open it, referring to the incident, tenderly, as a lovers' quarrel.

"The window just fell into the apartment," he said. "I thought, My God, how can this be happening?"

He announced his intention of becoming a policeman, as a start, he said, toward achieving some position of authority in life and to satisfy his urge to help people. To this end he enrolled at Monroe Community College, taking courses in police science and psychology. The first subject fit his vocational goals; the psychology courses fed his one consuming interest, himself. Psychology also attracted him as an attitude to life more appealing than the harsh insistence of Roman Catholicism on personal responsibility for one's actions: he found in modern psychology an agreeable tendency to see man as victim of impersonal forces which could be explained but not really controlled, man as acted on rather than acting. But he attended classes only sporadically and, true to form, took advantage of the school's medical facilities, complaining of migraine headaches and other afflictions. When he did apply for a job with the Sheriff's Department, he was rejected, but he regarded this as a momentary setback, blaming the nature of the test. Undiscouraged, he landed a job as the next best thing to a policeman, a security guard, a position that had the advantage of requiring no rigorous course of study.

Another advantage of being a security guard was the excellent opportunity it afforded him to take what he felt belonged to him, the merchandise. Kenny was naturally light-fingered. He stole clothing and jewelry, showering girlfriends with looted trinkets; but his larceny, never proved but often suspected, forced him to change jobs often, an imposition he resented. His selective readings in psychology helped him to cope with dismissal, however, providing him with explanations —excuses—for his acts and failures. He had his needs. The urge to steal he compared to the urge to urinate, a build-up of forces which required release. If his employers fired him for theft, they had suffered a failure to understand his needs. For a time he also worked as an ambulance attendant, gaining early experience with dead bodies, saying that the job met his need to help people; but the hours proved inconvenient.

He was going nowhere, and by 1973 the idea of California had begun to lure him. At that time he was working as a security guard at J. B. Hunter's Department Store and was pursuing Susan Moore, who also worked at Hunter's. She saw that he stole. When he would present her with costume jewelry, she would remonstrate with him and tell him that she even knew which counter in the store it had come from. Yet she felt for him; she could see how bright and animated by dreams he was. Someone like Kenny should not waste away his talents in an inferior position. He proposed marriage to her, but she resisted, telling him that he had to find himself, show that he was on track toward a steady life, demonstrate the reliability of a family man. Only then would she consider succumbing to his romantic rush. Kenny's mother objected to Susan, who in ways not specified was somehow not good enough for her son.

Kenny knew that he was in a rut. His thoughts radiated elsewhere, away from Rochester, away from his mother. He imagined other worlds, New York City, Hollywood. Finally, at the start of the new year in 1976, he made his move. He would go to California in search of a new start, a better life. Through his mother and Aunt Jenny, he made contact with Cousin Angelo, who agreed to take him in temporarily.

Like millions before him, Kenneth Bianchi moved to California because of the appealing images he harbored of the place. He would leave winter behind. A one-way plane ticket would buy him June in January, the good vibrations of the Beach Boys, surfers and healthy inarticulate women, Acapulco gold and Gallo Hearty Burgundy, orange-blossom-scented naked rap sessions. Linking these sunny images in his mind was an idea of freedom no different in its vagueness from a child's vision of the wonders waiting beyond any fence. Out there in the sleepy, salty beach towns, he would stake out his umbrella and feel renewed, happy, and himself. He would achieve California by dispensing charm, of which he had oodles.

To be exact, it was Bianchi's second trip to California. In 1957, when he was barely six and Angelo was just married to Candy, Kenny's parents had brought him to Los Angeles for a month or two to visit relatives. All Angelo remembered of him was that he had been a restless nuisance who kept wetting his pants, but he figured Kenny had learned to control himself by now. He gave him the spare bedroom on the stipulation that he would get a place of his own as soon as he landed a job.

Immediately Kenny found Cousin Angelo's way with women impressive. The house in Glendale may not have been a Malibu mansion, was a good hour's drive from the beach of Kenny's dreams, but he could not imagine a movie star's getting more attention from the ladies than Angelo did. Tonya, Twyla, Melinda, Antoinette, and all the others seemed drawn to Angelo like kittens to milk, and yet he showed them none of the chivalry Kenny compulsively bestowed on girlfriends. So awestruck was Bianchi by Angelo's success with women that he decided Angelo must know something. Kenny determined to learn as much as he could from an obvious master. Within a week of his arrival, Kenny had his first California date, a broad-beamed blonde he had encountered near the Orange

Julius stand at the Eagle Rock Plaza. Chatting her up in his usual smarmy way, he talked her into visiting his cousin Angelo. Kenny wanted the Buono imprimatur on Sheryl. He and Sheryl found Angelo in his shop unreeling a length of cord from a big wooden spool.

"Angelo, I'd like you to meet Sheryl Kellison. Sheryl, this is my cousin Angelo."

Angelo looked Sheryl over from tip to top, like a breeder at a brood-mare auction.

"Okay," Angelo said. Sheryl had passed muster.

Sheryl and Kenny went out for hamburgers, which she paid for, and then returned to Angelo's house to watch TV.

Thus was Kenny's life as a pursuer of California women launched. But his encounters were not always so formally initiated. During the first weeks of Kenny's stay, which was to last, much to Angelo's annoyance, until July, Angelo Anthony Buono III, the eldest son by Candy, was also living at the house, paying his father rent for the privilege of sleeping in the den. Soon Angelo would raise the rent, driving his son, called Anthony, out; but for a time a certain conviviality, a familiar camaraderie, vigorously primitive, reigned. Other sons would drop by with their girlfriends, who presented opportunities for both Angelo and Kenny. Sometimes everyone would watch pornographic movies together.

"There's one thing about the Buonos," as Candy was fond of saying. "They share everything."

Peter Buono, who was hooked on angel dust, brought his girl April Ritter over, and in Peter's absence Kenny managed to coax April into bed, saying that he was a much better stud than Angelo. Peter, who was smoking five Shermans (dark cigarettes soaked in a PCP solution) a day, never caught on, but he had his drugs and, now that he was out of the Marines, a developing career as a thief on his mind. Son Danny would drop by, too; and daughter Grace would occasionally stop in after cheerleading practice and spend the night on her father's water bed. Angelo had a special devotion to Grace. He monitored her dating, objecting to a boy she wanted to marry as being not good enough for her, and occasionally he took her to dinner at Henry's. Once he drove her out to Palm Springs to visit, so he told her, Frank Sinatra; but Sinatra was out of town, unaware of the courtesy call, so Angelo left a box of firecrackers as a present on the doorstep.

One Sunday evening, the first of February of that year, Angelo, Anthony, and Kenny were sitting around with nothing to do. It had been a dull weekend. On Saturday night, Kenny and Anthony had driven over to Hollywood to look at the girls and rip off a bottle or two from a liquor store, but other than that, nothing had gone down.

"Got an idea," Angelo said. "We get a girl over here."

"A prostitute?" Kenny asked. "We just call one up? Great. A call girl. Super."

They scanned the *L.A. Free Press*, a journal that had begun in political radicalism and progressed toward the more profitable fringes of pornography, for an outcall advertisement and selected one among a dozen. Kenny telephoned, asking for someone who could handle three guys. You could order a girl that way as easy as a pizza.

When the girl arrived, Angelo, as paterfamilias, claimed first dibs on the water bed. Anthony took seconds, and then, while Kenny completed his turn in the spare bedroom, Angelo looked through the girl's purse, which she had left on the dining-room table.

"Five bucks," Angelo said, stuffing the bill into his pocket. "Tell you what. This is one dumb cunt. She didn't take no money up front. That is the first rule they teach you. You know what? She's so dumb she ain't worth paying. She ain't that good, neither."

"We don't pay her?"

"That's what I said. Just watch."

Kenny came out of the bedroom with the girl, smiling at her as though he were going to ask her to the senior prom.

"You ain't worth shit," Angelo said to her. "Here. Take your purse and get the hell out of here."

The girl protested. She said that they had made a legitimate deal. They owed for three lays and two blowjobs. They couldn't get away with this. Fair was fair.

"Yeah?" Angelo said. "You'd be lucky giving it away. Tell you what." He pulled out his wallet and showed her his police badge. "You don't get out of here fast, you're under arrest. What's it gonna be?"

The girl left.

"That badge really works wonders," Kenny said.

"Very useful item," Angelo said, grinning.

They sat around congratulating themselves. Bianchi told his cousin how much he admired what he had done. It had taken real balls.

"You can't let a cunt get the upper hand," Angelo said. "Put them in their place. She wasn't worth shit."

It was now eleven at night. Angelo switched on the news. The phone rang, and Anthony answered it. He heard this:

"You all got a real nice house . . . real nice. Tell you all what I'm gonna do. I'm gonna mess you all's house up. I'm gonna mess it up real good. I'm gonna blow up that nice house of you all's. You gonna be flying high 'cause I'm gonna send you to the sky and you gonna die, motherfucker. You don't pay for your play, man, you ain't gonna see another day. I tell you what, son, recreation can be real expensive." The caller hung up.

"Who was it?" Angelo asked.

"Jesus," Anthony said, "some nigger says he's gonna blow up the house."

"He what?"

"Says we got a real nice house and says he's gonna blow it up. It was some nigger."

"Must be her pimp," Angelo said. "Fuck it, he's bluffing. Where's he gonna find dynamite this time of night? He's jiving."

"You sure?" Bianchi asked.

"Calm down," Angelo said. "It's just a little excitement. Passes the time."

"What if he's serious?"

"Be cool, man. You'll shit your pants. Ain't nothing but some jive-ass pimp. Watch TV. Shut up."

Sitting in the den, they caught sight of headlights as a car pulled into the driveway and honked its horn.

"I'll see who it is," Angelo said.

He opened the front door onto a yellow cab.

"Call for a taxi?"

"We didn't call for no taxi," Angelo shouted. "Must be a mistake." He shut the door and set the deadbolt. The telephone rang again. Angelo answered it, and this time the voice said that the house would be blown up at midnight. It was a quarter to twelve.

"The asshole's trying to bother us," Angelo said.

"You think he's serious now?" Bianchi asked.

Angelo did not reply. He strode over to the gun case in the den, removed three rifles, and handed one each to Kenny and Anthony.

"I tell you what," Angelo said. "If that nigger gets within ten yards of this place, he's gonna be one dead nigger." Angelo distributed ammunition. He was showing some agitation now. He told Bianchi to watch the side door. He and Anthony would watch the front. There was no way anyone would come from the back. They took up their posts.

Headlights appeared again in the driveway. Angelo and Anthony crouched down and readied their rifles.

"Who is it?" Bianchi called from the back of the house.

"Shut up!" Angelo said. "Jesus Christ, it's the cops! No it ain't. Shit!"

From out of a white van with red lights spinning atop it stepped a white-coated ambulance attendant. Angelo unbolted the door and opened it. The attendant approached.

"We didn't call you," Angelo said, hiding his rifle behind the door. "Must be a mistake. Ain't nobody sick here."

Angelo closed and bolted the door again.

"Goddammit," he said. "That motherfucking nigger is at it again. Who's he gonna call next?"

"He might call a hearse," Bianchi said.

"Shut up."

The phone rang again. Angelo grabbed it.

"Your house will blow up at midnight," the caller said and hung up. It was now only a couple of minutes before twelve.

Angelo could no longer conceal his fright with tough talk. He did what any alarmed citizen would do and dialed the police. Somebody was making bomb threats against him. No, he had no idea who the caller was. He had no enemies that he knew of. It might be some customer at his shop who figured it was easier to throw a bomb than pay his bill.

The police arrived. They told everyone to keep calm and put away the guns.

"I'm a businessman," Angelo said. "I don't want no trouble." He signed a complaint, on which he was listed as the "victim" of a bomb threat. The police watched the house that night and kept an eye on it for the next few days. Nothing happened.

Such swift police action inspired Kenny Bianchi to apply for a job with the Glendale Police Department. He had done nothing about job hunting since moving to California, and Angelo was starting to get after him. "I don't want no lazy bums around here. Move your ass." Bianchi's application required him to be fingerprinted, and he was asked to write a brief essay describing his reasons for choosing police work as a career. His creative writing skills took over:

"My reasons for wanting to be a police officer," he wrote, "are simple and varied." He listed five: he wanted to be able to help people, and he thought people needed help in today's troubled world; he enjoyed working with people, certainly something that would be important for a policeman; he also preferred working out of doors, because he was not the sort of person who could see himself being cooped up in an office all day, and he liked the idea of being active in various parts of the city; he felt that the job of police officer offered both a challenge and a chance to assert his individuality, two things which were very important to him, because a man never knew what he could accomplish until he was challenged, and too many people permitted themselves to be just faces in a crowd; and finally, most important, he wanted to contribute to the task of making America safe for people who believe in law and order.

In spite of this eloquence, he did not do well on

further examinations, and the Glendale P.D. turned him down. Undaunted, he tried to join the Los Angeles Police Department Reserves. He managed to get himself invited to participate in a "citizen's ride-along," joining officers on patrol in a squad car, and on his application this time he reached new heights of earnestness. "The main concern," he wrote, "is to be exemplary in conduct off duty as well as on." A police officer must remember that, no matter where he is, whether wearing his uniform or not, whether at work or engaged in recreational activities, "he is always representing the Department."

He was turned down again, partly on the basis of suspicions about some of the references he listed from Rochester. But Kenny had other irons in the fire. He got Sheryl Kellison, to whom he was now hinting of marriage, to drive him over to Forest Lawn one day, saying that he had heard of a job opening there; but when they arrived, he refused to get out of the car: the atmosphere was too depressing. He began to talk of setting up shop as a psychologist. He would have brochures printed up and call himself the "La Brea Counseling Services," and he began checking psychology books out of the Glendale public library to hone his skills in the discipline. The books included *Teaching Young Adolescents to Think* and several of Freud's works. There were people on the radio in Los Angeles who advised distressed callers on every sort of problem—divorce, homosexuality, whether to have an abortion, how to deal with death and terminal disease, toilet training, impotence caused by unemployment, mothers-in-law—and he figured he could do as well as these disembodied gurus. He had discovered that Southern California was both enamored of psychology and blessed with dozens of diploma-manufacturing establishments, where you could buy a ready-made college degree without bothering with the time-consuming irritations of study, and he purchased a couple of these with some of the spending money his devoted mother was sending him.

But Angelo was not impressed. He had already gotten rid of Anthony, and it was time for Kenny to get out. Angelo could tell that Kenny would stay forever if allowed. Angelo enjoyed the way Kenny deferred to him and so obviously admired him. It was like having a woman around the house. But that was just the trouble. Like a woman, Kenny needed to be put in his place, and like a woman, if you didn't watch out he could wheedle his way into taking over your life. He was like a woman or a dog, it was all the same. Angelo knew that if he let Sparky into the house, which he never did, Sparky would be all over the place, sniveling and cringing and licking his master's feet; if you kept him outside and used him for what he was worth, a deterrent to burglars, he was just fine. It was the same with Kenny. He could be of use, but Angelo was certainly not going to support him. Let the jerk find his own house.

Facing eviction, Kenny submitted to an actual job with the California Land Title Company. He was assigned to pursue research in property ownership at the Hall of Records in downtown Los Angeles, and soon he was promoted to title officer at the company's main office near Universal City in the San Fernando Valley. Without a car, he at first managed to get rides to work with a fellow employee, Mary Forsberg, who shared his interest in marijuana; but soon his mother, pleased at his progress, sent him enough money for the down payment on a car, the 1972 Cadillac four-door sedan that would prove so useful in the months ahead.

Things were looking up. In July, Bianchi found his own apartment at 809 East Garfield Avenue in Glendale, a convenient six blocks from Angelo's, in a one-story U-shaped building resembling the California auto courts of days gone by, complete with palm trees. Not only the rent and the location but the other occupants suited him, for they included young, single women. His next-door neighbor, Kristina Weckler, who was an art student in Pasadena, shunned him, telling a friend that Bianchi reminded her of an incompetent used-car salesman. But a girl across the courtyard, Angie Holt, proved more appreciative. His range had now expanded to include the ever-cooperative Sheryl Kellison, the Garfield residents, the floodtide of girls at Angelo's, and the girls at work. He tried as best he could to cover all this ground. If he was as yet no Angelo, still he had advanced. California was beginning to live up to his expectations.

Yet he pined for Susan Moore, or so he told her in letters and telephone calls back to Rochester. He had never formally withdrawn his proposal of marriage to her, and he renewed it several times over in passionate entreaties for her to visit him. He had done what she had asked of him, established himself with a steady job. He had proved his independence by pulling up roots and putting down new ones. And only now, he told her, in this strange place so far from home, had he come fully to appreciate her. The girls out here in California were not for him. This entire society was corrupt, not what he was used to nor what he longed for. The girls, he said, were loose. They thought no more of making love than of eating a hamburger. Even their clothes he found disgusting, cheap, sluttish. They had no sense of personal modesty and were as ready to surrender their virtue as a dog or a cat. He needed her. He wanted her to come to him and marry him. His prospects were good, better than they had ever been in Rochester, but he needed her, Susan, for his own forever.

Susan agreed to visit him but said that she would reserve judgment on marriage. Kenny sent her a one-way ticket and met her at the Los Angeles airport in his Cadillac. Susan was impressed.

But trouble between them started as soon as she entered his Garfield apartment and noticed the fake degrees on the wall. He tried to explain them away as "novelties," but when he admitted that he was thinking of starting a sideline as a psychologist and was preparing a brochure offering his counseling services at cut rates, she told him that, much to her disappointment, he had not changed at all and was just as impractical as ever. When she asked him whom he was dating, and he replied no one, she did not believe him; and when she told him frankly about her romantic life in Rochester, he lapsed into the same old jealousies and resentments, telling her that she was no better than the California sluts. When she reminded him that they had always fought over his absurd possessiveness, that he had become angry when she so much as danced with someone else at a party, his anger increased.

They argued through the night, and by morning, Susan announced that she was leaving. Kenny burst into tears. She wasn't giving him a chance. She did not understand the depth of his love for her. He was lost without her and might kill himself if she left him. They were perfect for each other and no man could love her as he could. She telephoned for a reservation on the next plane out.

On the way to the airport, Kenny pretended to get lost, saying he was bewildered by the freeway system. But Susan persisted and found another flight leaving a couple of hours later. She managed to talk him into writing a check for the ticket. He sulked as they sat in the departure lounge, and as the time of her flight approached, he began to cry, then sob, forcing his head into her lap like a son forsaken, ignoring her protests that people were watching. She made her flight this time. She had spent less than twenty-four hours with him, but something had told her to get out.

Chapfallen, Kenny took solace in other women. Sheryl was distressed to discover that he was also involved with Angie Holt but helped him distribute his psychologist flyers in the neighborhood and for several months saw him three or four nights a week. Angie, finding him refreshingly polite at first, a real gentleman, soon tired of his possessiveness, and when she brought in another young man to share her apartment with her, she told Kenny not to bother her any longer. He expressed shock that she could treat him so cavalierly. They had, after all, been intimate. He grew incensed at her rejection and hounded her, knocking on her door at all hours, following her around the building, confronting her in the laundry room and berating her as she tried to wash her dirty linen. She told him to grow up and lay off.

Stung, he broke into her apartment, found her diaphragm, punched a hole in it, threw it on the floor, and urinated on it. For good measure he stole her boyfriend's television set and sold it immediately to avoid being caught with it. As a final gesture symbolic of his pique, he slipped over her doorknob a semen-filled condom.

EIGHT

But for Kenneth Bianchi in California all was not defeat. He kept his job at Cal Land into the new year, 1977; there was nothing there for him to steal. At a New Year's Eve party he met Kelli Boyd, a plump, hazel-eyed blonde from the state of Washington who was also working at Cal Land. After weeks of movies and dinners out, a Dodger game, TV at Angelo's, an evening shooting pool with Angelo and one of his girls, and the occasional night spent with Kenny at his apartment, she agreed to move in with him on Garfield. By May she was pregnant.

Kenny wondered about fatherhood. It might be just what he needed to settle down, and it might be cause for escape. As was so often his habit, he proposed marriage, and, given Kelli's condition, he had every reason to expect that she would accept him, but she declined the offer, saying she needed time to think it over. She was sure she wanted to have the baby, but she was unsure about Kenny. He was thoughtful, kind, gentle, attentive; he wrote her cute little poems and brought her flowers; but sometimes he would not come home until very late. He said that he needed his freedom and that he liked to take long drives and walks by himself. She understood, but that was not what she wanted in a husband. He was also inordinately jealous of her friends, even of her brother Gerald and his two best buddies, all three of them men without women. He was neither punctual nor regular in his attendance at work, because, he told Kelli, he was suffering from cancer. To prove his illness, he sometimes would have her drive him to the hospital and tell her to wait in the parking lot while he pretended to go in for chemotherapy. Kelli reasoned that it would not make sense to have a husband who might drop dead before the honeymoon was over.

Kenny managed flings with some of the other girls who worked at Cal Land, never letting on to Kelli. He took special delight in coaxing one girl into Angelo's water bed when he was out: Angelo had strictly forbidden either his sons or Kenny to desecrate the water bed; Kenny was to use the spare bedroom for his trysts. Through another of the girls, Mary Forsberg, Kenny had access to plenty of marijuana, smoking some of it and selling the rest at a profit.

And there were additional small pleasures in his work. In the files at Cal Land he found intriguing tax assessment information which he enjoyed sharing with Kelli, bringing home the addresses and assessments of Sonny and Cher, Groucho Marx, Telly Savalas, Jerry Lewis, George Peppard, Lee Marvin, Dean Martin, James Caan, and other celebrities. Sometimes material about unknown people amused him. The name Frank Horney, for instance, tickled his funnybone. He laughed to think how irritated all these people would be if they knew what Kenny Bianchi had found out about them. Why, if he wanted, he could drive right up to their doors and say hello, maybe pretend he was the tax assessor. If he were not an honest man, he told Kelli, he could use the information to pull off burglaries. You would think that after what Charles Manson and his gang had accomplished in Bel-Air, this kind of stuff would be kept private. People could not be too careful.

When his supervisor found marijuana in Bianchi's desk drawer at work, Kenny was asked to resign. He protested that someone must have planted the pot, but he found another, similar job at Stewart West Coast Title in downtown Los Angeles. He and Kelli then decided to move to an apartment at 1950 Tamarind Avenue in Hollywood, so that they could live halfway between his work and hers in the Valley.

His schemes for getting extra money now included the psychologist's office he rented from Dr. Weingarten, where he often sat at night waiting for the phone to ring. It seldom did. One evening a man called in saying he was about to commit suicide, and Bianchi thoughtfully referred him to a hot line that specialized in such cases. He administered Rorschach ink-blot tests on Kelli, guided by a textbook on the subject, and he advised one of Kelli's friends about her weight problem.

Bianchi was anxious to find other ways of picking up extra money. When Angelo suggested that they find some girls to work for them as prostitutes, Kenny thought it a great idea. Kenny could use his gift of gab, Angelo said, to recruit the girls. Angelo would find the customers. They could clean up. Ninety percent of the whores in Los Angeles were controlled by black pimps. Why shouldn't a couple of good white American boys like them rake off a little of the action? Kenny should keep his eye out for possible recruits.

It did not take Kenny long to find the right girl. At a party at Mary Forsberg's which Kelli did not attend, he met Sabra Hannan, a sixteen-year-old from Phoenix, who had come out to Los Angeles looking for modeling work. She told Kenny that she had done one picture session for Evinrude outboard motors but that nothing had turned up since.

"You're a beautiful girl," Bianchi said. In this he was sincere. Sabra Hannan was blond with large, round eyes and a full lower lip that gave a little pout to her smile. And from what Kenny could tell she would look even better with her clothes off. "You ought to be making plenty of money modeling. You just haven't met the right people. I've got a lot of contacts in that business. Matter of fact, I can guarantee you five hundred dollars a week, easy."

Sabra said that she would think it over. She was going away to visit friends in Lubbock, Texas, and then on to Phoenix for a couple of weeks. If he would give her his number, she would call him from there if she decided to accept his offer.

When Sabra Hannan did call Bianchi from Phoenix in June, she said that she had run out of money. She remembered what he had said about five hundred a week. If he would pay her fare back to Los Angeles, she could reimburse him out of her first check.

"No problem," Bianchi said. "I'll have my secretary arrange for a plane ticket. Just pick it up at the airport. By the way, you need a place to stay?"

"As a matter of fact I do, for a few days."

"I'll take care of everything. I'll meet you at the airport. Gosh, you know, I have a feeling about these things. I have a feeling you're really going places, Sabra."

Kenny told Angelo the good news. Sabra Hannan was coming back to L.A., and she was broke. Wait till Angelo saw her. She was prime. She was first-class. About five-four, blond, and he would bet natural, great face, kind of pert and real slender but terrific tits. He hadn't actually seen her tits but he could tell. They stood right up and winked at you. But, Kenny wondered, how were they going to talk her into whoring? She thought she was getting some modeling deal. She didn't look whorish at all. Real clean-cut. He hadn't even said anything to her about posing nude.

"Just watch," Angelo said. "We're paying her plane fare, that's the first thing. She's already in hock to us, see? We already own her. Leave it to me. We'll be getting gold out of her ass in no time."

Kenny was to bring Sabra straight to Angelo's. When he picked Sabra up in the Cadillac, she remarked on what a nice car it was.

"Sometimes you need to impress people in this business," Bianchi said. "You know, you drive a cheap car and they think you're a nobody. You must be thirsty after your flight. Have some of this." He handed her a paper cup of what appeared to be orange juice.

By the time they arrived at Angelo's, Sabra was asleep. Bianchi had spiked the juice with a sedative. He left her in the car and went in to see Angelo, who told him he had decided Sabra should be left for the night at one of the motels down the street. That would soften her up, gain her confidence for the time being.

Bianchi got her a room under his own name at the Sands Motel, signing the register "Kenneth A. Bianchi, Ph.D." He managed to wake her and helped her to the room. Inside, he showed her three diamonds and told her that if she worked for him and his partner, his cousin Angelo Buono, for six months, she would get one of the diamonds as a bonus.

"I can't believe my luck," Sabra said. "Yesterday I was broke."

"We believe in taking good care of our employees," Bianchi said. "It's better for morale. Here, try one of these on." He handed her two frilly nightgowns.

Sabra changed in the bathroom and climbed into bed. She said she would see him in the morning. She didn't know why she was so tired.

But Bianchi climbed onto the bed with her and started pulling down the covers and unbuckling his pants. Sabra rolled away from him.

"No," she said. "I don't really know you. Not now."

"Come on. You're acting like a virgin. You can't fool me." He wished he had given her a stronger dose of the sedative. He had been thinking about making it with her for two days. He had thought about her with Kelli, and it had been better than usual.

"No. Please. Let me sleep."

Bianchi decided not to press the point. He would behave like a gentleman for now; there would be plenty of opportunities later.

The next morning Bianchi took Sabra to meet Angelo at the Trim Shop. Angelo sat behind his desk in the little office he had constructed inside the garage. Behind him the wall was covered with photographs of the classic cars he had worked on. He looked Sabra over, without rising from his chair, and smiled. He reached into his pocket, pulled out the fat roll of bills he always carried, and peeled off a hundred-dollar note and handed it to her.

"This'll get you some clothes. You working for us now?"

"Thank you. I guess I am."

"Okay. What that means is, your word is your bond to us for one year. Get it?"

"Sure."

"Your word is your bond," Angelo said. "Remember that. Don't forget it."

"Okay."

Angelo told her that she would move into his spare bedroom for the time being, until she got on her feet. Kenny would be telling her more about what kinds of modeling jobs she would be doing. In the meantime, she was not to go anywhere without telling them. If a job came through, they would need to know where she was. Sabra said she understood. She wouldn't want to miss any opportunities.

Over the next few days they softened Sabra up. At first Kenny told her that the modeling business was slow that month. It was July and a lot of people were on vacation. Then he told her that he had found her a job, but that it would involve some nude poses. Sabra said she had never done that kind of modeling before, but when Kenny told her it was high-class stuff, art work, nothing pornographic, she agreed. He told her they would need some shots of her in the nude right away, to show the customer what he was getting. Otherwise it would be like buying a pig in a poke. Sabra took off her clothes and posed on the water bed while Angelo snapped some Polaroids.

"You don't mind this," Angelo said. "Give us a smile."

But Kenny was sorry to tell her two days later that the job had fallen through. He asked her if she had ever considered prostitution. She said that she had not and that she had no intention of becoming a prostitute.

"Think about it," Angelo said. "Meantime don't go nowheres without telling me. You got that?"

But Sabra did not yet take Angelo's warnings seriously. She still figured a modeling job would turn up. They had promised her five hundred a week, hadn't they? One afternoon she decided to go over to the Eagle Rock Plaza to buy some clothes. She still had not spent any of the hundred dollars. They had been taking her out for meals at Henry's. She left Angelo's house without telling him and started walking east on Colorado Street. After a couple of blocks a car pulled over and a young man gave her a ride to the Plaza. She spent most of the hundred and walked back to Angelo's.

He was waiting for her, as was Kenny, who had taken yet another day off from work.

"You left without telling me," Angelo said.

"I just went to get some clothes. Look. Do you like this skirt?"

"You walked down Colorado," Angelo said. "Then you got a ride with some guy. You know him?"

"No. I could see he was nice."

"When you was at the Plaza, you talked to a guy. You know him?"

"No."

"Lying cunt whore. Kenny, get the towel. Take off your clothes, bitch. Do like I said!"

The look in Angelo's eyes and the knowledge that he had been following her or had had her followed terrified Sabra. She undressed. Kenny appeared with a bathtowel that had been soaked in water. Angelo told Sabra to get her ass into the spare bedroom. He had already explained to Kenny the virtues of a wet towel: it left no bruise marks.

Bianchi swung the towel hard against her back and buttocks and breasts while Angelo watched, smiling, telling Bianchi to see if he could hit a bull's-eye on her sex. This was a first for Kenny. He had never beaten a woman before. He found that he enjoyed it a lot.

"Now," Angelo told her as she lay on the bed whimpering, "you're gonna suck my dick."

When he was finished, Bianchi demanded the

same. He complimented Sabra afterward, saying that he had never enjoyed it more.

They now told Sabra that she was working for them as a prostitute. She had no choice. She owed them money for the plane fare and for the clothes she had just bought, and she would have to pay it back out of what she earned as a whore. If she behaved, everything would work out fine. But she must remember that she had given her word as bond for one year.

Angelo explained to her some inside procedures of the trade. She would always have a nailfile with her, in case a trick got too weird or violent. She was to stick the nailfile in his eye and get out of there. If the trick was not paying Angelo or Kenny directly, she should always take the money first and then hide it. Sticking it on chewing gum under a sink was a good idea. And she was to cut all the labels out of her clothes. That way, if the trick happened to be an undercover cop, she could not be traced to a neighborhood: this if she was working outcall, which they would arrange in time.

"You try to run away," Buono told her, "you're a dead pussy, understand? You can't escape. I got friends in the Mafia will find you. You know what we do to girls who try to run off? I'll tell you. We cut off their arms and legs and put them in a box and ship them out to the desert. You want that to happen to you, cunt?"

At first Sabra worked in Angelo's house. Angelo would show a Trim Shop customer her nude pictures, ask the man if he wanted "some of that," take his money, and lead him in to Sabra. Not only was he getting money as a pimp, which he split with Bianchi, he noticed that his upholstery business picked up when word got around about the extras you had available when you took your car to Angelo's. Men from the glass shop and the car wash next door started making use of Sabra, too.

Angelo did not give Sabra any of the take, nor did Kenny. And to complete the circle of servitude, sometimes when they took her out for a meal, they would not permit her to eat anything. Angelo would order a plate of his favorite stew at Henry's and then grin at

114

Sabra, saying he bet she was real hungry. The techniques of intimidation worked splendidly. Every day either Angelo or Kenny reminded Sabra what would happen to her if she tried to escape.

Both Angelo and Kenny had sex with Sabra, Angelo every day, even if he had other girls around. Sometimes Sabra would be awakened in the middle of the night by Angelo's harsh shout from his room: "Get in here and give me a head job." She would obey; she was as enslaved as any harem girl. The one thing she had managed to resist was anal intercourse. He was too big and she was too small. She had never done that and did not want to do it.

But Angelo was determined to break Sabra in to sodomy. One evening, with Kenny present—as Kelli's pregnancy advanced, Kenny was spending more and more time with Angelo—he handed her a big dildo and commanded her to force it up her anus. If she refused, she would be beaten. Naked and afraid, she tried to comply. She sat on the floor of the spare bedroom, Buono and Bianchi looming over her directing her, spitting obscenities at her and playing with themselves. But she failed to accomplish the act. She wept, but Bianchi beat her anyway, thrashing her with the wet towel as Angelo looked on, grinning. Angelo told her to keep the dildo with her and to practice with it.

Among the many girls still seeing Angelo while Sabra lived in the house was the devoted Antoinette Lombardo, now a senior in high school, none the wiser for an abortion and a miscarriage, still hopeful that one day Angelo would be her groom. Angelo, beginning to tire of her matrimonial obsession and anxious to teach her a lesson, told her that he could not possibly marry her unless he could be sure that she would not screw around when she became his wife. There was only one way to be sure of her devotion. She had never been with anyone but him. What if she went for another guy? What if she liked it with somebody else? Maybe she was just like other women, hot to trot, indifferent to loyalty, randy, ready and willing.

"You got to screw somebody else," Angelo said.

"Tell me if you like it. You don't like it, we get married. Got it?"

Antoinette said that she did not want anyone else. Angelo was her true love and he could always trust her. But Angelo pressed his argument. Antoinette gave in, saying that she would do anything for him. He was the man she had always dreamed of, strong, alone, defiant.

"I'll arrange it," Angelo said.

"But Ange, I don't see nobody else. Who would I go with?"

"That's okay. I'll arrange something."

Angelo had something in mind. Through contacts in his upholstery business, he had agreed to supply girls for an afternoon's orgy at the Triple AAA Paper Company box factory in Cudahy, a municipality in southeast Los Angeles County, the industrial heartland of Southern California, a treeless wasteland distinguished by the post-Assyrian architecture of the gigantic and abandoned Uniroyal rubber-tire factory. There would be about half a dozen men present. Sabra was good, but there was room for an extra cunt, Angelo calculated.

When Angelo and Kenny arrived at the box factory with Sabra and Antoinette, seven men awaited them, swarthy fellows congruous with the odor of cardboard. They included the box moguls and assorted civic dignitaries: Pete Werrlein, revered city councilman from the city of Bell; Red Fertig, the police chief of Huntington Park; and Warren Schmucki, chief aide to a member of the Los Angeles County Board of Supervisors. Angelo and Kenny ordered the girls into separate offices and directed traffic.

As the more experienced and proficient whore, Sabra dealt with five customers according to their wants. Sabra was also much prettier than Antoinette, so a majority of the men requested her. The orgy went well. Sabra was rewarded with an unprecedented cash payment, sixty dollars. Antoinette got nothing for her display of fealty except accusations from Angelo that she had shown signs of enjoying her work and might not be a good candidate for wifehood after all.

In the parking lot afterward, the men talked of

their satisfaction and the desire for another orgy at the earliest possible opportunity. Kenny noticed a decal, the seal of the County of Los Angeles, on Warren Schmucki's windshield, and Schmucki said proudly that it entitled him to free parking in county lots. He promised to send one to Bianchi.

Sabra was working out so well for Angelo and Kenny that they decided they should expand their operations. They told her that if she could recruit another girl, she could go free; otherwise she had another ten months to go on her contract. When Sabra said that she had a friend in Phoenix who might be interested, they gave her permission to fly there on condition that she stay no more than a week and return with the new girl. Could she attend the Led Zepplin concert in Phoenix? Sabra wanted to know. It was her favorite group. Yes, Angelo said, but she would be watched. "The boys" were strong in Phoenix and would find her and kill her if she tried to run off. And she could forget about going to the police. He had friends in law enforcement who owed him favors. He showed Sabra his badge to assure her of his connections. Meanwhile, in Phoenix she should keep practicing with the dildo.

Sabra returned with Rebekah Gay Spears, a fifteen-year-old biker's daughter who was eager to leave home for a new life in California. Angelo and Kenny had refused to send the girls air fare, so they turned a trick at an airport hotel for the money. Becky was a tiny girl with a large, sad mouth, mousy but frail and defenseless-looking in a way that appealed to Angelo. He was also gratified that Becky, once threatened with death, acquiesced readily to anal intercourse. He installed Sabra in a nearby apartment and moved Becky into his house so that she would be available to him daily and nightly, when she was not earning money for him. So brutally and frequently did he attack Becky's rear that he tore her sphincter muscles, and she resorted to wearing a tampon in her rectum to control her bowels.

Angelo made use of Becky's compliance, but sometimes she was too passive for him. He would hit her and shake her, trying to get her angry, saying,

117

"What's the matter with you? Ain't you alive? Fight me. Tits is better than you." Tits was his nickname for Sabra. When Becky did dare complain, he would tell her about shipping disobedient girls into the desert, delimbed, and ask her if she wanted to be beaten as Tits had been. As for Sabra, he reneged on his promise to free her, saying that she had to earn more money for him and Kenny before she would be let go.

The pimping now became more sophisticated. Angelo arranged through J. J. Fenway, owner of the Foxy Ladies outcall service, to have Becky and Sabra visit clients at home. Foxy Ladies would take a 15 percent cut of any call; Angelo and Kenny would get 60 percent, with 25 percent left over for the girl, in theory, although she rarely received anything but sneers and a little food. Becky and Sabra continued to work in Angelo's house for neighborhood clients and the Trim Shop customers, but on most evenings the Foxy Ladies driver would deliver them to men all over the city. And they played a return engagement at the box factory, Antoinette absent this time, after which Angelo had Kenny beat Becky, on grounds of her failure of enthusiasm.

The girls were proving a healthy source of extra income for Buono and Bianchi, and Kenny found owning women more gratifying than he could have imagined, although he continued to press Kelli to marry him and told her how much he looked forward to becoming a father. As her pregnancy progressed, Kelli grew irritable, but Kenny did not really mind: her bad moods gave him ready excuses for staying out late, and when he wanted sex, Sabra and Becky were his to do with as he wished. Yet his prosperity and happiness proved short.

It happened one August night that David Wood, a lawyer lonely and libidinous in his loneliness, locked up within the electronically guarded splendor of his Bel-Air house, telephoned the Foxy Ladies and asked that a girl be sent to him. Within an hour Becky Spears had been driven westward from the bungalowland of Glendale, on to Hollywood and the rich hush of Beverly Hills, along Sunset Boulevard past UCLA and through the rococo gateway of Bel-Air. This is a district that surpasses even Beverly Hills in the illusion of remoteness from the ordinary city. It is dark with trees, bright with meticulous flowerbeds, all hills and winding streets with names like Copa de Oro and Belaggio and houses forbiddingly huge and apparently impregnable, though the Manson gang had found otherwise: one of their victims, Sharon Tate, had lived on the cusp of Bel-Air and Beverly Hills, high up in secluded Benedict Canyon, just a stone's throw from a street called Angelo, a cul-de-sac. When Becky arrived at David Wood's house on Roscomare Drive, she was overcome by a serenity and security that tapped her emotions and loosened her tongue.

David Wood was not in the habit of summoning women in this way, but that night he thought he would try something effortless and anonymous. The evening turned out to be neither. The small girl with the downturned mouth emanated such sadness and dejection that, in spite of his worldliness, Wood started asking her variations on the most threadbare of all questions addressed to whores: How did a nice girl like you . . . ? Becky did not offer him any of the usual responses, such as "I only do this in my spare time" or "I perform a special service" or "How else would I earn four to five hundred dollars a night?" Becky let go. She told him she was the prisoner of two men. She told him about the beatings, the relentless sodomy, the threats of delimbing and death. She said that she believed it was only a matter of time before Angelo Buono and Kenny Bianchi would kill her. She knew Angelo wanted to kill her. The way he forced himself down her throat until she vomited or almost passed out told her that. The way Bianchi laughed when he beat her told her that he wanted to kill her, too.

Through his law practice, David Wood knew the criminal class. He was not naive. But Becky's tale shocked him, and her frail, sexually unattractive desperation made him want to help her. That this visitor from the moral sewers of the city had intruded on the order and expensive serenity of his home disgusted him, and he wanted to throw her out and go take a long, hot bath; but pity for her overcame disgust. Not for a second did he doubt that she was telling the truth.

He knew that the Foxy Ladies driver would be coming back soon, so he drove Becky to his office and telephoned for a plane reservation to Phoenix: it was not that Becky's family, from what she told him of it, offered decent refuge, but at least she knew Phoenix and had friends there. She had nowhere else to go. The plane was not leaving until early in the morning, so David Wood talked through the night with Becky at his office. The more she told him, the better he felt about what he was doing. He tried to reassure her that she would be safe, once out of the city. No two-bit auto upholsterer and his perverted cousin would have the resources to track her down. He did not believe in Buono's boasts about the Mafia or the boys or whatever he called them. The Mafia would not bother with such a small-time operation. In the morning he drove her to the airport and waited to put her on the plane. As they said goodbye, he took her father's telephone number and gave her his, telling her to call him if she felt she was in danger. And he told her never to come back to Los Angeles unless she heard that Buono and Bianchi were dead or safely locked up.

When the Foxy Ladies driver telephoned Angelo to tell him that Becky and her trick had left Wood's house and gone somewhere, Angelo was annoyed but not alarmed. The trick was probably one of those guys who liked to talk to whores and had taken her out. Becky should have telephoned, those were the rules, and he would have Kenny beat her, but Angelo figured she would return in the morning. And she had better have plenty of money to show for the full night.

But when Becky did not appear, Angelo had the Foxy Ladies driver take him and Kenny to David Wood's house for a confrontation. Wood was not home. Angelo telephoned his office. When Angelo told him he had better tell where the girl was or suffer the consequences, Wood hung up.

Once Angelo and Kenny realized that Becky was not coming back, they became enraged. Just so Sabra would not get ideas, they stuffed Becky's abandoned clothes into a box with a dead cat and showed the box to Sabra. Did she get the message? Dead pussy. That's what Becky was going to be and that's what Sabra would be if she tried to leave. Then Angelo set about trying to ruin David Wood.

He called Wood and told him that he was going to bring charges against him for having sex with a fifteen-year-old girl. Again Wood hung up. Angelo then had flowers sent to Wood's employees, with a note saying that David Wood was leaving the profession of law and that his employees were being terminated.

David Wood was angry, but he was not intimidated. He called one of his clients, a three-hundred-pound bouncer named Tiny, and said he needed a favor. He told Tiny what Buono was up to and told him about Becky. Tiny said he would take care of it.

Angelo was working inside a car when Tiny walked into the Trim Shop accompanied by four friends almost as big as himself.

"You Angelo Buono?" Tiny called. Angelo continued working and gave no response. So Tiny reached one arm through the open car window, grabbed Angelo by the shoulder, and started dragging him out of the window. "Now do I have your attention, Mr. Buono?"

Angelo crawled out and struggled to his feet. Tiny picked him up under both arms, gave him a vicious shaking, and said:

"David Wood's a friend of mine. You messing with him, you messing with me, Tiny. Get it? I don't like people messing with my friend. You don't want to see an instant replay of me."

Angelo said he understood. Tiny threw him down and left. Angelo did not bother David Wood again.

Angelo and Kenny were still angry, and they were worried. They figured Becky had made fools of them. It was bad for morale. Somebody was going to have to pay, one way or another.

"Some girls don't deserve to live," Angelo said.

They had no concrete plans as yet, but in the next six weeks they suffered further blows to their professional pride and their rage doubled. In September, Sabra escaped. Wisely she left the state, disappeared one day without telling anyone. Now, with his extra income gone, Bianchi started missing payments on his Cadillac, and fights with Kelli became more frequent. He stole the letterhead stationery from Universal and talked of the talent-scout scam. He and Angelo told each other over and over that they could not let the girls get away with this, and for the first time they began talking about killing a prostitute to set an example. They would rape her and do her in.

"I'm gonna get my hands around some cunt's throat," Angelo said. "Some cunt that don't deserve to live."

"Me too," Kenny said, anxious to let Angelo know that Kenny was really one tough guy. Angelo's rage fueled Kenny's, and Kenny made sure Angelo noticed, the cousins igniting one another.

"Let's go get some whore and get it over with," Angelo said one night late in September.

They cruised over to Hollywood and picked up two teenage girls. It was easy. The girls got into the car, and everyone agreed on a price. They drove up Curson Street into the Hollywood Hills and parked, and then Angelo showed his badge. If the girls did not cooperate, they would be busted. But after having sex with them in the car, they pushed the girls out, naked, and let them go.

"You chickened out," Angelo told Kenny later.

"No I didn't. Honest, Tony, I would have done it. I thought you didn't want to. I thought, you know, with two of them."

"Yeah? Bullshit. Okay, we'll see what you're made of tomorrow night."

The next night they drove down Highland and spotted two girls walking. It was not clear whether they were prostitutes or just out for a stroll. At the corner of Hawthorne and Highland, Angelo swung the Cadillac around in front of the girls as they were crossing the street. One of them took off, but the other stopped when Angelo flashed his badge.

Bianchi, standing in the street with the girl, who was barely five feet tall and wearing glasses, began interrogating her:

"Vice squad. Let's see some identification."

"My wallet's been stolen," she said. "Here. I have my citizenship papers."

When Bianchi looked over the papers, he saw that the girl's name was Catherine Lorre. She had been born in Germany, and her father was listed as Peter Lorre, film actor. The daughter of a man who, forty-four years earlier in Germany, had achieved international fame and Hollywood offers for his role as a rapist and murderer of little girls in *M* was now being sized up as a potential victim on a Hollywood street corner.

"Hey," Bianchi called to Buono, "look who we got here. It's Peter Lorre's daughter!"

A couple of photographs fell out of Catherine Lorre's purse onto the street. Bianchi picked them up. They showed Catherine at nine years, with her father at Christmastime. In one, Peter Lorre, looking like a small Papa Bear, was tickling his daughter, who laughed wildly. Wrapped and beribboned presents were strewn at their feet. In the other, father and daughter posed happily before the Christmas tree. "What do you know," Kenny said. "It really is Peter Lorre's daughter." He handed the snapshots to Angelo, who gave a big grin.

"Where are you going?" Kenny asked her.

"Home. Home from school. I have a ride. There." She pointed to a car parked down the street.

Kenny checked with Angelo, who shook his head, signaling that they should let her go.

"Okay," Kenny said. "Take care of yourself. Be careful now. You shouldn't be out walking like this at night. Be good."

Catherine Lorre walked briskly off, glad that she had had the presence of mind to lie about having a ride nearby, when in truth she was headed down to Sunset to wait for a bus. She wondered whether those men were really police officers.

In October, Angelo and Kenny suffered further setbacks. Angelo's mother was operated on for vaginal cancer, and the prognosis was glum. That the woman he had always called a cunt would end up dying from a disease in that region was a coincidence that did not occur to Angelo, but when he visited her in the hospital, sometimes accompanied by his old buddy Artie Ford, he found himself torn between love and hate, or emotions for which no strong enough words exist. He calmed himself, or tried to, by indulging in the satisfactions of stealing objects from the hospital—syringes, hypodermic needles, a stethoscope—but the thought of his mother's having pieces of malignant tissue cut out of her vagina intensified his already primordial emotions and impulses. He arranged with his sister Cecilia to visit Jenny on alternate nights.

He and Kenny found another girl, Jennifer Snider, to work for them and installed her in the spare bedroom. Sabra had given them Jennifer's number before escaping. And from Deborah Noble, an experienced prostitute, Angelo purchased a list of men known to frequent whores, a trick list, as it was called, of a hundred and seventy-five men at a dollar a name. Deborah Noble delivered the trick list to the Trim Shop, accompanied by three other prostitutes, one a tall, expensively dressed black girl named Yolanda Washington.

Angelo asked Deborah Noble whether she was certain that this was an outcall list. He did not want hundreds of strange tricks showing up at his house at all hours. Deborah Noble assured him that it was an outcall list.

Angelo made his usual cocky, joshing conversation with the girls, and in the course of it Yolanda Washington mentioned that she worked the north side of Sunset near Highland. That was her turf. She could be found there practically every night.

On the night of October 17, Jennifer Snider lay in her bed in the spare bedroom. She could hear Angelo and Kenny talking in the living room. They sounded angry. She had been living in Angelo's house for three days, spending most of her time calling, as she had been told to do, the men on the trick list. But something was wrong. All the men on the list wanted to come to her, not have her go to them. Deborah Noble's outcall list had turned out to be an incall list. Angelo and Kenny had been cheated, and they were furious.

Kenny came into the spare bedroom, took off his clothes, and, without saying a word, began to have sex with Jennifer. He had an ugly look on his face, and he started to get rough, pinching her and slapping her breasts. Jennifer asked him to ease up, but instead, he grabbed her by the hips, turned her over violently, and tried to sodomize her.

"No," Jennifer said. "I won't do that. No. Stop it."

When he persisted, she managed to turn herself over and throw him off onto the floor. He looked at her as though he was going to kill her. But she leaped out of bed and showed her nails to him, indicating that she was ready to fight. Kenny grabbed his clothes and left the room.

In the living room he told Angelo what had happened and suggested killing Jennifer Snider right then and there. First Becky and Sabra had run off, then the bad trick list, and now this, a bitch who wouldn't cooperate. It was time to teach everybody a lesson.

"I been thinking," Angelo said. "We can't kill Snider, you dumb shit. She could be traced here easy. Ain't you got a brain? I thought you was so smart. Listen. Remember that nigger whore was with Noble? We can't find Noble, but we'll get her friend. She told me where she works. We'll use my badge and handcuffs. Pretend we're arresting her, right? Then we snuff her. Noble'll get the message."

"Let's go," Bianchi said. "I'm ready for it. Kill the bitches."

"*Mi numi,*" Angelo said, looking Bianchi in the eye.

Kenny felt that Angelo approved of him, and it made him feel good. Now he would show Angelo that Kenny Bianchi had guts.

In the spare bedroom Jennifer Snider lay shaking, terrified that both of them would come in and beat her. But she heard the door open and shut and a car start in the driveway and back out. She let a few minutes pass, then checked to see that they were gone.

She tried going to sleep, but her anxiety mounted. She was asthmatic, and she began to feel an attack coming on. She took her pills, but the attack became worse, choking her. She could not remember ever having felt such anxiety. She went into the living room and, by the light of the fish tank, telephoned a boy-friend and then her mother. The sound of her mother's voice calmed her down. She told her mother that she was staying at a friend's temporarily but was leaving tomorrow. The atmosphere here did not agree with her.

While Jennifer Snider was talking to her mother, Kenny Bianchi was strangling Yolanda Washington to death in the backseat as Angelo drove north on the Hollywood Freeway. Bianchi had already stripped the girl and raped her on the freeway. Now he was show-ing Angelo that he was no chicken. He tried pulling back on her throat with his forearm first, then used a rag Angelo handed him. She was handcuffed, but she managed to kick Angelo in the head, so he held down her legs, draped over the back of the front seat, with his free hand until Kenny had finished the job.

When she was limp, Kenny surreptitiously re-moved a large turquoise ring from her left hand and slipped it into his pocket. He thought it would make a nice present for Kelli.

Then Angelo drove to a spot on Forest Lawn Drive, below the Oakwood Apartments he had once lived in. They dumped Yolanda Washington's body beside the road, near a rockpile and the entrance to the graveyard, across the way from a Warner Brothers set depicting a peaceful New England village.

So it began.

NINE

Thanksgiving week, 1977, will be remembered as the time of the greatest horror and panic in the history of Los Angeles. No one, except Frank Salerno and a couple of other officers, had paid attention to similarities between the Judy Miller and Lissa Kastin murders; and as for Yolanda Washington, she had been dead for more than a month and might soon have been written off as just another murdered prostitute. But now, in a mere nine days, five more bodies, all of them nude young women or girls, turned up on hillsides in the Glendale–Highland Park area, and connections among them were obvious to everyone. Buono and Bianchi's acts, though not their identities, had finally penetrated the consciousness of the city. Not a morning or an evening passed for the citizens without their being confronted in the newspapers and on radio and television with news of the killings and the fear, even the certainty, that the Hillside Strangler, as Buono and

Bianchi came quickly and collectively to be called, would strike soon again.

The term "Hillside Strangler" seemed to spring up spontaneously once police began referring to the "hillside murders," with no one able to claim sole authorship. Nor did police object to use of the singular, though they were convinced that there had to be more than one strangler: the less the killers thought was known about them the better. As a phrase, "Hillside Strangler" captured and even intensified the spreading terror in Los Angeles and soon drew recognition across the nation. In the city, women became afraid to drive their cars alone at night; parents feared for their daughters; self-defense classes for women multiplied; city parks were deserted; sales of Mace, tear gas, and guns took off. The usual conversational mundanities gave way to "I look over my shoulder and around corners" and "Everyone I talk to is petrified" and "I run into the house when I leave my car" and "I sleep with a hammer under my pillow and carry a steak knife" and "That's all anybody's talking about at school." Women debated what they would do if confronted by the Strangler. Was it better to try to run away, to fight, to scream, or to cooperate so as not to make him angry? Some people thought that the stranglings were a message from God, vengeance on a valueless city. The *Times* soon ran a feature story carrying the headline:

THE SOUTHLAND'S NEW NEIGHBOR: FEAR.

Such headlines and stories proliferated in all the media. They increased, of course, the fear they reported, but they reflected reality. No phrase could better describe the mood of the city then and for months to come than the title of the 1950 Richard Widmark film *Panic in the Streets*. Hollywood had caught up with Hollywood.

On Sunday, November 20, Sergeant Bob Grogan had planned an outing on his boat, but for him there was no possibility of deep-sea fishing that day. He mildly cursed when, reading the Sunday paper while his wife was off at mass, he got the call to go immediately to the corner of Ranons Way and Wawona Avenue in the hills that separate Glendale from Eagle Rock; had he known that he was embarking on what would become an obsession that would consume six years of his life, he would have cursed more vigorously.

Bob Grogan could find any address in Los Angeles as quickly as anyone, and he drove everywhere, even when going for a loaf of bread, as though he were chasing or being chased, a Mario Andretti of the freeways, trying to break the sound barrier in his beige unmarked Plymouth or, off-duty, in his baby-blue Coupe de Ville. But he had some trouble locating this body site, enough to make him think that whoever would dump a body there must know the area very well. It was all twisty little streets among low hills, not the sort of place a killer could get away from quickly unless he knew it as well as his own neighborhood. The dead girl lay on her side under a small tree. Opposite was a vacant lot, but elsewhere modest houses lined the streets. Had it not been a Sunday, the body would have been discovered earlier. Grogan arrived just after noon.

Approaching the body, Grogan thought immediately of his own teenage daughter and tried to banish the thought. He noticed the ligature marks at the neck, wrists, and ankles. When a coroner's assistant turned her over, blood trickled from her rectum, and Grogan had no trouble making deductions from that: it was his belief, based on his investigations of scores of rape-murder cases, that the victims were very often sodomized and often so after the murder itself. Necrophilia, Grogan felt sure, was a far more common human activity than generally believed. Because almost anyone would sooner admit to murder than to enjoying sex with dead bodies, it was a difficult crime to prove. Neither the public nor most people who wrote about crime would want to believe it anyway.

Small bruises showed around her breasts. And then, examining her more closely, Grogan noticed something that made him think at first that he was looking at the body of a drug addict: puncture marks on the inner arms. For a second, he was a little relieved. He would always rather deal with the murder of a drug addict. Addicts died young anyway. But there were only two puncture marks, none of the usual scars and needle tracks of the addict. The rectal bleeding and the absence on the body of any obvious signs of a dissipated, druggy existence suggested to Grogan that she might have been tortured before, during, or after the killing, maybe all three.

He stepped back and looked about. He noticed no footprints or disturbances of any kind on the ground around her, and the body showed no signs of having been dragged. He concluded that she had been placed where she lay, probably by more than one man, removed from a car that had then sped off. But the driver must have known the neighborhood.

While Grogan was writing up his preliminary report and speaking to the coroner's office that afternoon, learning that no drugs had been found in the body, a small boy was making another discovery. At about four o'clock on the other, western side of the Elysian Valley, Armando Guerrero, nine years old, was playing in a trash heap on a shady slope, about fifty feet below the obscure little street called Landa. Armando liked playing there because it was a secret place. Hardly anyone ever drove on Landa Street, although it emptied onto Stadium Way, the route to the eastern side of Dodger Stadium; Landa was dark and damp and a little scary, a great place for a kid to sift through trash for treasures. That afternoon, as the November light began to fail, Armando thought he spotted something unusual in the trash pile along with the old mattresses and bottles and cans.

Armando saw two department-store mannequins lying head to foot together amid the junk. Great things to take home! He approached one, reached down to tug at its foot—but then he noticed a dark circle around the ankle, with ants feeding in it.

Armando was frightened. He uttered a prayer to the Blessed Virgin and ran home to tell his brother. When the brother, Alonso, seventeen, touched the mannequins, he telephoned the police, saying that the mannequins were very stiff but that he was afraid they were real. He thought he had seen blood on them.

At first the policeman also thought they were mannequins, but when he touched them he recognized rigor mortis. These were two little girls, so fragile, helpless, dead, rot working away at their faces. Through the greenish slime on one mouth he saw blood-clotted braces on the teeth. He summoned LAPD Homicide.

It was Bob Grogan's partner, Dudley Varney, who examined the bodies. Sergeant Varney estimated at once that the girls had been dead for a week. He noticed the ligature marks, the absence of any clothes or jewelry, the smears of dried blood, the armies of ants. Los Angeles was having a November heat wave, and the stench in Angelo's "cow patch" was higher than usual. Sergeant Varney retreated around a hump on the slope and threw up.

Looking up toward Landa Street, Varney speculated that the girls' bodies had been tossed from there and had rolled down onto the trash heap. One man could have done the job, the girls were so small, but that seemed unlikely.

Varney asked the boys whether they recognized the girls. They said no, but the older brother said that he had heard that two girls were missing from St. Ignatius School. A poster had been distributed offering a reward for information about them. Varney checked and learned that a priest from St. Ignatius had distributed the poster, offering an unspecified reward for information about them, showing their school pictures and giving descriptions of them. They were Dolores Cepeda, twelve, weighing ninety-six pounds, and Sonja Johnson, fourteen, four feet eleven inches tall, weighing eighty pounds and wearing braces on her teeth. Varney glumly contemplated the contrast between their school pictures, which showed happy smiling faces on the brink of life, and the sight of their stiff, bruised bodies and ravaged faces in the trash heap, images that in spite of his experience of homicides haunted his sleep for months.

His investigation failed to discover a murder scene. The girls had boarded a bus at the Eagle Rock Plaza. They had disembarked, Varney learned, at a stop on York, not far from their homes. A boy who had been a passenger on the bus said that he had watched the girls through the right-side rearview mirror as the bus boarded new passengers, and he had seen them go up to a car and speak to someone on the passenger side of a car. Under hypnosis the boy recalled the car was a large sedan, either light on top and dark on the bottom or the reverse.

Varney also learned that the girls' parents had searched frantically for them in the neighborhood that night and the following day and that the priest from St. Ignatius had turned the school into a search headquarters all that week.

Varney and Grogan compared notes on the three bodies and were in no doubt that the same killer or killers had been involved, probably two men. Certainly if Dolores and Sonja had approached a car on the passenger side, there had been a passenger. One of the girls was said to have been frightened of strangers but very trustful and admiring of policemen—that might be significant.

The girl Grogan had examined was identified the following afternoon. She was Kristina Weckler, twenty, an honors student at the Pasadena Art Center of Design, a highly respected school. A friend and fellow student of hers, alarmed at Kristina's absence from classes on Monday, had gone to her apartment. The two girls had promised each other always to check up on each other, for safety's sake, and Kristina's friend persuaded the manager of Kristina's apartment building, at 809 East Garfield Avenue in Glendale, to let her into the apartment. Kristina had lived there for over a year. Her parents, who lived in Sausalito, had helped her choose it, and it had seemed to them just right for her, an older, U-shaped, tree-shaded building in a peaceful neighborhood. Kristina's friend had found the apartment empty and Kristina's old Volkswagen parked in its usual place. She then called the police.

When Bob Grogan visited the apartment on Garfield that evening, he questioned the manager and all the other residents. No one mentioned, of course, that Kenneth Bianchi had lived in the same building until that past August, in an apartment not fifteen feet from

Kristina's. All Grogan learned was that Kristina was a quiet, studious girl who was often alone at night, working on her drawings, which had put her at the top of her class at the Pasadena Art Center. Her friend told Grogan that Kristina had been disappointed not to have been invited to a party on Saturday, the night of her disappearance. It was to be a pot party and Kristina did not approve of marijuana smoking, her friends knew, so she was left out.

Inside Kristina's apartment, Bob Grogan's rage began to grow. It did not take much to ignite Grogan's furious indignation, and the sight of Kristina's apartment made him want to explode. He knew that he would not be able to relieve these feelings until he had found Kristina's killer and had gotten him sentenced to death, if that was still possible in California. Here was Kristina's drafting board, paints, inks, brushes, and pens arrayed beside it, a light adjusted above it for long hours of work. There, in the bathroom, were her nightclothes neatly laid out, bath oils and lotions lined up on shelves. The bed was turned down tidily, ready to receive a young woman who obviously cared about keeping her life in harmonious order. On a table he found a paperback book on astrology, predictions for lives in the coming year, 1978, which Kristina would not see. She had been a girl who thought about the future. And next to this Grogan found Kristina's notebook, a kind of diary, filled with colorful little drawings and paragraphs about herself and the things she cared about, books, friends, favorite artists, family. How glad she was to know that her parents loved her.

Grogan, alone, waiting for the fingerprint men and police photographers to arrive, sat down at Kristina's drafting board and read the notebook through. He could feel the girl's presence and hear her voice. He thought of her alive in this room, planning her days, her future; and he thought of his own daughter, another idealistic, loving, and admirable young woman. With a twinge of fear and conscience, Grogan thought of his daughter walking and waiting alone for buses at night in Los Angeles, these killers and others running loose; he resolved to buy her a car the next day.

The notebook made Grogan swallow hard. When he had finished reading it, he put it in his pocket. He was required, of course, to turn in all evidence; he knew that he could get himself into deep trouble for doing what he was about to do. Suppressing evidence. But Grogan cared more for justice than for legal niceties. The notebook was too private and painful, and it would have no bearing on a conviction, except perhaps to sway a jury's emotions. It said nothing of boyfriends, lovers, potential killers. It was testimony simply to Kristina's love of her work and her family. Her parents should have it. Grogan felt he already knew them, and he already trusted and admired them. The notebook might help them to survive Kristina's death. Nothing would help them get over it.

Bob Grogan, huge and brash, was a man of fierce sentiments and loyalties, and more than most detectives he tended to allow himself to get personally involved in his cases. All homicide detectives did this to an extent, if they were any good; you could not be wholly detached and succeed in this work. But Grogan let himself go more than others, for fear of cracking up, dared. When he told Frank Salerno that a homicide cop had to have some means of getting away from his work, of cleansing his mind of blood and of what the frequency of murder said about human nature, he meant it. Only two kinds of people, Grogan was fond of saying, understood human nature: homicide detectives and whores.

To escape, Grogan now had his boat, which he took out from Long Beach every weekend he could, and he had his large collection of jazz records and his electric organ. Late at night, his head filled with corpses and the indifference of killers, he would pour himself a shot of Jameson's, put a Duke Ellington record on the machine, and sit down at his organ to play along with the music. The driving rhythms and romantic melodies made sleep possible. He also played golf regularly at the California Country Club, enjoying the green peace of fairways and chit-chat that had no more violence in it than a solid tee shot.

At home with his wife, daughter, and son, it had long been an agreement that he would keep the details of his job to himself. Murder was not discussed. This was his wife's wish, and he was happy to accommodate it, sure that she knew better than he what made for a tranquil domestic scene. Grogan and his wife shared a common background—they had been together since Boston—but in personality they were unalike, she quiet and religious. Around her Grogan not only did not speak of murder but tried, to the extent that he was able, to banish strong words and phrases from his vocabulary. He did not mind splitting his life in two for her sake. On the contrary, he felt it gave him something to believe in. But once he was on the trail of Buono and Bianchi, he began to find the daily switch from war to peace more difficult.

The next day Charles Weckler flew down from San Francisco to identify his daughter's body. Grogan was immediately drawn to this shattered father, identifying with him. He asked Mr. Weckler whether he would like to go someplace for a drink. Mr. Weckler said he would, after he telephoned his wife.

Grogan took him to the Nightwatch, a bar in Pasadena. It was early afternoon, and the place was not yet crowded. The two fathers, one twice the size of the other, sat in a corner booth and ordered doubles. Mr. Weckler told Grogan to call him Charlie.

"Charlie," Grogan said, "we're going to get this bastard, I promise you. I know that doesn't help much for me to say that, but I want you to know that I am going to nail the fucking animal who killed your daughter. I don't suppose you would have seen the *L.A. Times* this morning?" Charlie Weckler said he had not. Grogan told him that the *Times* had carried a story about how the police were teaming up on this case. Grogan himself had been talking to Frank Salerno of Sheriff's Homicide that morning. Kristina had been the victim of a multiple murderer. There were several other cases that were tied in. The *Times* had listed eight, including two little girls who had been found the same day as Kristina. Grogan himself put the count at five, but there was one detective with the LAPD, Bill Williams, who wanted to include a sixth, Yolanda Washington, a black girl who had been found back on October 18. The location checked out; Williams was probably right. And another thing. Grogan was certain, as were Salerno and others, that there were two killers. But Grogan would appreciate it if Charlie wouldn't say anything to the press about that or anything else Grogan told him about the investigation.

"I don't want to talk to the press," Mr. Weckler said. "I don't intend to ever talk to the press. I know about the press. We will never talk to them."

"Very wise idea," Grogan said.

Mr. Weckler was a professional photographer, successful in his work. He had done features for *National Geographic* and other large-circulation publications. He knew all about publicity and knew that it would only add to his family's tragedy. But he was happy to tell Grogan anything. His daughter had been such a quiet, serious girl. He could not imagine what had led her into the killer's path, what had led her outside her apartment, without her car, on a Saturday night. She had not been with any of her friends.

"We'll find out," Grogan said. "The only thing we can think now is that somehow these guys are getting women to trust them. We think they might be posing as cops. But we don't want the media to know that yet. If they tell everybody that, then nobody'll trust a cop. But we may have to tell them."

Grogan ordered more drinks. Then he brought out Kristina's notebook from his suit pocket and handed it to Mr. Weckler. Grogan said he thought that Kristina's family should have the notebook, and he was not going to turn it in as evidence, unless he had to. But one of Kristina's friends might mention it, and Grogan might then be forced to discover it, so he would hang on to it for now, until he was sure it was safe to give it to the Wecklers.

Mr. Weckler thumbed through the notebook, straining to read his daughter's handwriting in the dim light of the bar. He drained his drink. He broke down. Grogan ordered more drinks. Then Mr. Weckler, acting from some deep paternal urge, took out his pen and wrote out, slowly and carefully, at the top of each page of the notebook, "Copyright © 1977, by Kristina Weckler."

"That way," Mr. Weckler choked out, "nobody can steal Kristina's work. At least her work can be safe."

Jesus Christ, Grogan thought, if I could find those murdering bastards right now, I'd kill them with my own bare hands.

"I wish I were a more religious man," Mr. Weckler said.

"Well," Grogan said, "I never had much luck with the church myself." He decided he had to try cheering Charlie up a bit, futile though the effort would be. Maybe he needed to try to cheer himself up. He went on: "I remember when I was in the sixth grade back in Boston, about 1946 it was, I had to serve a high mass for Cardinal Cushing, remember that bastard? *In nomine Domine . . .*' " He imitated Cardinal Cushing's Boston accent, even more nasal and flat than his own. "Anyway, it was this high mass for Rose Kennedy, you know? That's right, the President's mother, for Christ's sake. Of course, the Kennedys were a big deal in Boston even then. Old Joe. Anyway, it's a fucking historical event there, and here I am serving for the cardinal, and I did pretty good, got the Latin right, didn't spill the wine, didn't fall down genuflecting with the big book or anything. So afterwards, what do you know, the old bastard, the cardinal reaches into his scarlet robes and pulls out a twenty-dollar bill and gives it to me. Listen, that was a lot of money in those days. So what I did was, I ran right out and bought myself the best baseball glove I could find, a real thoroughbred mitt. And a ball, too. So I ran right home and showed the ball and glove to my father, I was so proud. So you know what my father did? I'll tell you what. He beat the living shit out of me, that's what he did. He said, 'Don't lie to me, Bobby, I know you stole that ball and glove. You expect me to believe Cardinal Cushing gave you twenty bucks? How stupid do you think I am? That son of a bitch never gave nothing to nobody!' "

Grogan laughed. "So you see, Charlie, I never had much luck myself with the church at all."

Mr. Weckler managed a smile and a small laugh. He reached across the table, took Grogan's hand, squeezed it, and looked into his big red face. Then he handed Grogan back Kristina's notebook.

The next day Jane King's body turned up, looking like a doll lost in April and found again in November. She had been discovered by a highway worker who was clearing brush on the Los Feliz offramp of the Golden State Freeway. Dudley Varney was assigned to be the primary investigator on Jane King. From the size of the maggots which completely covered her face, the coroner determined that she had been dead for about two weeks. Her pubic hair had grown out to about an eighth of an inch.

The LAPD announced that a special task force had been formed, which the media quickly termed the Hillside Strangler Task Force, headed by Lieutenant Ed Henderson of the LAPD but consisting of officers from the Sheriff's Department and the Glendale Police Department as well. On Thanksgiving Day, November 24, the *Times* reported that Jane King's murder might be linked to as many as ten others, saying that the police would not reveal the common method of strangulation; but on the following day the paper suggested that the strongest links seemed to exist among four victims: Yolanda Washington, Judy Miller, Lissa Kastin, and Kristina Weckler. Their age, where they were found, their nudity, and that they had been sexually molested seemed to connect them. Jane King had been older and it was not clear whether she had been raped.

Each day the newspapers and television offered varying reports, adding and subtracting victims from the Hillside list, increasing the public's confusion and alarm but, it must be said, accurately reflecting the confused state of the investigation. Thirty officers were now making up the task force. Grogan, Salerno, Varney, and Williams had most of the responsibility and would have preferred to have had all of it, sensing that the greater the manpower, the greater the chance for foul-ups. But the task force was soon flooded with phone calls and clues, almost all of which turned out to be worthless, and dozens of officers were needed to handle them. Eventually the task force grew to a hundred officers, and they would put together over twelve thousand "clue packages," labeled envelopes containing all the information on a given lead. When the task force added a computer called PATRIC (for Pattern Recognition and Information Correlation), Grogan said, "Holy God, that's all we need. I'll tell you what that goddam computer is. It's nothing but a fifty-thousand-dollar filing cabinet."

The killers took the Thanksgiving holiday off, but early Tuesday morning, November 29, Grogan was called again to examine a body in the hills of Glendale, this time in the Mount Washington area. Again the location, a steep, twisting little street called Cliff Drive, was difficult to find, but the body itself could not have been missed by anyone driving down to work that morning. She was on her back. The upper part of the body was lying in some brush, but the legs stuck out onto the pavement. Grogan noticed first her long red hair and the paleness of her redhead's skin. The five-point ligature marks told him immediately that Kristina Weckler's killers had murdered again. And there was another link to Kristina, along with the nudity and the proximate nature of the location. This girl's hands, which appeared to have been wrapped in some sort of tape, adhesive still sticking to her skin, bore strange lesions on their palms, dark bluish-green double lines. Grogan looked closely at her palms and could not figure out the lesions. They looked somewhat like burns, but it was impossible to tell how they had been made. What did seem likely was that the lines, which were about an inch and a half long, and the tape tracings on her hands indicated that the girl had been tortured, in some way as yet mysterious. The lines, like the puncture marks on Kristina Weckler's inner arms, suggested that the killers were refining and elaborating their methods. Grogan figured that they were getting bored with simple rape and strangulation. He was certain that when the killers were ready to act again, they would entertain themselves with a new twist of some kind, a torture, a method of abduction or execution, something.

Grogan noticed nothing else on the body except a shiny, sticky substance, through which a column of ants marched, on one of her breasts. It could be saliva or possibly semen, what the police called "pecker tracks." But tests on semen found on or in the other bodies had revealed nothing except the blood type of the victims. Ordinarily an antigen was secreted along with semen, as with saliva and other bodily fluids; the substance could be analyzed to determine the blood type of a rapist. But twenty percent of males were nonsecretors of the antigen, so that sort of identification, always chancy because of the quick deterioration of bodily secretions when exposed to air, was often useless. The laboratory would also try to analyze the marks on the palms and the adhesive on the hands. There was nothing else to go on.

Later that day, the girl's parents identified her. She was Lauren Rae Wagner, eighteen, a student at a business college in the San Fernando Valley, where she had lived in a house on Lemona Street, near Sepulveda Boulevard, with her parents, two sisters, and a brother. Grogan spared Joe and Judy Wagner the direct sight of their daughter's body, permitting them to view it on closed-circuit television at the morgue. That night Grogan went to visit the Wagners at their house.

Grogan sensed immediately that this family would never recover from the murder. Their closeness would help them endure it, perhaps, but that very closeness made the loss all the more intolerable. When he arrived, he found their house lit up outside by swarming television crews, Joe Wagner on the front steps trying to answer reporters' questions.

"Mr. Wagner, why do you think your daughter was abducted?" a reporter asked.

"I don't know," he replied, his voice quavering. "I guess because she was a girl."

Grogan urged Mr. Wagner inside, telling him he did not have to talk to these people. He told the reporters to go home. Couldn't they leave the family in peace? But they hovered around for hours.

Joe Wagner did most of the talking for the family. He said that the night before, Lauren had said she would be home by nine o'clock. She was not the sort of girl you had to set a curfew for; she was always home when she said she would be, and never after midnight. The family had gone to bed, and he had not noticed her missing until the morning. Then he had looked out the window and seen her car parked across the street, and when he looked in the car, he had found the door on the driver's side ajar and the interior light burning. He immediately started questioning neighbors, and Beulah Stofer, who lived across the street in the house in front of which Lauren's car was parked, told him that last night, at about nine o'clock, she had seen Lauren's car pull over, followed by another car, driven by two men. The other car had drawn up beside her. The men had gotten out and there had been some sort of an argument. Then, Beulah Stofer had said, Lauren had gotten into the other car and driven off with the men.

"Why didn't this woman contact you or the police?" Grogan asked.

"She said she wasn't sure it was Lauren. I don't know."

Grogan questioned the Wagners about their daughter. She had been a wonderful girl, they said. She was so loving and giving. She had cooked the family Thanksgiving dinner last week. She made clothes for her sisters. She was already working on Christmas presents, dresses for her sisters and a pantsuit for her mother. She was so helpful, but she liked to be independent. She had worked at a Taco Bell at night, but a robbery there made her quit. She worked two nights a week at a dime store. She always wanted to help out if she could.

"I used to take her car out and fill it up with gas," Joe Wagner said. "She tried not to take money from me."

"I told her to be careful about this Strangler business," Mrs. Wagner said. "The night before she left us. . . . In the kitchen, she was all dressed up. And I looked at her, and she looked so bright and so trusting and vulnerable. And I put my hand on her face and I touched her."

"I'm sure Lauren was a great person," Grogan said. "From everything you say, Lauren was wonderful."

"That's good of you, sergeant," Mrs. Wagner said, "calling her Lauren like that."

"What else would I call her?"

"Oh, everybody else seems to call her 'the victim.' You calling her Lauren, that shows you know she's still alive for us. Always will be. Our family has to have our Lauren."

Grogan told the Wagners that he would be in constant touch with them and reminded them that they did not have to talk to reporters. If the media refused to let up on them, they should call him and he would see what he could do.

As Grogan walked across the street to talk to Beulah Stofer, he was prepared to despise her as yet another example of the sort of person who, witnessing a crime, fails to report it for fear of getting involved. To Grogan such behavior was itself criminal, but he did not expect most people to act otherwise. He approached Mrs. Stofer's house. A Doberman in the front yard barked at him. Mrs. Stofer opened the door and told the dog to be quiet when Grogan identified himself.

One close look at Beulah Stofer softened Grogan's judgment of her. A sickly-looking woman in her late fifties, she was breathing heavily and appeared near collapse, her eyes watering and rolling nervously behind glasses. Her hands trembled. She managed to gasp that she was having an asthma attack. Her husband was in the back, not feeling well. Could Sergeant Grogan have some coffee and cookies while she recovered herself? She was sorry to receive him like this.

Grogan sat down and ate a cookie. "Gee," he said when she returned, "these are great cookies. You make them yourself?"

"Yes. Have some more."

Grogan asked several irrelevant questions to try to calm her down. He told her to call him Bob. She said to call her Beulah.

"I had a terrifying phone call just now," she said. "I thought I should tell the police."

"Yeah? A phone call?"

Mrs. Stofer said that a voice on the phone, a very

rough, male voice, with some kind of accent, maybe New York, had said to her, "You the lady with the dog?" When she had said yes, that she did have a dog, the voice had told her that she had better keep her mouth shut about what she had seen last night. If she talked to anyone about it, she was as good as dead.

Grogan told her not to worry. He would see that she was protected. What was it that she had seen last night? She repeated what she had told Joe Wagner.

"Did you know it was Lauren being abducted?"

"I didn't know it was an abduction. How could I have known that? I thought it might have been a quarrel, you know, with a boyfriend."

"With two boyfriends?"

"Sergeant Grogan, I am from the South. I believe in—" She started coughing, straining for breath again.

"It's okay, Beulah. Just tell me, what about the dog? What does the dog have to do with it? You tell me this voice asked if you were the lady with the dog."

Mrs. Stofer said that her Doberman, Caesar, had started barking. Caesar was her protection when her husband was out, but her husband had been home. He was in the back, taking a bath. He had not seen anything. So when Caesar had started barking, she had gone to the window to look out. As Grogan probed, Mrs. Stofer got more specific. The other car had been a big, dark car, with a white top. The two men had argued with Lauren, and one of them had dragged her from her car into theirs, and she had heard Lauren cry out, "You won't get away with this!"

"But you didn't call the police or tell the Wagners?" Grogan asked quietly, not wanting to upset Mrs. Stofer by accusing her. She was his best, his only, witness so far.

She struggled for breath. She wept. Then, Grogan would later testify, she told him that she had been raped when she was young. What she had seen last night had brought back all the terror of that. She had been paralyzed with fear. She had sat up all night. She had not even been able to tell her husband.

Grogan comforted her. He asked her whether she thought she would be able to identify the men.

"One of them had bushy hair," she said. "One of them was taller and younger than the one with bushy hair. He had acne scars on his neck."

"But do you think you could identify them if you saw them again?"

"Yes," Mrs. Stofer said. "Definitely."

Grogan ate more cookies. He drank some coffee. Mr. Stofer appeared briefly and confirmed that he had been taking a bath and had neither seen nor heard anything. Grogan stayed for nearly two hours chatting with Mrs. Stofer. He commented on what a nice house Beulah had, how, being from the South, she must find it difficult living in Los Angeles, how his wife made cookies, too, but to tell the truth, Beulah's were superior cookies. And he got her to go over her story several more times. She stuck to it, adding that the shorter man was "Latin-looking," and repeated the threatening telephone conversation exactly as before. He believed her, or almost.

Outside, Grogan paused to look around the front of the Stofer house. Like all the houses on the street, it was set back from the curb by a strip of grass, a sidewalk, and a front lawn, in this case a fenced yard for Caesar. The window through which she said she had seen Lauren Wagner's abduction was a good thirty feet or more from the street, which was not brightly lit. Mrs. Stofer obviously had poor eyesight. Yet she said that she could be certain of identifying these men, even though she also said that she had not been sure she recognized Lauren Wagner, her neighbor. And how, inside her house, with her dog barking outside, could she have heard Lauren tell the men, "You won't get away with this"?

Gauging again the distance from the window to the street, Grogan concluded that Mrs. Stofer, out of shame and fear, was not telling everything. What actually had happened, he felt certain, was that Caesar had barked and Beulah had gone outside to see what was the matter. She had witnessed the struggle and had probably snuck up to her fence, behind some shrubbery, to get a closer look. She had been within ten feet of what was happening, had recognized Lauren, gotten a very good look at the men, and heard

Lauren's futile warning to them. Then, terrified and, as she had said, paralyzed, she had retreated into her house and sat there all night.

Probably Lauren's killers had seen Beulah. Why else would they have called to threaten her? This was further evidence, Grogan concluded, that Beulah had been outside. The killers had traced her telephone number somehow and, when she had answered, had asked whether she was the woman with the dog. Grogan hoped that they would be stupid enough to come back to try to harm her, but he doubted it. He would have her house watched for the time being. He would not tell Beulah what he had figured out. He did not want to frighten her more; she looked near enough to collapse already. He needed her. He would talk to her again. He hoped that she would agree to be hypnotized.

Grogan did not sleep that night. He did not even try to play his jazz records, and he sensed that he would not be playing golf or going fishing for some time to come. He sat up with images of the bodies and of Charlie Weckler and of the Wagners, huddled bewildered in their house, before him. Lauren's and Kristina's faces merged in his mind with his daughter's face. He imagined Lauren at home on Thanksgiving, cooking. The first thing he had noticed, he admitted to himself, when he had seen her body, was how beautiful she was, the pale, long legs, the waist dramatically small, the brilliant hair. She had gotten the red hair from her father. Grogan had not told the family about the strange marks on her palms or about the evidence of sodomy the coroner had quickly noted. Nor had he told the family that he had already found out what Lauren had been up to from late that afternoon until she had driven home, or almost home, at nine. A word from her sister had led Grogan to Lauren's boyfriend, an older man married but going through divorce, he said. Lauren had spent those hours in bed with the boyfriend. There was no need to tell the family that.

She had driven home, probably, to judge from the conservative atmosphere at the Wagners' house, feeling good but a little guilty about what she had been up to, had gotten within yards of her front door, and had been carried off, raped, strangled to death, and dumped way off in another part of the city. Her mother had warned her about the Strangler. Lauren had sensed who they were the minute they approached her. That was why she had said, "You won't get away with this." What a ride she must have had to wherever they had taken her. She would have known her fate all that time. Had anyone ever felt greater terror?

That Lauren had been abducted from the Valley, so far away from any of the other girls, worried Grogan more than anything else. At least up till now the killers had confined themselves to Hollywood and the Glendale area; now they might find a victim anywhere. Probably they knew the heat was on in Hollywood. The whores would be wary of them, too. They might try anywhere next. That would heighten the city's panic, and soon enough the panic would turn to anger at the police, if something didn't break quickly. It gave Grogan some solace to think that he had found time in the frenzy of the past week to buy his daughter a car. But Lauren had had a car. He told his daughter to keep the doors locked, to park in well-lighted places, and to drive off if strange men approached her. At least she was not living alone, like Kristina Weckler. He could not imagine what had caused Kristina to leave her apartment that night. She had been worried by an obscene phone call she had received earlier in the week, Grogan had learned from Kristina's friend.

A dark, big car, white on top, Beulah had said. That might tie in with their posing as policemen. The press should know that now; women should be warned. At least Grogan knew that there were two of them. Latin, Beulah said. Mexican? A pair of Juan Coronas? Mexican Mansons? Grogan tried to picture them and could not. A psychiatrist would say that they hated women. So what else was new? Nobody would ever explain acts such as this. They were out for kicks. They had gotten away with it once, twice, again. By now they felt invulnerable. Grogan thought on, his emotions fluctuating wildly between rage and pity for Lauren and Kristina and their families.

By dawn he was ready to get back into the hunt. He left his house before his wife and children were up, taking the morning paper with him. The front page carried a map of where bodies had been found, beginning with Yolanda Washington, and Grogan noticed that the sites formed almost a circle. What he could not notice was that at the center of that circle was 703 East Colorado Street.

But when, later that morning at his desk in the Glass House, as Parker Center, the LAPD headquarters on Los Angeles Street, was called, Grogan saw the headline on the front page of the late final edition—

FATHER OF SLAIN GIRL ADMITS
KIDNAP STORY HOAX

—he wanted to lob a grenade into the men's room of the *Times*. The headline was to Grogan infuriatingly misleading and insulting to Joe Wagner, who of all men on the face of the earth deserved better at this moment. When he had noticed Lauren missing and had talked to Beulah Stofer Tuesday morning, he had tried to file a missing-person report with the police; but when the police informed him that a twenty-four-hour waiting period was standard before they acted in such cases, he had told them that he was sure his daughter had been abducted by two men from in front of his house the previous evening. This was hardly a hoax. By that time Lauren's body had been discovered.

Before Grogan was able to tell a friend of his on the *Times* what he could do with that headline, Joe Wagner telephoned. Late last night, Mr. Wagner said, a reporter from the *Times* had telephoned to ask about rumors that there had been witnesses to the abduction. The police would not reveal the names of the witnesses. Would Mr. Wagner, the reporter had wanted to know, reveal the names to help with the story?

"That prick!" Grogan screamed. "Jesus Christ, Joe," Grogan said. "You didn't tell him, did you? If they start bugging Beulah Stofer, she'll drop dead. If the killers don't get her first."

Mr. Wagner had declined to talk to the reporter.

"What's the asshole's name?"

Mr. Wagner gave it.

Grogan dialed the *Times:*

"Hey, how's it going? Listen, you working on the Lauren Wagner story? Right. I think I got something for you. Can't give it to you over the phone. It's real hot. Come on over here to Robbery-Homicide, room 321. And bring your editor. On the double. I'll be here. Sergeant Grogan."

When the reporter arrived with his editor, Grogan, all cordiality, ushered them into an interviewing room and closed the door. Then he began:

"You want some coffee? No? Good. Because let me tell you something. You're not getting anything but shit from me." He began shouting. "You are the most unethical son of a bitch I ever saw! What the fuck do you mean asking Joe Wagner about witnesses, you rotten prick? You want to fuck up the investigation? You want to get them killed? Don't you think the Wagners have suffered enough?" And so on. When the reporter said that he was only doing his job, getting a story, Grogan threw a chair against the wall and screamed that as far as he was concerned, this reporter would never get anything out of the Los Angeles Police Department except traffic tickets.

Two days later, at Lauren Wagner's funeral, the priest deplored in the course of his eulogy that Lauren had been killed because, in the new culture that had corrupted the city and the country, "everything is justified if it fulfills one's own desire."

TEN

If happiness is doing as one likes, Thanksgiving was a joyful season for Buono and Bianchi. Not only did they accomplish two fresh murders; they at last received the recognition they felt due them, publicity beyond a flak merchant's dreams, the entertainment capital of the world enthralled by their acts. As they watched the news together they took particular pleasure in learning that the media, and presumably the police, were crediting them with two or three murders they had not even committed, including a girl way out in Pomona. "They'll have us in Nevada soon," Angelo said.

Bianchi paid more attention to the publicity than Buono, who had always been indifferent to fame. Kenny subscribed to the *Times* and read all of it every day. A man who understood the value of information, he reveled in the spotlight. It was better than having a hit movie, and as nothing much else was going on in the world except the Egyptian-Israeli peace negotiations, Kenny could rightly feel that he was the center of everyone's attention. At work, he would hear the office girls chattering nervously about the sex-mad murderer who was loose in the city. Coyly, impishly, ever the tease, he would wink and say to them, "You never know. He could be anyone. Why, I could be the Hillside Strangler. . . ." That would get a rise out of the ladies every time.

For nearly two weeks after Lauren Wagner, publicity and the still-warm memories of their most recent killings were enough to buoy the cousins. They had accomplished so much, even the virgin they had decided should follow Jane King. That Sunday at the Eagle Rock Plaza they had noticed Dolores Cepeda and Sonja Johnson boarding a bus and had decided to follow them. A double play! The possibility of capturing both girls multiplied pleasurable anticipations: an orgy, then a twin killing. When the girls got off the bus on York Boulevard, Angelo and Kenny motioned them over to the car, flashing their badges. Kenny told the girls that a burglar was loose in the neighborhood. He was armed and dangerous. The girls had better accept a ride home from the police.

Dolores and Sonja, who had just stolen about a hundred dollar's worth of costume jewelry from a shop at the Plaza, were anxious to cooperate for fear that their crime would be discovered; and at first, when they were told to strip down at Angelo's "satellite police station," they thought that they were being searched.

Angelo and Kenny, after getting their sexual fill of the girls, each of them raping and sodomizing both, murdered Sonja first in the spare bedroom. When they came into the living room to get Dolores, she asked plaintively:

"Where's Sonja?"

"Don't worry," Angelo said. "You'll be seeing her soon."

The jewelry the girls had stolen was a great temptation to Kenny, but Angelo was watching too closely and made sure that it went into the dumpster along with their clothing and the jewelry they had been wearing, ceramic pins of unicorns, cloudbursts, rainbows, a thin gold-plated necklace with charms—a floating heart, a teddy bear.

Kenny happened to be driving Kelli's Mazda station wagon this time, and it proved convenient transport. With the two bodies laid out in the back under a blanket, Angelo directed Kenny to the cow patch. It gave Angelo particular pleasure to dump the bodies there, an arbor alive for him with bittersweet romantic memories, trysts, courtships, and later family picnics.

Then came Kristina Weckler. They had driven over to Hollywood and observed the heavy concentration of police, and they knew that there were others undercover. They required something nearer to hand. Kenny, remembering Kristina as a girl who had spurned him at 809 East Garfield, checked to see whether she still lived there by making an anonymous phone call to her, telling her he would like to eat her underwear, while Angelo stood by the phone, grinning. A few days later, on that Saturday night, with Angelo waiting in the Cadillac, Kenny knocked on Kristina's door and, showing her his badge, said:

"Hi. Remember me? It's Kenny Bianchi. I used to live next door. How's it going? Listen. I'm a member of the Police Reserve now. See"—he chuckled, shaking his head self-deprecatingly, emanating a gee-whiz sincerity—"they even give you a badge. I was just patrolling the neighborhood and I noticed your car, the VW, right? Well, wouldn't you know it, looks like somebody's crashed into it, right there in the parking lot. If you'll come out and help me write up a report, it might help you collect on your insurance."

That was all it took. But having done everything sexually they could think of to Kristina, finding themselves at the moment for murder, they agreed that they ought to try something different, for the sake of experiment and to confuse the cops. Angelo said he had just the thing. He fetched from his cigar box a hypodermic syringe that he had stolen from the hospital during a visit to his mother, filled it with Windex, and injected the fluid into both of Kristina's arms and into her neck.

The Windex produced convulsions, but Kristina failed to die. So Angelo came up with another idea.

He had recently bought a flexible gas pipe for a stove from Antoinette Lombardo at her parents' hardware store. The stove itself he had not yet purchased, so there was no difficulty in dragging the bound and gagged Kristina up to the gas outlet in the kitchen, placing the pipe against her neck, slipping a vegetable bag over her head, and sealing the bag with cord. While Angelo turned the gas on and off, off and on, Kenny pulled on the cord. They managed to kill Kristina by two methods at once.

With the holiday approaching, Angelo and Kenny paused for the traditional celebration. Kenny, however, suffered a blow to his pride that week. He and Kelli had not been getting on at all well as her pregnancy advanced. Sex between them had come to a standstill, and to Kenny, Kelli seemed intolerably cranky, even allowing for the discomforts of her condition. On the night before Thanksgiving Day, they got into a shouting match, and Kenny, losing his cool, took a swing at Kelli and knocked her to the floor. He was instantly awash with tears and apologies, but Kelli said that he had gone too far this time. Violence was one thing she would not tolerate. Something was definitely wrong between them. He was always out at night. He cared more for playing pool or whatever he did with Angelo than for her. What kind of a father would he be for her child? She packed her bags, her eye blackening, and went to stay with her brother.

So, despite the killings and the notoriety they brought, the holiday did have its melancholy side for the abandoned Kenny, but at least he had the comfort of sympathetic relatives to see him through. He telephoned his mother in Rochester. She had married again, and Kenny got a good pep talk from her and his stepfather. He celebrated Thanksgiving itself at Angelo's mother's place. Jenny, temporarily released from the hospital, cooked the turkey. She was now married to George White, the Indian. Nobody said grace, but all in all the dinner went well, an Italo–Native American ritual that provided the cousins a breather between murders. With all the news in the paper and on television about the Hillside Strangler, there was plenty of material for conversation. Angelo professed concern for his daughter Grace. He did not like the creep she was going with, and he hoped she had the sense not to hitchhike or walk the streets alone at night. He had warned her to watch out for this Strangler guy. Angelo said he figured the killer was probably some weirdo escaped from an institution.

By Monday, the joys and depressions of the holiday worn off, Angelo and Kenny were ready to roll again. They agreed that branching into new territory would be the smart thing to do, a way of avoiding and confounding the police. Angelo suggested Malibu, then decided that would be too long a drive. He said he knew the Valley well, and they settled on it, only a reconnaissance trip perhaps, but they would see what turned up. There were plenty of girls in the Valley, that was for sure.

They were cruising Sepulveda when Angelo spotted Lauren Wagner getting out of her Mustang at a doughnut shop. Angelo liked red hair. They waited for her to drive off again and then followed her. They had their badges and the handcuffs, and this time Angelo had stuffed a .45 automatic into his belt. Kenny was driving the Cadillac.

When Lauren turned onto her own street, Lemona, things happened just as Beulah Stofer described them to Bob Grogan. Bianchi brought the Cadillac alongside Lauren's Mustang; Angelo held his badge up to the window and pointed forcefully for her to pull over. Kenny got out and told Lauren they were going to have to take her in. When Lauren said that they would have to talk to her father, who was in the house just over there, Kenny dragged her out of her car and into his, and she shouted that they would not get away with this. By then Caesar was barking, and as they drove off, Angelo spotted what he thought was a woman crouching near the dog.

It was a thirty-five-minute drive back to Colorado Street. Lauren had plenty of time to meditate on her situation, and somehow in her terror she decided that her only hope lay in cooperation with these men, who she had no doubt were the Hillside Stranglers. Angelo won the coin flip, and in the spare bedroom with him, Lauren told him that he had nothing to worry about.

She liked sex, she said. She had spent hours in bed with her boyfriend that evening and was ready for more. When Angelo passed her over to Kenny, Angelo said that this was the best one so far. She knew what she was doing; she enjoyed it; Kenny would have a great time.

Then, as with Kristina Weckler, Angelo suggested that they try something new. He brought in an electrical cord from his shop, pared away the insulation on one end, separated the wires, taped them to Lauren's hands, and plugged in the cord. She trembled and moaned behind her gag, but the shock did not kill her. Angelo rewrapped her hands and tried again, repeatedly putting the plug in the socket and pulling it out, but again she refused to die. "We might as well go back to the old method," Angelo said.

In the next two days enough information reached the media to put a little scare into Buono and Bianchi. It had been reckless, they admitted to each other, to take the girl from almost directly in front of her parents' house. Their car, the *Times* reported, was said to have been a black-and-white sedan, leading police to suspect that the Strangler was posing as a policeman. Remembering the barking dog and the crouching woman, Angelo drove over to the Valley in one of his customer's cars and sped past Beulah's house, noting the address. Then through an old girlfriend who worked for the phone company he traced Beulah's number and made the threatening call to her. "That should shut her up," he told Kenny, who recalled that a car had come up behind them just as they had been pulling away. But they were not much concerned. The more the news reports increased, the more pleased with themselves they became; but they agreed that next time they would try an entirely new approach. The abduction should be made from a completely safe place.

Kenny spent a lot of time during the next two weeks trying to coax Kelli into coming back to live with him at 1950 Tamarind. He missed her, and he could not afford to rent there all by himself. On several nights he slept over at her brother's place, but on the couch, not with her, and she remained adamant, saying that at least a trial separation was in order. She needed peace and quiet during the last couple of months of her pregnancy. Meanwhile Jenny Buono returned to the hospital; Angelo visited her there nearly every other night, and he was also occupied with getting his Christmas-tree lot open for the season. But by Tuesday, December 13, he and Kenny had a new scam ready.

Kenny had noticed an apartment vacant on the ground floor at 1950 Tamarind, number 114. He had gotten the manager to show him the place, saying that he was thinking of moving down from his third-floor spot. On one of his inspections of 114, he was careful to leave the sliding glass door unlocked, and he brought Angelo over to case the location. The idea was to get a call girl to come to the vacant apartment. An ad in the *Hollywood Press* of December 9 ("A Sexual Freedom Publication") had given Kenny his inspiration:

Sexy Young Nude Model!
CLIMAX

We offer, for your discreet pleasure, young, lovely, sexy girls, who have your desires in mind. One will come to your home, office or motel, to fulfill your most erotic fantasy and wildest expectations. She is very anxious to please you. Describe your dream girl, and she'll be on her way to you immediately.

(213) 467-2932
7 Days-24 Hours
LA & Orange City

The ad carried a photograph of a baby-faced, pouting blonde. Kenny suggested that they call the Climax outcall service from a pay phone, ordering a girl to apartment 114 at 1950 Tamarind. Then they would tell her she was under arrest and take her back over to Angelo's. The police would trace the call to 1950 Tamarind; that would pull the whole investigation back to Hollywood and the prostitution scene there and help mess them up even more. Angelo added that since apparently the Cadillac had been spotted last time, they would use a different car. He had a white Mustang that a woman had left with him to sell. It would do just fine.

That evening Kenny made the phone call to the Climax service from a phone booth in the lobby of the Hollywood public library on Ivar Street, across from the Ivar Theater, which had once been legitimate but now offered live sex shows. Bianchi gave the name Mike Ryan—he remembered the name, he thought, as that of a police officer he had met during his attempts to join the force—and the Tamarind address, asking for a blonde with black underwear, agreeing to pay a hundred and fifty dollars in cash. The whore-dispatcher at Climax asked for his phone number: she would contact the girl and then the girl would call back to verify the time of her arrival. Bianchi looked at the number on the pay phone and read it off: 462-9794.

"Is that a pay phone?"

"No," Bianchi said. "This is my home number."

"Numbers with nines in them are usually pay phones."

"Gee," Kenny said, "I'm not that hard up."

In a few minutes a girl calling herself Donna telephoned, saying that she would arrive within half an hour.

While Kenny was telephoning, Angelo was lurking in the stacks, menacing a woman he had spotted in there, just for the fun of it. He peered at her around corners and through the shelves of books. He was excited, thinking about the new scam that would go down later. Just when the woman would think he had disappeared, he would maneuver up behind her in her blind spot; then she would notice him, give a start, and he would glare at her like a predator stalking its prey in a forest. The woman cut short her visit to the library, but Angelo saw her again in the parking lot and pointed her out to Kenny, telling him gleefully about the game inside. Bianchi, wanting in on the thrills, walked over to her car and stared at her through her window. As she drove off, Kenny and Angelo climbed into the Mustang and laughed about the woman. It would probably be a while before she felt like doing more research at that library.

At 1950 Tamarind, Angelo, as they had discussed beforehand, parked the Mustang in the basement garage and went out front to await the girl's arrival. Kenny slipped in through the sliding glass door of apartment 114 and lit a candle he had left there. The apartment was furnished, but the electricity had been shut off. He waited there in the candlelight, rehearsing his part, until he heard a knock at the door.

She was a blonde but rather larger than Kenny had expected, about five foot eight and stocky. She gave her name as Donna. He ushered her into the apartment, apologizing for the lack of lights, saying he had forgotten to pay his bill. Within seconds Angelo appeared; they showed their badges and told Donna that she would have to come with them.

"This is a bust," Angelo said, taking her hands and quickly slipping on the cuffs, grabbing her purse, and then shoving the purse into her cuffed hands behind her. They started to lead her out the door.

But in the hallway, Donna suddenly tried to wrench free and screamed, "Help-help-help!" Angelo quickly took hold of her, one long arm around her waist and the other up between her legs, and hurled her back into the apartment. Her purse flew down the hallway; her body crashed against the apartment wall, and her head hit the floor as she fell. Angelo crawled frantically back into the hall and gathered up her purse and its scattered contents, while Kenny held her down inside, covering her mouth with his hand and telling her that if she uttered one more sound, she would be dead. Just as Angelo got the door shut again, they heard noises in the hallway, doors opening, voices. He joined Kenny on the floor with Donna. He took out his keys and pushed one into her back. "Feel this? It's a knife. One sound and you've had it." Donna, her head bleeding, said no more.

They waited, panting, not moving, until they heard the voices cease and the doors shut again. Again threatening Donna with death, they led her out the sliding glass door and down to the basement parking garage, and they were off to Glendale.

"I'm sorry I screamed," Donna said in the car. "I was just scared. I'll do anything you want. Please don't hurt me. I have a little boy. He's at home waiting for me."

"Just shut up," Angelo said, glaring at her through the rearview mirror as he drove.

Beside her in the cramped backseat, Kenny advised, "It's probably best that you just sit there and don't say anything."

Angelo won the coin toss again. "Lousy fuck. Just lousy," he said when he was done. After Kenny had finished, Donna asked if she could go to the bathroom. Angelo, figuring it was the simplest way to guard against soiling his carpet, led her into the bathroom, unhandcuffing her so that she could use the toilet paper. Meanwhile Kenny was in the living room, rummaging through her belongings. He snuck her gold ram's-horn necklace into his pocket, figuring he would present it to Kelli, telling her it was an Italian good-luck charm. That might win her back.

No experiments this time. They dumped her on a steeply inclined vacant lot along a little-traveled extension of Alvarado Street, not far from Landa, on a hill within sight of City Hall.

It had been a close call, and they knew it. They took pleasure from the front-page photograph of Kimberly Diane Martin, Donna's real name, lying spread-eagled on her back halfway down the slope in the morning light. It was said that the body seemed to be pointed right at City Hall. Was the Strangler getting bolder? Was he mocking the authorities, the city itself? All this pleased them, but they knew that her screams at Tamarind could have been fatal for them. Angelo blamed Kenny for a scheme that had almost betrayed them, and he said that this would be the last scam, at least for the time being.

When the police came to interview everyone at 1950 Tamarind—it had been easy for them to get the address from Climax, and, as the paper reported, they were also trying to talk to everyone who had been at the Hollywood library that night, where Climax's records told them that the phone call summoning Kimberly Martin had been made—Bianchi had to agree with Angelo that at least a break in the killings would be a good idea. Kenny told the police officer who talked to him at his third-floor apartment that yes, he had heard something going on the previous evening. He had heard screams. But it was nothing unusual. Wife-beating was not all that uncommon, sad to say. When the screams had stopped, he had gone to sleep. Of course he would contact the police if he learned anything more or heard any rumors. His story jibed with that of many of the other residents, although he was the only person on the third floor who reported hearing screams.

A week later Kenny moved out of his apartment. He had been fired from his job at Stewart West Coast Title for missing work too often; his employer had finally checked out Kenny's chemotherapy excuses, found Kenny a healthy liar, and dismissed him. It was a tough Christmas for Kenny. It would have been worse for him but that Kelli took pity and invited him to accompany her up to her hometown, Bellingham, Washington, to visit her parents. The excursion raised his spirits a little, made him feel somewhat wanted, but when they returned to Los Angeles, Kelli still refused to live with him. He hoped his luck would change soon. If it did not, he might even lose his Cadillac. He got to feeling pretty sorry for himself.

He moved in with Kelli's brother's two close male friends, on Corona Street in the Glendale hills. He did not, he told Angelo, like the idea of living with men he was sure were homosexuals, but with no money and no job, what other choice did he have? Angelo just laughed at him and ignored the hint—that he should take his cousin in again. If he did, he might never get rid of him. Kenny had begun to get on Angelo's nerves more than usual. If the near-disaster of the Kimberly Martin scheme was any indication, Kenny was not as clever as all his faked degrees and fast talk might indicate. They had almost been caught, and then the police had interviewed Kenny.

To tell the truth, Angelo thought, the guy was a little nuts. He had no home; he couldn't hold a job; he let the broads run him around; he sometimes got a wild look in his eyes; he was beginning to wear thin. Lately he had begun pursuing his two-bit movie-talent-scout scam again, telling Marlene Katz, the daughter of the deli owner across the street, and a friend of hers that he was going to get them parts in the *Star Wars* sequel and in commercials for General Motors and Dial soap. He had sent the girls Christmas poinsettia plants, like some Hollywood big shot. They would catch on to him.

He and Kenny had carried out some great shit together, but the way Angelo was beginning to feel, if the guy weren't a relative, he would tell him to kiss off. Kenny took too much pleasure in all the Strangler publicity, Angelo thought. What did he think he was, a fucking starlet? He could sit all day at Angelo's reading the papers and waiting for more Strangler news on the TV.

Both of them got a kick out of all the reward money that was being posted by the City Council, the County Board of Supervisors, station KTTV, and a Glendale lawyer, more than a hundred thousand dollars all told, and they enjoyed Police Lieutenant Ed Henderson's description of Los Angeles as "a city of concern," but Kenny, in Angelo's sober view, was getting off on all this stuff too much. He was acting as though he would like to start making public appearances, maybe get himself a shot on the Johnny Carson show. Angelo was particularly incensed when Kenny told him that three days after they had murdered Kimberly Martin, he had gone on an LAPD ride-along, still trying to join a police force, and had asked the officers to show him the Hillside Strangler sites. Fortunately neither officer knew them, or Kenny might have spilled something. Angelo told Kenny not to do anything that stupid again.

Meanwhile like a sap he was making a fuss about this kid of his that fat bitch Kelli Boyd was about to deliver. Kenny was sounding like one fucked-up bimbo. Angelo told Julie Villaseñor, son Danny's girl-friend, who would sometimes spend the night with Angelo, leaving her kid in the spare bedroom while she shared the water bed, to stay away from Kenny. "He's nutty," Angelo said.

Nor were the holidays any picnic for Angelo. His mother died after the New Year, done in at last by the disease that had begun in her vagina. Angelo mourned. Jenny might have been a cunt, but she was his mother; he had been so close to her, had visited her faithfully, had never in his life lived more than a couple of miles from her, had relied on her, he knew, for comfort during the traumas of his divorces. No matter what—trouble with cops or women—Jenny had been there. Now of the immediate family only Cecilia was left.

But Angelo was not a guy to let life's inevitable changes of course get him down. He had plenty of upholstering to do. He had his house to tidy, the fish to feed, the rabbits to stroke, and he had the faithful Sparky, who was always there to greet him and to roll at his feet. Of course there was plenty of female company, too. Peaches moved in just after Christmas and stayed for most of January, other girls came by for quickies, and in the evenings Angelo would scout the waitresses at the Robin Hood Inn or the Red Vest. Henry's, his favorite, had closed, but there were al-ways new hunting grounds. And he comforted himself by finishing work on a new Excalibur car he had built for himself from a kit. Cream-colored with a tan can-vas top, a long hood, running boards, and gleaming chrome reminiscent of the glory days of motoring, the Excalibur bucked Angelo up. It was probably the only Excalibur in Glendale, the sort of car only a million-aire would normally drive, and here he had put it to-gether with his own deft hands. He was so pleased with it that he rented a separate garage for it. Angelo was blessed with what a psychologist would call a healthy mechanism for accepting and adjusting to grief.

Weeks passed. Heavy rains came to Southern California, ending a three-year drought. Even had An-gelo and Kenny been inclined to another murder, the wet weather would have put a crimp in their scam. Kenny found a menial job at Alma Lodge, a nursing home. Kelli returned to Los Angeles, quitting her job so that she could collect government assistance to care for the expected baby, still refusing to live with Kenny. But she was pleased that he seemed so excited about "the little person," as he affectionately termed the fetus, which was due in the middle of February. He even attended natural-childbirth classes with her, proving to her that he really cared and showing evidence that he was willing to assume the role of a truly contemporary father, involved, above stereotypical role models, announcing that when the time came he would be happy to change a diaper. They discussed names for the little person. They decided that if it turned out a boy, they would call him Ryan, after the title of their favorite soap opera, *Ryan's Hope*.

Kenny also got a kick out of the idea of calling his son by the same name he had used to ensnare Kimberly Martin, but he kept that little joke to himself.

He kept quiet to Kelli about his other women, too, content to appear to her the downcast, faithful lover, waiting for the word that she had forgiven him for his aberrant act of violence toward her, promising that his only interest now lay in his new family, trumpeting his belief in traditional family values. "I want nothing but the best for you and the little person. That gives me something to strive for." But away from Kelli he fended off celibacy by getting in touch with Sheryl Kellison, his first California girlfriend, who, so he told her, still occupied a special place in his heart. Sheryl was delighted to resume their relationship; Kenny was the most interesting man she had ever met, so sensitive, and it was no trouble at all to forgive wandering in a man who was deeply engaged in finding himself. When Kenny was with neither Kelli nor Sheryl, he followed Angelo's example and made inroads into the Glendale high school scene. He brought high school girls over to the Corona house to smoke pot and watch pornographic movies. He took girls into a deserted house he had discovered on Vista Superba, a dark, big place, ideal for a clandestine rendezvous, sex, and the inhaling of Rush, a bottled stimulant then popular with teenagers.

One night Kenny enjoyed a memorable double date with Liz Ward, a fourteen-year-old, and a teenage couple. The rain had paused, it was a starry night, the kids suggested a drive to a secluded place. They loved riding in Kenny's Cadillac, and they gave him directions up into the mountains on the Angeles Crest Highway north of Glendale, passing around a bottle of sloe gin. About four miles up they told him to park the car at a turnout.

Pine forests, rough granite boulders, chaparral and manzanita bushes and fragrant sage, the city a blanket of light below, the sky an astronomer's dream, California offering its everything above the crowded city. In the chill, dark January air, in a hollow on a hiker's path just off the road, young Liz Ward warmed Kenny up with oral sex. So remote and desolate and dark—Kenny thought what a great place it would be to dump a body.

But then the Cadillac days ended. At the beginning of February the car was repossessed. Since Sabra Hannan and Becky Spears had deprived him of extra income by their disobedient departures months before, Kenny had been unable to make the payments, and only his moving around had enabled him to keep the car as long as he had. He did not have the heart to tell his mother that he had lost it.

A man without a car in Los Angeles is a man without dignity. On the morning of Thursday, February 16, skipping work as usual, Kenny dropped by Angelo's, walking down from Corona, and complained about the way things were going for him. His car repo'd, his crummy and depressing job at the nursing home, Kelli's insufferable independence. How was all this happening to him, to a man of his inherent talents? There were people in Beverly Hills with half his smarts driving a Mercedes. He knew he had made some mistakes, but surely he deserved better than this, surely one day his ship would come in. Angelo told him he was a lazy shit but suggested that maybe a spin in the Excalibur would cheer him up. He would even permit Kenny to drive. The sun was out. The rain had let up. Who knows, they might come onto something.

Kenny turned up the radio and headed the Excalibur over toward the Valley, nipping in and out of traffic, feeling like a million or at least as though he had borrowed a million. Someday he would have a car like this! It made him feel a man again. He'd bet you could pick up any kind of a girl with wheels like this. He was Prince Valiant, rolling along in a car named after King Arthur's magical sword. Angelo, indifferent to mythologies, said that he was hungry for pussy.

They were driving along Riverside Drive in Burbank at about noon when they caught sight of a girl sitting alone at a bus stop. A blonde. Young. "She needs company," Angelo said. Kenny pulled over. Angelo asked the girl whether she'd like to go to a party in Hollywood. The girl said no. Angelo persisted, and when she still shook her head, he leaped out, grabbed her by the wrists, and started pulling her into the car.

At that moment another car drove up behind the Excalibur and stopped. Angelo now had the girl by the upper arms, wrestling with her. A woman in late middle age got out of the other car and rushed up, waggling an index finger at Angelo.

"You leave her alone! What are you doing? You come with me, dear. Don't let these men bother you. Let her go! I'll get the police!" Her tone and manner suggested a schoolteacher breaking up some rough-housing on a playground.

Angelo, startled, released the girl. Glaring at the woman, fixing her with his most vengeful stare, he said to her:

"God will get you for this!"

In the rearview mirror, driving off, Kenny saw the woman comforting the girl and cursed. He and Angelo were not pleased to have had their sport ruined by a busybody. They drove home in a snit. Angelo said that it was lucky for that old lady that she wasn't worth a rape.

Angelo returned to work. Kenny walked back up to Corona Street, borrowed one of his hosts' cars without permission, and drove over to the firm, near downtown, that had repossessed the Cadillac. He wanted to claim some books and clothes that had been taken with the car. He was angry. He felt his pride had been towed away with the Cadillac. He blew up at the manager of the tow yard, insisting that his scuba gear was missing. He would file a stolen-property report with the police. He would sue their ass.

The manager told Kenny to go to hell. In fact Kenny had never owned any scuba equipment, though he would have liked to own some. Scuba diving was the sort of thing he thought he ought to be doing; it fit his image of himself or the image he imagined for himself, not a carless nursing home attendant down on his luck but a muscled stud emerging from the Pacific with a tank on his back and girls at his feet. A man out of a Winston cigarette ad. But that he owned no scuba equipment was not the point. His protest was his way of standing up for his rights. He believed in consumer advocacy. You could not lie down and let these people run over you. At least that manager would know that he had not been dealing with a nobody. Kenny thought he probably would go ahead and file a claim with the police. He might just get some money out of it.

His two hosts were angry with him for borrowing their car. But what was a guy supposed to do? Take a bus? Hitchhike? Kenny stalked out, down toward Angelo's again. More and more, Angelo was the only person he felt truly comfortable with. Angelo gave him a lot of shit, but there was a bond there. They had their secrets. Together they had the city at their mercy, if only they chose to use their power, and that made up for any number of insolent managers at repossession lots. It was after five o'clock. Kenny was out of sorts, resentful of life's inequities. Maybe Angelo would buy him some dinner.

Kenny did not like hanging around the Corona house anyway. To each his own, but he did not approve of that style of life. Fags. Nobody could call Kenny Bianchi a fag. He hoped he might be able to talk Angelo into going cruising that night. Kenny was in the mood, and Angelo seemed to be, judging from the Excalibur escapade that day. It had been a long time, nearly two months. Obviously nobody was on their trail. All that had happened for weeks was that the police had arrested some demented actor and let him go. Kenny figured that he and Angelo had proved themselves invincible. On the chance that Angelo would be willing to try again, Kenny had stuffed into his pocket a false beard he had bought at a Hollywood novelty shop. Wearing a disguise on the prowl sounded like super fun.

When he arrived at Angelo's, he saw a bright new orange Datsun parked in the driveway behind the white Mustang. Next door at the glass shop and on the other side of the house at the car wash the workers were starting to go home for the day. In the Trim Shop he found Angelo seated behind his desk, talking to a girl, smoking a Kool. The Buzzard in his roost. The girl looked good to Kenny. Shiny, long strawberry-blond hair, scrubbed face. Her figure looked great in black slacks, her stomach flat.

"Shirley," Angelo said, "this is my cousin Kenny Bianchi."

"Not Shirley," she said smiling, pleasant. "It's Cindy. Cindy Hudspeth."

"I ain't so good with names."

"I want Mr. Buono to make me some floor mats for my new Datsun."

"Call me Angelo. Or Tony or Ange. Everybody does. Why not be friendly?"

"Sharp car you've got," Kenny said.

"Cindy used to work over at the Robin Hood," Angelo said. "I seen her in there. She waited on me, so I gives her my card. See? Advertising pays off." He grinned. "Say, Kenny, I need to talk to you a second. Wait here, Cindy. Be right back."

Angelo led Kenny into the house.

"Can you believe this?" Angelo said. "Can you believe the luck? What a cunt. One gorgeous cunt. So she walks right in at closing time. Listen, how about we pull a scam?"

"Okay with me."

"I been talking to her. She's working nights over at the college. She's on her way to work now. She wants another job, she says. Wants more money to go to college. Says she's giving dancing lessons, can you beat that? Wanna dance?''

"I've got it, Tony. Listen. Tell her, you know, you've got a list, that's it. You've got a list of people with jobs, but it's in the house. Get her into the house, we've got her.''

Angelo looked out a side window. Everybody had gone home from the glass shop.

"Okay,'' Angelo said. "That'll work.''

"But wait. What if somebody knows she came here? She might have told somebody.''

"No, she says she's just driving by and sees the shop and remembers the card. She just come in here by chance on the way to work.''

"Perfect.''

Angelo returned to his office and told Cindy Hudspeth that it was time to close up his shop now but that he could give her some job openings if she would come into the house. She was grateful for his help. Once she sat down in the brown vinyl easy chair, her hours were numbered. Kenny kept her occupied with small talk while Angelo fetched the gag, tape, and cord. When she said that she lived in an apartment at 800 East Garfield Avenue, Kenny said that that was quite a coincidence. He had lived right across the street last year. "It's a small world,'' Kenny said.

Kenny won the coin toss this time. But before raping her, he agreed to Angelo's suggestion that they tie her arms and legs to the legs of the bed. The spread-eagled sacrifice appealed to both of them. They used her for nearly two hours. At Angelo's urging, Kenny did the actual strangling.

They agreed that her car was a problem. They would have to get rid of it. Angelo went outside to look it over and found his business card on the floor on the driver's side. He tore it up and threw it in the dumpster. Meanwhile Kenny contemplated stealing her jewelry, but Angelo returned too quickly for that.

"I know a super place to dump her,'' Kenny said. "Hey, let me pick the place this time. I know a great one, way up on Angeles Crest. We can push the Datsun off a cliff.''

"Okay, *mi numi*. It better be good.''

"Promise."

They put Cindy Hudspeth's body into the trunk of her car, folding in her arms and legs. Kenny remarked how much better the Cadillac had been for this purpose. Kenny would drive the Datsun, and Angelo would follow him in the Mustang. To guard against fingerprints, Angelo, always prepared, presented Kenny with a pair of rubber surgeon's gloves he had stolen from the hospital.

Kenny attached his false beard, and they headed up toward Angeles crest in tandem. Kenny found the turnout where, a month before, he had enjoyed his tryst with Liz Ward, and he pointed out the hiker's path to Angelo, bragging about what had been done to him. "I don't care about your fucking head job," Angelo said. "Let's get this thing over with." They pushed the Datsun front first over the side of the road, the body still in the trunk. The car turned over once, spun around, and came to rest against some logs partway down the cliff.

On the way home Angelo stopped for cigarettes at a mom-and-pop store on Glendale Avenue, where Kenny dropped the rubber gloves into a trash basket outside.

Exactly one week later, Kelli gave birth to a boy. Complications with the delivery prevented Kenny's being present at the blessed event. He felt it was a shame that he had wasted all that time at the Lamaze classes. He would have been there had he been allowed: he was not killing anyone at the time. But he was delighted, as he said, that the little person had emerged a little man, Ryan. And he was gratified that Kelli bestowed on the child the surname Bianchi, making it officially an Irish-Italian crossbreed. Kenny was so proud to be a father that he arranged for a photograph to be taken of the new family, Ryan's hope in life. With Kelli looking on, Kenny posed, the beaming daddy, holding his baby.

ELEVEN

The woman Angelo had cursed as the old lady not worth a rape, the busybody, the interrupter of the Excalibur episode, was Jan Sims, a teacher at the Heritage School in Glendale, just off Colorado Street. After she had frightened Buono and Bianchi into taking off, she shepherded the girl into her car, comforted her for half an hour, and put her safely onto a bus, learning neither her name nor her destination. But seeing the girl safe and away was not an end to it for Mrs. Sims. She then went straight to the North Hollywood police station and told her story, describing the Excalibur and Angelo and Kenny, right down to Kenny's leather coat and acne scars and Angelo's warning that God would punish her. With all of this talk about the Hillside Strangler in the city, Mrs. Sims expostulated, surely this incident ought to be investigated.

Unfortunately the officer in charge took it upon himself to classify her as a fantasizing schoolmarm.

"Oh, lady!" he said to her. Did she really expect him to believe that two guys would try to abduct a girl in broad daylight from a crowded Burbank street in a fancy sports car? Did she realize how many calls they were getting about the Hillside Strangler? Everybody's brother was the Hillside Strangler. She should go home and sleep on it. A few hours later, Cindy Hudspeth was dead.

During the next week, Mrs. Sims telephoned the North Hollywood station. She was sure, she said, that she had seen the car in question parked on Colorado Street in Glendale. She had spotted it as she was on her way to work at the Heritage School. "Oh, lady," the officer said. He would file a report to go along with her original statement. His tone of voice told Mrs. Sims not to bother the police again.

So it was that, as she brooded on the incident, she did not try to tell the police about what else she had concluded. She was sure that she had seen the driver of the Excalibur before, the younger one, the one with the leather coat and the acne scars on his neck. Some weeks earlier, she had been waiting for her daughter in the parking lot of a building on Lankershim in the Valley. As she thought about it, she was certain that the same young man, this time dressed in a dark three-piece suit and carrying an attaché case, had approached her car, leaned on the window, and asked her what she was doing there. When she had explained that she was waiting for her daughter to get off work, the young man had said that he was just checking. He was in charge of security for the building, he had said. Something about the young man's manner, his bravado, the look in his eyes, had unnerved Mrs. Sims then, and now she was sure that he had been driving the Excalibur. Aware that yet another girl had been killed by the Strangler on that day, she wanted to call the police again, but what was the use? They obviously were paying no attention to her. She was too embarrassed to call them again.

Mrs. Sims had encountered Kenny in the parking lot of the building where he rented his psychologist's office from Dr. Weingarten. Had she been able to convince the police of the truth of that and of her other eyewitness accounts, the chances of finding Bianchi and of solving the entire case at that point would appear to have been excellent, because Bianchi's fingerprints were already on file along with dozens of others taken from the telephone booth at the Hollywood public library and at apartment 114, 1950 Tamarind, following the Kimberly Martin murder.

Back in December another woman had experienced similar frustration with the police, then in connection with Kimberly Martin. She was Dr. Lois Lee, a sociologist and the founder of CAT (California Association for Trollops), a kind of guild for whores that lobbied for the legalization of prostitution and offered legal services and counseling for prostitutes. Near eleven o'clock on the night of December 13, the Climax outcall service telephoned Dr. Lee to inform her that Kimberly Martin had not returned from a nine-o'clock call at 114 Tamarind and gave her the number Bianchi had given them. Dr. Lee traced the call to the library, rushed over to 1950 Tamarind to find the apartment empty, and located Kimberly's abandoned Oldsmobile down the street. She telephoned the West Hollywood sheriff's office only to be told that a missing-person report could not be acted on for twenty-four hours and that since the person was just another prostitute, nobody really cared anyway. The remark was callous but also betrayed ignorance of and indifference to the Hillside Strangler investigation, since two of the known victims had been prostitutes. Dr. Lee went directly to the sheriff's office herself and demanded action. The deputies telephoned the LAPD Task Force headquarters, but an investigator failed to arrive until one-thirty in the morning. By that time Kimberly Martin's body was already splayed on the hillside, and even immediate police action would not have prevented her death. But when most of this information, not including the initial response of the deputy on the telephone, reached the media, it did little to encourage public confidence in the police. Dr. Lee did not hide her anger.

These and other police errors resulted from several causes: the poor judgment of individual, lower-level officers; the public's panic, which sparked thousands of false leads, some of them no doubt inspired, as County Supervisor Ed Edelman had predicted, by the huge amount of posted reward money; and the size of the task force, which by February 1978 had grown to ninety-three officers. While Grogan, Salerno, and the other primary investigators could not have handled by themselves the mass of information coming in, at the same time ninety-three officers could not be expected to communicate effectively with one another, and a majority of these officers lacked extensive homicide experience—other senior homicide detectives had to be assigned to other murder cases. PATRIC, the computer, proved inept at cross-referencing, validating Grogan's opinion of it as an overpriced filing cabinet. Grogan and Salerno, who were now meeting often to compare notes and theories, circumventing the traditional Sheriff's Department–LAPD rivalry, agreed that they could be working more effectively if left alone. They especially dreaded and resented what they regarded as the useless and too frequent general meetings of the task force at the Glass House, and they kept some important information to themselves, including the identity of their few and precious key witnesses, lest that leak to the media, tipping off the killers and endangering additional lives.

There were many times when Grogan complained, and not quietly, that the press and television cared far more about selling papers and drawing ratings than whether the killers were caught or more women murdered. He considered the task force largely a capitulation to media pressure and hysteria, and sometimes the press and television fouled up the investigation directly and, Grogan thought, unethically. After Kimberly Martin, for instance, the police had flooded the Hollywood area with undercover cops, male and female, and were able to get the cooperation of prostitutes and pimps, who were suddenly more concerned than usual with personal safety. But some "media asshole," as Grogan phrased it, broke the LAPD code, and the undercover operation was thwarted by the presence of reporters, including TV cameras and lights. Grogan, called "Walrus" after his mustache and immensity, had to get a new code name.

It was Grogan's idea to equip a young policewoman with a radio transmitter, called a Fargo, so that she could work undercover trying to tempt the Stranglers into abducting her and yet remain protected. On her first night out she was approached by a man on Hollywood Boulevard. He asked her to come to his motel. When she refused, though not too vigorously, got into her car, and drove off to an apartment the police had rented, he followed her and tried to go into the apartment with her. The police, waiting inside, jumped him, threw him to the ground, landed a few good punches, and handcuffed him. He turned out to be a Marine on leave from Camp Pendleton, carried away by the policewoman's beauty and what he had taken as at least a halfhearted come-on. He was good-natured about being beaten up, however, saying that it served him right for trying to pick up a girl off the street. As a Marine he was glad to have had the shit kicked out of him if it helped catch that Strangler.

Early in February, before Cindy Hudspeth, Grogan was asked to take down the confession of one of the several men who had phoned the police or written the mayor claiming to be the killer. Most were dismissed out of hand as nut cases, but this one was so insistent that the police obliged him by booking him—the first man booked in the case. He was an actor named Ned York who had played minor roles in such television dramas as *Starsky and Hutch*, a cop show, and *The Courtship of Eddie's Father*. In "Murder Ward" Ned York had played an orderly in a lunatic asylum who dealt in drugs, in "Nightmare" a cop. He claimed to have known Kristina Weckler before murdering her and to have had an intimate friendship with a male student at the Pasadena Art Center of Design. He was a born-again Christian, separated from his wife, and his personalized automobile license read "RE 3:20," a reference to Revelations 3:20, which advises, "Behold, I stand at the door and knock; if anyone hears My voice and opens the door, I will come to him and dine with him, and he with Me."

"You know," Grogan said, "that's the right Biblical reference for an actor. I bet that license plate gets him a lot of free grub between roles.'' Was York confessing for the publicity?

Grogan ushered Ned York, whose arm was in a sling from a dog bite and whose frantic manner meant cocaine to Grogan, into an interview room on the third floor of the Glass House. Grogan's partner for the interview was Sergeant Sherman Oakes.

Within minutes Grogan knew that Ned York was making up his confession out of what he had learned from the media and from his own grotesque fantasies. This is one crazy motherfucker, Grogan thought, another tribute to Hollywood's favorite pastime, cocaine. Nothing he said squared with inside information, notably not the method of strangulation: Ned was accomplishing it all with his bare hands.

He asked for a hamburger and a Coke. Grogan thought, sure enough, I will dine with him and he with me, and, beginning to feel sorry for him, brought him the hamburger and Cokes for all three men. Ned York rambled on, mixing his sorrow at being separated from his wife with his regret for the lives of his victims. He said his little friend at the Art Center had been Kristina's boyfriend. Well, Grogan thought, he'll really have something to be sorry for after this, the poor bastard. He's probably never hurt anybody, but I don't see him getting any more TV roles. He gave Ned York a cigarette.

Suddenly Sergeant Sherman Oakes, whom Grogan knew to have a quick temper, stood up and splashed his Coke and ice right into Ned York's crotch. Grogan was surprised and confused. What in hell had this pathetic creature said that could have pissed Oakes off like that? What could make a guy angry at Ned York?

Then Grogan smelled burned cloth and saw little wisps of smoke rising from between Ned York's legs. York had tried to set fire to his own crotch with his cigarette.

''Jesus Christ!'' Grogan shouted. ''Let the poor son of a bitch out of here! He hates his dick so much he wants to burn it off!''

There were not many such light moments. Cindy

Hudspeth's murder brought the count to ten, although the press still counted twelve or thirteen, unaware of the distinctive ligature marks; and her murder brought few fresh clues, heightening if possible the public's fear and police frustration. Relations between the police and the media hit bottom. Grogan complained to anyone who would listen that reporters were not constrained by the rules of evidence and were free to print hearsay. They were interviewing witnesses, sometimes before the police could get to them, coloring witnesses' perceptions, endangering them, sometimes misrepresenting themselves as policemen just to get interviews, using composite drawings not developed by the police. Station KABC TV had broadcast a drawing of "the fugitive" that bore no resemblance to anything then known, based on some very dubious reports. And when the *Valley Daily News* quoted Glendale Police Chief Duane Baker as saying that the victims had been sodomized, Grogan was equally furious with the paper and the chief and hoped neither the Wagners nor the Wecklers saw the story.

On the afternoon of February 17, Frank Salerno had received the call to go up to Angeles Crest just beyond the Glendale-Pasadena city line. The pilot of a Forest Service helicopter, who scanned the area regularly to check for fires and cars that had plunged off the road, had spotted the Datsun. Then a rescue worker noticed the nude body through an aperture on the side of the trunk where a reflector had been torn away in the plunge. By the time Salerno arrived, at three o'clock, the rescue team had already hauled the car up onto the highway, and the body lay in the coroner's van. One look at the ligature marks told him that this was another Hillside victim, although the lines on the wrists, being unbroken, did not look to Salerno as though they had come from handcuffs this time. As for other kinds of evidence, there were none. The tire tracks and footprints on and around the turnout were too numerous to be significant.

At the morgue Salerno watched as the body was taken out of a plastic bag, blood oozing from a laceration on the scalp as attendants laid her out on a gurney. The blood dripped onto her shoulder and down her back as she was being moved. Salerno figured that the wound and some others might likely have come from the body's being knocked around in the trunk as the Datsun went over the cliff. There was a puncture wound on the bridge of her nose; markings ran down her cheeks from the corners of her mouth, and her lipstick was smeared, indicating a gag; there were four long abrasions, ranging from ten to four inches, on the outside of her right breast and along her stomach and numerous small marks on the back of her right arm and on her shoulder. At the autopsy, Salerno watched as bits of chaparral were removed from her vagina. These might have lodged, it was agreed, during the difficult negotiation of the body up forty feet of steep cliff.

Cindy Hudspeth's roommate on Garfield identified the body; she had reported Cindy missing the morning of the 17th. Salerno did his best to comfort Cindy's mother, who lived alone in Echo Park and had long been divorced from Cindy's father. She and everyone else Salerno could find described Cindy as a sweet, hardworking, ambitious girl; she had hoped to go to college in Northern California at Humboldt State or at Sonoma State, away from the frenzied congestion of Los Angeles. Bartenders and other waitresses at the Robin Hood Inn and the Red Vest in Glendale, where Cindy had worked part-time, said that she had been friendly, efficient, and rather naive for a twenty-year-old Californian. She had been much liked by the customers, many of whom would request that she wait on them. Her boss at Glendale Community College, where she worked nights answering the phone in the adult education section, said that she was "just the kind of girl you would always want around." She had loved disco dancing, had won several dance contests, and was planning to give dancing lessons: she had had business cards printed up. But she had not been able to decide where to give the lessons; she was afraid to bring strangers to her apartment. She had been, like everyone else, worried about the Strangler but had felt safer now that she had a new car. She had been planning a holiday in Mexico with friends.

No one had any idea how Cindy, a cautious, conservative young woman, had met up with the Strangler. She had left her apartment between four-thirty and five, after paying her rent, and would normally have turned west on Colorado Street on the way to the college on Glendale Avenue. Somewhere between her apartment and the college, she had been abducted.

One possible witness did contact the police. Janice Ackers said that on Thursday night she had driven off the westbound Foothill Freeway onto the Angeles Crest Highway northbound into the mountains. At first there had been no cars behind her, but then through her mirror she had noticed a car coming up behind her very fast with a second car following it. As she stopped to make a left turn, the first car, a small reddish-orange sedan, sped past her on her right and the driver had stared at her through his window. He had a wild, strange look in his eyes, Mrs. Ackers said, and he had a full beard. Then the second car passed, about eight car lengths behind. She watched the two cars speed up the hill, the second car gaining on the first. She did not notice anything about the second driver or about his car. The incident had occurred at about nine o'clock.

If Mrs. Ackers could be believed, and she appeared rational, this was yet another confirmation of what Salerno had deduced from the moment he had seen the position of Judy Miller's body, that two men were involved. The time and location and the color of the lead car checked out.

But the information did not fill Salerno with a rush of optimism. From talking to Bob Grogan he knew that Beulah Stofer had not seen a beard on either man. It had been nearly three months since Lauren Wagner's death, long enough to grow a beard, but Salerno was conscious of how little, really, he had learned since his own involvement had begun with Judy Miller. He and Grogan met often at the Code 7 bar or at more out-of-the-way places to exchange information and, after sufficient drink, to commiserate. They felt as did the new chief of the LAPD, Daryl Gates, who had been reduced to giving press conferences apologizing for the lack of progress, saying that he hated to look at himself in the mirror when he shaved. "I come to you with empty hands," Gates would report to an increasingly hostile press.

Grogan and Salerno agreed that the fact that Cindy Hudspeth and Kristina Weckler had lived across the street from each other, although they had not known each other, meant that the killers probably lived in Glendale; this explained the remoteness of many of the dump sites. As for physical evidence, the bit of fiber on Judy Miller's eye had led nowhere: a polyester fiber, origin unclear. The marks on Lauren Wagner's palms were almost certainly electrical burns. How they had got there no one could tell, but they indicated torture, as did the puncture marks on Kristina Weckler, who clearly had not been taking drugs. Some fibers had also been found sticking to the adhesive on Lauren's hands—again untraceable—along with some animal hairs that appeared to have come from cats. The Wagners had no cats. As for eyewitnesses, Salerno now had Janice Ackers. He had discounted Pam Pelletier but believed Markust Camden and had kept in touch with him, interviewing him again in February, finding his story consistent. Grogan had Beulah.

"I must have visited her thirty times so far," Grogan said. "I never ate so many cookies in my life. But I can't get her to admit she was outside and saw everything closer up than she says."

He had gotten Beulah to agree to hypnosis, but it had not worked. Every time she looked as though she was about to go under, she had been overcome by an asthma attack. Another neighbor, Evelyn Wall, also admitted seeing the abduction. She lived right next door to Beulah and had said that she had heard a man "hollering" that night. Evelyn Wall's recollection was at first vaguer than Beulah's, but under hypnosis Mrs. Wall said that she had gone outside to see what the noise was about, hiding behind the corner of her house. She had seen two large figures and a small figure in a big car that had been light on the top and dark underneath and another, smaller car, with no one in it. As the big car had driven off, one of the large figures had pushed down on the head of the smaller figure. Later that night she had gone out to check on the smaller car and had found the interior light burning but no one in it.

A third witness claimed to have been driving past and to have seen two men pulling a girl into their car. But this witness would be useless. "He's the only guy I know has a certificate from the state saying he's not crazy," Grogan said. He was a convicted murderer who had been declared cured of insanity by the Atascadero state hospital for the criminally insane. He would not make a good impression in court.

Grogan and Salerno agreed that their biggest breakthrough was probably having the fingerprints from the phone booth and the apartment on Tamarind: one set matched. None had been found in Cindy Hudspeth's car, except her own, other than what might be a palmprint or a footprint on the outside of the trunk lid.

The biggest of many missing pieces was the site of the murders themselves, or possibly the several sites. The size of the city, both in population and in geography, was working against Salerno and Grogan and the others. The task force made things worse by pulling the files on every unsolved murder of a female during the past couple of years, even from places as far away as Bakersfield. The numerous municipalities, each with its own police force, which made up the greater Los Angeles area also fouled things up: Salerno and Grogan were sure that many multiple murders were never identified as such because a killing done in one town might never be correlated with one committed in another. And just as the freeway system had made Los Angeles the bank robbery capital of the nation, the city of the quick getaway, so it was plain that the Stranglers were taking advantage of the freeways, covering far more territory than would have been possible in, say, New York or Boston, sketching the arterial form of the city in the geographical pattern of their abductions and dumpings.

"I'm going to write a goddam novel," Grogan said. "It'll outsell Joe Wambaugh. I'm going to call it *I Hope My Mother Is Never Murdered in Los Angeles.*"

When psychiatrists began offering theoretical portraits of the killer or killers, Grogan and Salerno paid attention, although their experience with psychiatrists in court had not inspired confidence in that profession. When they agreed with a psychiatric diagnosis, they invariably found that they had already arrived at the same conclusions themselves, without the obfuscations of a technical vocabulary. And in court every psychiatrist saying one thing was contradicted by another saying the opposite, so what was the use of them except to confuse a jury?

Now in interviews with the press, psychiatrists suggested that the Strangler was white, in his late twenties or early thirties, and single, separated, or divorced—in any case not living with a woman. He was of average intelligence, unemployed or existing on odd jobs, not one to stay with a job too long. He had probably been in trouble with the law before. He was passive, cold, and manipulative—all at once. He was the product of a broken family whose childhood was marked by cruelty and brutality, particularly at the hands of women. Early signs of trouble were chronic bedwetting, cruelty to animals, arson, vandalism, and poor relationships with other children. It was generally agreed that the strangling itself was the sexual kick. Murder might, however, be only foreplay, with sex coming afterward. One psychiatrist asserted that sex murderers usually do not perform normal intercourse under any circumstances.

Dr. Louis Jolyon West, chairman of psychiatry and behavioral sciences at UCLA and director of that university's Neuropsychiatric Institute, told the *Times* that this was a man living on the fringes of society whom no one would suspect. He liked danger but believed himself invincible. "It would be most unlikely," Dr. West said, "to find this done by more than one person. Homosexuals murder by teams . . . but this type is most always the work of a single person. If not, then the relation between the two would be extremely unusual—a *folie à deux* [a psychiatric condition in which two persons usually related share the same delusions and act out the same psychosis]." Another psychiatrist reasoned that "the killer may not have had much dating experience." Dr. West suggested that a woman confronting the Strangler try to "blind him if you can. Stick a sharp object into his eyes."

But Grogan and Salerno knew that this advice was useless, since there were two Stranglers. They weighed the accumulated wisdom of the psychiatric profession, thought the idea that the killers might be related a possibility worth considering, but found little enlightenment in the constantly repeated idea that such killers hated their mothers. What else was new? That was the standard explanation for every screwed-up male, as predictable as ham on rye. "Gee," Grogan said, "all we got to do now is find a white male who hates his mother. Can't be many of those around!"

Psychics offered themselves to the LAPD for a fee or for the publicity. Fortunately, in Grogan's view, the LAPD had never stooped to hiring a psychic as other police departments around the country had done. Psychics simply hung around an investigation until the evidence was in and then took credit for solving the crime. Any homicide detective who believed in psychics ought to resign and join the priesthood or produce movies.

A private detective from Berlin wrote saying that he could and would solve the case for the price of air fare to Los Angeles. Grogan could never get the German's polysyllabic name straight, but he kept writing, so Grogan began referring to him as Dr. Shickelgruber. "Anything from Dr. Shickelgruber today?" Grogan would ask when he arrived at the office. One day Grogan was sitting at his desk talking to Charlie Weckler on the phone, trying to reassure him that the investigation was progressing when it was not, when another officer came up and announced that Dr. Shickelgruber had arrived from Berlin. He was waiting outside.

"You're shitting me," Grogan said. No indeed, the German detective wanted to talk to the principal investigators. He would solve the case.

Grogan, figuring he had better be polite to a man who had flown all that way at his own expense, ushered Dr. Shickelgruber into an interviewing room. Unfortunately the German spoke no English, so Grogan summoned the only German-speaking officer on the force. Dr. Shickelgruber requested a blackboard.

On the board he wrote in German:

Two Italians
(Brothers)
Aged about thirty-five.

Grogan thanked Dr. Shickelgruber and saw that he was driven to the airport. His Italian-family theory impressed no one.

In April Grogan was dispatched to Boston to bring to Los Angeles a prisoner, George Shamshack, who had implicated himself and another man in two Los Angeles killings still promoted by the press as Hillside Strangler cases. Grogan knew that neither of these women had been killed by the Stranglers—the m.o. did not fit—but he did not mind the trip to Boston, where he visited his mother and brother. He read the *Newsweek* of April 10 with rueful amusement: "A break in the case? . . . the cops are cautiously optimistic that at least two of the puzzling murders are solved. That would still leave eleven unsolved cases." Oh well, Grogan thought, let them keep counting.

By the summer of 1978 the investigation was having its effect on Grogan's family life. He had become caught up in cases before, but nothing like this, and there was no end in sight. He stuck to the agreement not to discuss his work at home, but he had been home hardly at all for months and could think and talk of nothing else. He had practically become a member of the Wagner family, visiting them often, eating with them, trying to keep them from cracking. Lauren's sister was angry at Grogan for not telling her all the horrible details of what had been done to Lauren, but it was Joe Wagner, an earnest, rather naive man, who bothered Grogan the most. He took Joe Wagner to play golf and had long conversations about Lauren's death with him at his house. Grogan sensed that he was helping Joe, offering him faith at least in the integrity and concern of the police, but this father seemed unable to assimilate what had been done to his daughter. Such acts were beyond his comprehension, beyond what his religious faith and his belief in fellow human beings permitted him to accept. One evening as Grogan was leaving the Wagners, Joe took him aside in the hallway and said:

"Bob, I've got to ask you something. Please tell me. What is sodomy?"

Grogan was astonished. He did not want to answer. "Just bad sex, Joe," he said. "You know. Sex with hate."

With Charlie Weckler the conversations were freer though equally difficult. Charlie was dealing with his despair by means of anger. He had developed a stutter since his daughter's murder and sometimes became speechless with fury, clinging to Grogan as his one hope for vengeance. He would fly down from Sausalito, Grogan would take him to play golf, and then the two men would drink together at the Nightwatch, cursing the Stranglers, modern life, the press, Los Angeles. Charlie had heard that a national television network was planning a program about murders of prostitutes, using the Hillside Strangler case as an example of such homicides, and he told Grogan that he was suing the network to stop the program, because his daughter had not been a prostitute and treating the case that way would blacken her memory.

After a session at the Nightwatch, Grogan would pour Charlie onto the plane in the morning, and then in a few days they would start talking on the phone again: "At least you care, Bob. You really care. At least someone cares." And Charlie would fly down for more golf and drinks and talk. The two men developed a friendship born in death that would not falter. Charlie Weckler knew that Bob Grogan was devoting his life to solving Kristina's murder. At one point Grogan dreamed up the idea of an exhibition of Kristina's drawings and paintings at the Art Center of Design, the proceeds to go toward a scholarship in her name. He hoped that maybe the killers or one of them would show up, and he stationed undercover police all over the gallery and had photographs of everyone taken. The exhibition was a success but it trapped no one.

Everyone in the photographs could be identified as either the parent of a student, a student, a patron of the center, or a police officer.

It was strange, Grogan often thought, the way his life was being taken over. Salerno, equally conscientious but more emotionally detached, kept his family in place, Grogan could see, went to mass on Sundays with the wife and children, had to Grogan an admirable and enviable perspective: no matter what happened, the Salernos would go on, Salerno would do his work, the family would be intact. But Grogan was so involved by this case that the Wagners and the Wecklers began to haunt every moment of his life. What was Charlie thinking now? Had Joe found out what sodomy is? Grogan envied Salerno the coolness, the knack of turning off the job and embracing the family, permitting the family to triumph over the rest of life. He envied Salerno because he knew that Salerno was just as good at his job as anyone could be, just as dedicated a detective, yet he was keeping his life in one piece.

One afternoon at the Glass House, Grogan interviewed a woman who said she might have seen the Stranglers. She was agitated. The incident had occurred a month earlier, but she had been afraid to report it. Friends had persuaded her to go to the police. She had been drinking in a bar in Hollywood. She had gotten fairly tight. She was alone, and when she left the bar, she drove off at a pretty good clip, "my bra flying from the radio aerial," as she put it. A couple of blocks away, two cops pulled her over. They had a red light, but it was an unmarked car. There had been stuff in the paper about the Stranglers posing as police officers, so when one of these guys came up to her window, she really let him have it. She cursed him, let out a stream at him. He showed her his badge. She took off, gunning it. She had worried about the incident. The men had not followed her, but she had wondered ever since whether they might be the Stranglers.

Grogan had her hypnotized. Under hypnosis she said that she recalled the badge number. She gave

Grogan a detailed physical description of both of the men.

Grogan took the woman seriously. She seemed bright, and she was familiar with police work. She said that she had graduated from Reed College with a major in English and now ran a halfway house for men released from Chino State Prison. She knew criminals and had worked in various law enforcement agencies for years. She was in her thirties, tall and blonde with an alert, attractive face.

Grogan had a bulletin sent out to all the LAPD stations, and he decided to check out the story himself. It turned out to be accurate but so embarrassing to the police that, if it got out, the press would have a field day and the public might panic. Two officers working vice had tried to pick the woman up. They had made what was known among the police as a "pussy stop" after an evening of watching prostitutes. It was a common enough occurrence, but under present circumstances it was potentially disastrous. The woman had actually remembered the badge number in reverse, because it had a nine and a six in it and she had seen it upside-down.

Grogan reamed the officers out, told them they would be canned if their intended pickup pressed charges, and called the woman to explain what had happened. She was understanding. She agreed when Grogan told her that the pressures of working vice were considerable: you got turned on watching whores all night. She would not press charges. She knew what the police were going through with this case.

Grogan started babbling about the frustrations of the investigation. He told her about the Wagners and the Wecklers. He complained about the unethical irresponsibility of the media. He said that he could not burden his family with everything that was going on and that he was frightened every time his daughter left the house. It was no wonder that with a job like this cops were cracking up and dropping from heart attacks. It was like being in a war that never let up.

"You can talk to me, anytime," the woman said.

"That's okay. Thanks," Grogan said and hung up. I talk too much, Grogan said.

But he called her again, met her for a drink, and found himself unloading his emotions with a vehemence that surprised him. He could not stop talking to her, and when he told her about keeping Kristina Weckler's notebook, he knew that he had crossed a certain line. The woman turned out to be an ideal listener because of her familiarity with prisoners and police work, and, unlike Grogan's wife, she did not recoil from grisly details and violent language. She was tough, but he did not think her coarse. He let himself go. He would see her again.

He began an affair with her. He disliked himself for doing it, but he allowed himself to go ahead, and he worried that he might be falling in love with her. She lived fifty miles from downtown, so he did not see her except on weekends, but he began taking her out on his boat. The intensity of the case made it easy to contrive excuses. Every few days he would resolve to break off the affair, but he did not. At home he was silent and guilty. His wife did not know anything, yet, but sometimes the sight of her sad face on the pillow made Grogan go lock himself into the bathroom, despise his own face in the mirror, and feel like crying. He would have to end the affair soon, he said to himself. His children would hate him, too.

October 17, 1978. One year to the day after the murder of Yolanda Washington. Her death had started it all. The investigation was in the doldrums. Nothing new had turned up for eight months except hundreds and hundreds of false leads. The media had become bored with the case, and in a way this made life a little easier for the officers, but they could feel the public pressure on them, unresolved anger gathering, spreading blame in the air. The parents evolved from grief toward a craving for retribution, so they could make sense of their lives again or try to. Sonja Johnson's father attempted suicide. Over at the Glass House, Grogan, Dudley Varney, and Bill Williams, the officer who had convinced everyone else that Yolanda Washington must have been the first Hillside victim, decided that somehow they ought to commemorate the occasion. They ought to get drunk at least. They had to find some way to expiate their frustration for this one night. It was too late to go home. They had talked about the case all day and into the evening. Yolanda had been dead for a year this night.

Grogan, with his inclination to ritual, born of the mass-serving days in Boston, memories of Cardinal Cushing, the bread and the wine, suggested that they get a bottle and drink it where Yolanda Washington's body had been found—Forest Lawn Drive, across from the movie set. It was only right, he said. They had to do something. It was the anniversary, for Christ's sake.

They picked up the bottle and a pizza along the way. Williams brought a sheet from the morgue. He had taken it off a body in a moment of levity.

There at the very spot on Forest Lawn Drive they stopped, spread the coroner's white sheet on the hood of Grogan's car, opened the pizza, and drank, toasting Yolanda, cursing the Stranglers, and wishing on stars for clues. They invoked the names of the dead: Yolanda, Judy, Lissa, Jane, Dolores, Sonja, Kristina, Lauren, Kimberly, Cindy.

"You know," Dudley Varney said, "some people would think we're nuts, doing this."

Grogan gathered up the pieces of pepperoni, little Italian eucharists, on the pizza and laid them down again, spelling out her name: Y-O-L-I.

"Pass the bottle," Grogan said. "Here's to you, Yoli."

II
Disloyalties

What is possible is persuasive; so what has not happened we are not yet ready to believe is possible, while what has happened is, we feel, obviously possible: for it would not have happened if it were impossible.

—Aristotle, *Poetics*

TWELVE

February 1978 was an uneven month for Kenneth Bianchi, socially speaking. Although he achieved murder again and fatherhood, he was forced to change residence for the fifth time in the mere twenty-five months of his life in California when the men on Corona Street kicked him out. They were fed up with his irregular habits, his borrowing their cars without permission, his bringing high school students over to smoke dope and watch pornographic movies. They had invited him only as a favor to Kelli Boyd's brother, who was their friend, but they had expected Kenny to stay three or four days. It had now been over two months and no rent paid. When they discovered a California Highway Patrol badge among their guest's belongings, they decided he must go. They did not really suspect him, but the television and newspaper reports that the Hillside Strangler was probably posing as a police officer made them nervous; they had already concluded that Kenny must be lying about his degrees in psychology; this was not the kind of person they wanted as a nonpaying tenant. After Kenny left they told a neighbor who was a Glendale policeman about the CHP badge.

Kenny found an apartment for himself on Verdugo Road in Glendale. He was alone again. Kelli brought the baby over for Kenny to play with—he seemed to enjoy changing diapers on his little man—but refused to live with him. She was thinking, she said, of moving up to Bellingham to be closer to her parents and to raise Ryan in a healthier environment than Los Angeles. When Kenny asked her whether she wanted him to accompany her and the baby, she was noncommittal. Yes, she agreed that the boy needed a father. She was less sure that she wanted the father to be Kenny.

He bore these rebuffs to his love and paternal sense of responsibility with good grace. Surely Kelli would feel different once he began to prove himself. In the meanwhile he secured himself a new job cleaning, sterilizing, and delivering surgical instruments at Verdugo Hills Hospital. On his application he listed studies at Columbia in psychology and work at Strong Memorial Hospital in New York. As a character reference he named Angelo Buono, "re-upholsterer." His application so impressed the hospital that although he had asked merely for an orderly's job, he was given greater responsibilities at higher wages. With money borrowed from Sheryl Kellison he bought a car for four hundred dollars from a fellow employee. Things were looking up again. The true test of character, Kenny told himself, was whether you could endure setbacks and keep striving.

Nor did he worry much when the police came to interview him twice more. First a Glendale officer arrived at his apartment to ask him whether he owned a police badge. Kenny said he did not. That was that. The Glendale officer took his word. Then two LAPD officers, neither one a principal investigator on the Hillside Strangler case, came to call. Mrs. Wanda Kellison, Sheryl's mother, had telephoned the task force about Kenny. Her daughter was going out with this strange man, Mrs. Kellison said. She had argued about this man with her daughter, telling Sheryl that a man who borrowed money from a girl was no good to begin with, but Sheryl would not listen. Sheryl seemed to feel sorry for this Kenny Bianchi. Mrs. Kellison was worried. Bianchi had a strange look in his eyes. The task force should check him out. She could not say exactly why, but for some reason Mrs. Kellison thought that Bianchi might be the Hillside Strangler. For one thing, her daughter said that Bianchi talked about the Strangler all the time.

Mrs. Kellison was far from the only mother calling the task force to complain about a daughter's boyfriend. It had become a popular way for a parent to express disapproval of a prospective son-in-law. Grogan suggested that the task force set up a dating service; at least the computer could be put to good use that way. But the rule was to check everything out, so two junior officers were dispatched to investigate Bianchi. From the Department of Motor Vehicles they traced the address listed on his driver's license. One would think that 809 East Garfield would have inspired in these officers' minds an immediate connection to Kristina Weckler and Cindy Hudspeth. It did not. Nor, when they punched Bianchi's name into PATRIC, the computer, did his previous police interview at 1950 Tamarind show up. So off they went to trace Bianchi, figuring that this was another of the thousands of false leads that were multiplying daily.

At 809 East Garfield the landlord remembered Kenny Bianchi well. He had been an ideal tenant, quiet, so gentlemanly. You did not find many such young men these days. There had been this other tenant, Angie Holt, who had complained about him, but she was a troublemaker. Kenny was such a nice young man. He had kept in touch, had let it be known that he had become a father. He was so proud. If only all the tenants were like Kenny! He was living over on Verdugo Road now. They could find him there.

At the Verdugo apartment the officers told Kenny right away that his name had come up in connection with the Hillside Strangler investigation.

"Okay, fine," Kenny said, opening his door wide. "Won't you come in?"

The officers asked him whether he had been in town from October 1977 through the present time. Kenny said yes, he had been in Los Angeles since early in 1976. He had not been in jail? No, Kenny said, smiling as though the question were embarrassing, as though the very idea of jail were entirely alien to him. Had he ever been or was he now connected to any law enforcement agency? No, but he admired the police, the job they did, what they went through. In fact he had an application in to join the LAPD Reserves. He supposed he had not heard from them because of his changing addresses.

The officers thanked Bianchi and left. They did not ask him whether he had been interviewed before by the task force. The interview had taken less than ten minutes. Back at the Glass House the officers wrote up their report and filed it along with their photostat of Bianchi's driver's license. They did not bother to check on his LAPD Reserves application: his fingerprints were on that, and they could have been compared with the fingerprints from the phone booth and the Tamarind apartment, but these officers were not even aware of the phone booth and apartment prints.

It cannot be said to have been tough, but Kenny had handled the interview well. He knew Angelo would have been proud of him, and he hurried over to tell him about it. He found Angelo in the back stroking the rabbits, making Sparky jealous.

"Can you imagine," Kenny said, "I fooled the cops again."

"Keep your mouth shut," Angelo said. He told Kenny to go inside.

They sat down together in the den. Could you beat that? Kenny said. Three times now the cops had questioned him and they had not even come close. They never would. Not a chance.

"I was so cool. No sweat. Those idiots, they didn't even look at my driver's license." He took it out and showed it to Angelo. On the front, the Garfield address. He flipped it over and showed Angelo how he had written out in his own hand, duly accordant with the motor vehicle code, his subsequent address: 1950 Tamarind. Angelo stared.

"They didn't see this?"

"Are you kidding? They didn't see anything. I'm clean, Tony, clean and clear. They can't touch me."

Angelo slumped down, pulling on his earlobe. This was just great. Three times now the cops had been to see Kenny. They might really be on to something. They probably weren't telling all they knew. All of Angelo's misgivings about Kenny came back. The fuckup with Kimberly Martin. His telling the cops on the ride-along that he wanted to see the Strangler sites. His unhealthy lust for publicity. And now the cops were closing in on him. What else had Kenny said to people? What might he have said to Kelli or to the dudes on Corona? Angelo knew that he must act. He must get rid of Kenny.

"What's the matter, Angelo? You got something on your mind? I know you. The Buzzard's thinking something. The Buzzard's got a new scam. What's it going to be, Ange? What's going to happen? Hey, Angelo, say something. You're making me nervous."

Angelo said nothing. He walked over to the gun case, took out the .45 automatic, and shoved in a clip. Then he turned and pointed the gun at Kenny's head.

"I ought to off you right now," Angelo said.

"Hey, Angelo, hey, put that down. What's happening to you? Tony, why me? This is Kenny. This is your cousin Kenny. I thought we were partners. I thought we were in this together."

"I ain't in nothing, fuckhead, you stupid big-mouth fuckhead. How come the cops been to see you three times, they ain't been to see me once, huh? How come the cops know who the fuck you are, huh? You don't see no cops fucking around with Angelo Buono, right? What's the matter with you? You want to blow this deal? You talk too much."

Kenny hung his head in contrition. He apologized to Angelo, begged his indulgence, promised he would be cool from now on. Angelo calmed himself, put the gun away, went into the living room to stare at the fish. Kenny followed him, whining. Angelo told Kenny to leave him alone.

All through March and April, Angelo brooded, keeping to himself, fending off Kenny's regular phone calls, rejecting Kenny's suggestions to play pool or go cruising. He was relieved that the police did not visit Kenny again, but he was uneasy. He had broken, he knew, his cardinal rule, never to confide in anyone. He thought about Kenny, and the more he thought, the more his hatred for his cousin grew. Kenny was ready for more scamming, it was obvious. The fool had no sense at all. No timing, no feel for the right rhythm of things, no nothing. If it hadn't been for my dead cunt of a mother, Angelo thought, I never would have got involved with the jerk. Angelo was not inclined to introspection, but he sensed that he had overvalued Kenny's usefulness, relied overmuch on his servility, been induced by his willingness to please into sharing entirely too much with him. It was over with Kenny. But how to convey the message? Killing him would be too risky; they were too much linked together. Ignoring him seemed to draw him on. He craved abuse. He was like a woman who failed to read the score. Kenny reminded Angelo a little of Antoinette Lombardo. You could knock her up, turn her into a whore, shit on her in every way possible, and still she came back for more, a faithful dog waiting for another kick to the chops.

Angelo daydreamed of shooting or knifing Kenny, strangling him. Kenny, Angelo feared, was the kind of guy who would babble his way into trouble sooner or later. But Angelo, silent, watchful, clung to life with reptilian tenacity. Angelo blunt and rooted, Kenny homeless and euphemistic and absurdly hopeful: theirs was like a conflict between the ancient and modern worlds, with little enough to choose between the two.

As if to emphasize his determination to put distance between himself and his cousin, Angelo married again on March 29, affirming his impulse to survive and to go on with his own, separate life. The bride was Tai-Fun Fanny Leung, twenty-one years old, born in

Hong Kong. For her the marriage meant that she would be able to stay in the United States, and there was a practical advantage in the union for Angelo as well. Fanny's parents were sending her money to buy a house, and Angelo figured he would find a way to get his hands on that.

One afternoon in April, Kenny dropped by, the rejected suitor still hoping for attention. He announced, as though it were the end of something, that Kelli had abandoned him. She had gone up to Bellingham to be near her parents. It was terrible. His own son had been taken from him. How did Kelli expect the boy to grow up properly without the guidance of a father? What was wrong with women these days? Women's liberation had gone too far. Pretty soon women would have no use for men at all. Something had to be done to wake society up.

Angelo half listened. He was working on a car in the shop, music on the radio. Kenny droned on.

"Why don't you go up there?" Angelo said.

"What?"

"Follow the bitch, you love your son so much."

"I couldn't do that. What would I do? Leave L.A.? I'm going to the beach on Sunday with Sheryl."

"You better follow Kelli."

The more Angelo thought about it, the better the idea seemed. Getting Kenny away, out of the state. The guy was totally unreliable. Angelo wanted to be rid of him once and for all. He began encouraging Kenny to leave, but Kenny insisted that his future lay in California. Angelo pressed. At length he simply ordered Kenny to go. One day in May when Kenny was prattling about his psychology practice, how he was going to make it prosper at last, Angelo laid out the options simply and clearly. Either Kenny left the state, or Angelo would kill him. The evenness, the coolness, the directness with which Angelo delivered his ultimatum encouraged Kenny to pack his bags.

Still he dallied. He made a last stab at the psychology practice, placing an ad in the *Times* for an assistant. He listed his name as Dr. R. Johnson, gave the Verdugo address, and asked candidates with a degree in psychology to forward their college transcripts to him. He received several responses and selected the transcript of a Thomas Steven Walker, who held an M.A. degree in psychology from California State University at Northridge. Kenny, deciding that he ought to have college transcripts himself—with them he might land the very sort of a job he had offered Thomas Steven Walker—then sent a letter to the registrar at Cal State requesting "fully completed diplomas EXCEPT for my name. I have at additional expense retained a caligrapher [sic] that will print my name in a fancy script of my own choosing." He enclosed Walker's transcripts, which he had xeroxed, substituting his own name on the copies, signed the letter with Walker's name, and included a postal money order for ninety dollars. The registrar's office, exhibiting a surprising lack of skepticism, cashed the money order.

But before he could receive his new diploma, Kenny realized that Angelo would no longer tolerate his presence in Los Angeles. Maybe Angelo would mellow later, but for now Kenny understood that he had better get out. It took all of his persuasive powers to talk Kelli into the idea of his joining her. On the telephone he told her that he had come to a crossroads in his life. The birth of Ryan had altered his consciousness. Much to his surprise, he found himself welcoming the responsibilities of fatherhood. He now had something to live for, to work for; it was not easy, but he had come to understand his way of life up to this point had been selfish. Only through love could a person fulfill himself. And sometimes a change of scene was just what the doctor ordered. He had never liked Los Angeles anyway. It was decadent. Everything he knew about her home town, Bellingham, made it seem like the wholesome sort of place he needed. Kelli acquiesced.

Anxious, forlorn, wondering what he had done to deserve Angelo's turning on him like this, hoping that one day the closeness they had known could be restored, Kenny hit the road in late May in his four-hundred-dollar car. His employers at Verdugo Hills Hospital wished him well when he turned in his letter of resignation. He had written that he had decided to join his family up north, asking that the letter be kept confidential. He had no reason to believe that they would keep the letter from the police, but it was worth a try. He was not as worried about the police as Angelo appeared to be. There had been nothing about the Hillside Stranglers in the papers for weeks. Soon the whole thing would be forgotten; other murderers would grab the headlines. But he and Angelo had certainly had their moment. As he drove on up past San Francisco, past the meadows and forests and white peaks of Oregon, he felt sad and lonely, weary of wandering, dispossessed, wondering what his new life would bring. Angelo had been so insistent. What right had he to order Kenny out of the city? Now Kenny had only his clothes, his marijuana-leaf necklace, his college degrees and transcripts, his attaché case, his false beard, his bag of stolen jewelry, his psychology books. He was alone.

He drove straight through for two days, rolling northward, stopping at homey places where people praised the boysenberry pie. Bellingham would be some change. His experience of it at Christmas had made him wonder how much action a person could get from scenery. What could you do with pine trees and water? Meeting Kelli's parents, her mother and stepfather and her father, had been nice, but they were simple people, they had no conception of the kind of success that he knew would someday be his. No wonder Kelli had been tolerant for so long of all the time he spent with Angelo; she must have known he was bored with her, was lowering himself to be with her. But she and Ryan were family now.

He made up a poem as he drove along, improvising out of Robert Frost as imperfectly recalled from high school:

Long ago the snow-bent birches.
There is much winter sadness
Along a frozen lake under moonlight
For there one's memory tires of a squall of thought
Or a framework of white spines.

199

Death, he thought. The death of dreams. He continued:

> Caught within the icy waters
> We remembered what we once had.
> What once was mine and never
> Will be mine once more.
> I have it pretty good,
> Or so I'm told.
> Lord, why then this winter
> Weeping in my soul?
> A frozen lake under moonlight.

That's me, he murmured to himself, a lonely figure looking out over a frozen lake under moonlight. Not bad. If only the world would acknowledge his talent!

And so the banished acolyte, compelled into exile from the purlieu of Buono, entered a new state, the country of the pointed firs.

THREE OF THE VICTIMS

Lauren Wagner

L.A. HERALD EXAMINER

Kristina Weckler

Cindy Hudspeth

L.A. HERALD EXAMINER

L.A. HERALD EXAMINER

The "Hillside Stranglers": Angelo Buono (this page) and his cousin Kenneth Bianchi (next page). Together they raped, tortured, and murdered ten women in the Los Angeles area.
L.A. HERALD EXAMINER

The discovery of a victim's nude body—characteristically abandoned on a hillside.

L.A. HERALD EXAMINER

Sgt. Robert Grogan of the Los Angeles Police Department examines the body of another victim.

L.A. HERALD EXAMINER

(Above) Angelo Buono's house in Glendale, California, the scene of many of the slayings. Angelo's Trim Shop is at rear.
L.A. HERALD EXAMINER

Sabra Hanan, forced into prostitution by the Stranglers, lived to testify for the prosecution.
L.A. HERALD EXAMINER

Prosecutor Michael Nash won a conviction in the longest criminal trial in American history.

L.A. HERALD EXAMINER

Sgt. Grogan devoted himself to the case.

Judge Ronald George, whose controversial decision thwarted Deputy District Attorney Roger Kelly's move to dismiss the charges against Buono. *L.A. HERALD EXAMINER*

Buono with his attorney, Katherine Mader.
L.A. HERALD EXAMINER

THIRTEEN

Dear Sir or Madam,

My objective is a position in a community oriented facility or business setting involving responsibility for coordinating or supporting education, counselling, behavior modification or related programs in furthering human development and modality application.

Sincerely yours,

Kenneth A. Bianchi, Ph.D.

Affixed to the lower right-hand corner, a photograph of Kenny, Kelli, and little Ryan, the family group. Kenny, teeth bared beneath gently drooping mustache, appeared healthy and happy, vigorous, radiating that whole-earth outdoorsy optimism indigenous to the Pacific Northwest.

Kenny distributed this letter as he had the flyer for his counseling service, to advertise his merits in new surroundings. Its trendy, mindless phrasing did not land him a job doing whatever it was it proposed. Still his first few months in Bellingham showed signs of progress and stability. He and Kelli and Ryan settled into a small rented house on North Street, and Kenny got a job in charge of security for Fred Meyer's hardware and variety store. There he acted as a plain-clothes floorwalker and, sometimes, peered at customers through an aperture in the ceiling. There were, of course, wonderful opportunities for him to indulge in kleptomania, and he took equal pride in catching thieves and being one, but as word spread of his efficiency he landed a higher-paying position as a roving security officer for a company specializing in electronic alarm systems for private homes and businesses. He was given a company pickup truck for his patrols, and his business card proclaimed impressively:

Whatcom Security
Agency Inc.
The Total Security People
Captain Kenneth A. Bianchi
Operations Supervisor

Even better, his application for membership in the Whatcom County Sheriff's Reserves was accepted, and he began attending classes in police procedure: arrest technique, search and seizure, traffic regulation, firearm use, and so on.

To all appearances, family life and the move from Los Angeles were tonic to Bianchi. He was establishing himself as a respectable and socially responsible member of the community; he had the position of authority for which he had always longed. Yet all was not well with the inner Kenny.

Bellingham bored him. A town of about forty thousand inhabitants north of Seattle, less than fifty miles from the Canadian border, Bellingham lacked diversions appealing to someone of Kenny's sensibilities. It was situated on the Washington coast. No setting could be more beautiful, looking out toward the pine-covered San Juan and Vancouver islands and the Strait of Juan de Fuca. It was a paradise for the woodsman and the fisherman and for anyone fond of fresh air and water and the reassurance of a coherent community, where violent acts were neither common nor tolerated.

To Bianchi none of these virtues meant anything, and the very cohesiveness of Bellingham, its smallness, and its human scale were irritants. He could not be anonymous here. In such a place every citizen had an identity, an imposition painful to a chameleon, to a man who, himself being nothing, liked to pretend to everything. The people here were disconcertingly direct and sincere. The dramatic, primary blues and greens of the landscape and waterscape oppressed him, conjuring certainties, implying definitions. The blurry grays and browns of smog suited him better, the days of night; and at night in Bellingham the too-bright stars seemed to watch him like lidless eyes. There were no freeways here, no instant-access routes to anonymity where, sealed in his car with the music turned up, he could melt into the columns of millions on his way to another scam. Worst of all, in Bellingham there was no Angelo Buono.

Kenny longed for Angelo like a lover scorned. And as the days of the year began to shorten, bringing long northern nights and the steady rains of the Washington autumn and winter, Angelo came to haunt Kenny's thoughts more and more. He found himself thinking of Angelo day and night, images of strength and anger, Angelo grabbing onto some girl with his big hands, Angelo grinning, Angelo erect, Angelo taking what he wanted in front and behind, Angelo fingering a gun or deftly manipulating a roll of twine, Angelo a magnet to girls, Angelo looking on him, his own cousin, with scorn. Kenny's job, driving around checking on security systems, patrolling vacation houses left vacant until the next season, providing the illusion of safety to householders who were happily unaware that they had entrusted their lives and possessions to a murderer and a thief, offered few diversions. He had to content himself with stealing canned goods, telephones, gardening tools, books, light bulbs, storing everything in his basement, which soon resembled a fallout shelter. When Kelli would ask where he was getting all this stuff, Kenny would praise the generosity of the people of Bellingham, how neighborly they were, how everyone seemed to want to help out a newcomer. But he was lonely, his thoughts more and more drifting southward to Angelo as the winter darkness and dampness encroached, covering his thoughts like a shroud.

He did enjoy the authority of being Captain Kenneth A. Bianchi, Operations Supervisor, but the job left him much on his own, inviting him inward. At home he found that Kelli had lost her sexual appeal for him. At first he had made the excuse, to himself and to her, that it was difficult for him to see a nursing mother as a sexual partner, and Kelli had said she understood. Now he told himself that there was something inherently unappealing sexually about a woman who had given birth to his own child; and he and Kelli, when they were home alone together, were usually silent and distant from one another, Kenny browsing constantly in his psychology books. Lately, inspired by a pamphlet he had come across from the Bellingham Hypnosis Center, he had become interested in the subject of hypnosis because of the power it offered over others, and he was reading a book entitled *Handbook of Hypnotic Techniques*, by Garland H. Fross, a dentist.

His self-absorption and the absence of sex with Kelli led to masturbation, something his activities in Los Angeles had left little time for. A small rabbit-fur rug became his favorite masturbatory aid, because it reminded him softly of the great days with Angelo. He could rub the rug against himself even as Angelo had stroked his rabbits and dream of the spare bedroom or the orgy at the box factory or a girl being gagged in the brown vinyl chair. Once, after he had played with himself on the living-room couch and jerked himself off into the rabbit's fur, Kelli, cleaning house, found the rug stuffed under the couch, deduced what he had been doing, and confronted him with the gooed fur.

She was not angry, but she wanted to talk to him about it as a sign of their problems. Kenny denied everything.

"I'm sorry. I meant to tell you. I spilled some of that turkey gravy there. Just grabbing a snack. Wasn't that silly of me? I guess I was too lazy to clean it off. I've been working so hard. Sorry."

But the secret acts pleased him, and he continued with them. They belonged to him, and they were a way of recapturing memories more vivid than anything in his present life. A vision of Angelo with Sabra Hannan would always do the trick. Angelo's rough voice talking about Sabra's tits and telling her to shove the dildo up her ass was surefire. Beating Sabra. Angelo reaming Becky. Jane King resisting. Those little girls so hairless and helpless. The women and girls were merely characters to him; what mattered to him was that they pleased him. His memories served as a mental bank of videotapes that could be played at will for his morose delights.

These thoughts and acts came to sadden him, moving him to self-pity. He felt neither remorse nor anything like a post-masturbatory depression but a melancholy sense of the emptiness of his present life. Me then. And me now. It seemed that nothing could or would replace the days and nights with Angelo. To what new thrills was this new, regular family life of his leading? Where were the energies of the city, the slut-crowded boulevards, the evenings of promise? Was he now condemned to a lifetime of memories? Would he always be looking backward like some old man recalling the bold adventures of youth? As his spirits sank, his listlessness increased, and with it anger welled up in him, anger not at himself but at his circumstances and most of all at Angelo. Angelo still ruled his life. Somehow he must get rid of Angelo and at the same time prove to him that he, Kenny, was worthy of respect, had been the perfect partner all along and was also capable of autonomy. He must show himself his own man, deserving of recognition in his own right. Angelo must no longer think of him as a mere sidekick. But the more he tried to banish Angelo, the more he summoned him. Or did Angelo in some mysterious way will himself present to torture Kenny in reveries of painful pleasure across the hundreds of miles separating them? Kenny's obsession with Angelo intensified. He tried some new scams, telling girls he had met at Fred Meyer's store that he was going to open a photography studio, but his heart was not in it. He managed a couple of clandestine dates, achieving intercourse for a change, sending girls flowers and poems for Christmas, but memories of Colorado Street became all the more insistent.

Kelli got fed up. She told him that he was a zombie around her. A husband who changed diapers was nice but not enough. He did not seem to care even to take her to a movie. She wanted a man who could enjoy life. She suggested after Christmas that he move out. He begged to stay on. He wept, saying that his son was the most important thing in his life. He would get himself together, he said, urging her just to be patient.

Kelli's latest declaration of independence helped convince Kenny to act. He had somehow to prove that he was not a man to be trifled with. Gradually a plan formed in his mind. He would shake up this sleepy, complacent little town. He would bring a little of Los Angeles to Bellingham, a touch of California to Washington State. He would make a comeback.

With renewed energy, Kenny set his scam in motion. Captain Bianchi would use his position to achieve his secret goal, just as Angelo had used his badge and then his sheltered, secret house. How had Kenny failed to think of this before? Captain Bianchi had all kinds of houses at his disposal, empty vacation places just as safe and secluded or more so than Angelo's house had ever been. And he would out-Angelo Angelo. He would kill alone. He would make Angelo look like an amateur. Everything about the plan filled Kenny with eager anticipation. He moved swiftly to implement it, quickened by this new sense of purpose.

On Tuesday, January 9, Bianchi telephoned Karen Mandic, a girl he had met when working at Fred Meyer's hardware. Her roommate, Diane Wilder, answered, saying that Karen was out; Kenny left a message for Karen to call him. When Karen returned his call, he told her that he had a housesitting job for her if she wanted to make a hundred dollars. A new security system was being installed at the Catlow house on Bayside Drive, and the house would be without an alarm Thursday night. The Catlows would be away. If she would stay in the house, it would help him out. He suggested that Karen bring Diane along to keep her company. And one other thing. It would be better not to say anything about this to anyone other than Karen. The Catlows might not like the idea. She knew how people were. Karen said that she and Diane would meet him at the house at nine Thursday evening.

On Wednesday evening, Bianchi telephoned the Sheriff's Reserves office. He could not make the class on first aid Thursday evening, he said. Unfortunately he had to teach a class himself for his company.

The next twenty-four hours Bianchi spent in a dream. He made several trips over to the Catlow house to check everything out and made sure that their daughter, who was in town, was not going to drop by Thursday evening unexpectedly. He decided that the basement would be the best place for action and left a length of strong cord there. He did not think through the details of his scheme, so as not to spoil it. Improvisation had always played a part in Los Angeles, and not knowing everything that might happen added to his excitement.

It was cold and wet in Bellingham that night when Karen and Diane arrived at the Catlow house. Kenny was waiting for them outside in his Whatcom Security pickup. He suggested that Karen accompany him inside first to turn on the lights and check things out. They would only be a minute, he told Diane, and he was scarcely longer than that.

Inside, he urged Karen down the basement stairs —to check on the fuses, he said—and in the basement he grabbed the cord and wrapped it quickly around her throat from behind and strangled her with quick, fierce, and deadly force. She did not even have a chance to cry out. So great was his fury that the rope cut right through her flesh. He would worry about sex later. He hurried up the stairs to get Diane and wasted no time with her either. Once she stepped inside the door, he shoved her down the stairs and strangled her immediately.

It was done. Kenny was winded. He looked at the clothed bodies and pondered what to do next. He did not feel particularly aroused. More for form than from passion he opened his pants and masturbated over the clothed bodies as a last rite.

Where to dump them? He remembered a cul-de-sac near a school less than a mile away. He dragged the bodies one by one up the stairs and put them into Karen's hatchback Mercury. Then he drove the Mercury to the cul-de-sac, left it with the bodies heaped together in it, walked back through the rain to the Catlows', and drove his pickup home, disposing of the ligature on the way. It occurred to him that Angelo would have been useful during the dumping stage—as with Cindy Hudspeth's Datsun, Karen Mandic's car could have been driven to a more remote spot—but that seemed a minor inconvenience. Kristina Weckler and Lauren Wagner had been dumped almost as close to Angelo's house.

Climbing into bed, Kenny was careful not to disturb Kelli. He slept well that night, feeling disburdened, secure in the certainty that he had gained the headlines again and that he had done it on his own. He hoped the news would reach Los Angeles.

FOURTEEN

The news reached Los Angeles in ways Kenny had not anticipated. He was checking on security the next day at the South Terminal, a waterfront warehouse filled with canned salmon that he enjoyed stealing, when he was arrested on suspicion of double homicide. Karen Mandic had told her boyfriend about the housesitting job, mentioning Kenny's name, and in Karen's apartment the police found a note in Diane Wilder's handwriting saying that Ken Bianchi had telephoned. A search of Kenny's house turned up masses of obviously stolen goods, so the police booked him for grand theft as well, to make sure that they could hold him, first in the Bellingham City Jail and then at the Whatcom County Jail.

The Bellingham police, noting Kenny's California driver's license, telephoned the Los Angeles County Sheriff's Department to check on the suspect's background. They made no connection themselves between Kenny and the Hillside Strangler case, but their call was referred to Frank Salerno, who, once he heard Bianchi's Los Angeles address, knew what had happened. That telephone call was for Salerno a profane epiphany. In an instant the entire case broke open for him in a dizzying series of connections that had obsessed and eluded him since Halloween of 1977. From that moment Salerno knew that between the Hillside Stranglers and justice there stood only the law.

On Sunday, January 14, Bob Grogan answered a long-distance call from his partner, Dudley Varney.

"Where the hell are you?"

"Bellingham, Washington. I'm up here with Frank Salerno."

"What are you guys doing? Where in hell is Bellingham?"

Grogan was just unpacking from a trip to Greeley and Pueblo, Colorado. Another false lead to the Stranglers. A San Marino, California, socialite had charged her boyfriend with raping her in the Rocky Mountains. She said that the boyfriend had confided to her that he was the Hillside Strangler. Just another wacko, Grogan had concluded after interviewing the man.

"You better check on these addresses: 809 East Garfield, Glendale; 1950 Tamarind," Dudley Varney said.

"Check on those addresses? Dudley, are you kidding? Check on them? That's Kimberly Martin and Kristina. What's going on?"

Varney told Grogan about the phone call Salerno had gotten from the Bellingham police. Salerno had recognized what he was on to immediately when he traced Bianchi's driver's license. Now they were up in Bellingham and everything was breaking open. In Bianchi's house they had found a big stash of jewelry —rings, pins, watches, loose diamonds—and one of the rings matched the description of a turquoise one Yolanda Washington was supposed to have been wearing. A gold ram's-horn necklace matched Kimberly Martin's.

"What about the other guy?" Grogan wanted to know.

"There's a lead on that. Looks good. Bianchi's wife says his only friend in L.A. was a guy named Angelo Buono. It's his cousin. Some auto upholsterer on Colorado Street in Glendale."

"Kenneth Bianchi and Angelo Buono. Jesus Christ, Dudley, do you know what this means? That wacko German detective was right. Two Italians. He said brothers. Cousins is close enough. You said Bianchi has a *wife*, for Christ's sake?"

"Common-law. That's not all. He's got a baby. Little boy born right after Cindy Hudspeth."

"Excuse me," Grogan said. "I got to throw up."

"Yeah. I'm kidding Salerno about the Italian connection. Great family people."

Grogan immediately telephoned Joe Wagner and Charlie Weckler. The Wagners were moving up to Oregon, and the Wecklers were thinking of moving to Hawaii, hoping a change of scene would blur memories, but Grogan had kept in touch with both. Then Grogan got busy. He arranged for surveillance of Angelo Buono: an undercover officer would stalk him everywhere. Grogan checked Buono's address on a map. It made sense. 703 East Colorado Street was in the center of a circle formed by the locations of the body sites. Kristina and Lauren had been dumped almost in the same neighborhood as Buono's. But it was difficult to think of murderers living in Glendale, a peaceful community for Los Angeles, full of retired people and the silence of Forest Lawn. Casey Stengel had owned a house there and had died and was buried there beside his wife, and he seemed other than for his fame the typical Glendale resident, middle-American, down-to-earth, a relic of innocence.

Grogan telephoned Frank Salerno's new partner, Deputy Pete Finnigan, and arranged with him to go talk to Buono after Frank and Dudley returned from Bellingham with all their information. Bianchi was denying everything up there, including the two new murders, but Grogan was feeling optimistic for the first time in fourteen months.

In the next couple of weeks many of the pieces of the case fell together in spite of Bianchi's persistent denials. When LAPD Chief Gates gave a press conference announcing that a Strangler suspect was now in custody and released a photograph of Bianchi to the media, the undaunted Jan Sims telephoned the police again to offer her account of the Excalibur incident. This time Grogan and Varney interviewed her, and they believed her. David Wood, recognizing Bianchi's name, told a television reporter friend of his, Wayne Satz of KABC, about his experience with Becky Spears, and Satz talked Wood into flying to Phoenix in the company of a sheriff's deputy to interview her and Sabra Hannan, who was also living in Phoenix. They brought the girls to Los Angeles, where Salerno interviewed them and learned all the details of Angelo and Kenny's pimping operation and the names of other people who knew dark and valuable things.

Much to his relief, Salerno was able to persuade Wayne Satz not to air his videotaped interviews with Sabra and Becky until Angelo Buono was in custody. Grogan wanted to arrest Buono immediately, but Salerno's boss, Lieutenant Bullington, insisted that they needed more evidence first, ideally a confession from Bianchi. No one doubted that Buono was the other killer, but after all this time and the mistakes that had already been made, they wanted to be sure that they had the goods on Angelo when they took him. When Grogan learned that Bianchi had been interviewed so sloppily by LAPD officers in March 1979, he vowed to handle as much as he could himself from then on.

Grogan let only one day pass before going to see Angelo. On January 16 he and Pete Finnigan drove over to the Trim Shop, where they found Angelo seated behind his desk in his office. Finnigan, who had been Salerno's partner off and on since joining the Sheriff's Department in the early sixties, working his way up through vice and narcotics to homicide, had been assigned to the Strangler case the previous autumn. He had a special feel for the territory, having been born and raised in Glendale.

He and Grogan made a striking pair, this rare cooperative link between the Sheriff's and the LAPD, Grogan the looming Cro-Magnon, Finnigan about five nine, a fireplug with dark, curly hair, always a cigar in his mouth, his knobby face impassive, alert but unreadable dark eyes giving away nothing. Grogan as usual wore a light-colored suit, Finnigan a dark tweed jacket unbuttoned over his round belly. Only their Irish names made them alike. Grogan was garrulous and profane; Finnigan preferred to speak only when he had a point to make, and, like his partner Salerno, he rarely cursed.

It was only a preliminary visit this time, a way of feeling Buono out so they could decide how to go after him later. They found him cocky, not hostile but not giving an inch either. He pretended to want to cooperate. He admitted knowing Bianchi but implied that his cousin was pretty much a mystery to him. During this session they learned nothing except, to their surprise, that Angelo had married once more.

On January 28, they visited Angelo again. By this time Sabra and Becky had been interviewed, but again this was a preliminary session, so Angelo had to answer only general questions. They talked to him in his house and noted its extreme tidiness. Unaware as yet of the location of the actual murder scene or scenes, they could not apprehend the significance of the place. There was the gold-smoked mirror, the little sign saying "Please Remove Your Clothes," the brown vinyl chair, and, beyond the wall, the spare bedroom. They knew that they were talking to the murderer but not that they stood within the walls that had harbored his acts.

Angelo broke things off by saying that he had to go buy rabbit food. With his beak of a nose and his dyed black hair and crooked teeth and slurred, rough speech, he seemed repulsive to Grogan and Finnigan. As they drove away, Grogan said that he could not remember seeing a human being before who so closely resembled a piece of shit. Yet already they had learned of his reputation as a stud.

"Hard to imagine all those women going after that," Finnigan said.

"Must have a big dick," Grogan said. "We'll have to check his pecker out."

Salerno and Varney returned from Bellingham, and what were now the five principal investigators went over with one another everything they had on the case. They also consulted the Glendale Police Department. Bianchi, Salerno reported, was pretending problems with his memory, but the evidence against him was already conclusive as far as the Bellingham murders were concerned. And fortunately the courts in Washington were not as sentimental as the ones in California. Bianchi would get death unless they could get him to talk about the Hillside murders. Grogan and Finnigan prepared meticulously for their next interview with Angelo. They would lay everything they had on him and try to break him down. It might be that they could play one cousin off against the other.

One Tuesday, February 6, Grogan and Finnigan arrived at Angelo's at five in the afternoon, when they knew he would be closing up shop. They wanted no interruptions. Angelo had already figured out that he was being watched. He had popped into a police station one day to complain about it, the irate citizen invoking his civil rights. This time Grogan carried a little tape recorder concealed in the breast pocket of his suit. He switched it on as he approached Angelo's front door:

"Okay, it's two-six-seventy-nine and it's seventeen hundred hours. Peter Finnigan and Bob Grogan at 703 East Colorado, interviewing Angelo Buono. Maybe he's in the house."

Grogan knocked. No answer. He and Finnigan walked up the driveway toward the Trim Shop.

"Angelo," Finnigan called, "where are you hiding? There you are." Angelo was stitching the seat on a sports car. "How're you doing?" Music blared from the radio. Top-forty tunes.

"Hi, Angelo," Grogan said, affable as could be. "How're you doing?"

"Okay," Angelo grunted.

"Busy?" Grogan asked.

"Yeah."

"Well, that's good," Grogan said. "You're making money, anyhow. I wonder if we could take a little bit of your time and chat with you. I know it'll be a pain in the neck, but . . . ah . . ."

"Why not?" Angelo said. "I didn't have a good day anyway."

"We might as well put the finishing touches on it," Finnigan said, blowing cigar smoke.

"Gee," Grogan said, "that's a good car. Looks like an Austin Healy."

Angelo led them into his office, where they sat down, Angelo behind his desk. A buzzer went off on the wall. Angelo explained that that meant his wife was entering the house. That way he knew what was going on even though he couldn't see anything from his office. Grogan said that he understood that Angelo needed to watch his customers carefully. This guy, Grogan thought, lives like he's in a war zone. He remembered Becky and Sabra telling about how closely they had been watched. Grogan said that there were a few more things he and Finnigan wanted to clear up about Angelo's association with Ken Bianchi. The detectives asked Angelo about the restaurants he frequented, and Angelo named the Red Vest, the Copper Penny, and Henry's, before it had closed.

"Okay," Grogan said. "Did you ever go to the Robin Hood?" The question was important, because Salerno had found a waitress at the Robin Hood Inn who said that she had seen Angelo Buono talking to Cindy Hudspeth there, when Cindy had been a waitress. She had told Cindy not to give Buono the time of day; he looked unkempt and crude.

"Robin Hood? Where's the Robin Hood?" Angelo asked.

"Up here on Glendale Avenue."

"Is it an eating place?"

"Yes," Finnigan said. "Restaurant and cocktail lounge. Robin Hood Inn. You're not familiar with it?"

"It's on the left-hand side going up Glendale Avenue?"

"Yeah."

"Never been in the place," Angelo said.

"You've never been there?" Finnigan pressed. "Do you know if Ken has ever been there?"

"Don't know. I don't drink, so I don't go nowhere it has booze."

They asked him about other restaurants, about where he used to go with Kenny, about whether his father had been a policeman or a security guard, and about his new wife. Angelo seemed concerned that they believe that he was truly married. He brought out the certificate of his marriage to Tai-Fun Fanny Leung. The phone rang. "I'll get on his ass in the morning," Angelo said to whoever was on the other end of the line and hung up. Did he have his father's security guard badge? Angelo said no, he had never had it: "I didn't take nothing of my dad's when he died. They haven't sent me anything and I didn't ask for anything, and that's the way I left it."

"How about a gal by the name of Becky Spears?" Grogan asked abruptly.

"Becky?"

"Rebekah or Becky Spears." Grogan pulled a picture of Becky out of his pocket. "This gal here. Did you ever see her before?"

"The name don't sound familiar."

"How about a gal by the name of Sabra Hannan? We've got a picture here. See if you know her."

"What's her name?"

"Sabra. Sabra Hannan."

"I know her, Sabra."

"Where do you know her from?"

"From Kenny. I know her from Kenny."

"What's the relationship between Kenny and her? Do you know? Was it one of his girlfriends or what?"

"They had a thing going. They had a thing going."

"Who? Her and Kenny?"

"Yeah."

"Do you know J. J. Fenway?"

Angelo admitted knowing the owner of the Foxy Ladies outcall service and Fenway's driver, although he pretended not to recognize the driver's picture. He had met them "through another guy," he said. He continued to refuse to admit knowing Becky. To try to throw him off stride, Grogan then asked about Israel Katz, the delicatessen owner, and his daughter Marlene. Had Angelo helped Kenny with his pretending to be a movie talent scout to Marlene?

"No. He did that on his own."

"Were you there when it happened?"

"No."

"How do you know he did it then, alone?"

"How?"

"How do you know?"

"Her dad came over here asking."

"About what?"

"If Kenny was in the movies. I said I don't know what he's in, man. If he told you he's in the movies, he must be in the movies."

"Well, what did you think?"

"I think he was trying to, you know, fuck the guy out of something."

"Well, you knew Kenny wasn't in the movies. Did you tell her dad that?"

"No. I told her dad, if he said he was in the movies, I don't know, 'cause he came over and he asked me, you know, if your cousin was in the movies. I said wait, hey man, I don't know what he does. I said but, ah, you know, check on it. If he's in the movies, call the, you know, the studio."

"Well," Grogan switched back, "did you know either of those two girls, one who you said was Sabra?"

"Sabra."

"Sabra and the other girl who you didn't know the name of was probably Becky."

"Becky was—" Angelo stopped himself. "Sabra's friend was small. The girl was short. Short and thin."

"Well, we're doing a lot of fencing here with you, Angelo, and maybe, maybe we ought to stop fencing."

"Yeah. This is bullshit. Ask what you want to ask."

"And start telling you that we've talked to a lot of people."

"I assume you did and they all called me, man. Everybody you talked to calls me." Angelo was showing some irritation. Grogan hoped he was getting worried. "They went back over here and I talked to them."

"Hey, Angelo," Grogan said, "why don't we tell you where we're coming from, too?"

"Yes. Right."

"Well, we don't work prostitution or pimping or any of those crimes. We work murders, so we really don't care too much about prostitution unless it's directly related to what we're doing. Were you running broads?"

"Huh? No."

"Were you running broads?"

"No, I wasn't running broads. Kenny was running broads."

"Okay, did you ever have any sex with Becky Spears or Sabra Hannan? Here at your house?"

"Yeah."

"Were you aware how old they were?"

"Nope. The broads set up themselves."

"Out of your house?"

"Out of my house."

"And you knew it?"

"Uh-huh."

"You knew she was tricking out of your house?"

"Yeah."

"Which one?"

"Which girl?"

"Yeah."

"They both did."

"They were both tricking out of your house "

"Yeah, with Kenny's help."

"And Kenny was doing the pimping?"

"That's right. I don't have to pimp, man."

Grogan brought up J. J. Fenway again but got nowhere. He moved on:

"How about a girl by the name of Peaches?"

"Sure."

"Who is Peaches?"

"Peaches."

"What's her name?"

"I just know her by Peaches."

"Is she a whore or what?"

"Not that I know of."

"Did she live here for a while or what?"

"She used to stay here."

"Is she a black girl?"

"She is a Negro."

Grogan went around with Angelo about Peaches

but could not get him to pin down dates. The investigators had not found Peaches yet anyway and so had no idea what she might tell them. Angelo said that he thought she was probably someplace back East. Grogan had started to ask more about Kenny when a customer appeared.

While Angelo went out to deal with the customer, Grogan, first switching off his tape recorder, told Finnigan that he was going to try another approach:

"Okay, Pete. We're gonna squeeze the bastard. You can tell he's basically a coward. He's already trying to put everything off on Bianchi. He acts cocky but underneath he's yellow."

Angelo came back into his office and sat down behind his desk. Grogan stared at him, saying nothing for half a minute. Then Grogan got up, walked slowly over to Angelo, looking down at him, bulking over him. He began:

"You know about politics, don't you, Angelo? Right. Well see, we got a political problem here. We got one Strangler, we need to get the other, understand? And guess what. You're it. We don't even give a shit whether you did the murders or not, we've just decided you're it, Angelo, so you better start copping out, because if you don't, guess what, you're it anyway. Get me? You talk, maybe you won't get the gas chamber."

Angelo said nothing. The color rose in Grogan's face, and he started breathing heavily. Angelo showed some signs of alarm, looking down and away. I think I've got him, Grogan thought, I think the little shit is going to break. Suddenly Grogan reached down, grabbed Angelo by the shoulders, lifted him out of his seat, and screamed into his face, shaking him around like a toy:

"Listen, scumbag, you know what we know? Everything! No point wasting time! We know about Becky and we know about Sabra, we know about you beating them and threatening them and all of it! We got plenty to show you did the murders with your chickenshit little cousin! You keep shitting us you get the chamber, see, just like you electrocuted Lauren Wagner, just like you gassed Kristina Weckler!" He threw Angelo back into the chair. "I can't wait to watch you die, Angelo. We got enough on you now to fry you ten times. We know about David Wood, see, the lawyer you tried to fuck over. We even know where you picked up Judy Miller on Sunset, we got a guy saw you. You think Kenny's not ratting on you? You better get him first! We got somebody saw you pick up Lauren Wagner with Kenny. We got three people saw it. Talk! You motherfucking son of a bitch!"

"I didn't do no stranglings," Angelo said. "I never killed nobody."

Grogan knew then that he would never get Angelo to talk. For a moment there Angelo was so close to breaking, Grogan believed, so very close. But the only thing to do now was to get his lies on tape. If only I had just a little bit more on him, Grogan thought, I could break him. But the moment had passed. Grogan would have to play by the book from here on out.

"Okay," Grogan said to Finnigan, "if that's the way he wants it. Read him his rights." Grogan took the tape recorder out of his pocket, laid it on the desk, and switched it on again. Finnigan began:

"Two-six-seventy-nine, six twenty p.m. We're at 703 East Garfield."

"Colorado," Grogan corrected him.

"East Colorado, in Glendale. This is an interview with Angelo Buono, Jr." He went on to tell Angelo that he had the right to remain silent, to be represented by an attorney, through the Public Defender's Office if he could not afford one. "Do you understand these rights?"

"Yep." Angelo had looked frightened during Grogan's tirade, as though he wondered whether Grogan was about to execute him personally—correctly perceiving Grogan's fondest wish. But during the reading of his rights, Angelo had regained his composure, seemed even to have gained strength from having withstood Grogan's attack. He settled into his chair and started pulling on his earlobe, tilting his head as though he were about to entertain a business proposition.

"Okay," Finnigan said, relighting his cigar. "Do you want to discuss with us—"

"I will discuss anything you want to discuss."

"Without an attorney being present?"

"Why not?" Angelo lit up a Kool.

"Okay. Fine."

"That good enough?" It was as though Angelo wanted the detectives to think that he was doing them a favor. It took effort for Grogan to keep from bursting out again. His rage had been strategic, but it had not been an act. Watching Angelo, he thought of the Wecklers and the Wagners and wondered why anyone would think that this animal deserved constitutional rights when he had already forfeited his right to live. Simple execution was too good for him. He should be tortured first, have done to him what he had done to those girls, then killed and left in the desert to rot and be picked apart by buzzards.

Finnigan and Grogan now alternated asking Angelo questions. They started fresh, establishing that he knew Kenneth Bianchi and that Bianchi had lived with him at this address in 1976. Angelo fudged on Kenny's subsequent moves about town, but he admitted having been in the East Garfield and Tamarind apartments.

"Two times I went [to Tamarind], there was a girl there he was living with, a fat girl."

"Do you know Kelli?" Finnigan asked.

"Kelli?"

"The one that had his baby."

"Right. She was there two times or three times when I was there."

Angelo verified that Kenny had worked for a land title company and had applied to the LAPD Reserves, going on citizen ride-alongs. He acknowledged that Kenny had mentioned a Sergeant Mike Rhine in connection with his police applications. This explained to Grogan and Finnigan Bianchi's use of the name Mike Ryan when he had telephoned the Climax outcall service to lure Kimberly Martin. Sergeant Rhine had already said that people often confused his name with Ryan, and he remembered Bianchi as an applicant. If they weren't getting much on Buono, Grogan and Finnigan knew, at least they were building a good case against Bianchi. If they could do that, then it remained to tie the two cousins together. Grogan, not yet knowing about the inspirational role of a soap opera in the naming of Bianchi's son but having heard the boy's name, wondered whether Bianchi had been perverse enough to call his son after Sergeant "Ryan."

Angelo denied ever having owned a badge. He admitted having had handcuffs but said he had thrown them away when the key had broken off in them. Bianchi, he said, had never seen them. He denied having nude pictures of girls to show to customers: "No, I got girls with clothes on." He admitted having often ridden in Kenny's Cadillac and he remembered that the county seal on the windshield had come from one of his customers, a county employee. Had he ever seen Kenny with a police badge?

"He had something, but I could never swear it was a police badge 'cause you could go down to the swap meet and buy them. . . . They had everything in there, man, you could buy anything you wanted to. That's why I asked you guys, tell me something besides a badge 'cause those things are Mickey Mouse things, you can buy them all over town, man."

Had Kenny, Grogan asked, ever passed himself off "as a professional person, like an engineer, a lawyer, a doctor that you know of?"

"Yeah."

"Psychologist, psychiatrist?"

"Something like that, but then, maybe that ain't, it's something close to it, office he had or he was sharing or something with some guy, a professional guy, out in North Hollywood." He had visited the office. "And Kenny had things hanging on the wall like this other guy, certificates and things."

Grogan began turning the interview toward the Hillside Stranglings:

"Have you ever been to Forest Lawn Drive with Kenny Bianchi? Do you know where Forest Lawn Cemetery is off the Golden State Freeway?"

"Oh yeah. I take it go, when I go to Hollywood to visit my friend, I take that for a shortcut. . . . We might have took that road going to Hollywood or out there somewhere." It was faster than other roads, Angelo said.

Grogan and Finnigan named other locations: Angeles Crest, the Eagle Rock Plaza, La Crescenta. He had visited them all, Angelo said, with friends, with his children.

Grogan wanted to know what kind of a guy Kenny Bianchi was. Angelo provided this character analysis:

"Like I told you before, the guy'd give you the shirt off his back, he really would. You know, but he changed on me, he'd be a real nice guy when he wanted something and if he wants something and you don't give it to him, then he'd get upset, okay? He never got upset with me because, you know, I never had any reason to get him upset. You know, I used to loan him money, he'd pay me back. I'd never push him for the money because I knew he'd get kind of upset with me."

"Were you afraid of him? Did he have a bad temper?"

"Yeah, he had a bad temper. And I figure, you know, life is too short to get, you know, in a hassle for what, ten dollars, five dollars. I'd rather forget about it. Then don't loan him the money next time, see?"

Grogan showed Angelo photographs of the victims, one by one, naming them and asking Angelo if he knew them or recognized them:

Judy Miller:

"No."

Yolanda Washington:

"I probably saw her before. I might have saw her on TV. She's one of the girls who got strangled. . . . They had her picture on TV."

Dolly Cepeda:

"Kenny didn't bring her over . . . this girl was on TV."

Sonja Johnson:

"No, I don't know this girl. I think she was on TV, I'm not sure. They had a bunch of pictures on TV."

Lissa Kastin:

"She was on TV."

Jane King:
"No, she was on TV. This girl was on TV."
Kristina Weckler:
"I think she was on TV. I ain't sure."
Lauren Wagner:
"No. She might've been on TV. I ain't sure."
Kim Martin:
"I don't think I know her. I think she was on TV."
Cindy Hudspeth:
"She was on TV."

They pressed him on whether he had ever met Cindy Hudspeth, but he denied it. Grogan then asked Angelo specifically whether he was involved in or had anything to do with the Hillside Strangler murders, and Angelo denied it:

"Any knowledge I have is by the media."

Finnigan asked him whether he thought it possible that Ken Bianchi could have been involved in the Hillside Strangler cases.

"Could be, like I said before, you never know, the guy's mind could have jumped time or he might have had a revenge."

Grogan wanted to know whether, in watching coverage on television and in reading the papers, Angelo had formed any opinions about the Hillside Strangler.

"I don't buy no paper. Okay. Only thing I would know by the news media is with the TV if I don't fall asleep by eleven." But he went on to offer this interpretation: "I commented to friends of mine when they brought the subject up, and I said, you know, why didn't they look at two girls doing it or a guy and a girl. Because, you know, usually a girl will jump in the car quicker with a guy or a man and a woman in the car than with two dudes. Or she would jump in a car with two girls much easier. I don't hitchhike myself, never have. And you know, when a girl hitchhikes, she's taking her life in her hands, man, she doesn't know who she's getting in the car with. It could be a guy escaped from a crazy house and stole a car and driving down the street and see a girl hitchhiking and pick her up. What I tell my own daughter, my own

kids, even my boys and they can take care of themselves. I don't even do it."

"Did you ever discuss the Hillside Strangler
cases," Finnigan asked, "at the time they were on the
news, with Ken Bianchi?"

"Oh, we commented on it, Kenny commented on
it, I commented on it, like I said, I commented like,
you know, could have been two girls or a guy and a
girl doing it. And he didn't respond too much to it,
when I think back now. 'Cause my daughter just told
me he used to ask her, you know, he said you want to
go somewhere, I'll take you. So, you know, when, ah,
then he, ahm, used to see it on the news and comment
to me, he was kind of quiet about it. You know, he
said something, but not like me and you would talk
about it, you know, like two people would talk about it."

"Do you know of Kenny having any weird sexual
hang-ups?" Finnigan asked.

"I don't know. I haven't, ah, you know, been
double dating together and end up shacked up with
screwing the same broads. You know, everybody's
got funny things, you know."

Grogan inquired once more whether Angelo had
ever been involved in prostitution, with girls and
pimps and pimping.

"I never pimped any girls. If you call knowing
Kenny, hustling girls in my place, and that makes me
a pimp, then I'm a pimp. All the girls I know, if they
sell their butt, they're doing it without me. I ain't getting no money."

Finally, Angelo denied having contacted Kenny
since his arrest in Bellingham.

"No," Angelo said calmly. "I haven't even
talked to his mother and I'm surprised she hasn't
called me. She used to call all the time and ask me
how Kenny was getting along."

Grogan and Finnigan concluded the interview.
They had questioned Angelo for nearly two and a half
hours. He had contradicted himself at several points,
especially about whether he knew Becky Spears and
whether he knew about the prostitution, and of course
it was absurd for him to admit it had been headquar-
tered out of his own house and then to say he had

nothing to do with it. He had tried to paint Kenny as irrational and, absurdly, to depict himself as a concerned father. His theory about two women being the murderers was certainly unique.

"The creep will never admit to anything," Grogan said. "We might as well forget about that. He's the type would go to the gas chamber denying everything. And you know something? There are people out there would believe him. There are juries would believe him. They'd believe Angelo Buono is just a hardworking guy with all these kids to support. Just a guy who happened to get divorced and settles down with a nice Chinese girl twenty-five years younger than him. They would actually believe him."

Grogan got further insight into Buono's family life when he went to see Candy at the house on Glover Street. Candy was not reluctant to talk about her ex-husband, and perhaps the most important information she supplied Grogan was that Angelo knew Landa Street, the most obscure of the body sites, very well. She remembered his taking the family on a picnic to the "cow patch." She also described to Grogan the beatings she had endured, the threats against her life; she told him about Angelo's handcuffing her and tying her to the bed and about how Angelo would never give her any money for the children after the divorce. She doubted that her children would talk about their father. Her son Peter was afraid Angelo would kill him, and, in Candy's opinion, he would not hesitate to kill anyone who crossed him, including his own son.

When Grogan and Finnigan talked to Peter, he was so gone on drugs that he could barely speak, but he did manage to get out that his father would kill him if he talked. And when Grogan was interviewing Artie Ford, the story about Angelo's turning on the gas and not caring whether the kids blew up along with Candy came out, as did Angelo's boast that he and his sons had slept with his stepdaughter and Peter's statement that Angelo had had sex with him, too. Grogan wondered what else Angelo might have done; it was beyond imagining.

The police obtained a warrant to search 703 East

Colorado. They moved Angelo into a Holiday Inn for three days so that they could make the search as thorough as possible, but they found nothing. They used a chemical spray, ninhydrin, which was capable of revealing fingerprints even years old, but Angelo's tidiness paid off for him. No fingerprints of any age or kind showed up, not even Angelo's own. That a man could live for years in a house and avoid leaving a single set of his own prints seemed incredible.

Angelo bitched, of course, about being moved out of his own house, claiming that his rights were being violated, and he complained that his privacy was being invaded also by his being publicly identified in the newspapers and on television as a suspect in the Stranglers case. What if some nut should take it into his head to kill him, an innocent man? Angelo had good reason to be apprehensive about vigilantes. He received several anonymous threatening letters, which he turned over to the police:

> To Greaser Buono:
> You sure are guilty as hell. You are a perfect example of a sub-human mutation and your exist-ance [sic] is a disgrace to normal human beings. I pray to God someone kills you.

And:

> Mr. Buono, why don't you and your gook wife go back to New York where New York wops belong. We do not like your kind in Glendale.

Grogan hoped that no one would actually shoot Buono, only because there would be so much public sympathy for the assassin that it would create a messy public relations problem for the police who would have to arrest him.

Grogan now spent most of his days and nights interviewing anyone he could find who had had anything to do with either Bianchi or Buono, weaving together the hundreds of threads that bound the two. One Sunday he took his girlfriend—for so she had become and yet remained, the woman he had met through the case—out for a ride on the boat. He could not stop talking to her about Buono and Bianchi, and because the case had broken after Grogan and she had begun their affair, it gave them a common ground, far more than the usual connections for middle-aged lovers, more like the violent intensities of a wartime romance. When Grogan was not actually working on the case he was thinking and talking about it; at night he dreamed about it, reenacting the stranglings as he imagined them, Angelo's flesh-crawling voice ever in his ear.

That Sunday he piloted *Sunny* ten miles out toward Catalina Island and cut the engine, letting her drift. He sat in a deck chair in swimming trunks, a baseball cap on his head, fishing for yellowtail, drinking a Cape Codder, vodka and cranberry juice, a link to home. Here he was happiest, or as happy as he could be with his life messed up, rocked by the swell, breathing in the salt, thinking that this was the California he loved. Out there on the sea he liked to look back toward shore and imagine what the city had been before all the human beings had fouled it up. The California Indians had been so content, Grogan had read, that they had forgotten what war was and had been easy prey for the Spaniards and their militia-backed missionaries. Then there was the pueblo that became the City of Our Lady Queen of the Angels, a paradise for a while of sun and sea. But everything was only for a while. The good old days had lasted about sixty years. Looking windward, Grogan observed Catalina, a hump of the state preserved, owned for years by Wrigley, the chewing-gum mogul, a remnant, a deep-green bushy haven rising softly out of the ocean, beyond it nothing till Hawaii. Often he had dived for abalone there, spent cool-damp nights on the boat, moored in the quiet harbor of the isthmus, forgetting everything. But now he could not get Angelo Buono out of his mind.

"That is the coldest, most dangerous son of a bitch I have ever met," Grogan shouted at the sea. His girlfriend listened as she sunned herself on the deck. He rattled the ice in his glass. "That guy would stop at nothing, and look, he's lived in this town for forty years. Forty years! Like a snake. Waiting to strike. And look who he strikes. Lauren and Kristina. A guy like that, gassing's too good for him. You wouldn't believe how cold. And all those kids of his! But you just wait. Some nitwit is going to come along and say Angelo's mother was mean to him. Poor Angelo! I tell you this world is so fucked up it isn't even worth saving. We ought to never leave this boat.''

Another thing Grogan said he could not understand: how could all those girls go for Buono? He was so ugly! Slimy! But more girls were turning up every day. Frank Salerno had found another one. Frank had been over at the Trim Shop and Angelo had actually introduced him to her. She was Melinda Hooper. It so happened that she lived on Alta Terrace, just down the street from where Judy Miller had been found, so it was a great break in the case, it linked Angelo to another dump site. But what did all these girls see in Angelo? "I mean, this guy has shit coming out of his pores," Grogan said. "How do you figure it, K.O.?" Grogan called her by her initials, because, he said, she was a knockout. Sometimes he called her T.K.O.

K.O. said that she did not find Angelo's attractiveness to women so difficult to understand. It was like *Beauty and the Beast*. Even Quasimodo had his appeal. Some women thought ugly men were cute, like newborn babies, which was what Quasimodo's name meant in French. She started to explain, but Grogan cut her off:

"You're talking like a goddam English major."

But K.O. said that she could explain without recourse to literary references. Grogan had been talking so much about Angelo that her curiosity had gotten the better of her. She had decided that she had to get a look at the guy herself.

"You didn't go over there?" Grogan swung around and stared down at K.O.

"Yes, I did," K.O. said. "I went over to the Trim Shop."

"You must be out of your mind!"

"I pretended I needed some upholstery work done on my car."

"You talked to him?"

"He was talking to some other customers, they must have been. He gave me a look. I'll never forget it. He looked right through me. I must have been standing about ten feet from him. If I hadn't known who he was . . ."

"Yeah? You what?"

K.O. grinned. "I might have taken my clothes off right there. No kidding. The guy is magnetic."

"I suppose you think he looked like a newborn baby!"

"Well, not exactly."

"Jesus Christ! Don't you ever go near that place again! Don't you know we're getting calls from the neighborhood? People are afraid. They should be! Are you nuts? Are you kidding me?" K.O. shook her head. "Oh, Lord, what is life? Why didn't my mother tell me about life?"

Grogan put down his fishing pole and his drink and hurled himself over the side, disappearing, breaking the surface snorting, swirling and splashing, the large-hearted walrus.

FIFTEEN

Locked up safely in the Whatcom County Jail, Kenny Bianchi had little opportunity to indulge his inclinations to evil, but he could still lie. And he found several people important to his fate who were ready, for one reason or another, to believe him. His initial, foundational lie was that he could remember nothing about the night of January 11 except that he had gone out for a drive. He told his court-appointed lawyer, Dean Brett, that he was so concerned about his situation, so distressed about his apparent amnesia, and so horrified at the possibility, which he could scarcely imagine, that he had killed two people, that he was considering suicide. Worried about his client, Dean Brett called in a psychiatric social worker, John Johnson, to counsel Kenny.

John Johnson spent a great deal of time with Kenny during February and found it difficult to square his mild, intelligent, and sensitive personality with that of a multiple murderer (by this time Kenny had been publicly identified as a prime suspect in the Hillside Stranglings as well). After listening for weeks to Kenny's sorrows, his love for his mother, his concern for Kelli and Ryan, his shocked disbelief in the possibility of his guilt, his desire to regain his Roman Catholic faith, his belief in his fellow man, his love of children, his affection for nature, the pride he had taken in his work in Bellingham, his admiration for his deceased adoptive father, his respect for his mother's present husband, the high regard in which he held womankind—after weeks of this John Johnson ruminated on the various categories of neurosis and psychosis into which Kenneth Bianchi, murderer, might fit. How best, Johnson reasoned, proceeding deductively on the basis of his psychological training, could one label a man who had committed acts so at odds with his observable personality and his social and moral values, as manifested during so many hours of discussion? How could one reconcile Kenny's obvious concern for the welfare of his wife and child, who were visiting him regularly in jail, with his strangling to death at least two women?

His amnesia, Johnson thought, might well be a key. It just might be that Bianchi was suffering from a multiple personality disorder, a condition in which more than one person or personality appears to inhabit the same physical body. Certainly multiple personality disorder was a possibility worth investigating. Just as there had been *The Three Faces of Eve,* there might be three, four, or five faces of Kenny, each one unaware of the others. Johnson told Dean Brett about this possibility and hinted at it to Bianchi.

Kenny took the hint, leaped at it. He remembered having seen the movie of *The Three Faces of Eve* years before, and his considerable readings in psychology and psychiatry told him that here just might be a golden opportunity to beat this rap with an insanity plea. He would have to be careful. He would have to pretend complete ignorance of his supposed illness and yet manage to behave exactly as someone suffering from it might behave. This role would be quite a challenge, perhaps the greatest of his life, but if he could fool Dr. Weingarten into believing that he,

Kenny Bianchi from nowhere, was a bona fide psychologist and renting him an office, why couldn't he convince another shrink that he was suffering from some fantastic lunacy? As usual, Kenny had faith in his abilities and undying hope that somehow everything would turn out all right for him. And after all, he had already apparently convinced a highly educated psychiatric social worker without even trying, without even knowing what disorder was supposedly afflicting him. The rest might be a snap.

At John Johnson's suggestion, Dean Brett called in a forensic psychiatrist, Dr. Donald T. Lunde, author of *Murder and Madness* and a professor at Stanford University, to examine his client. The first interview was scheduled for March 11, and Bianchi tried to prepare for it by pumping John Johnson. Kenny was nervous. This new scam might be all that stood between him and the electric chair. In Washington, he knew, they still fried people.

But then fortune smiled on Kenneth Bianchi. On the evening of March 9, just two days before his session with Dr. Lunde, Kenny was flipping the dial on the television set in his jail cell and stopped at Channel 8, BCTV, whose signal came to him from across the border in Canada like a protective blessing from his guardian angel. The Friday Night Movie was, to Kenny's delight, the story of a multiple personality case, *Sybil*, starring Joanne Woodward, who had played Eve in *The Three Faces of Eve* and this time played the psychiatrist, and Sally Field, who played Sybil and her other personalities, including Vicky, Peggy, Marsha, and so on. What a break.

Kenny watched *Sybil* with all the intensity of a college student cramming for a final examination. He noted that as the mystery of Sybil's illness unfolded, tremendous emphasis was placed on the role of early childhood traumas. According to the movie, Sybil had been sexually abused, and her music teacher had been a tyrant. As an adult Sybil suffered from monstrous headaches accompanied by terrific noises in the head, and she endured frequent nightmares, many of them featuring little animals and fantasies of pursuit and entrapment. Dreams and headaches, Kenny told himself, headaches and dreams, I am going to have to have plenty of both. Watching Joanne Woodward brought back memories of *The Three Faces of Eve* which assisted Kenny in his research, and now he studied the kinds of questions she directed at Sybil, asking her what other personalities were inside of her and how she felt about one or another. "Marsha is going to kill Sybil someday," Sybil said. "Marsha is the only one with any *joie de vivre*." He watched as Sally Field skillfully took on the radically different characteristics of the various personalities. He concluded that he would have to invent someone opposite from his own sweet-natured public self, someone surly, foul-mouthed, and arrogant. Someone rather like Angelo. For the moment, he did not worry about naming this other self. A name would come to him in due time. He knew that if he overprepared, he might come off phony. After all, he was not supposed to know about these other selves yet. His performance, like Sally Field's, would have to suggest a tormented voyage of interior discovery.

As it happened, Dr. Lunde did not try to investigate the question of multiple personalities. He focused on Kenny's apparent inability to remember anything about the Bellingham murders, and he suggested that either amytal, a barbiturate sometimes given to reduce anxiety, or hypnosis be administered to explore Kenny's faulty memory. Kenny, of course, preferred to be hypnotized or rather to be given the opportunity to pretend to be hypnotized. He had read a book on the subject and he knew that no one could be hypnotized against his will. There was no telling what he might say if drugged, but if he could fake being hypnotized he might be able to convince anyone of anything. To his relief, Dean Brett decided to call in Dr. John G. Watkins, who had had extensive experience for over thirty years in the field of dissociative reaction, including amnesia and multiple personality.

Although it is the generally held view among psychiatrists and psychologists that multiple personality disorder is an extremely rare phenomenon, Dr. Watkins was one of a growing number of clinicians who believed that it was not nearly so rare as had been supposed and that amnesia could, more often than one might think, be a sign of the disorder, since one personality was typically unaware of what another had been doing, resulting in amnesic gaps. At least twice as many cases of multiple personality had been reported since 1970 as during the previous hundred years. Medical literature had become full of controversy about the phenomenon, with skeptics arguing that doctors themselves tended to induce the disorder by making implicit and explicit suggestions during therapeutic sessions, which usually involved hypnosis. The skeptics argued that too many therapists, egged on perhaps by the appeal of the phenomenon to the gothic corners of the popular imagination and insulated from criticism, or so it appeared, by the reluctance of professionals to call one another quacks, were finding multiple personalities with increasing frequency. A rapist, William Milligan, had used multiple personality disorder as a successful not-guilty-by-reason-of-insanity defense in Ohio in 1977.

Dr. Watkins, who was a professor of psychology at the University of Montana and a diplomate of the American Board of Professional Psychology and the American Board of Psychological Hypnosis, and who, like Bianchi, had a degree, although a genuine one, from Columbia University, was a firm believer in the prevalence of multiples. When Frank Salerno learned that Dr. Watkins was being called in to examine Bianchi, Salerno and Pete Finnigan rushed up to Bellingham to be present at the session. They knew that Dr. Watkins's participation represented a move toward an insanity plea, and they greeted that possibility with dismay; but they hoped they might catch Bianchi lying and that, perhaps under hypnosis, he would confess and implicate Angelo Buono.

On March 21, Dr. Watkins began interviewing Kenny in a small room at the county jail in the presence of John Johnson, Dean Brett, Salerno, and Finnigan. The detectives were there with the permission of the defense lawyer. A videotape machine recorded the session and all subsequent sessions.

Dr. Watkins began by telling Kenny that John Johnson and Dean Brett "felt that maybe I could be

235

of some help to you. I don't know if I can or not but maybe if we talk a little bit together, I could be of some help."

To Salerno and Finnigan, this statement was already a bad sign. Was Dr. Watkins here to make a diagnosis, regardless of the outcome, or was he here, as he said, "to be of some help"?

"I'm just here as a consultant and as a psychologist that may or may not be of some help to you," Dr. Watkins went on. "I know that you're in a lot of trouble and . . . it's not pleasant, I know, but how've things gone since you've been here?"

It's not pleasant for twelve dead girls, either, Salerno and Finnigan thought.

Kenny said that it was very hard on him. He had never been in jail before. He was trying "to make do and keep calm and keep my wits as best I can."

"You worry a lot, though, of course," Dr. Watkins said.

"Constantly."

"Do you dream much when you sleep?"

"Sometimes. It varies from time to time. There are some days when I can remember two or three dreams."

Kenny had the right dreams ready, but for the moment Dr. Watkins passed on to touch on Kenny's past life:

"John was telling me a little bit about your life . . . I understand it's been kind of a rough one, it hasn't been all peaches and cream, your life, all together. I thought maybe you might tell me a little bit more about you. . . ."

Kenny was prepared. He knew that he would have to come across as an abused child and that he somehow had to wriggle out of all the nice things he had said to John Johnson about his mother, so he began:

"If you would have come and talked to me about three, four weeks ago, you could have talked till you were blue in the face, for example, about my mother, trying to discredit her, and I would have fought you tooth and nail, thumb and screw. I mean, I would have disagreed with whatever you had to say bad about her because I've always had a respect and a deep love for

236

her. And on what foundation, I don't know. It's just something I've always felt, all these years. But now . . . seeing that I had problems, some more serious than others, which could develop into serious problems . . . it leaves a question there . . ."

"You mean," Dr. Watkins encouraged him, "you feel that maybe you've kind of forgotten the unpleasant sides of the pictures that might have happened then? . . . You're beginning—what you're saying in a sense is that the picture isn't as rosy as you thought of it . . . it's a lot less pretty than you thought it was. It's a possibility, you know."

"I know. I thought about it. It's like skeletons in a closet," Kenny said aptly.

Dr. Watkins praised Kenny's courage in facing up to his "problems" and his unrosy family life: "You've started on the road to becoming a more authentic person." (Salerno and Finnigan winced at this.) Dr. Watkins wanted to know whether Johnson and Brett had told Kenny anything about him.

"Ah, yes," Kenny said. "Your credentials preceded you." Indeed they had. One of Kenny's many psychology texts, *Handbook of Clinical Psychology*, even had a chapter in it written by Dr. Watkins.

Dr. Watkins remarked modestly that it was difficult to live up to one's credentials. What about hypnosis? Did Kenny know anything about that? What did he think about it?

"Well, I don't really know much about it," Kenny lied. "I've read a few things about it, but it was very minor, just in a small pamphlet once."

"And movies," Dr. Watkins said, "have a lot of scary stuff about [hypnosis] and so on and so forth and television."

"Oh," Kenny jumped in, "I don't pay much attention to what's on TV. Just a lot of junk, you know. I—the thing I feel bad about is that I'm locked in a little cell and I not only have to contend with myself, I have to contend with—the boob tube, you know."

"Yeah," Dr. Watkins agreed.

"It rots your brain," Kenny said ruefully.

"Yeah."

"But it consoles me once in a while."

In truth Kenny had had the chance to study *Sybil* yet again before meeting Dr. Watkins. The movie had been shown again on BCTV the evening of March 12, the day after the session with Dr. Lunde. When Dr. Watkins said that now he would explore Kenny's feelings about hypnosis, Kenny said that it would be a new experience for him and that he was fearful of what might happen, what he might find out about himself.

"It sometimes hurts," Dr. Watkins said. "It isn't always pleasant."

"Life isn't easy," Kenny philosophized.

"Huh?"

"As they say, life isn't easy."

"No, that's very true. . . ."

"Well, my curiosity has really been aroused."

After some brief discussion about how Kenny felt when he learned that he was adopted, about his father's death and about his dreams—"I imagine that some of the dreams you have are sort of upsetting and frightening," Dr. Watkins suggested—Dr. Watkins began his hypnotic induction, telling Kenny to take a few deep breaths, to stare at his hand, to feel heavy, "to really go down into the most beautiful and relaxed feeling," and so on. The induction took about half an hour, and then Dr. Watkins said:

"But I would like to kind of talk to you. And I've talked a bit to Ken, but I think that perhaps there might be another part of Ken that I haven't talked to, another part that maybe feels somewhat differently from the part that I've talked to. And I would like to communicate with the other part. . . . Part, would you please come to communicate to me? . . . And when you're here, lift that left hand off the chair to signal to me that you are here. Would you please come, Part, so I can talk to you. Another Part, it is not just the same as the part of Ken I've been talking to. . . . Part, would you come and lift Ken's left hand to indicate to me that you are here?"

Slowly Kenny raised his left hand.

"All right," Dr. Watkins soothed. "Part, I would like for you and I to talk together—we don't even have to—we don't have to talk to Ken unless you and Ken want to. But I would like for you to talk to me.

Will you talk to me by saying 'I'm here'? Would you communicate with me, Part? Would you talk with me, Part, by saying, 'I'm here'?

"Yes," Kenny said, his voice lower than normal.

"Part, are you the same thing as Ken or are you different in any way? Talk a little louder so I can hear you. Huh?"

"I'm not him," Kenny said.

"You're not him. Who are you? Do you have a name?"

"I'm not Ken."

"You're not Ken. Okay. Who are you? Tell me about yourself."

"I don't know."

"Do you have a name I can call you by?"

"Steve."

"Huh?"

"You can call me Steve."

"I can call you Steve, okay. Steve, just stay where you are, make yourself comfortable in the chair and I'd like to talk to you. You're not Ken. Tell me about yourself, Steve. What do you do?"

Kenny had had plenty of time to think up the right answer to that question. He sat slumped in the chair with his head bowed and swaying, feigning hypnotic drowsiness, sensing that his moment had come. He knew the evidence against him in Bellingham, and he knew that by this time both he and Angelo were prime suspects in Los Angeles. Finnigan and Salerno, who had been identified to him as Los Angeles detectives, were looking on. He knew that he now had to establish an alter personality at odds with himself, and so he answered straight away:

"I hate him."

"You what?"

"I hate him."

"You hate him. You mean Ken," Dr. Watkins asked helpfully.

"I hate Ken."

"You hate Ken. Why do you hate Ken?"

"He tries to be nice," Kenny said, letting his head roll around.

"He tries to be nice. I see. Well, tell me about, how do you mean—"

"I hate a lot of people."

"You hate a lot of people."

"He tried to be friends."

"He tried to be friends. Who do you hate?"

"I hate my mother."

Having put in place that foundation stone of analysis, Kenny rushed ahead to construct a conflict between Ken and Steve and to establish that Steve had forced Ken to commit the Hillside Stranglings:

"I fixed [Ken] good when he went to California."

"How'd you do? How do you mean? What'd you do?"

"I can't tell you."

"Huh?"

"I can't tell you. You'd tell Ken."

"He won't tell me," Dr. Watkins said, "so you got to tell me."

"I was with him one night," and Kenny paused to laugh, rather sneeringly, rather like a movie-version psychopathic killer. "He walked in on his cousin Angelo."

"Yeah?"

"And Angelo had a girl over." Kenny laughed again.

"Yeah."

"Ken walked in in the middle of Angelo killing this girl."

"Walked in on the middle of what?"

"Angelo killing this girl. I made him feel like he was a part of it."

"Now, who's Angelo?"

"Ah, some turkey he knows. His cousin."

Not content with supplying, along with his psychological alibi, the link between himself and Angelo, Kenny quickly went on to explain how Steve had supplied Ken with a motive, one neatly consistent with basic psychological theory as derived from Freud:

"I made [Ken] think all these real morbid thoughts."

"Like what?"

"Ah, like there was nothing wrong with killing

240

'cause it was like getting back at his mother, and I made sure he didn't really know what was going on. . . ."

"Did he go kill a number of them?"

"Yeah. He—I made him do it."

"You made him do it."

"He thought it was his mother, and he thought it was people he hated." This was a slip, since Kenny, as Steve, had already said that Ken did not hate anyone and was always trying to be nice, but if Dr. Watkins noticed the slip he said nothing about it.

"Yeah," Dr. Watkins said. "You fooled him."

"Oh, yeah, he couldn't figure out later what he had done and why." Here Kenny laughed again for effect.

"Did he forget it then that he did it, or not?"

"Yeah, I wouldn't let him remember that. . . . I made him strangle them all."

Kenny then went on to say that Steve had also made Ken strangle the girls in Bellingham. He made one more slip. In response to Dr. Watkins's saying that he must like to kill women more than men, Kenny, forgetting for a split second the distinction he had established between the two selves, explained why:

" 'Cause Ken hates women." But he caught himself, quickly interjecting: "I mean, I hate women." Again, if Dr. Watkins noticed the discrepancy, he said nothing about it. For good measure, Kenny had Steve say that he wanted to kill Ken, and he would make Ken die, somehow, echoing the dialogue from the film when Marsha says she wants to kill Sybil.

As he brought the hypnosis session to a close, Dr. Watkins gave Steve, or Part, or Kenny as Steve, or whatever Kenny had wrought, all the credibility Kenny could have wished for:

"Well, Steve," Dr. Watkins said, "I guess you can go back where you need to go. Just go back and sit down." Kenny was already sitting down. Had Steve been standing all this time? Can one personality sit while the other stands? Kenny, at any rate, stayed seated. "And I want to talk to Ken. You can stay under hypnosis, but Ken, I want to talk to you. Will you come back? When you're here, say 'I'm here.' "

"I'm here," Kenny said.

"Ken, do you know anything about Steve?"

"Steve," Kenny said, drawing out the vowel, knitting his brow.

"Does that mean anything to you?"

"Who's Steve? . . ."

Dr. Watkins told Kenny that "during the coming weeks" he would come to know more about Steve and in so doing become "stronger and stronger and stronger with each passing day," while Steve would become "weaker and weaker and weaker." He, Ken, would find out more and more "through thoughts, memories, dreams, and so forth" until he fully understood "what has happened." He would have more energy: ". . . more of the energy of your whole body is going to flow into Ken, give him strength and courage and memory, until pretty soon, there is just Ken. Do you understand that?"

"Okay."

Dr. Watkins counted to five, telling Kenny that he would be wide awake and alert. "Open your eyes."

"Hi," Kenny said, shaking his head. "God, what happened? I feel in a daze."

Dr. Watkins told him that he would come to understand in his own way, through his own strength, that it would be up to him to discover himself.

"Okay. Real good," Kenny said. "Thank you, sir. Thank you very much."

Watching all this, Frank Salerno wrote down in his notebook a succinct judgment: *"Bullshit."* That evening he and Pete Finnigan went to dinner with some members of the Bellingham P.D. at the Bellingham Yacht Club. Over many drinks they discussed what had happened, how Dr. Watkins had appeared to swallow the whole act, how Bianchi had slipped up a couple of times, forgetting whether Ken or Steve was supposed to be the good guy. When they telephoned Grogan to tell him what was going on, Grogan said:

"Okay, I got a great idea. The judge says to Bianchi, 'Mr. Bianchi, I tell you what I'm going to do. I am going to let Ken off. Ken is acquitted. But Steve gets the chair.' "

SIXTEEN

The detectives, sickened as they were by the prospects of having an insanity plea by Bianchi, could take some solace in his having finally fingered Angelo Buono. In anticipation of this break, Salerno had already contacted Markust Camden, tracing the itinerant bounty hunter all the way to Indiana a week after Bianchi's arrest. Salerno had several telephone conversations with Camden, who complained of problems with a wife or girlfriend; Salerno, commiserating with him, got Camden to agree to come to Los Angeles at some future date for another interview. Informed about Bianchi's arrest, Camden said that he recalled Judy Miller's introducing him to a "Kenny" at the hot dog stand in Hollywood, a guy who she had said was "strange" and "liked sex a lot." This turned out to be a false lead, but on April 11, during a break in the Bellingham psychiatric evaluations, Salerno got Camden a plane ticket to Los Angeles and flew down to interview him at the Gala Inn motel on Figueroa Street downtown.

Salerno arrived prepared with two mug runs—each a lineup of six photographs of male faces arranged in two rows of three—one run including a picture of Bianchi, the other one of Buono. Camden failed to respond to the run that included Bianchi, but when shown the other, he pointed immediately to the middle picture on the top row. "That's your man," Camden said. It was Angelo. Then Salerno showed Camden a blowup of the photograph of Angelo. How sure was he that this man was the one Camden had described earlier as a Puerto Rican who had driven Judy Miller away from the railroad diner in a limousine?

"I'm positive," Camden said. He added that he would be willing to affirm the identification under oath in court. Salerno put Camden on the plane back to Indiana, asking him to keep in touch if he moved again. He would definitely be needed at the trial.

All this was promising except for one unfortunate factor. Camden had been staying at the Richmond State Hospital in Indiana, a mental hospital. He had checked himself in, he said, voluntarily because he had become upset about troubles with his wife. To Salerno, Camden's stay in the mental hospital did not compromise his credibility—his story was the same as it had been before, and he had picked out Buono's picture with no hesitation whatsoever—but a defense lawyer might make something of it. Nothing about this case was simple.

At about the same time, Bob Grogan called again on Beulah Stofer—his seventy-fifth visit to her, Grogan estimated. He too had mug runs, but as soon as he suggested to Mrs. Stofer that she try to pick out one or both of the men whom she had seen abducting Lauren Wagner, she started wheezing and asked Grogan to leave. Grogan immediately withdrew, but in the next few days called her repeatedly, trying to calm her and telling her that she was in no danger but that what she knew was vital to the conviction of Lauren's killer. Grogan tried everything with her, but she was too frightened to cooperate, and she said she was worried that her asthma was getting worse. But finally she agreed to try to help. It had been her doctor, she said, who had convinced her. She had confessed to him what was on her mind, preying on her, and the doctor had advised her to go ahead and try to help the police. Holding back was making her condition worse, the doctor said. Her health required her opening up.

Again Grogan sat with her, soothing her, chatting aimlessly about anything that came to his mind, and then he brought out the mug runs. She immediately picked out both Buono and Bianchi.

Although from one point of view Mrs. Stofer had now become twice as good a witness as Camden—she picked out both suspects and was a more credible sort of person—from another point of view she posed serious problems. Grogan still could not get her to say what he believed was the truth: that she had gone outside her house to get a very close look. She had poor eyesight, and it was doubtful that a jury would believe that she could have seen Buono and Bianchi clearly enough through her window to identify them, particularly at night, when light reflections from inside would have made seeing even more difficult. Worse, shrubbery had begun to grow up in the yard near the fence, obscuring the view of the street, and by the time of a trial it might obscure it completely. And what would happen to her on the stand? She might have an asthmatic seizure and collapse entirely.

Meanwhile, Kenny, performing again as Steve for Dr. Watkins, added that the killings had taken place at Angelo's house, named Kristina Weckler as a neighbor at the Garfield apartments, alluded to dump sites off the Golden State Freeway, and spoke of alternating with Angelo in doing the actual stranglings.

He improved his characterization of Steve, building on his received hypothesis that Steve was supposed to be an alter ego, as opposite as possible from the kindly Ken. He added sprinklings of profanity—"They're fucking bugging me, damn it, leave me alone! Fuck what a drag, you know I just want to be me! Fucking shrinks!"—and a snarl to his delivery; and he laughed frequently, like the villain in a melodrama. The more extreme this bizarre impersonation became, the phonier it appeared to Salerno and Finnigan. Salerno wrote "bullshit" twice more in his notebook. But Dr. Watkins showed not a sign of disbelief.

Ken, Steve spat, was "an asshole" and "a motherfucker" whom Steve controlled totally. Steve had tricked or forced Ken into bad habits, not only murder but "thinking dirty" and smoking cigarettes. Kenny also had Steve develop a spontaneous case of faulty grammar—"We didn't keep no tabs"—and turned on the sympathetic, solicitous Dr. Watkins, calling him "a drag."

"All right," Dr. Watkins shrugged, "I'm a drag. I'm sorry."

The primary source of Kenny's creative characterization of Steve was Angelo Buono, the one person he had ever been close to who acted consistently like a classic tough guy and who certainly could be said to have functioned as Kenny's alter ego in Los Angeles. Angelo was indeed the perfect model for Steve, so like any artist Kenny was able to draw a character from life. But art too begets art, and Kenny also had in his mind the example of Sally Field portraying one of Sybil's alter egos as a rough-edged prostitute, the flying nun become a whore. Although his theatrical methodology was sound enough and his performance was convincing to Dr. Watkins, Kenny would never have passed a screen test. Or, to be fair to him, his acting never rose above the level of a primitive television series or the outsized gestures of the villain in an old B western. He might have been cast for a minor part in a high school production of *Guys and Dolls*. Still, as they say in Hollywood, you don't argue with success.

When Dr. Watkins dismissed Steve again for the day—"Well, nice talking to you, Steve. Why don't you just go wherever you need to go. I'd kind of like to talk to Ken now"—Kenny switched back immediately to his accustomed role as Mr. Nice Guy:

"Nice talking to *you*. Thank you, doctor. Have a nice trip, now."

Although he had now betrayed Angelo, Kenny had not done so without deliberation. After his arrest his first impulse had been to cement the pact of silence with Angelo and, he hoped, to use his cousin as a character reference just as he had done on job applications. Between the two of them, Kenny thought, alibis at least for the Los Angeles killings could be cooked up. He quickly wrote Angelo a letter alluding to their family ties. But Angelo's response had been a phone call to Kenny threatening to kill Kelli and Ryan if Kenny snitched. (Angelo used cryptic language, assuming that the jailhouse phone was bugged, which it was not, but Kenny got the message. When Kenny later disclosed the threatening call, Grogan and Finnigan knew that they had caught Angelo in another lie, since he had denied contacting Kenny in Bellingham.) On February 27, Kenny tried to reach Angelo indirectly. "Dear Mom and Dad," Kenny wrote to his mother and her second husband:

> Angelo took me in sight unseen [in 1976]. He's a loner and took me in. He may have been a criminal years ago, but he's got two [?] legitimate businesses and although not always Kosher, he's not a terrible egg. None of us are perfect. I want you to call him for me, see how he's doing. I wrote him to say hi. Tell him this, that I wish he could write the letter I asked him to write. . . .

> P.S. Don't tell Kelli. She dislikes Angelo because he used to tease her all the time.

Had Kelli known what Angelo had threatened she would have had a better reason to dislike him.

When even this roundabout approach to Angelo failed to produce so much as a friendly note—Angelo was not about to "say hi" to his accomplice—Kenny knew that his only hope to save himself lay in implicating Angelo; if he could incorporate the betrayal into the multiple personality act, he might walk. But, like almost anyone facing possible execution, Kenny was willing to try anything, and he could hardly be sure the multiple personality scheme would work. An alibi would be even better. He wrote again to his mother, this time enclosing a crudely hand-printed, supposedly anonymous letter that implicated a boyfriend of one of the murdered Bellingham girls. He implored his mother to fly to Seattle and mail the faked letter from there to the Bellingham police. She did not comply with her son's request, although she did come to Bellingham to see him. Alone and face to face with him, she could only weep, unable to doubt his guilt, feeling sorry for him but ashamed. Eventually she broke down and told the police that her son had been a liar as far back as she could remember.

But Kenny, ever resourceful, tried another woman. Angie Kinneberg, one of the girls to whom he had sent Christmas flowers in Bellingham, came to see him in jail, and he managed to slip letters to her, fifty-seven in all, and three postcards. He begged her to give him an alibi, to say that he had been with her on the night of the Bellingham murders: "If I had come over I could have you testify under oath of my whereabouts Thursday night. I have no alibi from 8:10 till 9:50 p.m." To Angie he maintained his innocence: "I could never take another's life. I was set up . . . I keep dreaming like an old Perry Mason show that all of a sudden somebody steps up to say I was with them the night in question." "Please help me if you can, I'm begging for my life. When I read the autopsy reports I became sick. Karen was a nice girl when I knew her several months ago. I'd like to get my hands on who did this to these girls." "If you can find the strength in your heart to help me you can include the times in your letter along with the place." To try to tempt her, he began talking to her about collaborating on a book about himself and alluded to a possible hundred-thousand-dollar advance. He professed his love for her and, of course, proposed marriage. Angie told Kenny's mother about the proposal; his mother said that Kenny would never get out of prison, so Angie might as well accept to make him happy.

Angie did go so far as to write Kenny a note that provided him an alibi, but, conscience-stricken, she told Dean Brett that it was a lie and asked him to tear it up. As Kenny's multiple personality ruse began to look as if it might work, he dropped the search for an alibi and admitted to Angie that his "other self" might have done the killings. He had been merely a "watchful voyeur." He could never take a life. That was the reason he had avoided going into the army. Even the thought of something like prostitution "turns me off. I've never condoned the selling of one's body for any reason. The body to me is sacred and I'm not even religious." He asked her to go to the library and read up on everything she could find on multiple personalities, to help him understand himself, he said. At the same time he began seeing a Catholic priest, Father Don Warner, and spoke of regaining his faith. Father Warner gave him a rosary, and Kenny began carrying it and displaying it during subsequent interviews with psychiatrists.

Two more doctors arrived to interview him, one at the request of the court, the other called by the Los Angeles County Public Defender's Office, but since neither employed hypnosis Kenny had to keep Steve under wraps. He concentrated on trying to depict his mother as "very stern on punishment," mindful that he had to appear to have been an abused child, and on inventing Sybil-like dreams. Like Sybil and Eve, he also announced that he was suffering from headaches.

To add to these orchestrated impressions, Kenny began keeping a diary, knowing that it would be read by his doctors. He managed to write down something in it almost every day, and by the time he was finished with it he had scribbled more than twenty-five thousand phony words. He emphasized lurid dreams modeled on Sybil's dreams, with recurring themes of entrapment, pursuit, violence, visions of escape or death. And he made sure to mention his mother frequently, always portraying her as a villain, himself as her victim.

Kenny's approach to his situation was something like that of a spy caught behind enemy lines. He knew what role he was supposed to play if his captors were finally to be convinced that he was genuinely what he was trying to appear to be. He knew the value that the enemy would place on documentation. If the documents were lacking, he would supply them:

I was running down a dark hallway—I could
see a light at the end—but I wasn't reaching it for
some reason—I ran and ran and finally reached the
end of the hallway, lighted and I couldn't move
forward.

At an amusement park I was on a roller coaster
ride, it never seemed to end.

He varied entries about such dreams with complaints
of headaches, and since he knew it was vital that the
doctors perceive him as helpless, he added vignettes
of himself as a timid little tyke:

There was a song popular on the radio—I used to
be afraid to go to bed at night—the name was
"one-eyed, one-eared flying purple people-eater."
My mother controlled all my relationships.

Occasionally his prose approached babytalk:

. . . for a while I had a pet duck—until it grew too
big. I used to like to pick those flowers that if you
suck on them they were so sweet. I remember having to go to bed if I didn't eat everything. . . .
When I was sick once my aunt brought me 4 books.
I remember being disappointed because she didn't
bring me a toy.

Kenny knew that it was important for him to try
to establish that he was capable of understanding himself—in the light of the already assumed perceptions
of the doctors—and therefore of becoming one day
"integrated" or cured. And so, in writing specifically
about his alter ego, Steve, he was careful to suggest
that he, Kenny, was making progress and that he was
beginning to figure out Steve's origins:

The name Steve that keeps popping into my
head has been familiar. I think I know something
now about myself—there is another stronger person inside of me. I think he calls himself Steve. He

251

hates me—hates my mom—hates a lot. I feel this person wants to get me. I've had dreams of someone who is a twin but he was exactly opposite from me—for the past few days I feel like my insides were at war—for the past two nights just as I'm about to fall asleep bits and pieces have been forming—the name—the struggle, me against him—in my dreams it felt like the body of the twin was exactly mine but the attitude totally foreign. I feel stronger but scared. I feel hate but I don't feel like reacting to the feeling. . . . Why does he hate me so much? Where did he come from?

And always he slipped in that his mother had caused this warring split in him:

I dreamt of my mother. She was yelling, screaming. I was backing down some stairs—she was slowly pursuing.

For good measure on April 17 Kenny began adding poems to his diary. Poems had been effective with women; they might make a doctor more sympathetic, too. In them he tried to create the impression that his poetry showed that through art he was able to express a new integration of personality—a somewhat clever idea, when one considers that from Freud on the psychoanalytic community has always considered art the expression of personality and analogous to dreams in its unconscious expression of inner conflicts:

I'm scared
   my stomach hurts
there's no place to run
now,
it was easy to run away
before.
I feel strong, in control
but still unsure
of someone I've come to know,
someone I don't understand

as well as I know myself now. . . .
I'm so alone now, somewhat
I feel naked.
I'm knowing me.
I wish I were free of him.
I want help.
I don't care for him
and he doesn't like me.
I feared confinement but
I'm thankful for it now.

Here Kenny picked up on Dr. Watkins's prediction that he would get stronger, become an "authentic" person. Kenny was clever enough not to suggest that he was already cured—he knew that that would appear premature—but that he was ripe for healing. He wanted to present himself as eager for treatment, so as to lay the basis for a verdict of not guilty by reason of insanity, to be followed by treatment in a mental hospital and a return to the world as a cured maniac. He would try to take advantage of a contemporary willingness on the part of the courts, the doctors, and, to a lesser extent, the public to forget about the real victims and to see the criminal as victim.

With Dr. Watkins's blessing, Bianchi and his lawyer made known to the court that they intended to enter a plea of not guilty by reason of insanity. The court, recognizing that whether Bianchi suffered from a multiple personality disorder now represented the crucial issue in determining his ability to stand trial, called in Dr. Ralph B. Allison, a psychiatrist from Davis, California, who had the reputation of being an expert on multiple personalities and was at the time completing work on a book entitled *Minds in Many Pieces*. Dr. Allison began interviewing Kenny on April 18. That morning Kenny wrote in his diary that he had had a dream the night before about his "twin":

He told me life wasn't what I thought it was like, he said there are no rules, you have to make your own, he said he wanted to get me away from people

I was leaning on for help. . . . He said he would hurt my kid. I became angry. I stood up and grabbed him, told him I didn't like him, I punched him, he broke free, I ran after and reached to grab him and he just disappeared. I felt an easy cool breeze, slowly it turned warm.

As if he worried that the doctors would be unable to interpret the significance of this invented dream, Kenny decided to help them out by suggesting an interpretation, which he added in the margin: "This doesn't feel like a dream, like the dreams I use[d] to have of my father it seemed so very real, too real. . . . If this person is more real than just my dream and if this is the same person haunting me, which is more than likely, then this person could have been responsible for the uncontrollable violence in my life, the instigator of the lies I've done, the blank spots I can't account for and the deaths of the girls; all the ones in California and the two here. But if he is insane, then he killed them using me—why can't I remember for sure I want to know if this is so." Make sure you don't miss this, doctor, the entry beckons.

But there was no chance that Dr. Ralph Allison would miss it. Dr. Allison was alert to every hint of the presence of multiple personalities. His new book was about them and he had already published five articles and for a time had issued a newsletter on the subject, and for the past three years he had moderated programs at the American Psychiatric Association meetings on multiples, as they were called in the trade. Dr. Allison thought that multiples were about the most exciting phenomenon current in psychiatry, and if anyone was going to recognize one, or them, when he saw it, or them, surely Dr. Allison would. Before the session he read over Kenny's diary, perused his medical records, and viewed the videotapes from the sessions with Dr. Watkins. He had seen Steve. He was ready, and Kenny was ready for him.

In a gentle, avuncular voice, Dr. Allison sat opposite Kenny in the small interviewing room and began by asking general questions about Kenny's life, tracing his movements from the East to California and up to Bellingham. Then he told Kenny to respond to certain finger signals which would, supposedly, trigger his unconscious memory. The number of fingers held up represented the years of Kenny's life, and when the fingers added up to a year that contained some memory, Kenny was supposed to tell Dr. Allison about that memory. At nine, Kenny began talking about his playmates at that age, and when he said that he had enjoyed playing games of hide and seek—"I like hiding. It's easy to hide away from everything"— Dr. Allison took the bait. If John Johnson and Dr. Watkins and *Sybil* had given him early leads and suggestions, he was now able to lead Dr. Allison—progress of a kind. Dr. Allison asked:

"Did you ever hide inside your own head?"

Kenny knew where to go from there:

"Sometimes, just to get away."

"What do you do in there?"

"Talk."

"Anybody else in there to talk to?"

This was getting to be old hat for Kenny now. But again he was duly cautious, not naming Steve yet. Kenny knew that he had to make Dr. Allison feel that he, the doctor not the patient, was bringing out the alter ego. Kenny identified the other person as simply "my friend."

"Who's that?" Dr. Allison asked obligingly.

"Stevie," said Kenny, adding the diminutive in consonance with a juvenile memory, or rather the invention of one. "He's my second best buddy."

So now Steve had an origin as Stevie.

"Does he have a last name?" Dr. Allison asked.

This question posed a challenge for Kenny. He had not anticipated being asked for a last name, and he did not want to screw up now, having come so far.

"He did have a last name," Kenny stalled.

"What was it?"

"I can't remember."

"Well, what's Stevie—"

"Walker," Kenny mumbled, barely audible.

"Walker," Dr. Allison repeated. "Where'd he get that name? Do you know his parents?"

"He didn't have any parents. Stevie was alone."

After further infantile excursions, Dr. Allison asked Kenny to grow up to his current age and said that he wanted to talk to Stevie now. "What's your name?"

"Steve."

"What's your last name?"

This time Kenny decided not to play the last-name game. He was uncertain about the wisdom of giving Steve a last name and decided to concentrate instead on getting into character as quickly as possible, so he replied:

"You're the motherfucker who's been trying to get me to leave [Ken]."

"You can't," Dr. Allison said.

"Fucker."

"What's your last name?"

"What business is it of yours? What're you, writing a fucking book?" To divert Dr. Allison further from the surname question, Kenny took out a cigarette and ripped off the filter, lighting the butt with his best macho manner.

"Ashtrays are in the chair over there," Dr. Allison offered.

"I know where the fucking ashtrays are, you don't have to tell me. Oh, fucking assholes, you know, I was doing fine, I come out whenever I fucking felt like it. Now you got to stick your goddam nose in this whole shitty mess. I was doing fine, you know. Now I can't even fucking come out when I want to."

Snarling and ranting, Kenny as Steve attacked Ken: "Fuck him, his mother too."

"She was pretty weird . . . ?" Dr. Allison offered helpfully.

"Fucking cunt."

"She was quite a bitch, wasn't she?"

"She was a fucking cunt. You know, he still puts up with her shit a little bit. You know, I mean, granted, I can't come out, but I can see what he's doing, and fuck, man, he has got to wise up."

"But you did get yourself in a jam."

"He got himself into a jam. I fucking killed those

broads, you know, to smarten him up, to show him that he couldn't push me fucking around.''

The idea of Ken pushing Steve around, rather than the reverse, was new, but Kenny pretended to rave on. He said that he, as Steve, had killed the Bellingham girls to get rid of Ken, to ''get him out of the way.'' This concept derived, of course, from Kenny's attempt to banish Angelo from his thoughts by doing murder on his own; in this sense Angelo remained Kenny's constant inspiration, acting not only as the model for the Steve character but as the source of Steve's motives, as Kenny invented them.

''Let me clue you,'' Kenny said, ''it's a fucked job you got.''

''True,'' Dr. Allison said, ''and that's—''

''You know, you should go out and live a little bit.''

''I find [my job] interesting.''

''I bet you do.''

''How about down in L.A., with Angelo?''

''Angelo. Now, he's my kind of person,'' Kenny said, silently indicating the Angelo-Steve identification but not so that Dr. Allison would notice it as the source of fiction.

''Um. How so?''

''He just—he doesn't care a fuck about life. . . . It's great. Other people's life. Doesn't give a fuck. That's great. That's a good attitude to have.''

Kenny went on to elaborate on the Angelo-Steve connection, describing how Angelo and Steve had killed the girls in Los Angeles, with Ken an innocent bystander. It was, with all the evidence against him, as close as Kenny could get to blaming everything on Angelo. But then, pride surpassing discretion, Kenny suggested that Steve had given Angelo the idea in the first place and that Steve had killed the first girl—''some black broad''—on the freeway.

When Dr. Allison began to press for details of the killings, Kenny, not wanting to reveal too complete a capacity for recall too soon, decided to heighten the impression of Steve as a wildly irrational creature, menacing, out of control. He jabbed the air with the defiltered cigarette and stood up, shouting:

"That's [Ken's] problem! It's not my fucking problem. I want him out of the way! You don't really know, you don't fucking understand that I want him out! I don't want to sit here anymore!" He took a swipe toward the videotape camera. "I don't want no fucking cameras! Turn that shit off!"

"Just sit down, sit down, sit down, sit down, cool off, cool off . . ." Dr. Allison held up his hand, as if trying to calm an evil spirit. "You don't have to talk to me anymore."

"That's right, I don't. And I don't fucking want to either!"

"Okay, you can go back where you came from."

"I don't want to. I want to stay now."

Kenny slumped back into his chair and pretended to fall into a trance.

"Ken's going to have to come out," Dr. Allison said, urged, seemed to pray. "Ken is going to have to come out! Come out Ken! Come out Ken! Ken?"

"Yeah."

"You here?"

"I'm here."

Dr. Allison pointed to the cigarette in Kenny's hand.

"When did I take this out of my pack?" Kenny asked in his sweet-tempered Ken-voice, acting for all the world like a bewildered child. "I don't remember taking it out of my pack."

"That's right," Dr. Allison reassured him. "You were in a trance at that time."

"Why's the filter broken off?"

"Just a hand broke it off. Don't you break off filters?"

"No," Kenny said, his voice rising in wonder, "I can't smoke a nonfiltered cigarette." The delicate boy.

"I guess somebody around here smokes without a filter," Dr. Allison suggested. "You ever found that before? Where and when?"

"At different times, you know, around apartments I've had."

Kenny was simply reacting to the law of supply and demand: if Dr. Allison wanted to know where and

258

when, Kenny would supply him with an answer. And Dr. Allison's voice was so soothing and encouraging. Dr. Allison said that it looked as though Steve had been at work again, as though Steve were a mischievous leprechaun. All at once Steve was now playing devilish little tricks on poor Ken.

Dr. Allison was relieved to be talking to Ken again instead of Steve. The doctor, although he had diagnosed many multiple personality cases before this one, had never talked to what he believed was a multiple personality who was also a murderer until Bianchi. The doctor had been frightened by what he perceived as Steve's murderous anger and was glad that, as he believed, he had succeeded in banishing Steve at a crucial moment. Dr. Allison considered himself lucky, although he also prided himself on his skill and bravery in dismissing this monster. He had feared that he was about to become Steve's next victim. Kenny's act had been that successful.

Before sending Kenny to his cell, Dr. Allison asked him to try to dream that night about Steve, unusual though it was for a psychiatrist to suggest the subject of a dream to a patient. He asked him to dream how "to cope with Stevie, with the aid of the highest elements of helping power inside [Ken's] mind. That will be the job for tonight." Dr. Allison's voice was soothing. He added: "I want you to keep that diary going! That's very, very important." Kenny could not have agreed more.

The next day Dr. Allison asked Kenny to see whether he could talk to Steve directly. Kenny responded with a rambling stream-of-consciousness monologue, or rather a bizarre imitation of one, in which he pretended to reminisce about childhood. He acted like a medium making contact with a dead relative, pausing from time to time to permit voices to pass over the great beyond. Dr. Allison was impressed. He said that it had been like listening to someone talk on the telephone without knowing what the party on the other end of the line was saying.

On the following day Dr. Watkins appeared again and presented Kenny with yet a new opportunity to dissemble. He administered a Rorschach ink blot test to Kenny; or, to put the matter more precisely, he administered the test first to Kenny as Steve and then to Kenny as Ken. Kenny, of course, knew the test well but pretended ignorance of it, not mentioning that he had often amused himself by administering it to Kelli and others and that he knew what sorts of responses would produce the right results. As Steve he pretended to see in the blots such intriguing phenomena as "two elephants fucking each other." In another blot he pretended to discern something "like somebody eating out a cherry broad."

"Eating out a what?" Dr. Watkins inquired.

"Cherry broad, man."

"Okay. Anything else?"

"Do you understand me?" Kenny asked, not sure that Dr. Watkins was up to Steve's vocabulary.

"Of course."

And on to another blot:

"Looks like Siamese twins, doesn't it, but it's not. It's a big dick. . . . It's two broads getting it on. . . . Looks like an abortion."

Then Dr. Watkins summoned Ken.

"Hi, Dr. Watkins. Have I been sleeping or something?" As he pretended to awake from the trance, Kenny made a fuss over finding his rosary on the table, saying he had no memory of putting it there and drawing a parallel between this mystery and that of the torn cigarette filter with Dr. Allison.

"What do you think happened?" Dr. Watkins asked.

"Steve again."

"Yeah," Dr. Watkins agreed. What would Steve think of next?

Kenny complained sorrowfully about the headaches he had been having.

"That's [Steve] trying to get out," Dr. Watkins said.

"I wondered why, 'cause I usually don't get headaches."

Now it was time for Kenny as Ken to take the Rorschach test. Where Steve had seen elephants fucking and so on, Ken saw people dancing in a discotheque, children playing London Bridge, two men carrying a bucket, a butterfly, a snail, a moth, a steamboat on the water, two little Indians, a leopard, rocks beside a pond, and the Asian continent. For good measure, not to appear absurdly saccharine, he added two dogs fighting over a bone and "an unborn fetus" as photographed by means of a "radioscoptomy."

"You, Ken, are getting stronger every day," Dr. Watkins said before leaving. "I don't know how everything's going to come out, but I suspect you'll be able to handle things better."

"It hasn't been easy for me," Kenny said.

To Dr. Watkins the Rorschach tests substantiated a diagnosis of multiple personality; but to verify the results, he forwarded them to Dr. Erika Fromm, professor of psychology at the University of Chicago. He told Dr. Fromm nothing about Bianchi, permitting her to assume that the subjects, identified simply as "Mr. K" and "Mr. S," were two persons.

Dr. Fromm wrote formal evaluations of the tests, finding "Mr. K" to be "on the whole . . . a near normal man, mildly neurotic, mildly introverted, who possesses a great deal of fantasy." "Mr. K" also "has greater creative ability than he actually makes use of in his ordinary life" and "spends a great deal of time in daydreaming." Of "Mr. S's" responses she wrote, however, that "this is one of the sickest Rorschachs I have seen in working with this test for more than 40 years. It is clearly that of a patient in whose mind sexuality and violent aggression against women are fused. I would expect him to be a rapist and a killer. . . . For the sake of society—as well as for his own sake—he should either be in prison or in a closed ward in a state hospital." Yet he was "not a psychopath."

Since she knew nothing of Bianchi's background, Dr. Fromm was not in a position even to guess that he might have faked both tests; her evaluations suggest that Kenny had managed to give precisely the impressions he had intended. In an informal, covering letter to Dr. Watkins, Dr. Fromm said that she wondered why she had been sent two such radically different personalities to evaluate: one seemed to her likely to be a criminal, but the other seemed so normal that she could not imagine why he should be in court. Was it possible, considering Dr. Watkins's interest in multiple personalities, that the two tests represented different personalities of the same man? One response by "Mr. S"—"Some cat got hit by a car"—made her wonder whether "Mr. S" might be a black man. The word "cat" might be black slang, "cat" referring to a man. If so, "Mr. S's" aggression would be directed against men as well as women. Yet he was clearly not a homosexual.

Dr. Watkins was now sufficiently confident of his diagnosis to give an interview to *Time* magazine. In the issue of May 7 he was quoted as saying that Kenneth Bianchi, "a very pure psychopath," had a *Doppelgänger* inside him who from time to time "seized control of the normally mild-mannered Bianchi." Dr. Watkins stated that he himself had been afraid of being attacked by Steve, who had first emerged when Bianchi was nine years old and was a product of Bianchi's unhappy childhood.

The *Time* interview was too much for Bob Grogan. Alarmed by what Salerno and Finnigan had told him about the goings-on in Bellingham, Grogan had been monitoring the videotapes of the psychiatric sessions: under Washington law "discovery" worked both ways; both defense and prosecution were entitled to review any evidence before it was formally introduced in a trial. Grogan had already formed a low opinion of Drs. Watkins and Allison. He was certain that Bianchi was putting on an act, and now, on a piece of plain stationery, identifying himself simply as an outraged citizen, he wrote a letter to Dr. Watkins in Montana. He attacked Dr. Watkins for the *Time* interview, calling him "a bush league unprofessional turkey" and accusing him of trying to get national publicity for himself at the expense of a fair and effective trial for a murderer. The sanity hearing had not yet been held. What right, Grogan asked, did Dr. Watkins, in violation of any sort of legal or medical ethics, have to give out his ridiculous diagnosis to a national newsmagazine at this point? At least the other doctors had been discreet. He signed the letter simply "Bob

Grogan," not wishing to take advantage of his police affiliation nor to end up being accused of trying to intimidate a witness.

Dr. Watkins replied, defending himself. When asked about Dr. Watkins's letter, Grogan said: "I counted nine typos. I'll bet because I called the guy a turkey he probably thinks my mother took away my Thanksgiving dinner. Maybe I shouldn't have pissed the guy off. If I ever murder anybody I might need him. I think I've got another personality inside me. His name is Derrick and he plays with his pee-pee and has a thing for shrinks."

SEVENTEEN

Kenny was delighted with the way things were going. He read Dr. Watkins's *Time* interview with pleasure and pride and said in a tape he sent to Kelli: "Things are looking really good. Dean [Brett] and a lot of other people know now that I'm not guilty. It's just a matter of getting all the data together." But just to be sure, he kept up the elaborate fiction of his diary, adding dreams and feigned realizations. When Kelli wrote him about an article she had read about Sigmund Freud, Kenny took the opportunity to give himself the benefit of a spontaneous Freudian analysis in his diary:

> In 1923 [Freud] finally set out his well-known triad
> of id, ego and super-ego. He proposed that the id
> is unconscious and the instinctional without moral
> judgment. That the super-ego is partly unconscious
> and represents the rules instilled by one's parents

and society—the voice of guilt. And the ego is the conscious ego which is able to relate and adapt to the outside world.

I think that the problem that's been is that . . . Steve could be part of the id . . . because the id is unconscious and instinctional without moral judgment. That's really an interesting hypothesis. Anyway, just thought I'd mention it at this time.

As always, modern psychological theory offered him an agreeable escape from personal responsibility. And he liked playing in his diary with the word "responsibility," as though it were something apart from himself, an idea, a thing, a curiosity, occasionally toyed with and questioned but never *assumed:* "I'm filled with this false sense of responsibility, not meaning that the feeling is false, meaning that I really shouldn't blame myself for what has happened. . . ." Always "what has happened," never "what I have done." To Kelli he said, as if congratulating himself, citing as usual a psychological authority: "John [Johnson] mentioned that in actuality I am a victim. . . . If you ever have any questions or don't understand anything about dissociative reaction, I'm not an expert but I'm gaining a lot of personal knowledge. . . . I hope the book I'm going to write will help people. This will be my repayment for what has happened. Now that I'm aware of what has happened, I would trade my life for bringing all those girls back. But that's not possible. Dean says I shouldn't blame myself. I wasn't responsible for what happened.

"Anyway, when you get the film for the camera, take a picture of the kitty for me. You know, I never realized before I can get shots for my allergy [to cats]."

He spoke to Kelli of his plans for the family after he was released. They would sit in the park and enjoy the air. He missed her cooking. Money would be no problem: "When I get out, honey, I know that the publishing deal's going to go through." The book would be a best-seller, and once it hit the best-seller list, there would be still more money: "That's the reality of publishing a successful book, a popular book." Fortunately "I won't even have to have the book started before they come across with the money. Just a contractual obligation."

Of course, Kenny did not tell Kelli that he had already proposed marriage and a book to Angie Kinneberg, nor did he tell her that he had asked Angie to spy on Kelli, whom he suspected of two-timing him. Perhaps Kelli could become his full-time secretary when he got out. As she knew, "every worthwhile thing in life is won with hard work and practice and patience."

Kenny always remembered his "dear son Ryan" in these letters and tapes:

> . . . Well, sweetheart, I think I'll end this for now. When I think of you and Ryan I have a tendency to get mushy. I don't want to get too mushy here. I don't know how you'll take it. . . .
>
> This part is for Ryan. *Ryan* [Kenny crooned, called], *Rrrryyyaaannn*. Daddy's here. Come on, Ryan. Talk to Daddy. Say hi. Say hi, Ryan. Come on, say hi. Come on, *tinkers*. My little *tinkers*. *Daddy's little man*. Perhaps Daddy will be home soon, sweetheart. I love you and miss you, you little man. Bye-bye. Bye.

The detectives were as depressed by the way things were going as Kenny was pleased, but they were not giving up. Meticulously they scanned the videotapes of the Watkins and Allison interviews, trying to spot a significant slipup. Not that they had any hope of convincing the doctors that Bianchi was pulling a scam. The doctors, Grogan said, obviously had a will to believe Bianchi. Grogan called them "true believers" and compared them to religious enthusiasts. He said that they approached the multiple personality idea as the church faithful view an apparition of the Virgin Mary. Bellingham was becoming like Fatima or Lourdes, and the next thing you knew Bianchi would start healing cripples. A political analogy also occurred to Grogan: "They believe in this thing like my father believed in the Democratic Party. It's like I told my dad, 'You'd vote for Mao Tse-tung if somebody told you he's a Democrat.' " But the prosecution was going to call in its own psychiatrists. Grogan knew one of them by reputation and predicted that this doctor, Saul Faerstein, would help to turn things around: "Faerstein's no fool. Faerstein's a hard-ass. He'll nail the bastard. I predict."

Then at last Salerno and Finnigan thought they might have caught something on the videotapes. It was indistinct, mumbled, but with the volume at full blast they heard Bianchi give Steve the surname Walker, and they heard Dr. Allison repeat the name. It rang a bell. Somewhere in Bianchi's papers, the ones discovered in his attaché case, they knew they had come across a reference to a Steven Walker.

They searched through the papers and found what they needed: the letter to the registrar at California State University at Northridge asking for a diploma with the name not filled in, signed "Thomas Steven Walker." The letter said that a ninety-dollar money order was enclosed, and the registrar or his clerk had stamped the letter "paid." The detectives also found Cal State transcripts with Bianchi's name on them. This was obviously another one of Bianchi's scams and fit in with all the other fake degrees and diplomas he liked to collect.

Salerno and Finnigan hurried down to Los Angeles and on to Northridge. They showed Bianchi's supposed transcripts to the registrar, who checked out the social security number and confirmed that the transcripts were actually those of Thomas Steven Walker. Then they traced Walker to his apartment in Van Nuys and, interviewing him, learned that he had responded to an ad in the *Times* and had forwarded his transcripts in applying for a job. A search of *Times* back issues revealed the ad, in which Bianchi had represented himself as "Dr. R. Johnson" but had given his Verdugo address.

They now had everything they needed to show that Bianchi had made the mistake of giving his phony alter ego the name of an actual person, but to round out the picture of Bianchi as the con artist of psychology, they went to see Dr. Charles Weingarten: Kelli and other witnesses had confirmed that Kenny had rented an office from a legitimate therapist, and his counseling-service flyers had listed the address. Salerno and Finnigan wanted to establish that Kenny had been able to fool a professional psychologist even before Bellingham. Dr. Weingarten, who had a gentle, even fragile manner, said that Bianchi had identified himself as a marriage, family, and child-guidance counselor and had said that he needed temporary space while he built up his practice. Dr. Weingarten described Kenny as "very sincere and pleasant" and said that the young man had discussed Gestalt therapy and transactional analysis with obvious expertise. The interview had taken about fifteen minutes. Dr. Weingarten had been reading about Bianchi's multiple personalities. "From what I've read about Steve," Dr. Weingarten said, "I feel I met Ken." Somehow it had not occurred to Dr. Weingarten that even as he had been duped, other doctors were being fooled now. But neither Salerno nor Finnigan had the heart to deepen Dr. Weingarten's disillusionment by asking him what on earth made him think that Steve wasn't just another Bianchi con.

By the time Salerno and Finnigan had completed all this important work, the prosecution had brought in a very big gun to train on Bianchi. He was Dr. Martin T. Orne, head of the Unit for Experimental Psychiatry at the Institute of Pennsylvania Hospital in Philadelphia and a professor at the University of Pennsylvania. Among other distinctions, Dr. Orne, who was Vienna-born, was considered the world authority on hypnosis and had written the definitive historical and clinical article on the subject for the *Encyclopaedia Britannica*. In that article, published in 1974, Dr. Orne took a cautious view of the uses of hypnosis and warned of its limitations and potential abuses. "In general," Dr. Orne wrote, "hypnosis cannot be induced against an individual's will." Of equal significance to the Bianchi case, Dr. Orne warned that "when unhypnotizable subjects are asked to simulate hypnosis, their performance can deceive experienced hypnotists. Simulating subjects convincingly perform extraordinary feats of strength and memory. . . ." Dr. Orne was also aware of the controversies in medical literature surrounding diagnoses of multiple personality disorder, and he was mindful that a defendant facing a charge of murder would have much to gain by faking insanity. Dr. Orne approached Bianchi with an open mind and in a truly scientific spirit, assuming nothing except the scientist's responsibility to prove or to disprove a hypothesis. In the forensic context of Bianchi's statements, Dr. Orne knew that he had to be particularly alert to possibilities of malingering. Diagnosis in such a situation, he knew, was a very different and more difficult problem than in the ordinary therapeutic context.

After reviewing the Watkins and Allison videotapes, Dr. Orne decided that his primary task would be to determine whether or not Bianchi had in fact been hypnotized. He noted that Steve had first appeared under (apparent) hypnosis when Dr. Watkins had said that he believed there "might be another part of Ken that I haven't talked to" and proceeded to summon that part. Dr. Orne also noted that Steve appeared to change or to intensify as the interviews progressed. In addition, Dr. Orne went through masses of material accumulated by the police which indicated that Bianchi was an accomplished liar. If Bianchi was faking being hypnotized, it would not prove that he was also faking the symptoms of a multiple personality, but it would obviously suggest that this was the case.

Dr. Orne had developed certain procedures which could help to determine whether someone was actually hypnotized or was simulating the state, and he decided to apply these to Bianchi without, of course, telling Kenny what was going on. Dr. Orne called these procedures double hallucination, single hallucination, suggested anesthesia, and source amnesia. Kenny's responses to three of the four indicated that he was faking being hypnotized.

At first Dr. Orne asked Kenny to imagine that Dean Brett was sitting next to him in an empty chair. Kenny did so, pretending to speak animatedly to his lawyer. Dr. Orne then pointed to the real Dean Brett.

Kenny explained that the hallucinated Brett was no longer there. But he overacted, rattling on in a manner that Dr. Orne knew was inconsistent with actual hypnosis: "Dean, Dean! How can Dean Brett be in two places?" and so on. In true hypnosis, the subject does not question the logic of the hallucination, and it was obvious to Dr. Orne that Kenny was trying to prove to him that he had actually experienced the hallucination, when he had not. Kenny also made the mistake of getting up and pretending to shake hands with the imagined Dean Brett. It was unprecedented for a hypnotized subject to attempt to have a physical exchange with a hallucination. Equally telling was Kenny's insistence that Dr. Orne himself "must be able to see" Dean Brett: the truly hypnotized subject simply assumes the induced reality. Kenny's final error was to ask the phantasmagorical Dean Brett whether he would mind being touched. Again, the truly hypnotized subject would assume that the hallucination would not mind if, as Dr. Orne did, the hypnotist says that it would not mind. The hypnotized subject accepts reality as defined, within limits, by the hypnotist.

The suggested-anesthesia procedure also worked on the principle that the truly hypnotized subject acts according to the logic of the hypnotized state, as defined by the hypnotist, not according to waking, normal logic. This test involved Dr. Orne's drawing an imaginary circle on the back of Kenny's hand and telling him that he would feel pressure when touched outside the circle but feel nothing when touched inside the circle. He was supposed to say "Yes" when touched outside the circle and, even though he could supposedly feel nothing, say "No" when touched inside the circle. By normal, waking logic, of course, the subject, supposedly feeling nothing when touched inside the circle, would say nothing. Kenny, seeing the test in this way, trying to prove he was really hypnotized, said nothing when Dr. Orne touched him inside the circle. But he was wrong. The truly hypnotized subject would have gone along with the hypnotist and said "No" when he was supposedly feeling nothing. Dr. Orne knew at that moment that Kenny was faking. Kenny thought that he had outsmarted Dr. Orne when in fact he had demonstrated that he was being logical and fully awake.

Kenny's reaction to the source-amnesia procedure, however, was inconclusive. In this test Dr. Orne asked Kenny three easy questions (including "What is the capital of the state of New York?") and one difficult question: "What color does an amethyst turn when heated?" Kenny did not know, and Dr. Orne gave him the answer: yellow. Dr. Orne then told him that when he woke up he would not remember yellow as the correct answer. Kenny did not remember, but this was an inconclusive response. About one-third of all deeply hypnotized subjects do recall the correct answer but cannot remember the source of their knowledge: sometimes they make up a source, such as a book or a college course. Thus Kenny's pretending not to remember the correct answer at all did not prove by itself that he was faking, only that he had failed to give absolute proof of having been deeply hypnotized, as he would have had he remembered the correct answer but not the source of it. Some hypnotized subjects behave as he had, failing to recall the correct answer altogether, so this test could not be used as certain evidence of his lying.

In sum, however, the tests added up to conclusive proof that Kenny was malingering, as Dr. Orne would phrase it, and his behavior in general convinced Dr. Orne that here was an actor. Kenny went through, as Steve, his cigarette-tearing routine again, once more expressing a childlike bewilderment afterward when he pretended to notice for the first time a heap of filterless butts in the ashtray. To Dr. Orne this was transparent fakery, not only because of the obvious overacting but because, having gone through the cigarette routine before with other doctors, Kenny, had he been telling the truth, would not have been surprised that the mischievous Steve had been at work again. He would have remembered what had supposedly happened with Steve before, since he had been told about it when awake, as Ken. And since he was faking amnesia now, Dr. Orne concluded, he had doubtless been faking amnesia from the beginning.

What had been obvious to commonsense detectives from the start had now been proved scientifically.

Kenny, unaware that Dr. Orne had tricked him into betraying himself, continued to add baloney to his diary:

> I just had my first session with Dr. Orne, nice guy. Strangest thing happened, we were doing the test for hypnosis and it seemed that I was dreaming that Dean came into the room only it wasn't clear. It was like I was seeing him in a strobe [light], and it looked like he was standing next to Dr. Orne.

There remained for Dr. Orne the question of multiple personality disorder itself. Dr. Orne cagily admitted to Kenny that there might be a problem with the multiple personality diagnosis. Although Dr. Allison had asked whether there were more than two personalities involved, so far only Ken and Steve had emerged. "That's pretty rare for there to be two," Dr. Orne suggested. Usually, he said, there were more than two. Three at least and sometimes eight or ten or more. Dr. Orne conducted this discussion when Kenny had not been hypnotized, or rather without giving Kenny the opportunity to pretend to be hypnotized. Dr. Orne wanted to establish that Kenny was reacting to cues and clues thrown out by the doctors. If Kenny was faking multiple personality, he would find a way to invent a third personality. Dr. Orne hinted that it was an important matter and that he was worried about there being only two parts.

Dr. Orne went through a hypnotic induction again and summoned Steve. He then sent Steve away and began exploring whether or not a third personality might exist. Kenny crouched down into his chair and began whimpering.

"Are you Steve?" Dr. Orne asked. "Tell me about yourself. What's your name?"

"I don't know."

"It's all right. Tell me."

Kenny began crying, like a frightened child, and pleaded, "You're not going to hit me, are you?"

"No, I'm not going to hit you. It's all right. I'm not your mother. She hit you a lot?"

"Yes."

All this was Dr. Orne's way of setting Kenny up. All he had to do was throw out a cue, and Kenny would pick up on it. Deliberately using the same language as Watkins and Allison, Dr. Orne then asked to talk to that "part" that was trying to get out, a "part" separate from Ken and Steve. Kenny was having trouble coming up with another name. Mewling about, he finally called his new self Billy. But poor Billy was afraid. Billy needed more time to come out. That was just fine with Dr. Orne: as far as he was concerned, Billy could keep his own schedule, there was no need to rush. Dr. Orne suggested that they break for dinner:

"Billy, all right. I will soon wake you and the next time, you may talk to me. Is that all right?"

"Yes," Kenny said, whining. Dr. Orne offered him a Kleenex.

Kenny had two hours to get his new self together, and, sure enough, after dinner Billy emerged right away. He was a little bitty boy. He did not know his last name. Did he know Steve?

"He's a bad egg," Kenny said in his new Billy-voice, small and scared, full of infantile metaphors. Billy did not get into trouble like bad Steve. Billy did not know foolish Ken. Billy liked to eat tuna fish, yum-yum. But under Dr. Orne's questioning, which deliberately suggested more of a role for Billy than a mere baby Kenny, Billy grew up a little and took responsibility for the psychologist scam in Los Angeles. He had just done it for fun, he said, posing as a psychologist. Dr. Orne told little Billy not to worry himself. That was not a serious crime. With his faint German accent that made sarcasm easy but not blatant, Dr. Orne remarked:

"Los Angeles people don't take these things that seriously. There are so many quacks." No doubt Dr. Orne was thinking of one or two quacks he had encountered himself.

"I was introduced to the existence of Billy," Kenny wrote in his diary that night. "I wonder what he's like."

Dr. Orne had proved that Kenny had been faking multiple personality disorder. All one had to do, he saw, was to suggest a new self and Kenny would invent one, given enough time and sufficient guidance. But, unlike Dr. Watkins, Dr. Orne did not take his findings to the press. Rather he kept them to himself until the appropriate moment in the judicial process, working over his conclusions and phrasing them precisely.

Dr. Orne was not one to criticize his colleagues; he was content to let his work stand on its merits. He went so far as to invite Drs. Watkins and Allison to write up their own diagnoses of Bianchi for Dr. Orne's *Journal of Experimental Hypnosis,* where he published his diagnosis as well. But later Dr. Orne did say publicly that it was probably easier for someone to fool a professional than a layman when it came to hypnosis.

Although they were deceived by Bianchi's multiple personality hoax, Drs. Watkins and Allison can in no way be accused of unprofessional conduct. In truth they were being so thoroughly professional that what was obvious to the layman was not to them. The detectives saw the fraud at once; a BBC producer who was filming a documentary about Bianchi sensed the fakery after viewing the videotape of one session with Dr. Watkins; a writer who was doing a book about the Stranglers recognized the sham at once; the writer's daughter, who was fifteen at the time and who knew nothing then about the case, happened to see five minutes of a tape showing Bianchi playing Steve for Dr. Allison and commented of Kenny, "What a lousy actor!"

How can it be that professionals were so easily hoodwinked? A key lies in Dr. Watkins's comment to the skeptical BBC producer that Bianchi could not possibly have known enough about hypnosis and psychology to fake multiple personality syndrome. Dr. Watkins said Bianchi would have to have had "several years of study in Rorschach [tests] and graduate study in psychology for him to be able to do that." So great is the belief of some professionals in the intricacy and obscurity of their specialty that they can become blind to the obvious. Nor was Dr. Watkins impressed by Bianchi's library of psychology texts. After all, Bianchi did not have a degree.

Fortunately not all professionals have so deep a belief in credentials. Kenny sensed right away that however friendly Dr. Orne had appeared, this psychiatrist might be less gullible than others. He actually seemed to be looking for the truth. Nor had Dr. Orne said anything about trying to help Kenny or even to cure him, as had Drs. Allison and Watkins. Dr. Orne was alarmingly precise and dispassionate. Kenny started trying to cover himself. He wrote in his diary:

> I don't envy [Dr. Orne] his position. I don't have any real ideas except I don't see how he can reach a definite conclusion. I'm beginning to wonder if the personality I've been told about is not being truthful with me (the Dr's that is). What bothers me is I'm told I have a problem, I'm told what it is. I'm told because I don't know, now I don't know what to think. . . .

In other words, Kenny was already trying to find a way of blaming Drs. Allison and Watkins for the entire scam, just in case he was found not to have multiple personalities. Something in Dr. Orne's manner—his scientific approach—had made Kenny begin to worry.

Dr. Saul Faerstein, who followed Dr. Orne, did nothing to reassure Kenny. Dr. Faerstein simply made Kenny talk, as Kenny, about his past and about the murders, and elicited a history of lies. "I had my first day with Dr. F[aerstein]," Kenny wrote in his diary on June 1st:

> He's not very objective. I can't help what my past was. . . . I know what he's shooting for and I don't blame him. But I don't understand what's happening to me. . . . I dislike it when people make up their minds before they get into a situation. He doesn't understand that there's a difference between knowing of doing something and having no control and *not* knowing of doing something, there-

fore having no control. He's definitely not objective. I don't think he really understands what's been happening in my life. . . . Dr. F[aerstein] feels, I believe, that if I have knowledge of things now, I've had such knowledge all along. . . .

When Kenny wrote that Dr. Faerstein was "not very objective," he expressed a quite reasonable fear that Dr. Faerstein was being entirely objective and was disturbingly, to Kenny, immune to the Bianchi charm and alert to the Bianchi lies. Dr. Faerstein's indifference to the Steve and Billy charade worried him, and after a second session with this alarmingly skeptical doctor, Kenny wrote a new kind of entry in his diary:

I, Kenneth A. Bianchi, being of sound mind and body, do hereby write this, my last will and testament. To my son Ryan I leave all my worldly goods, as little as that may be, it goes to him with my deepest love. It is profound to me that I have had to experience more confusion and mistrust and insincerity in society, if only the right people had been wise enough to follow through with their responsibilities, during the years of forming me into the mold of adulthood, I wouldn't be where I am now. There's a sadness in misunderstanding, an emptiness like a hollow egg. The egg which can produce life in two ways, one in creation and one in sustenance [sic] and not realizing the potential of either.

Of course, Kenny did not have to write a will to leave his son the only Bianchi legacy, malignity and shame. But the will does serve as testament to his final thoughts whenever he would come to breathe his last: Whatever I have done, be sure to blame someone else. The will is in its own way and with its banal final simile an eloquent statement of an approach to life not unique to Bianchi in the twentieth century.

But if Kenny felt discouraged, Dr. Allison did not. Dr. Allison reviewed the videotapes of Dr. Orne's interviews and, ignorant of Dr. Orne's techniques and conclusions, saw there not a refutation but further confirmation of a multiple personality diagnosis. Why, a third personality had emerged! Billy! If Billy would talk to Dr. Orne, surely Billy would talk to Dr. Allison. Here was a challenge. Now that Billy had arrived, could additional personalities be far behind?

Dr. Allison began his new interviews on June 28. (Bianchi had now been talking to psychiatrists and psychologists for three and a half months.) He began by telling Kenny at great length about the history of his involvement with multiple personality cases: the articles he had written, the book he was preparing, the oceanic vastness of his experience in the field. "I was the communicator between the psychiatrists around the world. I've been in India, Germany, United States, Canada, Austria. I sort of became the coordinator of passing information around because they were all very lonely out there. Nobody understood them. You think *you're* not understood: the psychiatrist who's treating such folks is also not understood by the other psychiatrists. . . ." Dr. Allison wanted Kenny to know that Dr. Cornelia Wilbur, "also known as Connie," was a personal friend. She was the doctor who had treated "Sybil." Did Kenny know that book or had he seen the movie? No, no, Kenny said. He thought perhaps Kelli had seen it, he was not sure. Well, Dr. Allison said, *Sybil* was "a super best-seller" as a book and "since that time they've made a movie out of it with Joanne Woodward playing Dr. Wilbur and I forget the name of the young girl who played the patient. She was formerly the flying nun."

"Sally Field," Kenny said helpfully.

"Sally Field, right. . . . Well, anyhow Dr. Wilbur got to be friends with me and when this case came up your attorney presented the defense that there might be another personality in there doing these dastardly deeds." Dr. Wilbur had actually recommended Dr. Allison for the present case, because she was seventy years old and he was on the West Coast and, after all, he was such an expert: "I have collected up to now fifty cases I've seen, which is not a world's record, but it's close to it. I know another psychiatrist who's had about sixty-five back in Philadelphia [and] one that had that amount in Honolulu. The three of us have the largest numbers. . . . I've got three in therapy right now in my clinic." (By 1984 Dr. Allison himself was up to seventy and closing fast on the Hawaiian.) Dr. Allison told Kenny that, sad to say, some psychiatrists were skeptical about multiples. Kenny shook his head. Gee, weren't all psychiatrists open-minded?

"No, I have to say that's not true. Well, anyhow, you're learning about psychiatrists. We can't help exposing some of ourselves when we expect you to expose yourself."

"I've already picked out my favorites," Kenny said coquettishly.

Having exposed himself at length, Dr. Allison now brought up a touchy issue. Why had Billy talked to Dr. Orne but not to him, Dr. Allison? "Somebody lied to me," Dr. Allison said.

"Steve," Kenny offered.

"I'm not trying to lay blame. I consider it like military secrecy. You got to have the secrecy clearance," Dr. Allison said. Why had he not received clearance? His goal now was to get that clearance and to find out more about Billy.

"I like you, Dr. Allison," Kenny said. "I feel comfortable with you."

Dr. Allison suggested that they would talk to Billy during the next session. He concluded this interview with a lengthy digression on the collective unconscious according to Carl Jung and further digressions on the "transpersonal self," seven levels of consciousness "and five more about that," Freud and ego theory, and "the source of all wisdom that we need to solve all these crazy problems while we live in this crazy world. . . . And heavens to Betsy," Dr. Allison said, "we all have to have some help for that!"

The next morning, preparing Kenny for the appearance of Billy, Dr. Allison told Bianchi to imagine that he had inside of himself a special force, almost like another person, whom he was to call Inner Self Helper, or Ish, for short. Ish would help him get in contact with Billy. Ish was strong and not a bit neurotic. Was he ready? All right:

"So now we want you to call out Billy. He's back

in there. He must respond to your call, and I want to hear both of you this time because I don't want only one side of the conversation. You call, 'Billy! Come on, Billy. I want to talk to you, Billy.' "

"Billy?" Kenny called. "Billy? Billy? Nothing, Dr. Allison."

Dr. Allison now assumed the voice of a kindly but firm schoolmaster:

"Billy? You get in there! Get in there right behind his eyeballs and you answer Ken's questions. Enough of this hiding! Time to get to work! I've never met you, but that's not important. . . . Get your rear end up there and get to work!"

"Nothing, Dr. Allison," Kenny said, teasing the eager doctor.

"Come on out, Billy! Billy! Come on, Billy." Now Dr. Allison sounded like a man calling a puppy dog. "Come on out, Billy! I know about you, Billy. *I know you met with Dr. Orne!*" Still Billy refused to budge. "Come on, Billy. Come on, Billy. Come on, Billy. Come on, Billy. Now is not the time to be shy, Billy! Come on out, Billy. Billy. Come on, Billy. Come on, Billy. Come on out, Billy."

Kenny, who had been sitting slumped, eyes half closed, now began to stir, raise his head. He looked Dr. Allison vaguely in the eye.

"You are Billy!" Dr. Allison said happily.

"Dr. Allison," Kenny said, very much like Stanley meeting Dr. Livingstone. This was a slip. Billy was not supposed to know who Dr. Allison was. But Dr. Allison corrected:

"You have not seen me before, have you?"

"Glad to meet you. No, sir."

"You hid out the last time I was here."

"Yes."

"Why did you do that?"

"I don't know. Just curious."

"Will you sign in, please?" Dr. Allison handed Kenny a pencil. It was just like the old TV show *What's My Line?* Kenny signed "Billy" on a piece of paper in childish script. It seemed to satisfy Dr. Allison.

Before he was through, Dr. Allison found yet another personality, which Kenny called Friend. Now there were Ken, Steve, Billy, Friend, and, if you wanted to count him, Ish. Quite a crew.

But Dr. Allison wanted to make sure that all these personalities would not disappear again. He made each one of them promise that he would return if summoned, even if asked to emerge by another doctor. Ken and Steve and Billy all promised to come back, and Friend promised to help. To dramatize this, Bianchi conducted a conversation among all of them: "Just call me," Steve said, "and I'll come out, if it's okay with you." "Okay," Ken said, "now I want to talk to Billy. Billy? Are you there?" "Yeah, Ken. What can I do for you?" And so on. Dr. Allison was delighted. Now would all the fellows write notes on pieces of paper?

"Sure. It's okay with me, doc," Kenny said. He scrawled a few lines for each personality, each in a different handwriting.

"A good job, Ken!" Dr. Allison said. "All hunky-dory!"

Alone in his cell the next day, Kenny, his hopes once more up, wrote in his diary.

Had my second visit with Dr. Allison. Accomplished a lot.

EIGHTEEN

"Those whipsock shrinks!" Bob Grogan cried after he had seen the new series of Allison-Bianchi tapes. "Too bad the Marx Brothers aren't still making pictures! I'd buy the rights myself!"

Grogan was enjoying a couple of cocktails with friends at the Nightwatch, washing his rage in laughter and Jameson's.

"You heard of *The Three Faces of Eve?* I call this one *The Four Assholes of Bianchi*. Let's see. Groucho would play Steve, right? Chico, he always had a scam going, he'd play Ken. And Harpo would be a natural for Billy, you know, shy, can't talk, sensitive. Zeppo, he never did much anyhow, he could play Friend. Wait a minute. I forgot about Ish. Fuck, I could play Inner Self Helper. I come out and jerk everybody off. It couldn't miss. Call Paramount! Get me Zanuck! And we'll hire Allison and Watkins as technical advisers. A laugh a minute. Get Angelo to direct—he knows all the right moves. I tell you, I've worked hundreds of homicides. This is the first one started out a tragedy and ends up a fucking farce!''

Grogan was laughing, but as he left the bar early that morning he took out his .38 and shot out two streetlamps.

After that episode Grogan started leaving his gun in the trunk of his car. He did not like carrying it anyway and saw his shooting out the lights as proof of his belief that if you were wearing a gun you were all too likely to use it. He would wear it when the time came to arrest Buono or if some other threatening occasion turned up, but for now he would leave it in the car. A couple of months later someone jimmied his trunk and stole his gun. Whatever could go wrong in this case, he thought, would. He was surprised the thief had not stolen the car as well.

In Bellingham, Bianchi spent two more days with Dr. Lunde and then the doctors were through with him. He stopped writing in his diary as soon as the doctors were no longer there to read it.

Dean Brett entered a plea of not guilty by reason of insanity, and the doctors presented their findings. Drs. Watkins and Allison agreed that Bianchi suffered from multiple personality disorder and was not competent to stand trial. Had their advice been followed, Kenny would have spent some time in a mental hospital and then would have been released, when it was determined that his personalities had been ''integrated'' into one big happy Bianchi.

But Drs. Faerstein and Orne stated unequivocally that Bianchi should stand trial, and Dr. Orne's systematic dissection of Kenny's act proved decisive. Salerno and Finnigan's discovery that Steve Walker was an actual person living in Van Nuys and not inside Bianchi was also important, although the multiple personality advocates argued that multiples often took the names of alter personalities from real life.

The Los Angeles County District Attorney's Office offered Kenny a deal. If he pled guilty to the Washington murders and to some of the Hillside Stranglings, he would get life with the possibility of parole and he would be able to serve his time in California, where the prisons were supposedly more humane than in Washington. Washington's Walla Walla State Prison had the reputation of being one of the most brutal in America. In return, Bianchi was to agree to testify truthfully and fully against his cousin Angelo Buono.

For Bianchi the choice was between death in Washington or life in California. Since this time the life involved was his own, he chose life. Besides, Kenny thought, plea bargaining was also a way for him to buy time. You never could tell what might happen in the months to come. To test his credibility and his willingness to talk, the Los Angeles detectives would now interview him in the Whatcom County Jail. If he proved a cooperative witness, the plea bargain would be formally signed. Kenny braced himself for interrogations he knew would be less pleasant than the ones with the doctors.

Bob Grogan was delighted that he would now get the chance to question Bianchi face to face, but he wondered how much he would be able to extract from a man for whom lying seemed not second nature but first. Grogan went over everything that was known about the Wagner and Weckler killings. It was about these that he would be the primary interrogator, and he would have to be able to check everything Bianchi said against the known facts. And to further prepare himself, Grogan went to talk to a psychiatrist friend of his, a man who worked for the Rand Corporation in Santa Monica. What chance was there, Grogan asked his friend, that Bianchi would now tell the truth? A very good chance, Grogan's friend replied. A man like that, fighting for his life, might well tell the truth now. But only once. He might, he probably would tell the truth now; but after that, in the weeks to come, he would start lying again and would probably contradict everything. Grogan had better get it all down the first time, because that would be it.

All the principal investigators, including one sergeant from the Glendale P.D., now gathered in Bellingham to interview Bianchi in the county jail. Roger

Kelly, the Los Angeles County deputy district attorney who had been assigned to the case, also came up to Bellingham to participate in the interviewing, and this annoyed Grogan. He did not like Kelly personally, and it was his opinion that Kelly's reputation as a skillful prosecutor of murderers was ill-deserved. Kelly had an excellent record of achieving convictions, but Grogan believed that Kelly avoided difficult cases, taking only those that offered a great deal of incontrovertible physical evidence. Grogan felt that Kelly did not have the will or the stamina to pursue a case in which most of the evidence was circumstantial and in which the principal witness was both an accomplice and an accomplished liar. Grogan, being Grogan, made no secret of his opinions, which Kelly denied publicly and vehemently.

Grogan hoped for the best. If he and the detectives did a good job of getting Bianchi's confessions, they might overcome what he perceived as Kelly's deficiencies. Their chief hope was that Bianchi would tell them things which he could not have known without participating with Angelo in the stranglings; they also hoped that Bianchi would supply them with new information which could help to convict Angelo. Under California law, the accused could not be convicted *solely* on the testimony of an accomplice; but if the accomplice's testimony was corroborated by other evidence, direct or circumstantial, it could be used to convict.

The first interview, conducted by Williams and Varney, dealt with Yolanda Washington, and it was not promising. Bianchi, although maintaining his typically polite, mild manner, gave no motive for the original Hillside Strangling other than his and Angelo's desire to get sex from a prostitute without paying for it. He refused to acknowledge that the turquoise ring found in his Bellingham house belonged to Yolanda, and he said that when they had dumped the body, they had covered it with a big log. No log had been found on or near the body. The officers pressed, but Kenny insisted that there had been a log.

Salerno and Finnigan, however, got better results

when they questioned Bianchi for two days about Judy Miller. His description of the abduction from the railroad diner jibed with everything Markust Camden had said, with one irritating discrepancy: Camden had described the car as a limousine and had said that Kenny's Cadillac had not been the car when Salerno had shown him a photograph of it. Kenny insisted that he and Angelo had used the Cadillac that night. It may have been, Salerno and Finnigan thought, that Camden simply took the big four-door Caddy for a limousine and then failed to recognize it from the photograph, but any inconsistencies in Camden's statement might spell trouble.

Salerno and Finnigan were highly detailed in their questions. They wanted to know what kind of rope or cord had been used, how long the strangulation had taken, whose idea it had been to perform this or that act. Of great interest to Salerno was Kenny's account of how Judy Miller had been blindfolded and with what sort of material: the wisp of fiber Salerno had taken from Judy Miller's eyelid had yet to be traced. When Bianchi said that he believed it was a kind of foam Angelo used in his work, Salerno knew that a most important piece of evidence might now materialize.

Salerno and Finnigan concealed their revulsion as Kenny recounted every detail of the killing with no more emotion than someone talking about what he had eaten for lunch. The cool, inflectionless voice; the way Bianchi said "Judy Miller" over and over again, running the syllables together, indifferently, with utter detachment, as though the girl had been a thing, a toy of no consequence—it was chilling and, at last, incomprehensible. They could tell a little about his thought processes from his grammar: always he discussed his actions in the third person unless he was asked specifically about what he himself was actually doing at one point or another. "I'm squatted down. My butt is around the area of her knees, which would put my knees in the area of her chest. I did this and simultaneously he put the bag over her head." But "she was squirming and arching her back and groaning and making noises, you know . . . the bag was put over her head . . . the body was placed . . ." as though something or someone other than himself had been doing all of this.

Salerno managed to elicit vital circumstantial evidence from Bianchi about the dump site.

"When we first went through this," Salerno said, "you were having difficulty recalling the dump site, and then something triggered in your mind about why that dump site was picked."

"His girlfriend," Bianchi said.

Salerno already knew that this was Melinda Hooper. He asked Bianchi who this girlfriend was.

"I don't know if it was his girlfriend. Some girl he knew, or he had gone over there to dinner. He knew the location. I don't know her name."

"Tell us about that. How do you know he knew? What conversation led you to believe?"

" 'Cause I asked him how he knew the spot and he pointed down the street and he said, 'Down there is the house where this girl, I've been over there to dinner and I know her father.' He's either taken her out or wanted to take her out or something like that. She was apparently really attractive. She was young."

Salerno pressed him for several minutes, then showed him a photograph of Melinda Hooper's house, which Bianchi identified as the one Angelo had pointed out.

Bianchi also told Salerno and Finnigan about trying to pick up Peter Lorre's daughter. This was something entirely new; they would check it out, along with a few other leads Kenny volunteered. Anything that added to his credibility would help.

Grogan and Varney's interviews were equally revealing. Only Bianchi's version of how he lured Kristina Weckler outside her apartment did not seem to ring true. Kenny said that he had invited her to a party, but everything Grogan knew about Kristina and her opinion of Bianchi made it unlikely that she would ever have considered accepting such an invitation. It must have had something to do with a police ruse, Grogan figured, tricking her in some way. The bull about the party was Bianchi's bizarre pride showing up. He would for the most part tell the truth, this time, as Grogan's psychiatrist friend had predicted, but he would still fib here and there, for reasons of pride and for devilment. He refused to admit stealing either Yolanda's ring or Kimberly Martin's necklace for the same reasons. To him being a thief was less glamorous than being a murderer.

When Grogan asked Kenny about the needle marks on Kristina's inner arms, Kenny added a needle mark on Kristina's neck. The left side, he said. Finnigan, who was listening in an adjoining room, looked at the coroner's photographs of Kristina and found the mark. No one had noticed it before. Even more revelatory was Kenny's description of the gassing. No one had known anything about the gassing before this moment. Grogan asked Kenny about what sort of gas pipe had been used, and Kenny described everything in convincing detail, down to the absence of a stove in Angelo's kitchen, the location of the outlet, and how the gassing had been accomplished. When Kenny described how the flexible pipe had been placed alongside her neck and the plastic bag pulled over her head and tied off around the pipe, Finnigan again checked the photographs, and, sure enough, there was a vertical line on the flesh, a bruise from the pipe that, like the needle mark, had not been noticed before. All this was not merely new information, it was proof that Bianchi was telling the truth.

In talking about Lauren Wagner, Bianchi was similarly detailed about the attempted electrocution, and everything he said about the abduction squared with Beulah Stofer's statements. He quoted Lauren as having said, "I love sex. It's no problem. I'll do whatever you want. I enjoy it so much that I just spent most of the day with my boyfriend. We've been doing it all afternoon." Grogan said nothing, but he believed Bianchi. Grogan knew that Lauren Wagner had been in bed with her boyfriend just before the abduction, and there was no way that Bianchi could have known that then, nor could he have discovered it since. It was not something Grogan told the press or the family.

"Ken, there's something that's bothering me," Grogan said after hours of talk. "Prior to your coming to California, Angelo Buono lived there alone. We didn't have any strangulation murders till after you came on the scene. Now, I talked to Mr. Buono and I've had the opportunity to talk to you and, I mean, I put my money on you in terms of intelligence and organization any day, rather than on Mr. Buono. What you tell us is kind of hard to believe, that Buono's the organizer and you're the follower." Time and again Kenny had described how Angelo had led him, had figured out how to pick up the girls, how to kill them, and where to get rid of the bodies. "I don't think you're a follower, Ken. I think there's some problem in that area. I don't know if you're being candid with us or you're just trying to lay all the blame on Angelo Buono and you don't want to accept any of it. You want to comment on that?"

"Yes. I think it's best not to short-change Angelo Buono. There's more there than meets the eye. This has been very obvious to me. I've had pretty close contact with him throughout this thing. . . . He can come off as a real dumbo, just really off the train. And it's not him. He's not the most trained person around but he's very, very, very street-wise and he's also a little wise in other things, too. He can come off any way he wants to."

"How'd it all start?" Grogan asked.

"I'm not going to sit here and say that there perhaps wasn't something in the back of my mind as a fantasy sort of thing. It may have been just the chemistry between two people."

"Did this become a sexual motive? Why the sex?"

"I thought about this a lot. Was this a thing to get the thrill of killing and the sex was just an extra bonus, or was the sex the main thing and the killing was just a necessity afterwards? I'm not sure. It could be either one of those. It could be a variation of both of those."

How lucid, Grogan thought. How perfectly well formed his thoughts are. He knows as much about it as anyone ever will, and he is telling us so. Of course, Grogan knew, Kenny was leaving out the original or immediate motivation, to take revenge for Sabra's and Becky's running off and for the bad trick list, which by now the police had become aware of. But all in all, Kenny was telling the truth. Sex or murder or a variation on both.

Nor had Grogan really doubted that Kenny had been more of a follower and Angelo more the leader. Kenny, Grogan believed, was a nowhere man; he was whoever someone else wanted him to be. He would never have taken this or any initiative on his own. After the Lauren Wagner interview was finished, Grogan drew his chair up to Kenny's as the others were drifting out of the room and talking among themselves.

"This is off the record, Ken," Grogan said, "just between you and me." Grogan wanted to see whether he could break through Kenny's psychological defenses. With Angelo he had tried, and failed, with threats and a little physical persuasion. With Kenny he would try the buddy-buddy approach.

"There's no tape recorder going now, Ken, and I'm not taking any notes and this isn't going to affect what happens to you one way or the other. You know something, Ken, I think you and I are a lot alike, you know that?" He let this sink in. Kenny said nothing. "I'll tell you what I mean. Look at us. Two Catholic boys from the East, right? Me from Boston, you from Rochester; Catholic school, the nuns, doing what's right, you know what I mean. Okay, then we get to California, and what happens? I tell you what. I meet a bunch of cops and I join the police force and, well, here I am. We both had that Catholic guilt, right? Don't do this, don't do that. And you wanted to be a cop too. We wanted the same thing, had the same background. But what happened to you? You meet up with Angelo Buono, you live with the guy, and what happens? All that pussy! Instead of all that don't do this, don't do that, suddenly it's do whatever you damned want. Pussy, dope, money. California! You just couldn't resist. You gave in and then pretty soon, what do you know, here you are! See? We're really alike. I could have gone the same way. What do you think?"

Kenny said nothing. He just stared blankly at Grogan. This guy, Grogan thought, is completely dead inside. He can't even pretend to believe me, because he knows it won't help his case. He can't even pretend if he doesn't think he's going to get something out of it. The guy is a zero. What a fucking shame he won't be executed.

Grogan did not bother trying to get through to Bianchi again. But Finnigan and Salerno could not let Bianchi go without telling him what they thought of him. After the Cindy Hudspeth interview, which was the last and took two days, Salerno was drained, but his hatred for Bianchi gnawed at him. It had taken hours to get Bianchi to admit that he had been up at Angeles Crest a month before the murder, that this was one dump site which he had chosen—he did not quite admit the latter but he almost did when confronted with Liz Ward's recollection of sex with him on the mountain trail. Liz Ward had recorded the event in her diary. Salerno and Finnigan also had the idea that Bianchi might well have known Cindy Hudspeth or have met her before the killing and might have lured her to Angelo's, perhaps telling her that his cousin wanted to take dance lessons, but Bianchi denied any of this. At the same time Salerno and Finnigan, through various trick questions, satisfied themselves that on the whole Bianchi was telling the truth in his icy narrative of the events. They tested him on his memory of the interior of Cindy Hudspeth's Datsun, for instance, suggesting at one point that the upholstery had been torn. When Kenny emphatically denied this untruth, he verified his general credibility. He insisted that the car had been pushed over the cliff front first, even though it had been found with its rear pointing down the mountain, and his version eventually checked out with informed analysis of the car's plunge and final position.

Salerno and Finnigan mocked Bianchi's multiple personality scam with sarcastic questions, referring to their own discovery of the real Steve Walker.

"Do you realize now," Finnigan asked, "that it was probably one of your biggest screwups, using that name [Steve Walker]?"

"I have no idea what it was."

"Of all the names you [could have] picked, you picked the one that could be traced. What were you going to do with those diplomas?"

"I have no idea."

It was highly irritating to the officers, not that it mattered as far as their case against Bianchi was concerned. But here was a man who would admit to murder but not to an error in manufacturing a defense, even when the error was obvious. They asked him why, given his deviousness, he expected them to believe anything he had to say. Why would he be telling them the truth now when he had spent his entire life telling lies? "I've learned from John Johnson," Bianchi had the nerve to say, "that it's the truth that sets you free." Salerno and Finnigan restrained their laughter.

Salerno felt about Cindy Hudspeth much the same as Grogan did about Kristina Weckler and Lauren Wagner. Although he had not become emotionally entangled with her mother as Grogan had with the Wagners and Wecklers, Salerno did feel rage against Bianchi for Cindy's death, and somehow he wanted Bianchi to know it. But he knew Bianchi would not care a damn about a homicide detective's opinion of him, so he thought and thought about some way to get through to him and make him squirm. At the very least Salerno wanted to go on record as despising him. At last Salerno decided to try to burn Bianchi with whatever might be left of a Roman Catholic conscience in the black recesses of his soul. At the end of the last session, Salerno said:

"Are you seeing a priest?"

"Yes," Bianchi said. "Father Don Warner."

"On a regular basis?"

"Yes. Every Sunday at least and sometimes a couple times a week."

"Are you a practicing Catholic?"

Bianchi hesitated. "Practicing Catholic?" he asked the air. He took the question as though he were being asked by a bank officer whether he owned a Visa card. "Yes, I am," he said at last.

"Does Father Warner bring you communion?" Salerno was thinking that for a Catholic to take communion without having repented of his sins meant eternal punishment. "Do you go to mass?"

"He brings communion. I don't go to mass."

"They don't have a service for mass in here?"

"No."

"He's heard your confession and all that?"

"That is correct."

"Do you believe in God?" Salerno asked, his voice with an edge to it now. Salerno for this moment was no longer a mere detective but the Grand Inquisitor. It was time, Salerno believed, for a truth greater than a legal or any merely mortal truth to be served. Again there were seconds of silence.

"Yes," Bianchi said blandly, "I do."

"Do you believe in hell?"

"Yes, I do. Some form of punishment. Yes."

"You had better," Salerno pronounced. He stared at Bianchi, hoping but not believing that he had made some impression.

Pete Finnigan wanted to put himself on record, too. He could not try to weigh Bianchi down with the weight of religious conviction because he did not share Salerno's intensity of faith, but he could make clear his hatred.

"Just so you know where you and I stand," Finnigan said to Bianchi, "it really galls me to spare you your life. The only reason we're going through this bullshit, as far as I'm concerned, is so that we can lock you and Angelo both up forever."

"Yes," Bianchi said quietly.

"Okay?"

"Okay."

"Well, I'm through," Finnigan said.

That night the detectives gathered at the Bellingham Yacht Club for cocktails and dinner: Grogan and Varney, Salerno and Finnigan. Bill Williams had already returned to Los Angeles. They were in a good mood, and they kidded Varney as he consumed dozens of steamed clams: Varney always wore cowboy

292

clothes and boots but never ate meat. They talked about how slithery Bianchi had been in the interviews, how he would give them a lot and then hold back a little. Some of his revelations, such as that he and Angelo had tried to pick up Peter Lorre's daughter, they would have to check out in Los Angeles; others they knew they would never be able to prove. But the important thing was whether Bianchi would be consistent in testifying against Angelo, because there was far more evidence against Bianchi than against Buono. They thought the plea-bargain agreement was regrettably lenient but probably necessary: Bianchi would plead guilty to the two Bellingham murders and would serve consecutive life sentences for those; in California he would plead guilty to five of the Hillside Stranglings (Washington, King, Weckler, Martin, and Hudspeth), one count of conspiracy to commit murder, and one count of sodomy, for all of which he would receive a sentence of life plus five years. Theoretically parole was possible. No one believed he ever would be paroled, but the idea of it annoyed them. To a man they wished him dead.

But they were men used to making the best of what was. Tearing into slabs of salmon, they anticipated the pleasure of escorting Bianchi back to Los Angeles. Grogan had chartered a private jet for the trip. It was a shame, he said, that Bill Williams would not be along for the ride. After a couple more bottles of wine all the detectives agreed to chip in and pay Williams's way up from L.A., so he could be in on the fun. "It's only right," Grogan said. He rushed off to telephone Williams.

Back at the table Grogan became philosophical. The world was turning rotten. In the old days men like Buono and Bianchi would have been hanged without claptrap and decent people could go on with their lives. Yet he wondered. The problem was with human beings, the world was populated by shits, history was nothing but betrayal and killing. He had been reading a book, *The History of the Irish Race,* by Seamus MacManus. "We were a great people," Grogan said. "Read that book. What happened?" He ruminated about what cold bastards Bianchi and Buono were. They were the worst he had encountered, but the world was full of such people. Not all of them murderers, but everywhere you looked there were cold sons of bitches who would as soon cut your throat as ask the time of day. His wife was a decent person. Did he know any others? The devious sleek self-gratifying phonies were conquering the world. You met them every day of the week. Businessmen. Reporters. Politicians. Policemen and hypocritical priests. Half-wit lying psychologists. Whores. Married whores. Fake waiters. Self-serving two-faced owners of newspapers. Everybody had a gimmick. America was Hollywood. If the truth were known, Grogan said, sipping, there were not a hell of a lot of good people in the world. Look at all the Hollywood assholes. Look at the Latin American community in L.A.: if he ever told the press, he said, what he knew about the Latins and their gang warfare, he'd be crucified. The Irish, they were always killing each other and stabbing each other in the back. It was funny. Strange. Everybody talked about how good people were, with all the evidence to the contrary. To listen to the Jews, you would think Auschwitz was an aberration. "It's not an aberration," Grogan said. "Don't people understand? World War Two was *normal!*" The truth was that it would be hard to find a table in the world like this one, with four good guys sitting at it and no sons of bitches. At least when they did something wrong, they felt guilty about it.

"You know, I kind of envy those two bastards. They can do anything and never give it a second thought. Me, I steal a newspaper and I feel like a shit. I must be an idiot. I look at another woman and I—"

"Okay, Grogan," Varney said, who knew about Grogan's girlfriend, K.O. "You're laying it on a little thick. Let's just say you're not what we call an asocial personality. Except I sometimes wonder about you."

"I'll tell you what it is," Grogan said, "it's my Catholic goddam guilt, and I know where it all started. I was a kid maybe fourteen, fifteen, back in Boston, see? That's when my guilt started. I walked into this shop, this little grocery store, and I was the only customer and this lady that owns the shop, she's standing in the back. So she motions to me to come into the back of the store. Okay, I go back there, and what do you know? First thing I know is, this lady, she was real attractive, about thirty, thirty-five, she's kneeling down and she unzips my fly and she starts sucking on my pee-pee.'' Grogan drained another glass. "And I didn't know what she was doing, you know, in those days, we didn't know from nothing. But it sure felt good. So afterwards I ran out of there and I went and told my buddies. They didn't believe me. They said, 'Grogan, you're nuts. No woman would ever put her mouth where a guy pees!' Anyway I knew what happened was a sin, see, it had to be a terrible sin. But I didn't know what it was called. Maybe nobody had ever done it before! Maybe I had committed the worst sin there was! I looked in my catechism and there wasn't any name for what I'd done. I knew adultery wasn't it. Maybe getting your pee-pee sucked was the sin against the Holy Ghost! So how was I going to confess a sin without a name? I couldn't see myself actually *describing* what had happened to some priest, he'd throw me out. So I never confessed it. I just kept it secret on my soul and it's been there ever since and that's why I feel so goddam guilty all the time. So who do I blame? I'll blame the Pope, he can take the heat! Pass the wine. Let's have cognac.''

The detectives discussed the mysterious relationship between Buono and Bianchi, what Kenny had referred to as the "chemistry" between them, as always viewing human behavior as the result of impersonal forces. Dudley Varney stressed a homosexual link and argued that Buono and Bianchi had actually been having sex with one another. Grogan doubted this, while accepting that Buono was basically a sodomite and didn't care what sex he plunged into. To Grogan, Buono and Bianchi had been engaged in a sexual competition, each one trying to prove to the other what a master he was of women. A competition like that was obviously homosexually inspired, but actual sex between the two would have spoiled the game. Of all the detectives, Salerno was most content simply to call Angelo and Kenny evil.

Neither the detectives nor anyone else had picked up on a revealing tidbit Bianchi had unknowingly dropped during the Lissa Kastin interview. He had said that Buono often called him by an Italian name during the killings. Bianchi had mispronounced the phrase, not knowing how to spell it nor its meaning:

> It's Italian. It's slang. *Minuni*. It means—I don't know—I can't really interpret it. It's more a feeling. It's a slang word in Italian and it has all different types of meanings. It means—it's not something really nice. It's not cussing somebody out, but it's not real nice. Like Dumbo or something like that, you know, it's just *minuni*. He used to call me *minuni* and he did that with Antoinette [Lombardo]. Called her *minuni*. She understood it better than I. You know, I've always had a feeling for what it meant, but she seemed to understand what it meant, and I never asked her about it.

No one followed up on the term; it seemed so trivial. The implications of *mi numi* remained hidden.

The mystery of the Buono-Bianchi relationship continued to haunt everyone, especially Grogan. Back in Los Angeles, he asked everyone who was willing to talk about it, and what he heard more than anything else was that the two cousins had appeared to hate one another and that Angelo especially was contemptuous of Kenny, throwing him out of the house and continuously bad-mouthing him as a lazy bullshitter. Finally Grogan went to see George White, Jenny Buono's second husband, the old Indian who had seen the family from the inside, but not as a blood relation. George White tried to be loyal to his stepson and, like the others, said that Angelo had hated Kenny. But Grogan probed and probed:

"I know you don't believe Angelo did anything, George, but just suppose for a minute, just suppose he did. Just suppose he and Kenny actually committed these murders together. How do you figure, supposing that, that these two guys who hated each other so much actually got to be asshole buddies, you know what I mean, that they ended up killing ten girls together? How would you explain that, George?"

George White said nothing, looking every inch the wise old Indian who knew secrets of the earth but would not disclose them. Then he sighed and fixed Grogan with a stare and said:

"Well, Bob, you know those Guineas. They stick together like stink on shit."

NINETEEN

The small jet, leased from Continental Airlines, taxied up to the terminal at the Bellingham airport and Grogan sauntered out to meet it. When the pilot descended, he said that he was there to pick up the Grogan party.

"That's us," Grogan said and waved to the others to climb aboard. From out of the terminal came the other detectives, including Williams, who had flown up that morning, and Lieutenant Ed Henderson, who, as head of the Hillside Strangler Task Force, had felt that he too should be along for the ride. Bianchi, handcuffed, marched among them. As he said goodbye to his Bellingham lawyer, Dean Brett, Bianchi mentioned that he had been reading a wonderful book, *Blood and Money*, by Thomas Thompson. Bianchi hoped, he told Dean Brett, that someday someone would write such a book about himself. Maybe Thomas Thompson would be interested in the story.

"Who's the prisoner?" the pilot asked Grogan,

who, like a scoutmaster, was ushering everyone aboard.

"You don't know?" Grogan said.

"No. I just got instructions to pick up Grogan and his party."

"That's the Hillside Strangler," Grogan said. "We're taking him back to L.A."

"No shit. The Hillside Strangler! Hey, that's great. How about I take her up to about thirty-five thousand feet and we open the hatch?"

There were just enough seats for everyone in the little jet. The detectives, plenty hungover, were in a festive mood. Lieutenant Henderson wanted to know how and why the hell Williams was on board, since he was supposed to be on assignment in Los Angeles, and Grogan said that it would have been a travesty of justice for Williams to have missed the occasion and that the other detectives had paid Williams's way up to Washington. It was the first and maybe the last instance in the history of Los Angeles that the Sheriff's Department had given money to the LAPD.

Grogan spent most of the flight taking photographs through the windows, talking the pilot into swooping low over Mount Rainier and other scenic wonders, so, as he said, he would have something to show his kids from the trip. After an hour or so Bianchi said that he had to go to the bathroom.

"I'll take him," Grogan volunteered. "Let me have the honor."

He guided Bianchi back to the tiny lavatory at the rear of the plane, holding the door open to keep an eye on him, telling him that he sympathized with any guy who had to open his fly with handcuffs on, thinking silently about how Kenny and Angelo had let Kimberly Martin go to the bathroom before they had killed her, as Kenny had blithely narrated. As Bianchi urinated, Grogan could not resist taking a peek at what had caused so much trouble and grief. He called back to the other detectives:

"Hey, you guys! I got new evidence! Bianchi here can't be the one that did the sodomy! He ain't got the *cazzo* for it!" (*Cazzo* being a strong Italian word for "penis" that Grogan had picked up as a kid on the Boston streets.)

There were no other gibes at the prisoner during the flight, but as Bianchi was making his way out of the plane, Dudley Varney whispered into his ear:

"You better tell the truth down here, Ken. If you don't, I'll personally escort you up to Walla Walla and give you a little present of a jar of Vaseline so you can enjoy getting what you gave to Dolly Cepeda and Sonja Johnson."

On October 22 the posse finally captured the Buzzard, descending on Colorado Street accompanied by the press and television reporters and their lights and cameras. Angelo affected his usual jaunty cockiness, strutting about as though he were a celebrity, which he was. As Grogan put the handcuffs on him, he asked Angelo for his wallet.

"I never owned no wallet," Angelo said. "Never owned a wallet in my life." But with one hand still free he reached into his pocket and pulled out a big roll of bills, fifteen hundred dollars, which he said should be given to the owner of the glass shop next door, who would pass it on to Tai-Fun Fanny Leung Buono. The police honored his request.

Grogan had not expected Angelo to surrender his wallet. It had, Grogan assumed, now become methane gas in a rubbish dump, like the victims' clothing. But at that moment Bill Williams was snooping around the little office in the Trim Shop. He opened Angelo's desk drawer and there it was, a light tan leather wallet. Williams flipped it open and found no police badge but two pinholes on the leather and, on plastic windows holding photographs of young girls, the distinct outline of a shield-shaped badge. Williams rushed out to show his find to the other detectives.

No one could imagine how the cautious Angelo, the guy who had not left a single other clue, could have been careless enough not to have disposed of the wallet long ago. At last they now had at least one piece of physical evidence, of Angelo's police ruse if not of murder. It was not enough by itself, but it was something.

In the county jail, Angelo was put in a cell on B row in what was known as the Highpower or special security section, reserved for prisoners who were either a danger to others or themselves in danger, or both. Two kinds of prisoners were automatically placed in Highpower: snitches (informers) and baby-rapers (rapists of underage girls or boys). Buono was in the latter category and if not carefully guarded and protected would have been attacked sooner or later by other prisoners. His fellow inmates on B row included a member of the Mexican Mafia who had a contract out on his life; prisoners who had assaulted deputies; a man whose father was a judge; an FBI informer; a parricide; a man whose father was a member of the state parole board; a member of the American Nazi Party; and, for several months, Peter Buono, in for grand theft, who was given a cell next to his father's. The police had hoped that Angelo and Peter might say something incriminating to each other, but they hardly spoke, playing checkers with each other through the bars. Angelo did make the mistake of speaking at one point to another prisoner, however, Steven Barnes, a former member of the Aryan Brotherhood, a prison gang he had betrayed.

"How come you killed all those girls?" Steven Barnes asked Angelo.

"They were no good," Angelo said, braggadocio overcoming smarts. "They deserved to die. It had to be done. But I only killed a couple of them. I ain't worried. My cousin's gonna go into his little nut bag."

Barnes reported the conversation to the police. Such jailhouse confessions were generally not powerful evidence, since the prisons teemed with men anxious to help themselves by snitching on others, but this one might help a little. The language, as reported by Barnes, was pure Angelo; several other witnesses, including Bianchi, said that "some girls deserve to die" was one of Angelo's favorite phrases, and it was unlikely that Barnes, who knew nothing about the psychiatric interviews in Bellingham, could have made up the bit about the "little nut bag."

Indeed, Bianchi had already gone into that bag. He had a cell in a separate part of the jail with his own television set, and from there he began a series of long letters to Dr. Allison—"the epistolary Strangler," Grogan dubbed Kenny—contradicting everything he had said to the detectives, pretending not to remember killing anyone, and reviving Steve, Billy, and the rest of his cast of characters. He said, of course, that he had been misunderstood and that he had implicated himself with Angelo only because the police "in their black and white minds felt I was putting too much blame on Angelo." He had confessed only to save his life, to make the plea-bargaining deal. He wrote similarly to Angie Kinneberg. And when Deputy D.A. Kelly talked to him about these letters, he defended them, pretending renewed memory lapses, protesting his innocence.

Kenny's motives in changing his story were simple. Roger Kelly had five Los Angeles murder counts dismissed. Had Kelly not dropped these charges, they could have been held over Bianchi's head as a threat to make him stick to his plea-bargain agreement. Now he no longer had to fear the death penalty, since he had already been sentenced for the five other Los Angeles murders and the two in Bellingham. But as a snitch against Angelo he would be subject to the code among prisoners of death to informers. Therefore if he could make himself useless as a witness, he could avoid "having a K-9 jacket put on him," prison lingo for being fingered as a snitch, K-9 being the classification for imprisoned informers. Kenny also hoped that by making inconsistent statements and by feigning memory lapses again, he might yet be declared insane, placed under psychiatric care, and released sooner or later. As usual, hope never left him and never did he give up scheming and scamming. In his mind his most serious problem remained the two Bellingham murders, for which there was such an abundance of evidence against him. He might wriggle out of Los Angeles, but how could he get his Washington conviction reversed? In time he devised a plan that he hoped would be just the thing to solve the Bellingham problem.

Early in June 1980, Kenny received a letter, sent to him in care of the county jail:

> Ken,
>   You don't know me but I would like to visit you. My name is Ver Lyn. I am a playwright and I am currently writing a fictional play entitled *The Mutilated Cutter*.
>   The story is about a female mass murderer.

The letter went on to ask Kenny if he would be kind enough to read a draft of *The Mutilated Cutter* and to help her with the characterizations. The playwright had never met a mass murderer, she said, and wanted to make sure she got things right. The letter was signed "Veronica Lynn Compton, pen-name Ver Lyn."

Veronica Lynn Compton was indeed a playwright and a poet, of the sort bred by the idea of art as self-expression and of the artist as a tortured soul at odds with society—society being, so the concept evolved, at once healthier and sicker than the artist, who was to have it both ways. It was a concept at least two hundred years old, but in later years it had become especially popular in Russia and in California. Veronica was also an aspiring actress and had put together a portfolio of herself with the title *A Star Is Hiding*, consisting of glamour photographs in which she smiled, pouted, grimaced, and displayed herself in evening gown, bikini, leotard, and merry-widow-plus-garterbelt. The final photograph showed her sitting awestruck at the feet of the director of the Actors Studio and was inscribed, "For Veronica, With hopes & best wishes for the future, Lee Strasberg." She had acted in various little theater groups around Los Angeles, and another of her plays, *Night Symphony*, had been performed at a theater in Hollywood and reviewed, negatively, in the *Times* and other publications. When not pursuing art, she was sleeping with various Hollywood types, including a lawyer-agent who later became the victim of an unsolved murder.

The Hillside Stranglings and all the publicity attendant on them had inspired *The Mutilated Cutter*. Her idea for the play was to add a feminist twist to multiple murder. The heroine—she planned to play the part herself—would strangle a female victim and then traumatize the corpse's vagina with a specially designed hollow dildo through which semen, previously collected for the purpose, would be squirted, thereby foiling and thwarting the male-dominated oppressive forces of society and the law.

Kenny at first made no response to the letter, but Veronica persisted. In every sense, she was a striking woman. Twenty-three, in appearance a dark, Latin spitfire, her burnished flesh emanating equatorial heat, she had been baptized Veronica Lynn Barrera de Campero. Her figure merited an *olé;* she was a beauty except for her nose, which was upturned to the point of snoutishness and lent to her face a porcine effect. She wrote Kenny several times again in quick succession: she had seen him on television, and never had she been so moved. (When sentenced in Bellingham, Kenny, alert to the cameras, had put on a lachrymose act of contrition, blubbering that his entire purpose in life was now to put Angelo Buono behind bars.) She was committed to art, Veronica wrote: "I adore art. I live for art." Yet art was such a strain: "Whenever I complete a play, I get depressed." She believed in freedom and extended her beliefs to her parakeet, which, she wrote proudly, she permitted to fly about the house, his droppings a small enough price to pay for the exhilaration she felt at his liberty.

She wrote that she identified with Kenny and knew that fate had willed them to meet:

> Things of nature are meant to be,
> Such were two victims, a he, a she!
> Musical magic it dispossess!
> Rose-tinted fragrance is its dress!

Veronica, who was the daughter of the editorial cartoonist for a Los Angeles newspaper, had been briefly married and had borne a boy child, with whom she lived in a trailer park. Of her little boy, who was eight years old, she wrote:

> He enjoys a good robust nude by Picasso but prefers the marble sculptures of grand breasts and proud ass. He is terribly erotic (and no I do not condone *incest*) and loves to nestle and fondle my breasts. . . . He tries to court my female lovers. I am extremely discreet and he has only seen me in the act of love with his father (when he can sneak a peek!). I worship the little fellow with all the maternal zest of Mother Earth. At his school I turned down the P.T.A. presidency.

It took only a few such letters to convince Kenny that here was a woman worth meeting. He telephoned her —he had this privilege and his calls were not monitored—and agreed to see her in the visitors' room at the jail in a few days' time.

Now Veronica wrote Kenny that she was breathless with anticipation. She was counting the hours until their meeting. She could scarcely sleep. She knew that he was the man of her dreams who could calm her troubled soul:

> Years of tears have made my life
> Mistreated youth, unestimable strife.

She knew that somehow they would have a beautiful sex life together: she had had an orgasm when talking to him on the telephone. She would sweep him away to a place called Island Lost where "In and Out are non-existent as is the juxtapositional concept of Right or Wrong." Oh, the exquisite painful pleasure of imagining what their meeting would be like:

> Bring in the champagne, more caviar,
> I'm in love with Mr. Wonderful, Mr. Beautiful,
> You're the apple of my eye,

All day long I sigh.
My buttocks matched, so firm, robust,
Two dainty melons ripely just!

Her every dream was of him:

> My dearest,
>
> What a wonderful sex-filled night I had. It was so exciting. And the man was so mysterious. Took a long, hot bath at my house. And he looked so tempting as the steam rolled off his body. You will never guess who it is.
>
> All night he stayed here with me. I can't tell you how magnificent it was. It was simply outrageous.
>
> You know him well. In fact, you know him very, very well. Do you want to guess? Forget it. You can't in a thousand years. You know why? I will tell you. Because my lover was here in spirit, not in body. It was a dream, my precious, a dream about you.
>
> Do you realize it's only 51½ hours until we see each other?
>
> Did I excite you with curiosity in the beginning of the letter?

And then, like a pedantic creative writing instructor, Veronica explained her literary devices:

> Technique employed was suspense. Suspense adds to drama. Wait till you read *King Lear Revisited*. It is the play I am currently working on.
>
> I hope you like it. I hope you can appreciate the enormous amount of work I had to invest in it.

She went on to suggest that Kenny memorize Hamlet's "To be or not to be" soliloquy so that he could recite it to her when they met.

At last the fateful meeting. Their romance exfoliated like a bruise. They talked for hours through the jailhouse glass, long visitors' sessions being another of Kenny's privileges. Veronica told Kenny that she herself was an actual murderess as well as a playwright but that he alone now shared that secret. She was lying, but it helped to get their relationship off on an equal footing. Kenny told her that her letters were among the most beautiful things he had ever read and that *The Mutilated Cutter* reminded him of Bram Stoker's *Dracula,* one of his favorite books. They discovered a mutual interest in necrophilia. Kenny envied openly her knowledge of literature. He wished, he said, to further his literary education, with Veronica as his guide. She suggested he start with Strindberg, Ibsen and Edward Albee. He was, he said, something of a poet himself. She entreated him to write love poems to her. She would visit him faithfully, play Juliet to his Romeo. They would write and telephone each other every day.

Kenny was not so caught up in the Shakespearean delirium of it all as he pretended. It was *The Mutilated Cutter* that had caught his fancy, not its author, and he began to formulate a plan to make use of Veronica with the plot of the play in mind.

But first he had to plight his troth. Poetry would be just the thing. He summoned his muse. He knew that for this literary lady he would have to rise above his usual plain style. Veronica required afflatus. He recalled from high school not Robert Frost this time but a romanticism of the sort favored by certain kinds of English teachers, and out of him poured these among many other verses:

[To Veronica]
Even as I walked towards you on that path,
in a field of marigolds, where a mist
gently caressed the earth, and
a warm breeze spoke softly of life
and love, I was almost home.
But nay, the *riata,* it held you out of reach.
You were but a sparrow's feather away.

Riata, a Spanish word for flood, stream, or freshet, he threw in as a bouquet to Veronica's Latin blood. In the margin of this poem he drew a Beardsleyish portrait of her as a long-nailed dragon lady. She responded:

> Your virginal neck is so very beautiful, what grace and wondrous structure. With expert precision my knife's razor edge skates across your jugular vein.
> And then comes the deep rich redness. I drink fondly.

And he:

> I keep thinking of the sunshine you bring to my life.
>
> That first step:
> Ah! the ecstacy of that
> first step to sensuous bliss!
> And the joining of two as one,
> as the earth meets the sky,
> as the oceans meet the shores;
> *inter nos* (between us)
> we meet as one.
>
> Your orbs are as deep as the oceans,
> Your labiums hold the enthusiasm
> of a thousand fires and ensure
> precipitous impatience
> of what you rejoinder next.
>
> To you I toast the wines of Eros'
> fountains and stand
> despotically majestic.

Always he kept this elevated tone. Occasionally he chose peculiar metaphors. The following appears to have been drawn from dentistry:

> The sheets do show
> the impression still
> of our finest moments.
> The aseptic instrument of
> peridental care stands perched

> in lonely solitude
> within the obscurity
> of our powder room.

Apparently Kenny was comparing his penis to a toothbrush, perhaps one equipped with a rubber gum massager ("peridental"). It was after this that Veronica suggested diplomatically that Kenny equip himself with a dictionary and a thesaurus. "You," he told her, "are a diamond in a pile of coal."

However inept, his poems wormed their way into Veronica's heart, and their conversations became increasingly intimate. He confided to her his pride in having killed so many women. He said that he believed in living for the moment and that his ideal would be to be at one with nature, free as a jungle beast. What was it like, she wanted to know, just to pick out girls at random and have sex with them and kill them?

"Well," Kenny said, "it's kind of like this, Veronica. It's like a kid going down the street and you see all these candy stores and you can pick any candy that you want and you don't have to pay for it and you just take it. You just do what you want. It's the greatest."

They discussed how delightful it would be to go on a killing spree together. Veronica suggested that they live together, kill dozens of people, keep the bodies in the basement, and then commit double suicide. "I know what we could do," she said. "We could cut off their parts and have a collection of cunts, clits, and cocks! We could keep them in jars and take them out to look at them!"

This was a little beyond Kenny's more wholesome approach to murder, but he went along with her. Soon she was saying that she was ready to die for him, and that was approximately what Kenny had in mind, although he warned her in avuncular fashion that she was "heading down a dangerous path." Still, if she really loved him that much, there might be something she could do for him. What he saw as the ingenious plot of her masterpiece, *The Mutilated Cutter*, might offer the key to his freedom. He could scarcely dare to suggest it, he said, but what if, just what if she were actually to carry out the plot of the play in real life, strangle somebody and make it look as though a man had done it? Not just any man, but the same man who had killed Karen Mandic and Diane Wilder in Bellingham. If she would go up to Bellingham and kill a girl and leave semen on her or in her, that would show that the police had arrested the wrong man.

Veronica agreed instantly. For her, she said, it would really be a form of research for her writing. She even ought to be able to write the trip to Washington off her income tax.

They made elaborate plans. They decided that if the plot worked and Kenny was absolved of the Bellingham murders, the next thing would be for her to provide him with alibis for each of the dates of the Hillside Stranglings. Let Angelo take the rap for them. Kenny gave her a list of the dates, with suggestions for alibis: they had gone to the movies, they had seen a play, and so on.

But first they would have to make sure that the new Bellingham strangling went off just right. Kenny had learned that his blood type failed to show up in his semen—Angelo also was among the 20 percent of males who were nonsecretors—and that meant that somehow he would have to supply Veronica with a sample of his own semen to leave with the body, so it would match that found on the Bellingham bodies. He would have to devise a way of smuggling semen out of jail. Meanwhile he advised her to pick as victim a girl with a car, so that she could leave the body in the car as he had Karen and Diane. She should be young, Kenny said, with "average tits," and she should weigh no more than ninety or a hundred and ten pounds, so Veronica could handle her. Veronica should try the campus of Western Washington University: Karen and Diane had been students there.

On the morning of September 16, Veronica came to visit Kenny. The plan was for him somehow to give her a sample of his semen and for her to fly up to Bellingham that afternoon. They talked together for about twenty minutes, and then Kenny handed her a book she had lent him, a hardbound collection of one-act plays, and he whispered, "When you're alone, pull the string." A piece of string, Veronica saw, dangled from the book's spine.

Kenny had hidden his semen in the book. He had masturbated into the finger of a rubber glove that another inmate had given him, sealed the finger with bubble gum, and tied the piece of string around the finger. The string had come from his rosary, from which he had stripped the beads and crucifix. Alone in her car, Veronica pulled on the string and from out of the book's binding emerged the semen-filled finger. What an ingenious lover she had! Now it was off to kill for him.

For her mission Veronica disguised herself with a blonde wig and large sunglasses, and she stuffed a pillow into her dress, believing that a pregnant woman would look less threatening. From the Bellingham airport she took a taxi to the university and wandered around the campus for a while, searching out a victim. She had dosed herself with cocaine, for courage, but she failed to find a promising co-ed, so she called another cab, bought a gallon of wine, and checked into a motel, the Shangri-la. She drank about half the wine, sniffed more cocaine, and decided to go to a bar for some real drinks.

At the Coconut Grove bar Veronica struck up a conversation with an attractive young woman and eventually invited her to try some cocaine at the Shangri-la. The woman declined but agreed to drive Veronica to the motel. This was going to have to be it, Veronica thought. Somehow she would have to get the woman into the motel and strangle her. Veronica bought several rounds of drinks to try to loosen the woman up. She tried to gain her sympathy by saying that the man who had got her pregnant had abandoned her.

In the car the woman pushed in a cassette. It was Stravinsky's *Rite of Spring*. Veronica knew the music and the ballet for which it was composed, an evocation of a primitive fertility ritual in which the lead dancer, portraying a sacrificial virgin, dances herself to death. Stravinsky's tempestuous rhythms encouraged Veronica. She would commit the act and from then on be able to write from experience. She would revise *The Mutilated Cutter* with a new confidence and act the principal role with a degree of faithfulness to the method style of acting that no one could match. She and Kenny would be able to live well. There would be a movie and she would be on the cover of *People* magazine. Even if she was caught and convicted, she thought, everyone would sympathize with a writer in search of material, an artist who had risked all for art. She might serve a little time, but the publicity would make her a star. A committee of artists would get her out of prison.

At the motel Veronica asked the woman to come in for a chat, pleading loneliness and melancholy, offering a glass of wine. The woman acquiesced, being a little drunk now and figuring that a glass or two might even her out.

Veronica went into the bathroom to fetch, she said, another glass. Behind the door she removed from her purse a length of stout cord and checked to see that the finger of semen was intact. She knew that as she came out of the bathroom, the woman would be seated with her back toward her and that this was the moment, it had to be now because the woman was bigger and probably stronger than she and surprise would be essential. She took a good grip on the cord, her fists spread apart on it, leaving a slack length between.

She reached the woman in two long strides, brought the cord down over her head and snapped it back against her throat, wrapping it once around, and started pulling.

The woman tried to draw air, tried to force a scream but only gargled, threw back her arms and grabbed at Veronica's wrists, held, dug nails in, pulled with everything she had, wrenching from side to side, and with one great effort flipped Veronica up and over her. Veronica lost her grip, cartwheeled, smashed the small of her back going down against the arm of the chair, and collapsed moaning onto the floor. In a second the woman loosened the cord and threw it aside and was out of the door and into her car and away.

Veronica lay on the floor. She had failed. How

would she face Kenny? Would the woman go straight to the police? Quickly Veronica gathered up her clothes and hurried down the street and around the corner to a pay phone, where she called a taxi. She made it to the airport and away.

It took Veronica's intended victim several days to recover from the shock. Her eyes had hemorrhaged and her throat was bruised; she was embarrassed by what she had allowed to happen, and bewildered by it at the same time. But finally she went to the police.

Again the rarity of violent crime in Bellingham made solving this case relatively easy, but Veronica helped by behaving peculiarly and creating a disturbance in the San Francisco airport, where she was meeting a connecting flight on her way home. She became hysterical, and police questioned her before allowing her to catch her flight. From that airport she mailed a letter and a tape to the Bellingham police, both accusing the authorities in the most obscene language possible of having arrested the wrong man (Bianchi) in the Bellingham murders and in the Strangler case, taunting them with the new strangling. All of these actions together with her being a well-known visitor to Bianchi in jail made her an instant suspect. When her airline reservations checked out and the San Francisco police verified a photograph of her, she was as good as convicted.

On October 3, Grogan and Salerno went to arrest her in her trailer in the city of Carson, an industrial suburb south of Los Angeles. Much to Grogan's irritation, Deputy D.A. Roger Kelly also tagged along. They found Veronica living in disarray with a dope dealer. (Her son was safe in the custody of her father, who had taken the child from her in desperation over her way of life.) They had a warrant for her arrest, but at first Grogan and Salerno, having discussed strategy beforehand, simply asked her if they could talk to her about Kenneth Bianchi, whom they said they knew she had been visiting. She let them in without any fuss, and for half an hour Grogan sat with her on her couch, asking her about her ambitions for a movie career, praising her good looks, joking with her, flattering her intelligence, and so on, generally softening her up. He was just getting her to the point where she might tell them, he hoped, some interesting things about Bianchi, perhaps in the (false) hope of extricating herself from a charge of attempted murder, which Grogan had been careful not even to mention as yet, when all of a sudden Roger Kelly, a small man who in voice and manner resembled the late Senator Joseph R. McCarthy, turned on Veronica and began yelling and screaming at her, accusing her of all the vile things of which she was of course guilty but uncharged. Kelly picked up some letters and drawings from Bianchi that were lying about and shook them at her, McCarthy-like, as he ranted.

Grogan wanted to slam a big fist into Kelly's mouth right there, but he had to sit silently as Veronica, turned off entirely by Kelly's accusations, clammed up. So much for that witness, Grogan thought. What was Kelly trying to do? There was nothing for it now but to arrest Veronica and have her extradited back up to Washington. Whatever use she might have had in the case against Buono—what might Kenny have told her about Angelo?—had been torpedoed. Had Kelly simply lost his temper, or what? Grogan wondered.

Afterward Kelly brushed aside Grogan's objections by saying that Veronica was too crazy to be of any use as a witness anyway. But even crazy people, Grogan said, can give you information, can provide leads; they did not have to be put on the stand to be of help. Kelly would not listen.

Grogan began to brood. First Kelly drops the outstanding murder charges against Bianchi, so there is nothing hanging over him, and now this. What is going on here?

Bianchi lost interest in Veronica as soon as their plot failed and she was arrested. But her love for him, as she called it, endured, and she complained to him about his "chump" passionless letters, which became shorter and less and less frequent. When she threatened to tell everything she knew about him, he responded with a grandly entitled "Letter to the World" —Bianchi never slighted his own significance—proclaiming his innocence and the abuse he had suffered

314

at the hands of a heartless society. "I haven't killed anybody in my entire life," he announced to the cruel world, but "the only ones that care are myself, my beloved Veronica and perhaps my mom and Dad. You win, Angelo 'Tony' Buono."

Veronica doubted his sincerity.

When news of her Bellingham exploit made the papers, she received a letter from another murderer, Douglas Clark, the Sunset Slayer, who was like Kenny being held in the Los Angeles County Jail and who commended her for her courage, saying that she and Bianchi were truly a modern Juliet and Romeo. Clark wished, he wrote, that he had a woman who would do as much for him.

Douglas Clark, who was later sentenced to death, was perhaps a more appropriate mate for Veronica than Kenny, in that Clark's crimes and predilections ran to more extreme forms of sadism. Clark's special talent was to force a woman to perform oral sex on him at gunpoint and, with nerveless confidence in his aim, to shoot her through the head as she brought him to orgasm. He would then chop off the victim's head, place it in his refrigerator, and bring it out from time to time for further oral sex. All this Veronica knew when she wrote to Clark in February 1981, as she was awaiting being sentenced: "We are falling seriously, crazily, dangerously, omnipotently, ubiquitously in love with each other. Doug, that can only mean two things in my mind. One, we seriously got (Oh God, I can barely bring myself to write the God blessed word. I am embarrassed to even suggest it to you in fear I'll look unchic, unsophisticated, unliberated and terribly corny. Shit, I'll say it.) married. I'm in a tomb barely alive waiting in a casket for you. Love me." She suggested that after they were released they open up a mortuary together: "Our humor is unusual. I wonder why others don't see the necrophilic aspects of existence as we do. . . . Nature is nature. What lives that does not live from the death of someone else? . . . For me it would be a great honor to have you love my corpse, dissect it, explore, oooh! You could dissect your favorite parts and put them in jars of formaldehyde and keep my skeleton. Every night you and your

315

house mouses could cuddle me." As a Valentine, Clark sent her a photograph of a headless female corpse.

But it was Kenny whom Veronica truly loved, or so she told him. She wanted to make him jealous. She envisioned a headline in the *National Enquirer*— "HILLSIDE STRANGLER DUMPED FOR SUNSET SLAYER" —that would infuriate Kenny and cause his passion for her to return. Clark appealed to her and excited her—"I take out my straight razor and with one quick stroke I slit the veins in the crook of your arm. Your blood spurts out and spits atop my swelled breasts. Then later that night we cuddle in each other's arms before the fireplace and dress each other's wounds with kisses and loving caresses"—but Kenny occupied first place in her heart.

At her trial she argued that she had been doing research, and she wrote to her victim, woman to woman and mother to mother, asking her not to testify, saying that she should understand how a child needs its mother: hers was playing Little League baseball and his mother should be there to cheer him on. But in March 1981, she was sentenced to life in prison for premeditated attempted murder: the citizens of Washington were not pleased that someone had tried to import what they saw as a Hollywood style of life to their state. Her earliest possible parole would be in 1994. Months after her conviction, Kenny wrote to her curtly that he felt "shock and sorrow," and Veronica flew at him, calling him an ingrate and worse. To Douglas Clark she suggested that he and she announce their engagement, saying of the faithless Kenny, "That weak-kneed fool. I have read into his silence and am inflamed!"

But neither prison nor disillusion in love stayed Veronica's literary ambition. Taking heart from the Hollywood axiom that any publicity is good publicity, she wrote to New American Library, the publishing company, and to the William Morris Agency, saying that she was the world-famous Copycat Strangler (newspapers had so named her) and suggesting that a joint edition of her and Kenny's poems, "with personal comments by both of us on our feelings and ideas of love," would make a best-seller. Both William Morris and NAL declined participation. Later she extended her literary-homicidal contacts by writing to Jack Abbott, the literary killer. Norman Mailer, leading a coterie of literati, had helped to spring Jack Abbott from prison, praising his prose style and promoting him as an artist victimized by a punitive penal system. Mailer had given Abbott brief employment as a researcher on *Ancient Evenings*, Mailer's Egyptian novel; but Abbott then murdered a play-writing waiter and was returned to prison. Veronica was so enthusiastic about Abbott and his book, *In the Belly of the Beast*, the tirade Mailer had endorsed, that she saluted Abbott as her "Dearest and most beloved Comrade":

I am still drying my face from the shower of tears that o'erswept me as I read your book.

I suppose that I should let you know that your book is voraciously consumed by a prison full of women. . . . And for what it is worth Norman Mailer has nothing on you!

She then told Jack Abbott about her involvement with Kenneth Bianchi and her attempt to get Bianchi released by murdering on his behalf:

I was a woman who ventured to do something that had never been done. If anything, I am a brilliant, exciting and vivacious woman.

The world would never understand her or Jack Abbott, she said. But:

There will of course be a minority consisting of Norman Mailers and Veronica Comptons who will cheer, rant and rave, applaud and revel in your enlightenment. You are *our* guiding light, the beacon of liberation. Carry on my friend. I love you well.

But this was a merely literary romanticism, authentic life with Kenny fast becoming a receding dream. Her letters might achieve the eloquence of an Academy Awards presentation, but her ratings were slipping. Parole was distant; what to do? Where could she audition? She sought for her name in the papers. She gained the admiration of other women prisoners by her Broadway vivacity. She tried lithium.

TWENTY

Bob Grogan sat in his apartment, his companions that night his jazz records and a book. From hour to hour as the music moved him he transferred his big body from the couch to the bench of his electric organ. For twenty minutes more or less he could forget the Stranglers by playing along with this band or that, forget too his missing family and his girlfriend, letting music and the occasional sip of whiskey banish his anger and his guilt. Then the record would end and in the silence the rotten emotions would return.

How it was that he had found himself living alone in this apartment he was not entirely sure, but often he thought that the case was robbing him of his sanity, more often he felt like a fool, and sometimes when he thought he was in love with K.O. he imagined a new life around the corner; but his longing for his family was too strong to permit that hope to flourish. He sensed that the case had caused him to let his family go out of focus, to dissolve into a background that was to be dealt with later; and then one day he noticed that he was out of his house and on his own again after twenty years of marriage, living in this apartment which, like most other new buildings in Southern California, had been designed for the young or rootless: impersonal furniture, a communal swimming pool, hanging lamps, colors derived from tropical fish, the whole thing suggesting a holiday from life.

Grogan was a poor liar and no good at keeping secrets, like those of a double life. Once K.O.'s existence was known, he had had to leave home, but the move at least for now was presumed temporary and he had not considered moving in with his girlfriend. Grogan did not really approve of what he preferred to call shack jobs anyway. Either you married someone or not, that was what marriage was for, and K.O. continued to live and to work fifty miles from him. But it was easier to see her than his children, who resented what he was doing and were barely speaking to him. He did not blame them, but he suffered under their scorn. His daughter had tried to understand but did not hide her hurt, and his son, Grogan felt, hated him. I have got to straighten out my life, Grogan said to himself several dozen times a day. Sitting in his second-floor apartment he felt up in the air in every sense, a floating object.

The apartment building happened to share a back fence with 809 East Garfield Avenue. Why had he chosen Glendale, why was he perched a mere hello from Kristina Weckler's ghost and Kenneth Bianchi's haunts? Why had he arranged it so that he could not drive to work without crossing Angelo's Colorado Street only two blocks from the Trim Shop? Grogan cited the reasonable rent. It was not easy to find a decent apartment anywhere in Los Angeles for less than three hundred dollars a month, and he had the family to support, mortgage payments and the boat to keep up. But it was as though he had taken roost there believing or compelled to hope that if he hovered daily near the scenes of evil, somehow the spilt blood would have to be avenged.

It was March 1981, and Grogan had just learned of Veronica Compton's conviction, but he took little pleasure in it. What he had found out about Veronica, her correspondence with Bianchi, her extensive sexual involvements with prominent Hollywood types who had enough money and enough lawyers to keep their behavior out of the papers, made Grogan less pleased at her conviction than depressed at what she represented. She might be crazier and more reckless and more desperate from drugs than most, but she was far from unique, only a visible example of a city that often seemed to be at war with everything that mattered in life. A city? Maybe an entire country, Grogan was beginning to think. *Vogue* magazine, as Veronica had pointed out to him during their too brief conversation in her trailer, had been featuring sadomasochism as a fashion motif. New music celebrated torture, self-mutilation, and death. Ugly was in. Maybe, Grogan thought, turning up the volume on the phonograph, I have ended up in an anachronistic profession. Maybe being a homicide detective is just whistling Dixie. Maybe I am just standing in the way of what everybody has decided is the really fashionable thing to do, kill one another. Maybe I have become like the guy still printing books by hand or the priest still saying mass in Latin. If that was true maybe he was meant to be alone.

He knew that he was alone in certain speculations about the case, especially about Bianchi's background and the question of how he had evolved from a difficult child into a killer. The psychiatrists, Grogan believed, had been off on a wild goose chase when they had tried to establish that Bianchi's adoptive mother had been cruel or even violent to him: Grogan was sure that Bianchi had made up all that stuff on the spot. Grogan believed just the opposite, that Bianchi's mother had been overprotective of her only, adopted child. Something a psychologist in Rochester had written in a report on Bianchi back in 1962 stuck in Grogan's mind:

> It would appear from Kenneth's viewpoint that his mother has related to him in such a way so that he feels his very survival depends on his being

in her good graces. In order to do so, he must maintain very rigid control over his masculine aggressive impulses. The need not to show any masculine assertiveness is so great that his basic identification is quite diffuse and contains as much of a feminine component as a masculine one. There is a tremendous amount of anxiety generated in all of this, so much so that one wonders how well Kenneth could maintain his psychological integrity if he did not somatocize it [experience frequent psychosomatic illness] in the way he does now.

The psychologist, Dr. Robert Dowling, had concluded his report:

It is thought that Kenneth would respond well to individual psychotherapy, but without simultaneous treatment of his mother, who it appears is not accepting of such a plan, the effects of such a course of action would be fleeting.

Dr. Dowling, Grogan believed, had been on to something, especially in suggesting that the mother needed treatment as well.

As for the case against Buono, the preliminary hearing in municipal court had been dragging on since the previous May. Dozens of witnesses were testifying to the kind of life Angelo and Kenny had led together. As it turned out, much of this material would not be admissible before a jury. Important new evidence had finally developed, however, thanks to the persistence of Kathy Vukovitch, a criminalist with the LAPD, who had established that the fiber found on Judy Miller's eyelid had almost certainly come from the Trim Shop. Chemists from the DuPont and the Monsanto corporations had found no significant differences between the Judy Miller fiber and the foam that Angelo used in upholstering, the foam Bianchi had mentioned as blindfold material. Vukovitch was working on the Lauren Wagner fibers as well.

This was a promising development, the only good piece of physical evidence so far, but there had been discouragements too. One day the previous November, Angelo's house had disappeared: bulldozed, apparently on the orders of the owner of the glass shop next door, to whom Angelo had signed over the deed. Sheriff's Department artists had constructed a precise scale model of the house, based on photographs and measurements taken earlier, but it would have been far more effective to be able to take a jury through the actual house, whenever a jury was at last chosen. Now 703 East Colorado Street was only a paved empty lot, the Trim Shop still at the rear but not a trace of the actual murder scene remaining. The owner of the glass shop denied any collusion with Angelo in the bulldozing, insisting that he had been losing money on the property, unable to rent it with the house still there.

But more disturbing, in Grogan's mind, was the behavior of the prosecutor, Roger Kelly. Having begun by doubting Kelly's will to carry through such a difficult case, Grogan now suspected Kelly of deliberately trying to scuttle it. The worst moment for Grogan and, he feared, for the case, came when at last, after what he estimated as at least a hundred visits (four hundred cookies, two hundred cups of coffee) to Beulah Stofer, Grogan had finally persuaded the woman to give a statement to Kelly. This visit happened by chance when Grogan, Varney, Williams, and Kelly were driving Bianchi around Los Angeles in a van, determining his ability to pick out abduction and dump sites. On Lemona Street Grogan suggested that they leave Bianchi guarded in the van and stop in to see Beulah.

More coffee and cookies all around. Mrs. Stofer recounted her story again, saying as usual that she had seen everything through the front window, Grogan as sure as ever that she had gone outside to quiet Caesar and to take a closer look. Shrubbery in the yard now obscured the street from the window, but she assured Kelly that she had been able to see clearly through it three and a half years before.

Kelly listened, and then, to Grogan's horror, he laughed at Mrs. Stofer. "You expect me to believe that?'' he said. ''You expect a jury to believe that? It's ridiculous!''

Grogan, asking Kelly to leave, tried to calm Mrs. Stofer down, assuring her that he believed her and that he would convince Kelly, who was just a little irascible today.

Outside, Grogan tore into Kelly, calling him a son of a bitch and asking him what the hell he was trying to do. Was he trying to ruin a witness? Grogan, looming over the little prosecutor, clenched his fists.

''You guys are crazy,'' Kelly shouted. ''That woman has no idea what she saw. Well, we'll have to throw that count out!''

Grogan lunged at Kelly, screaming as the other officers leaped to hold him back. From then on he found it difficult to speak to Kelly at all, and he vowed never to speak to him again once the case was over.

When Kelly did the same thing to Jan Sims, scoffing at her story about the attempted abduction in the Excalibur, Grogan knew that the case was in deep trouble. Kelly shouted at Mrs. Sims: ''Don't you know your testimony could send an innocent man to the gas chamber?'' Innocent? Grogan was speechless. Kelly told the police to stop trying to find the Excalibur—the vehicle registration records had turned up nothing, nor had a search of garages in Buono's neighborhood—because there was no Excalibur. Mrs. Sims was just fantasizing, Kelly said: her identification of Buono and Bianchi from photographs meant nothing.

The most charitable interpretation of Kelly's behavior was that he did not believe in eyewitnesses, but that was a rather unlikely position for a prosecutor to take, and Grogan did not believe it. Of all the eyewitnesses, only Catherine Lorre and Markust Camden now looked as though they might be useful, and Camden was hardly an impressive character, although criminal cases often had to rely on witnesses whose own lives were poor models of civic propriety. Catherine Lorre had confirmed Bianchi's story of her near-abduction and had reenacted the scene for Salerno and Finnigan, who took photographs with themselves acting Angelo's and Kenny's roles. Even better, on her own she had identified Angelo. In December 1979, she had been visiting a biker friend of hers at the county jail when she spotted Angelo, who was receiving a visitor of his own at the time, a faithful girlfriend. Catherine Lorre had immediately telephoned Kelly, saying that she was certain that this was one of the two men who had stopped her in Hollywood two years before.

Sergeant Bill Williams's persistence had turned up another witness who added something to Bianchi's credibility, a woman who acknowledged that two naked girls had disturbed her and her husband's sleep late one night in September 1977. The girls had asked for clothing, saying that they had been stripped and forced out of a car by two men. The woman's husband had since died and she had moved, but Williams had traced her through a neighborhood association of householders, who had remembered hearing her talk of the incident.

All this Grogan pondered that night in his apartment. The thought that Kelly might throw out the Lauren Wagner count seemed inconceivable, but that was what Kelly had said he was going to do. For the other count for which Grogan had primary investigative responsibility, Kristina Weckler, there was little on Angelo, only that he had purchased a flexible gas pipe from Antoinette Lombardo's parents' store before the murder. And Bianchi was continuing to change his stories from day to day, claiming renewed memory lapses, denying this and admitting to that, then reversing himself, making it clear that only a prosecutor determined to separate Kenny's lies from his truths with corroborating evidence would stand a chance of convicting Angelo. Grogan would have attempted to get Kelly removed from the case, but there was no chance of that now. He and the other detectives had tried that over a year earlier, even before Bianchi had been arrested, when in another case Kelly had publicly criticized the LAPD. They had said then that they found Kelly impossible to work with, and for a few days another prosecutor had been assigned to the Hillside Stranglers case. But, so Grogan believed, the District Attorney's Office then decided that the LAPD could not be permitted to choose prosecutors, and Kelly had been reinstated.

Grogan's mood was no better the next morning. He dreaded seeing Kelly in court and trying to be helpful to him: all the detectives were in court almost every day, either testifying or making suggestions to the prosecution, shepherding witnesses, listening for new clues or at least hints. That morning before going to court Grogan calmed himself, as he sometimes liked to do, by scanning what the LAPD called its Murder Books, a collection of files going back to the earliest days of the city, records of all the known homicides that had been committed in Los Angeles since the turn of the century. As the century had lengthened, the files had become more complex, and it pleased Grogan to look over some of the earliest cases from time to time. The directness and simplicity of the old entries amused him and soothed his nerves. That morning he read, flipping the pages in the big old book, the passages crudely typewritten with odd lines scribbled in some long-dead homicide detective's hand:

April 21, 1899

PALOMI JOHNSON, stabbed to death some time last night in rooms of M. CASTELLA, New High St.; suspect CASTELLA. Both drunk. CASTELLA captured.

Those were the days, Grogan thought. I bet they convicted Castella in a week. He read on:

February 19, 1915

HOR FOOK, alias BATTLING NELSON, China-man, resident of Chinatown, about midnight Feb. 14, 1915, beaten up with pick handle and badly wounded, dying on Feb. 18. On Feb. 19 officers Leland and McAuliffe arrested AL-FREDO GALLARDO on suspicion of doing the job. Four days previous to murder, GALLARDO gave Chinaman 50¢ to buy him opium but was given charcoal instead; GALLARDO remarked to Y Sam that the "Battler" had tried to poison him and would kill him for doing it. The day and night of murder GALLARDO was hanging around vicinity of the crime.... When informed the "Battler" was dead GALLARDO turned very red and seemed to get very nervous and then spoke of leaving town immediately.

ALFREDO GALLARDO charge changed to vagrancy. Sentenced to $100 or 100 days.

I guess Gallardo had a good lawyer, Grogan thought. He tried one more:

July 17, 1915

ETARO or GEORGE IGUCHI, Jap, shot by MRS. MABEL SMITH at her residence, 1700 West 43rd St., Apt. 3, at about 8:45 p.m. this date. He died in receiving hospital.... Mrs. Smith had been keeping company with Iguchi since Feb. 1, 1910, unbeknown [sic] to her husband.

Imagine that, Grogan thought. Iguchi and Mrs. Smith carrying on for five years, and Mr. Smith never knew. What a scandal.

Iguchi had come to her apartments to return some pictures he had taken of her, when Mr. Smith and the Jap were having some words over his being infatuated with his wife. All three started for the gun which was lying near. Mrs. Smith reached it first, shooting Iguchi. Mrs. Smith acquitted by jury.

Acquitted! Grogan marveled. Well, some things never change. But those were the days! Grogan got special pleasure reading about the first murder case in Los Angeles in which psychiatrists had been permitted to testify, arguing, of course, that the defendant was insane. Psychiatrists had been termed officially by the court "alien witnesses" then, an apt phrase in Grogan's view. The jury had sentenced the defendant to death.

Grogan tried to imagine what Buono and Bianchi's entry would look like in these files. The transcript of the preliminary hearing was already nearing seven thousand pages. Grogan felt himself a man out of his proper time. But it made him feel better to think that once there had been a better world.

Grogan had cause to rejoice when the ten-month-long preliminary hearing in Case No. A 354231, People of the State of California, Plaintiff, versus Angelo Buono, Jr., Defendant, ended with a decision by Municipal Court Judge H. Randolph Moore that the case should go to trial. At least that hurdle was past.

The case was now assigned to Superior Court Judge Ronald M. George, who began hearing preliminary motions. Because the Public Defender's Office was representing Bianchi, Buono required separate, private counsel, lest a conflict of interest in the defense take place. The supervising judge of the Criminal Division appointed Gerald L. Chaleff, who had already handled Buono's defense on the murder counts at the preliminary hearing, as Buono's attorney because of Angelo's alleged indigency. At Chaleff's request, Katherine Mader was appointed co-counsel for the defense. The lawyers' pay was adequate: sixty-five dollars an hour for Chaleff, somewhat less than that for Mader; by the trial's end, Chaleff's firm alone had been paid over half a million dollars by the County of Los Angeles. But not every criminal lawyer wanted to represent Angelo Buono. Chaleff's first choice as co-counsel had been another woman, who, after a conversation with Angelo, declined the opportunity. Chaleff, a Harvard Law School graduate who had had several years' experience as a public defender before going into private practice, was known as bright, tough, and tireless. Mader, a U.C. Davis Law School graduate, had the reputation of being a vigorous researcher and investigator. Grogan was not alone among observers in thinking that Angelo had gotten a definite edge over the prosecution in his legal advocates. And, as Chaleff later confirmed, Angelo himself had asked for a woman as co-counsel, with an eye toward affecting a jury.

Before jury selection began, however, Judge George's first task was to rule on various pretrial motions. He denied a defense motion to set bail for Buono, ruling that Angelo must remain in jail for the duration of the trial, but he sustained a defense objection to television coverage, accepting only still photography in the courtroom and denying a request by the television networks for live coverage. These and other motions occupied several weeks, and for all the publicity of the event, things proceeded in the orderly, sometimes dreary way of trials, until the defense moved to sever the eleven nonmurder counts against Buono (including pimping, pandering, sodomy, conspiracy to commit extortion, oral copulation, rape, and false imprisonment) from the ten murder counts. The motion argued that the nonmurder counts should be tried separately at a later, different trial.

Judge George was faced with a decision that could have an important, perhaps determining effect on the outcome of the murder trial. If the nonmurder counts were severed, the jury for the murder trial would be permitted to hear little about the life which Kenny and Angelo had led together before they had actually begun the Hillside Stranglings. The picture of a man who in league with his cousin had committed innumerable criminal sexual and violent acts would be but dimly perceived by the jury.

Judge George, who had studied the preliminary hearing transcripts in detail, was not yet convinced of Angelo's guilt, but the evidence before him certainly suggested a strong possibility of guilt. To sever the nonmurder counts now would, he knew, make conviction far more difficult. Yet legal precedent dictated that they be severed, the principle being that to try noncapital offenses along with capital offenses was wrong because the jury could be swayed toward conviction on the more serious charges simply because there was greater evidence on the lesser charges: the lesser charges could have a buttressing effect on the more serious ones. A jury should not, in other words, be swayed to believe a defendant guilty of, say, murder simply because he was guilty of burglary.

At the same time Judge George also knew that, one way or another over the course of a trial he estimated would last at least a year, the other evidence, the testimony of Sabra Hannan and Becky Spears and all the others who had suffered everything short of murder at Buono and Bianchi's hands might somehow work its way into the murder trial, through one gap or another created by the defense or the prosecution or a combination of both.

Judge George's task, then, as he saw it was to sever the nonmurder counts or risk reversal on appeal. At the same time he knew that the prosecution would be expected to be aware that somehow the severed material, or some of it, might later be admitted anyway. On June 11 he ordered the nonmurder counts severed but he also indicated, in response to questions from Roger Kelly, "that nothing the Court was saying would preclude a proper showing at trial. And that [it] might even develop by way of defense cross-examination or defense testimony [that something might be put at] issue that was not initially at issue." Roger Kelly appeared to take the hint that at some later point evidence might be admitted which initially was being barred. At least Kelly said that he might make a motion to that effect later on, and Judge George said that nothing he was now ruling would preclude such a motion. Judge George even had in mind, although he did not and could not say so, a specific piece of evidence, namely Sabra Hannan's testimony that both Buono and Bianchi had tried to force her to insert a dildo into her anus and that Bianchi had beaten her in the presence of Buono. This incident, which in a memo to himself Judge George called "The Sabra Hannan Dildo Incident," would be admissible because it specifically involved both Buono and Bianchi together in an act of violence against a woman and therefore had direct bearing on the charge that Buono had committed murders in league with his cousin. It was, in other words, not merely an incident from the past showing bad character.

But if Roger Kelly did take the judicial hint, his subsequent actions failed to show it.

On July 6, Bianchi gave what by now was his typical flip-flopping performance on the stand, contrary to his agreement to testify truthfully against Buono. He had no recollection, he said, of faking being hypnotized; yet, he said, he had "probably" faked being a multiple personality. When he had told the psychiatrists about committing the murders with Angelo, he was "not sure" whether he had been telling the truth or not. Then he said that he had "probably" been lying when confessing. "Probably" he had not been present during the crimes at all. At another point he acknowledged being present at the Los Angeles killings but denied those in Bellingham.

One week later, citing this and other contradictory days of testimony by Bianchi, Roger Kelly moved to dismiss all ten murder counts against Angelo Buono, to drop completely prosecution of Buono as the Hillside Strangler.

In making his motion to dismiss, Kelly told the court that Bianchi had been giving inconsistent versions of the crimes since he had signed the plea-bargain agreement, saying not only that he could not remember whether he or Angelo had killed different victims but sometimes that he had not been involved in any killings at all. An attempt to clarify Bianchi's status as a witness on July 6 had brought all these inconsistencies to a head, and now, Kelly had determined, prosecution of Angelo Buono was impossible. Kelly was making the motion with the full support of his boss, District Attorney John Van de Kamp, who concurred in the decision with Kelly and his co-prosecutor, James Heins. "It is the belief of the Los Angeles District Attorney's Office," Kelly said, "that the person [Bianchi] whose continued credibility is essential to the successful prosecution of the murder charges against Angelo Buono has lost such credibility. . . . The prosecution for murder now pending against Mr. Angelo Buono cannot be predicated on the evidence now in existence and should be dismissed."

Kelly went on to argue that the severing of the nonmurder charges made conviction still more unlikely—this in spite of Judge George's indications to him that evidence of the nonmurder charges might be admissible as the trial developed. Kelly moved that, the murder charges being dropped, Buono should be tried at a later date on the pimping and other nonmurder charges, with bail set at fifty thousand dollars.

Grogan believed that his worst fears and suspicions had been realized—no, worse than that, because he had never been able to bring himself to suspect that *all* the murder counts would be dropped. In Grogan's opinion, Kelly had given up, Van de Kamp had given up, justice had given up. Grogan felt, as he said later, as though someone had just pissed on the American flag. He could not bear to look at his fellow detectives. They were all there in court, Salerno, Finnigan, Varney, Williams, all of whom had just been told that they had wasted years of their lives in the mistaken belief that they had been acting in the interests of an outraged community. Even if Angelo could be convicted on all the other counts, he could get no more than ten years, would be given credit for time already served in custody, would have his term reduced by one-third for good behavior, and would be out on the streets in less than five years. Five years for ten murders. Never had Grogan felt so futile. What would he say to the Wagners and the Wecklers? He felt suddenly as if he had been conscripted into an army of deserters, tainted, compromised, sucked in unwillingly by some gross act of disloyalty. Kelly had mentioned the possibility of trying the murder charges at some future date, but he had also said that this was unlikely, and, as Grogan knew, a case gets weaker, not stronger, as the months or years pass, as memories dim and witnesses disappear. Justice, Grogan believed, had taken a dive.

It was impossible to read Judge George's reaction to this turn of events. Remote on the bench, he said simply that he would take the matter "under submission." He would not rule on it now. Court would be adjourned for a week. He would rule on the district attorney's motion on Tuesday, July 21.

Grogan and Salerno went directly to the Code 7 bar after court. There they encountered an investigator for Angelo's defense team, a man for whom they harbored contempt, who was in such an ebullient mood that he offered to buy the detectives drinks.

"I wouldn't drink your fucking whiskey," Salerno said, and retreated with Grogan to a corner.

Angelo and his attorneys were elated, agreeing to celebrate together with dinner at an Italian restaurant as soon as Judge George granted the motion to dismiss and Angelo walked out of court free. There was little doubt as to how the judge would rule, for it was routine for judges to accede to the prosecution's wishes in such matters. Only the previous March, Judge George himself had agreed to dismiss murder charges against a woman at the request of the prosecution, when new evidence had turned up implicating another suspect. What would be the point of ordering the prosecution to proceed with a case it said it could not win? Kelly, Heins, District Attorney Van de Kamp, Angelo and his lawyers—all had every reason to believe that the Hillside Stranglers case was at long last over.

But they had misjudged this judge.

III

A Resurrection of Faith

My God, my Father, and my Friend,
Do not forsake me in the end.
    Well may they curse their second birth,
Who rise to a surviving death!
        —*Dies Irae* [The Day of Wrath]

none. When this narrator ... she was sleeping with
various Hollywood types, including a lawyer-agent
who later became the victim of an unsolved murder.

TWENTY-ONE

Judge Ronald Marc George was the son of a Parisian father, who had immigrated to America in the late twenties, and a Hungarian mother, who had come to the United States a few years later. More quickly than is usual with an intellectually inclined American son, his views of life and of human nature had swung toward those of his European parents. By the time of the Hillside Stranglers trial he was forty-one, young for a judge, but youthful delusion of the kind that searches out goodness in everyone was already many years behind him. Unlike so many others of his generation, he was never a flower child.

Educated along with his younger sister at the Beverly Hills public schools and at the École Internationale in Geneva, where he discovered a love of languages, he had decided on a diplomatic career by the time he left high school. But in 1961, after graduating from Princeton University, where he majored in the Woodrow Wilson School of Public and International

Affairs, he entered the Stanford Law School, where his interest in the criminal law was kindled. He became fascinated by aspects of criminal behavior and the means of preventing or identifying it. But he had no wish to defend criminals, and, having received his law degree, he joined the staff of the attorney general of California as a deputy attorney general, specializing in criminal cases.

For the first time, now, Ronald George had direct experience with the criminal class, and the exposure changed his thinking as well as his politics, which had until then tended toward the liberal. The good intentions of liberalism melted away as he was forced to confront extremes of human violence and behavior. Nothing in his excellent yet exclusive education had prepared him for the shock of human behavior at its unremorseful worst, and he came to believe that he had lived the first twenty-five years of his life as a privileged naïf. He did not regret the privilege, but naiveté was no longer possible. Most of the assumptions of his liberally educated generation—the perfectibility of mankind, the belief in general and broad possibilities of moral rehabilitation, the efficacy of altruism—he abandoned as Maginot lines against barbarism. Hemingway's phrase "Isn't it pretty to think so?" took on more weight. The liberal-humanist tradition seemed to have grown desperate, the prayer of a man already half eaten by a shark.

He married a girl whom he had known in high school, moved into a house close to his parents, and fathered the first of three sons. He achieved a reputation in the Attorney General's Office as a brilliant legal scholar adept at oral argument. At the age of thirty he was chosen to present the case for the death penalty on behalf of the State of California, one of six cases he argued before the United States Supreme Court.

In 1972, Governor Reagan appointed Ronald George to the municipal court bench in Los Angeles, and in 1977, Governor Jerry Brown, entirely out of character with his other, very liberal appointments, elevated him to the superior court. Four years later he began presiding over the trial of Angelo Buono and immediately had to decide whether there was to be a trial at all.

Judge George had sensed from the manner in which Roger Kelly had been cross-examining Kenneth Bianchi, evoking, it seemed, Bianchi's contradictions rather than penetrating to the consistencies behind them, that something was about to emanate from the District Attorney's Office, perhaps even a motion to dismiss. But when the motion to dismiss all the murder counts was made, the judge was sickened. As different as they were in background, in education, in their stations in life, and in society, and though they had never spoken to each other, the judge's feelings at that moment ran parallel to Sergeant Bob Grogan's. It had been imaginable, even vaguely anticipated, but actually to hear the motion to dismiss was another matter. From the moment he heard it, Judge George had no doubt what he must do. He adjourned court for a week, he said, to take the matter "under submission," to make up his mind; but in truth he needed the time to construct a ruling that was legally watertight.

So unpredictable had the California Supreme Court and the Court of Appeal become, so inclined toward defendants' rights had the higher courts revealed themselves in recent years, that the judge had to take account not only of precedent but of what the courts were likely to do in future. Judge George did not mind these extra considerations: they simply added to the intensity of legal scholarship, which had over the years come to delight him more and more, much as the mysteries of texts once delighted monks. Nor did the shifting of legal winds lessen his respect for the established hierarchy of the court system. But he did not want to rule against the district attorney and Angelo Buono now only to have his opinion picked apart and reversed. He knew, as he liked to say, that as a superior court judge he was "engaged in the practice of preventive jurisprudence," as mindful of the possibilities of reversal by a higher court as of the correctness of his present rulings.

He also wanted to take the time to phrase his ruling in such a way as to make it understandable to the literate public as well as to lawyers and appellate judges. It was beyond his proper role to speculate publicly on the motives, or lack of them, behind Kelly's motion and the D.A.'s concurrence in it, whether it had been prompted by a lack of will or by fear of losing a highly publicized case, or by neither, or by a combination of both. But he did want to spell out in plain English his concern with what he regarded as a grave error by the District Attorney's Office in asking him to turn loose Angelo Buono without a trial. This, the judge believed, would be a misuse, even a circumventing, of the judicial process, and whatever the motives behind it, it suggested to the public an indifference to the most serious of crimes. Had society reached the point, the judge wondered to himself, where it no longer cared to defend itself? Had the murder rate in Los Angeles so numbed people that they were willing to acquiesce to killing as a part of the culture, like going to the movies and the beach?

As he worked on the ruling, the judge felt entirely isolated. No one outside his family, not a single broadcaster or reporter or columnist, was anticipating anything but his granting of the D.A.'s motion. Police Chief Gates had told D.A. Van de Kamp that he was getting bad advice and should reconsider aspects of the case, but this exchange had occurred in a private meeting, and the judge did not know whether he had a single ally in legal circles. One television commentator, Baxter Ward, a theatrical former county supervisor with a portentous, old-style radio announcer's voice, began attacking the judge *ad hominem* in anticipation of the ruling, saying that this was the judge who was going to set Angelo Buono free. His guess as to how the judge would rule was consistent with everyone else's.

On the morning of July 21, Angelo Buono, wearing a long-sleeved shirt to conceal his tattoos, entered a courtroom packed with newspeople. He swaggered to his chair before the bench, physically unchanged by his nine months in jail except that he was pale, and his hair showed a lot of gray, since he had been unable to dye it. His female counsel, Katherine Mader, whispered to him, slinging her arm around his shoulders. In the hallway outside the courtroom, cameras waited to convey his walk to freedom. Roger Kelly stared ahead, avoiding the contemptuous eyes of detectives. Salerno and Finnigan sat together off to one side, silent. Grogan exiled himself to a corner at the back, subdued by frustration. He had done some asking around about Judge George and had concluded that if any judge in the state might save the case, this was the one; but Grogan held out little hope, had already begun rehearsing to himself phrases of regret to the Wagners and the Wecklers, words he knew would stick in his throat.

All courtrooms are churches, the raised bench, so named since the Middle Ages, an altar of sorts; and as the robed priest of justice appears, the people rise as a congregation. That morning Judge George entered his courtroom and assumed the elevated place. He glanced down at the packed room through glum brown eyes set in a long, Manolete-medieval face, over a nose that veered toward the grandiose, and arranged before him a thirty-six page sermon. Gray hair made him appear older than his years, but he broke the silence with a youthful voice.

He began by citing the district attorney's motion to dismiss each of the ten murder charges, emphasizing that the motion specified that it was made "without the likelihood of refiling": without, in other words, the likelihood that Angelo would ever be tried for these murders. He noted that Buono, even if convicted on all eleven of the nonmurder counts, would serve less than five years, and he pointed out that the pending motions for dismissal and for bail "reach this court after twenty-two months of proceedings," the preliminary hearing alone having lasted ten months; and he quoted the prosecutor's statement of only two months earlier, in which Kelly had said, "We believe there is more than sufficient [evidence] to show presumption of guilt by Mr. Buono . . . and I think the evidence the People put on at the preliminary is sufficient to withstand any conviction, the jury believing Mr. Bianchi, and could convict Mr. Buono."

At this point Grogan took a deep breath. Was it possible that in underlining Kelly's former position in favor of prosecution the judge was getting ready to deny the dismissal motion? Grogan began to hope.

Judge George launched into a brief excursion detailing legal scholarship on the subject of the duty imposed by law upon a court in ruling whether or not to grant a prosecution motion to dismiss criminal charges. Citing various precedents, he summarized that "the common thread in this legal fabric . . . is the principle that a prosecutor has almost total discretion as to whether to file charges (and which charges to file), but that once he has made the decision to file charges the disposition of such charges is a judicial function." It was the judge's prerogative, in other words, to accept or not a motion to dismiss.

He then, again by way of reference to legal precedent and authority, reminded the District Attorney's Office that it was charged with grave responsibilities which demanded integrity, zeal, and conscientious effort in the gathering and presentation of evidence. He quoted the American Bar Association's standards for prosecutors: "In making the decision to prosecute, the prosecutor should give no weight to the personal or political advantages or disadvantages which might be involved or to a desire to enhance his or her record of convictions."

At this point spectators in the courtroom may have remembered that District Attorney Van de Kamp was planning to run for the office of attorney general of California, and Grogan also thought of Roger Kelly's pride in his record of convictions. Grogan now permitted himself something more than hope. He was beginning to believe that Judge George was going to rescue the case. The judge added that it was "the court's duty to dismiss pending charges only if it is apparent that dismissal would be 'in furtherance of justice.' "

Judge George now took up the matter of the

persistent contradictions in Bianchi's testimony, on which the motion to dismiss primarily rested. He accepted that there were such contradictions, but he concluded that "it is more significant that to the extent that Mr. Bianchi at any given time claimed personal recollection of a particular murder, the participants in the criminal conduct were always the same—Mr. Buono and Mr. Bianchi, and no one else. Furthermore, [Mr. Buono's] potential guilt of first-degree murder would not depend [under California law] upon whether he had done the actual strangling (or had had forcible sexual relations with the victim) or had merely assisted Bianchi in doing so." At no time, the judge pointed out, had Bianchi, in spite of his contradictions, ever represented that Angelo Buono was not involved in the homicides. Contrary to what Kelly had argued in his motion, no "novel infirmities" in the prosecution's case had lately arisen: Bianchi's flip-flopping had been a factor ever since his arrival in Los Angeles, and the prosecutor had been fully aware of the problem from the moment he had filed charges against Buono. "Basically the doubts and lapses which Mr. Bianchi expressed during the past several weeks amount to nothing more than a modest increment to the morass of contradictions which have characterized this case from its inception and which apparently left the District Attorney's Office unmoved enough to be able two months ago to characterize its case as one in which the proof of guilt was both evident and sufficient to sustain a conviction on appeal."

The judge then reviewed important evidence which the prosecutor had failed to mention in his motion to dismiss. Kelly had listed only the prior association between Buono and Bianchi, Catherine Lorre's testimony, and the Judy Miller fiber evidence. (Kelly had said nothing about the Lauren Wagner fiber evidence.) The judge added to these Markust Camden's testimony, and Deborah Noble's, Jennifer Snider's, and Antoinette Lombardo's, as well as the testimony of the driver of the Foxy Ladies van, that of a waitress at the Robin Hood Inn, and that of a man who apparently had witnessed the abduction of Yolanda Washington from Sunset Boulevard, an incident that had involved the use of a police badge. The judge cited also the evidence of Buono's wallet, which "has a cut-out area customarily employed in that type of wallet for the placement of a badge," and Buono's denial at the time of his arrest that he had ever owned a wallet, "possibly a false statement; if so, interpreted under the law as showing a consciousness of guilt." All of this evidence was certainly enough to meet the legal requirement that the testimony of an accomplice be corroborated "by such other evidence as shall tend to connect the defendant with the commission of the offense. Case law establishes that such corroboration 'may be slight and entitled to little consideration when standing alone. The requisite corroboration may be provided by circumstantial evidence.' " The judge added that convictions were routinely obtained on the corroborated testimony of an accomplice who had made inconsistent statements, and he cited the Manson case as one recent example. A jury would be free to decide which statements to believe and which to disregard.

Judge George now spelled out his conclusion:

> This court has the authority and the obligation to deny a motion by the District Attorney's Office to dismiss serious pending criminal charges where the court finds that dismissal would not be "in furtherance of justice." . . . nor is it the function of the court automatically to "rubber-stamp" the prosecutor's decision to abandon the People's case. . . . Applicable standards indicate that a prosecutor must under ordinary circumstances pursue the prosecution of serious charges where there is sufficient evidence for a jury to convict, without concern for the consequences to his reputation should he be unsuccessful in obtaining a conviction.

This second reference to the possibility that concern for reputation had motivated the motion to dismiss made Grogan want to cheer. The judge then employed language more stinging:

> This court would be abdicating the responsibility of its office were it to permit the District Attorney to abort this massive and costly three-and-a-half-year investigation.

It would be "spurious," the judge proclaimed, to dismiss the charges on the theory, as suggested in the motion, that new evidence might turn up later, since the motion had been submitted "without the likelihood of refiling," as the prosecutor himself had stated. Furthermore it would be "disingenuous" to suggest, as again the prosecutor had, that the murder charges be dismissed lest an acquittal on them have a negative effect on the trial of the nonmurder counts. "Disingenuous" was the judge's carefully chosen word here for "phony." In a dignified but sharp way, the judge was accusing the prosecutor of slinging bull.

> The court's decision is that our legal system should be permitted to run its normal course by appropriate submission of the issue of guilt or innocence to a jury selected from the community rather than leaving that issue to the disposition of the District Attorney as final arbiter of the case. . . . If in fact [this court's] obligation is merely to perform the ministerial function of giving "rubber stamp" approval to the District Attorney's decision to abandon this murder prosecution, let an appellate court so instruct this court. . . . This court finds that dismissal of the ten murder charges pending against defendant would not be "in furtherance of justice," and the District Attorney's motion to dismiss those charges is hereby denied.

Finally the judge took care of the matter of the reluctance of the District Attorney's Office to prosecute. He fully expected a vigorous and effective resumption of prosecution, he said, but:

. . . should such action not be forthcoming from
the District Attorney's Office, this court has authority to deal with that contingency by referring
the case to the Attorney General . . . or under certain circumstances by appointing a special prosecutor.

The sermon was over. It had taken the judge an
hour and ten minutes to read it out. Its message was
sufficiently unusual to cause some initial confusion,
but the confidence of his tone and the persuasiveness
of his logic were quickly apparent, nowhere more evident than in the simple phrase "this court has authority," an assertion no one was prepared to doubt. It
was as though a second-strike victory had been declared in a kind of legal war, one with strong political
consequences, although politics had not played any
part in the judge's motives. His denial of the motion
was a slap in the face not only to Roger Kelly but to
John Van de Kamp, whose office the judge, not subtly,
was accusing of "delegating to Bianchi the prosecu-
torial responsibility for defendant's case by allowing
Bianchi to scuttle the case." Words such as "scuttle,"
"spurious," and "disingenuous" were not mild, nor
had they been meant to be mild. And the judge's calm
affirmation that he was prepared to turn over the prosecution to the attorney general or to a special prosecutor was especially provocative. John Van de Kamp
was a Democrat who was running for attorney general, a post then held by George Deukmejian, a Republican who was running for governor.

Judge George gave Van de Kamp two weeks to
decide whether to resume prosecuting Buono. If Van
de Kamp withdrew and Deukmejian's office decided
to take over the case, it might appear as though the
whole matter had degenerated into a political issue,
one that might play a role in the 1982 campaign. If the
Republican attorney general won the case before the
election, it would make the Democratic candidate for
that office look weak and help Deukmejian to the gov-
ernorship. If Deukmejian lost the case, Van de Kamp

and Kelly would be vindicated, Deukmejian would look foolish, and the Hillside Stranglers case would become known as Judge George's folly.

Judge George regretted the political implications, because he wanted nothing to detract from the only important issue, which was justice. But controversy he neither courted nor shunned. Personally he enjoyed the composure of a man who had done the right thing, and in some respects the hullabaloo his action caused did not bother him. Perhaps a side effect of all the charges and countercharges would be to heighten public regard for the criminal justice system, which appeared to many to have become paralyzed by trivialities; and perhaps the legal community, which had become an arrogant society unto itself, might come to focus for the moment more on justice than on the law, which had become less the instrument of justice than, as it were, its strangler. With all this in mind, the judge repeated the statutory phrase "in the furtherance of justice" several times over in his ruling. For all its length and scholarship, the ruling had a bracing simplicity to it, like "Thou shalt not bear false witness against thy neighbor."

JUDGE NOT KNOWN FOR CONTROVERSY

announced the *Los Angeles Times* the next morning, calling the judge's action "extraordinary. Such prosecution motions are normally granted as a matter of course." Lawyers were quoted saying they could not remember in their experience a similar ruling. References to the balance of power abounded. "Nothing in George's background," the *Times* reported, "predicted this surprise rejection. . . . He simply had no track record of going against convention. Prosecution and defense lawyers were in agreement that the 41-year-old-jurist was a scholarly, fair-minded judge. . . . Deputy Dist. Atty. Roger Kelly agreed, saying, 'I've always respected him and admired him, at least until today.' "

As for Angelo, he and his attorneys had to cancel their plans for a celebratory dinner.

"Mr. Buono has been on the brink of victory so many times," Katherine Mader said, "that he just doesn't show any emotion and he probably won't until he walks out having been found innocent of being the Hillside Strangler."

TWENTY-TWO

When Judge George denied the motion to dismiss murder charges against Angelo Buono, the city was deeply affected. Television and radio editorials endorsed the judge's courage, although the *L.A. Times* made no comment, and he received many letters of praise. Within the legal community, however, opinion was divided over whether he had performed a courageous act or an arrogant one. Lawyers and judges who objected to his decision did so on the grounds that he had upset "the system," even though the judge had stated in his ruling that without a trial Angelo Buono's guilt or innocence could never be established by means of the criminal justice system itself.

His opponents argued that he was improperly assuming a prosecutor's role. One politically prominent lawyer, a former federal judge, suggested privately that while it was difficult for people to understand why the judge had acted improperly in this case, given the vicious crimes involved, what if the defendant were

Martin Luther King or Sacco and Vanzetti, who might be subject to the prejudices of a judge? If a prosecutor moved to drop charges, it was wrong for a judge to question that decision and amounted to a violation of judicial neutrality.

Judge George did not respond to such criticisms publicly, except to cite the ample authority for his unprecedented action. Privately he pointed out that while his every decision was subject to appeal, his critics were suggesting that a prosecutor should have absolute discretion and not be subject to the same kind of scrutiny. Surely this was an unbalanced notion, all the checks on one side and none on the other. And to raise at all in this case the issue of political or racial bias was a red herring, symptomatic of the kind of mentality that perceived all criminal defendants as victims. If the judge was not a prosecutor, neither should the prosecutor be the judge.

The central issue here was, as Judge George saw it, not whether the judge was stepping beyond his proper role but whether the prosecutor was performing with the vigor mandated by the constitutional responsibilities of his office. Where would society be if something called the system, itself a precious yet imperfect human construct, subject to all the errors of which the people who worked within it were capable, were permitted to become an impediment to justice?

The word "system" itself was probably a misnomer. In its constant use and overuse the judge sensed characteristics of a contemporary obsession with valueless technology. "System" had come to imply something static and hard, something as inflexible as a computer and as self-sustaining as the robots of science fantasy. To deny the legal and moral responsibility of a judge to make the system work, adjust it, force it if necessary, was to adopt a peculiarly technological approach to the law, thwarting justice with technicalities, permitting social disorder in the name of procedural rigidity.

Roger Kelly defended himself publicly, denying Grogan's and others' accusations against him. Somehow his thirty-two-page memorandum to Van de Kamp, in which he argued that the case could not be won, was leaked to the *Los Angeles Times,* which gave it prominent coverage. Most observers believed that Kelly himself was the source of the leak, but he denied it. The memorandum ignored much of the evidence against Buono, including new and highly promising conclusions about the fibers found on Lauren Wagner's hands and wrists. (Kathy Vukovitch, the LAPD criminalist, had by now pretty well established that the Lauren Wagner fibers matched the rug, made from automobile carpeting, in the spare bedroom where, Bianchi had said, he and Angelo had tried to electrocute Lauren. The rug had still been in place when Angelo had been arrested. Other fibers from Lauren's hands matched an accumulation of material found in the crevices of the seat of the brown vinyl easy chair—an unusual collection of fibers that acted like geological sedimentation as evidence of time and place. Only what had been identified as cat hairs, also stuck to the adhesive left on Lauren's hands, remained a puzzle, since Angelo had owned no cats. One LAPD chemist had identified these as rabbit fur, but for some reason his analysis was discounted.)

Bob Grogan condemned Kelly, despite Kelly's denials, for using the media to undermine the case and to try to save face. Nor did John Van de Kamp's comments to David Israel, a columnist for the *Herald-Examiner,* seem proper to Grogan. Asked by Israel whether he thought the decision to drop the murder charges would hurt him politically, Van de Kamp replied:

"Given what the judge did, it may have been politically more prudent to proceed with the prosecution. It's one of the chances you take. But I think we'll be vindicated in the long run."

"Does that mean you think Buono will walk?"

"I'm limited in what I can say."

When he read that, Grogan observed: "*Limited!* He says he'll be vindicated! How is Van de Kamp going to be vindicated unless Buono's vindicated?" Grogan also noted that by saying that it would have been politically more prudent to prosecute, Van de Kamp was making Buono sound like a political victim, something Buono's lawyers must have liked: they were already referring to a "conspiracy to convict" their client. Again Grogan began to wonder whether people really wanted homicide detectives to do their job or not. Did people secretly or unconsciously agree with Buono that the girls deserved to die? There seemed to be an indifference to or even an acceptance of murder that was a symptom of some grave psychological disease in society.

Neither Van de Kamp nor Buono's lawyers took up Judge George's challenge to have the ruling appealed to a higher court, nor did they seek to have Judge George remove himself from the forthcoming trial, something that Angelo urged his attorneys to do. The District Attorney's Office withdrew from the case. Attorney General Deukmejian appointed two deputy attorneys general, Roger Boren and Michael Nash, along with a special investigator, Paul Tulleners, to examine evidence to determine whether the case was worth prosecuting. When these three discovered how much of the evidence had been ignored in Kelly's memorandum to Van de Kamp and in Kelly's motion to dismiss, they decided that Kelly was so negative as to be worthless to them, and they did not even consult him.

Of all the factors Kelly had omitted, the Lauren Wagner fiber evidence seemed to them the most important, perhaps the key to winning the case: it not only connected the victim to Angelo, it placed her in the very chair in which Bianchi had said that she had been gagged and blindfolded and in the very room where she had been killed. It was exactly the kind of circumstantial evidence needed under California law to corroborate the testimony of an accomplice; it was a means of separating Bianchi's lies from his truths.

Boren, Nash, and Tulleners were quickly convinced that Buono was guilty; convincing a jury would be another matter, but they were sure that there was enough evidence for that, and Judge George's ruling, they perceived, could act as a kind of schema or preliminary script for the presentation of their case. Their only serious misgivings concerned whether, because of the circumstantial nature of much of the evidence, they could persuade twelve different citizens to a unanimous verdict, as required. You never knew what a jury might do. All you needed was one juror who hated the police, for instance, and you could forget about unanimity.

They presented their view of the case in a six-hour meeting with a panel of four nationally respected prosecutors—one of them had prosecuted Caryl Chessman—appointed by Deukmejian to advise him, who agreed unanimously that the Attorney General's Office should prosecute. In November the case went to trial, after a two-month continuance granted by the judge to permit the new prosecutors to prepare—a delay opposed by the defense, which argued that Buono's right to a speedy trial was being violated and appealed this ruling all the way to the California Supreme Court, which upheld Judge George six to one.

Immediately the judge faced another crucial ruling. In June the defense had made a "Motion to Exclude Hypnotically Induced Testimony and Testimony Influenced by or Related to Hypnosis." This motion, which argued for the exclusion of testimony by five witnesses, including Kenneth Bianchi and Beulah Stofer, would, if granted, effectively end the prosecution's case. The motion was occasioned by a case pending before the California Supreme Court *(People* v. *Shirley)* in which the court was expected to rule within a few weeks' time on the admissibility of the testimony of witnesses who had been hypnotized. For years hypnosis of witnesses by the police had been commonplace, but now it had become the subject of a national legal controversy, and the Minnesota Supreme Court had already ruled that a witness is incapacitated from ever testifying if hypnotized. Judge George's problem was to anticipate what the California Supreme Court would rule. Its most extreme possible position would be that any attempt to hypnotize a witness, even if totally unsuccessful, would cause that witness to be incapacitated: if that was the ruling, Bianchi would be barred entirely as a witness.

Judge George decided to assume that the California Supreme Court, however liberal, would stop short of the most extreme position and rule, at most, that witnesses who had been successfully hypnotized could not testify. That left him to decide who had and who had not been hypnotized and opened up the whole question of whether Dr. Orne had been correct in his conclusion that Bianchi had fooled Drs. Watkins and Allison, had faked both being hypnotized and the multiple personality syndrome. Since Bianchi had pleaded guilty and had never gone to trial, neither issue had been decided in a court of law. Dr. Watkins continued to maintain his original diagnosis, that he had hypnotized Bianchi and that Bianchi suffered from multiple personality disorder, was legally insane and not responsible for his acts. Dr. Allison had done a partial about-face. He still claimed that he had actually hypnotized Bianchi, but he admitted that Bianchi had fooled him, partially, on the multiple personality issue. Dr. Allison now testified that he believed that Bianchi had indeed been a multiple personality *while committing the murders* but that he had not been multiple when talking to Dr. Allison. Since interviewing Bianchi, Dr. Allison had become a prison psychiatrist, and now, he said, he realized that prisoners do tend to lie:

> That was a shock to me because I had been used to believing what my patients told me and working from that. But here I would meet a man as he was trying to go on parole and I'd find out that he's told one story when he got arrested to the police, another story to his own attorney, a third story when he got into court, a fourth story to his parole officer and a fifth story to me when I got him here, and now he wants to go on parole and he's got a sixth story. And there's no way, you know, that you can tell what's the truth when you have that kind of changing history.

Grogan, hearing Dr. Allison's change of heart, or partial change, wondered that it had taken Dr. Allison's becoming a prison psychiatrist for him to realize that criminals lie. Hadn't he ever seen a Jimmy Cagney movie? And did he really believe everything his regu-

lar patients told him? Didn't he know that fooling the
shrink was one of the favorite games of people on the
couch? Oh well, Grogan reflected, at least Allison had
admitted being fooled, halfway. As for Dr. Watkins,
who was currently giving public lectures about Ken
and Steve and Billy, he probably believed the Holy
Trinity was a multiple personality case.

Judge George ruled that Dr. Orne's analysis was
entirely persuasive, that Bianchi had faked both hypnosis and multiple personalities. The judge reached his
decision, he said, after studying the more than fifty
hours of videotapes of the psychiatric sessions and
their transcripts. Of Dr. Watkins the judge said:

> I find Dr. Watkins' methodology to be highly sus-
> pect based on the testimony of all the doctors and
> based on the literature submitted to this Court. . . .
>
> And I find that in particular his methodology
> was fraught with suggestibility and I think he . . .
> invited the emergence of or gave a cue for the
> emergence of the multiple personality in his re-
> marks in the first session, actually telling Mr. Bian-
> chi that there was a multiple personality.

The judge could not resist a further swipe:

> I think that Dr. Watkins shows incredible na-
> ïveté and made unwarranted assumptions in dis-
> counting any possibility of faking. And I find
> almost ludicrous Dr. Watkins' emphasis on the four
> different styles of handwriting, which Billy's or
> anybody else's earlier years [came] up with. . . . It
> [all] appears quite farfetched.

As for Dr. Allison, the judge, referring to his "rather
dramatic turnabout and substantially revised opinion," dismissed his continued insistence that he had
in fact hypnotized Bianchi. Judge George found that,
as Dr. Orne had argued, Bianchi had never been hypnotized in any session and had faked all the multiple
personalities, inspired by the suggestions of doctors
and a psychiatric social worker and aided by his exten-

sive knowledge of psychological theory and by viewing *Sybil* and *The Three Faces of Eve*. Bianchi's testimony was therefore admissible.

Regarding the four other witnesses in question—including a witness to the Yolanda Washington abduction and Beulah Stofer's neighbor, Evelyn Wall—Judge George ruled that all except Beulah Stofer had been successfully hypnotized by the police, and he was therefore required to bar their testimony. Mrs. Stofer herself, said the judge, had not been hypnotized and could testify. According to Mrs. Stofer and the police officers who had tried to hypnotize her, she suffered from asthma and emphysema and her coughing fits had prevented hypnotic induction.

The defense was pleased that Bianchi's testimony had been ruled admissible, because Chaleff and Mader believed that it would make it easier to prove him a liar. But the prosecution figured that Bianchi's lying was a given anyway and that they needed his testimony, the true parts of it, to convict Buono. So both sides thought that they had won this round. (It turned out that Judge George had anticipated the California Supreme Court's hypnosis ruling correctly. On March 11, 1982, the Supreme Court did at last rule that the testimony of witnesses who had been hypnotized could not be admitted. In June of that year, however, the Supreme Court added a footnote to this opinion stating that it was not ruling at that time on whether the decision was retroactive or applied to cases then at trial, throwing the matter back into doubt with reference to the Buono trial. To the extent that they excluded the testimony of any witness, Judge George then vacated his original hypnosis rulings, offering to take up the entire matter again, but neither the prosecution nor the defense sought to do so. Nor did either side then attempt to introduce witnesses whom the judge had already determined to have been hypnotized. The testimony of Bianchi and Stofer would remain admissible.)

Now, on November 16, 1981, jury selection began. Early in the process, Boren and Nash decided that Chaleff and Mader were trying to trick them into using up challenges of prospective jurors at the start, leaving the defense's challenges for crucial final selections. Instead Boren and Nash accepted a panel of twelve jurors and eight alternates as soon as they felt they had a reasonable group; and the defense, since it had let these candidates pass, was stuck with them. Of the jurors, ten worked in city, county, or federal civil service positions. One was a retired Dolly Madison Bakery employee and one a female Pan American Airlines flight attendant. They included, promisingly in the eyes of the prosecution, one woman with two daughters and another woman living near the Eagle Rock Plaza with a teenage daughter.

From the prosecution's point of view, the social and economic character of the jury was encouraging: these were working people, none rich, none idle. Such people tended to be more realistic than the privileged classes about extremes of human conduct. For the prosecutor trying to convict an Angelo Buono, the worst possible juror would have been someone isolated by wealth or status or both from the harsher realities of urban life—a Beverly Hills matron, say, or a young university professor or a Unitarian minister— who luxuriated in an exalted view of humanity, felt guilty about privilege, and was unable or unwilling to accept the idea of the ruthless. As Grogan said, the ideal jury to convict Buono would have consisted of homicide detectives and whores.

The jury as finally chosen included seven women and five men, among them—as nearly as can be surmised from names and physical appearances—six Afro-Americans, two Anglos, and four Hispanics. The alternates, of whom two eventually became jurors, were similarly mixed, with only Asian-Americans missing from among the chief ethnic population groups of Los Angeles. Ethnic and sexual balance had become important factors in determining the fair selection of juries, and this one appeared immune to scrutiny on appeal.

It took three and a half months (fifty-four actual days in court) to select this jury, delaying the actual start of the trial until the spring of 1982. The cause of this tedium and expense was California's cumbersome system of jury selection. A hundred and twenty prospective jurors were examined—these surviving from an original panel of three hundred and sixty, those who could not serve for several months being excused—with defense and prosecution both permitted twenty-six peremptory challenges. By law, both sides were allowed to examine each prospective juror directly, and the judge and counsel had to question each in individual court sessions from which all other jurors as well as members of the public were excluded. Interrogation covered such matters as whether he or she would vote for acquittal because of opposition to the death penalty. This time-consuming procedure—in many other states and in the federal system the judge alone, sometimes guided by written requests from the attorneys, conducted the examination of jurors—was the result of judicial decisions and legislative lobbying by attorneys, who got paid by the hour and were jealous of their prerogatives. Direct questioning of jurors by lawyers was permitted in *all* felony and misdemeanor trials in California and helped to clog the courts. During the Hillside Stranglers trial, jury selection in another Los Angeles murder case, this one involving only one count and one defendant, took from April of one year to February of the next, a full ten months. Judge George, who had lobbied for the system's reform, calling it "sick" and a prime reason for growing public contempt for the criminal justice system, said that he felt "disquieted" when fellow jurists congratulated him on getting a jury for the Buono trial in "only" fifty-four court days.

When at last the jurors were impaneled, they learned that the trial ahead of them was expected to last about a year. Court would meet from ten to twelve and from one-thirty to four-thirty, with time off for holidays, doctor's appointments, and funerals. The jurors' employers, including Pan American, agreed to pay full wages for the length of the trial. In addition the jurors received five dollars a day and fifteen cents per mile to drive to and from the courthouse. They had to pay for their own lunches.

Only two weeks into the trial itself, another important ruling presented itself to the judge. At issue were Bianchi's extended statements to the police in Bellingham, the interviews for which Salerno, Grogan, and the others had so carefully prepared and which had elicited minutely detailed accounts of the killings, much new information, and several items that Bianchi could have known only from being present at the murders. Without these statements the prosecution's case would be greatly weakened, but because they had not been made under oath and for other, technical reasons, the judge ruled them inadmissible. Only Bianchi's testimony under oath would be let in, the same "morass of contradictions" which had been the basis for Kelly's motion to dismiss.

But then Chaleff and Mader—in what was probably a serious lapse in defense strategy—exercised their right to cross-examine Bianchi on his Bellingham statements. The defense's intention was to underline Kenny's contradictions, but the result was to render admissible the Bellingham confessions in full and to permit the prosecution to show that much of what Bianchi narrated in Bellingham was, unlike his later obfuscations, verifiable: the needle mark on Kristina Weckler's neck, for instance, unnoticed until Bianchi had mentioned it, and his positioning of Lauren Wagner as confirmed by the fibers. Equally important was that audio tapes of these confessions were now played for the jurors, who could judge for themselves whether anyone, no matter how accomplished a liar, could have invented such a mass of details—dialogue, physical description of victims and locations, such things as the cigar box, itself an item of physical evidence, in which Angelo had kept the handcuffs. Boren and Nash had been struck by the convincing qualities of these tapes—including the tone of Bianchi's voice, even, matter-of-fact, so different from the histrionics of the psychiatric sessions—and they hoped that the jury would react similarly. They rejoiced that Chaleff and Mader had opened the door to letting in these tapes and that Judge George was quick to admit them.

Another opening which Boren and Nash had hoped for came when Chaleff and Mader brought in Tonya Dockery to testify that Angelo, far from being brutal and violent, had once tried to sodomize her but had stopped when she had protested. Although some evidence of Buono's harshness with women had already been admitted, Boren and Nash saw this attempt to show what a gentlemanly fellow Angelo really was as a breakthrough. As Judge George ruled, Dockery's testimony allowed into evidence Sabra Hannan's testimony that Angelo had tried to force her into submitting into sodomy, Becky Spears's testimony that Angelo had injured her by repeated acts of forced sodomy, and Antoinette Lombardo's testimony that Angelo had sodomized her. The judge kept out some details, including the orgy at the box factory and the attempted extortion of David Wood, but bit by bit the truth was now permitted to emerge.

Some witnesses found it more difficult to talk than others. Sabra Hannan, clearly relishing getting back at Kenny and Angelo, narrated her grotesque experiences in fluent and vivacious detail. She was married now and working as a dental hygienist. Becky Spears, by contrast, was forlorn, sickly-looking, clearly distressed at having to recapitulate her suffering. Perhaps most touching was Antoinette Lombardo, who had so naïvely loved Angelo and believed in a matrimonial future with him. She was now studying to be a court reporter. Her husband waited for her in the hallway as she managed to describe various horrors, and when she was finally permitted to leave the courtroom, he embraced her.

The work of Paul Tulleners, Boren and Nash's special investigator, added much to the prosecution's case. Tulleners was a demon researcher, and over the weeks and months he dug up material no one else had found. To begin with, very little was known about Angelo's life prior to his linking up with Kenny. Other than Candy, relatives stuck to a policy of *omertà*, some from fear and others, like Angelo's sister Cecilia, from loyalty; and Jenny was dead. Angelo, of course, said nothing, except that he did give an interview to a television reporter, Jim Mitchell of KNXT, whom he telephoned from jail saying he wanted to talk. At the jail Angelo told Mitchell:

"I didn't do nothing, and they're trying to put me in the gas chamber. If I killed somebody, they have a right to burn me. I believe in that. An eye for an eye, a tooth for a tooth. But I didn't kill nobody."

Angelo, whom the reporter described as "a forty-seven-year-old family success story," continued:

"I voted for the death penalty. If a guy did wrong, kill the son of a bitch. . . . You know that D.A. dropped the case. I didn't like Kelly but he didn't have no evidence. But the judge wants to keep it going. I don't know why. I think he's biased. Why am I in this courtroom? Because some judge thinks he's God. I've never been in a courtroom before. I don't know what's going on. . . .

"Hey, man. I'm getting gassed in that courtroom. I'm getting railroaded. This whole thing has been a political trip from day one."

Tulleners's work, however, dug up the truth about Angelo's background. His juvenile and later court records at first appeared to have been lost or destroyed, but Tulleners patiently hand-searched the files and was able to fill out the picture of a man who had been a bully and a thief since childhood and who had, contrary to his protestations, been in courtrooms and jails many times before.

Tulleners also found Angelo's first wife, verified Angelo's failure to support any of his eight children financially, and located Nanette Campina in Florida. He interviewed Nanette there. She was most reluctant to talk. Unlike Candy, she was still afraid of Angelo, and Tulleners could see that it would be impossible to get her to come to Los Angeles voluntarily to testify. Eventually she did begin to confide some stories about Angelo's brutality, about how she had escaped to Florida, and about how her daughter, Annette, had complained about Angelo's "advances" to her. But unfortunately Tulleners was accompanied by a young, greenhorn fellow investigator, who reacted with such ill-concealed shock and disgust at Nanette's revelations that she clammed up from embarrassment. Tulleners had heard enough, however, to conclude that Angelo had raped and beaten Nanette regularly and had certainly slept with his stepdaughter.

It was unlikely that all of this material would be admissible at trial, but all of it bolstered Boren and

Nash's confidence in their case and made them feel even more strongly that their cause was just. Of admissible evidence the most important Tulleners unearthed was the white Mustang Bianchi had named as the car used in the abduction of Kimberly Martin and in the dumping of Cindy Hudspeth's body. Bianchi had said that the Mustang had stains on the carpet on the passenger side, probably from a leak in the air conditioning. Tulleners checked through thousands of vehicle registrations, narrowed the search to a few hundred, began personally inspecting these, and finally found the right car, the carpet stains still visible. He was able to trace it back to the woman who had consigned it to Angelo for sale in 1977.

When Bianchi took the stand in June 1982, he became the two hundredth witness to testify. It fell to Michael Nash to examine him, and Kenny was less cooperative than ever. He denied remembering anything about any murders. He had been scheduled to testify for a month, more or less; now it looked as though he would be through in a day. But in a court session in which Bianchi's lawyer, but not Bianchi himself, was present, Judge George let drop the question whether Kenny was violating his plea-bargain agreement to testify against Buono. After all, hadn't Bianchi agreed to testify fully and freely? If he was found to be in violation of the agreement, he would have to serve his time in Walla Walla, something Bianchi had thought it worth bargaining to avoid.

Having had an evening to consider the prospect of Walla Walla, Kenny began talking again the next day, still contradicting himself but at least giving Nash the opportunity to catch him in lies or in inadvertent truths. Boren and Nash were so meticulously prepared—they developed a filing system that enabled them to locate any of the thousands of documents quickly, and they devised a daily summary of the transcript, which by October 1982 had grown to over twenty-five thousand pages—that they were able to elicit some revealing points from Bianchi, particularly about his association with Buono before the murders. Kenny always looked directly at Nash and never at Angelo. The only interchange between the cousins came when Kenny described having intercourse with a girlfriend of Angelo's on the water bed, something he knew Angelo would have been furious about had he known. As Kenny told of the event, obviously pleased with himself, Angelo quietly gave him the finger.

If Nash was skillful at eliciting from Bianchi elements of his relationship with Buono, Chaleff was also good at confusing matters when he questioned Bianchi, who was glad to help with contradictions. By the time Bianchi stepped down, after five months on the stand, most of it under cross-examination by Chaleff, Nash privately confessed himself ready to strangle the witness, and he worried whether the jury had become overwhelmed by all the testimony. If muddlement was Chaleff's strategy, he was doing well with it.

One afternoon after the day's session, Jerry Cunningham, Judge George's bailiff, a young sheriff's deputy with a fresh and open face, remarked to the judge that it was a shame that a guy as intelligent and articulate as Ken Bianchi had not put his talents to better use.

"A guy like that," Cunningham said, "he could have made something of himself. He could have gone someplace in society. Done something useful."

"Yes," Judge George said. "He could have been another Albert Speer."

Suddenly, in the middle of Bianchi's testimony in October, the defense made a major move. Katherine Mader had belatedly discovered that Markust Camden had spent time in a mental hospital, and the defense accused Frank Salerno and Pete Finnigan of deliberately withholding this information, in violation of California's discovery rule. Chaleff and Mader alleged that there had been "willful law enforcement misconduct which has made a sham of the prosecution of Angelo Buono" in that "specific critical impeachment information regarding Markust Camden's credibility was known by Sgt. Frank Salerno and Deputy Peter Finnigan in 1979, and [has] been deliberately withheld from the defense since that time." The motion also claimed that since Salerno and Finnigan withheld the truth about Camden from the magistrate who had issued the search warrant for Angelo Buono's house, all evidence obtained in that search, including the fiber and carpet material and Angelo's wallet, should be suppressed. Salerno and Finnigan were part of a "conspiracy to convict Angelo Buono." They were aware that Camden "has spent almost his entire adult life institutionalized in mental facilities." They were aware that he had been "hospitalized as 'delusional' and 'psychotic' at the time of Sheriffs' contacts with him in 1979. . . . Salerno and Finnigan, as a deliberate pattern of conduct, failed to maintain contact with potential witnesses who contradicted Markust Camden" (an apparent reference to the long-forgotten and discounted Pam Pelletier, who, since she had been hypnotized, could not now have testified). They had by allowing Camden to testify "and by not coming forward with information they possessed regarding Camden's mental capacity, perpetrated a fraud upon the court."

In light of these charges against Salerno and Finnigan, the defense moved to dismiss the case "due to denial of due process." If that were denied, the defense called for the declaration of a mistrial.

Headlines the next morning read:

COPS ON TRIAL
IN BUONO CASE?

TWENTY-THREE

Judge George took the new motion to dismiss under submission. The prosecution would have to be given time to reply, and he would need extensive preparation to make his ruling. Alleged police misconduct had become perhaps the most frequently stated reason for appellate reversals of criminal convictions in recent years. In 1976, for instance, the California Court of Appeal had reversed a defendant's conviction for burglary because police officers coming upon a burglary in progress had not stopped to knock at the door and announce their purpose before entering the house, arresting the burglar, and seizing the evidence. Mindful of his commitment to "the practice of preventive jurisprudence," the judge would have to construct a careful ruling in order to avoid having it overturned later by a higher court—especially if he ruled against the defense, as, after reviewing the facts, he was inclined to do. If Salerno and Finnigan could be shown to have deliberately concealed Markust Camden's mental problems, their conduct could easily be construed as grounds for at least a mistrial.

Meanwhile the trial poked along. In December, over defense objections, the jury was taken on a series of elaborately planned excursions to the locations central to the prosecution's case: 703 East Colorado, apartment 114 at 1950 Tamarind, 809 East Garfield, the railroad diner, Alta Terrace Drive, and all the other abduction and body sites. The prosecution and the detectives, including Sergeant Roger Brown of the Glendale P.D., who had original responsibility for the Lissa Kastin investigation, orchestrated these "jury-views" to demonstrate the plausibility of the killers' movements. Each juror was given an elaborate itinerary.

But the jury-views could not proceed before the judge resolved a dilemma. Angelo had the right to be present at these as at all phases of his trial, but security required that he be shackled when transported anywhere, as he was each morning and afternoon when he was taken to and from the courthouse and the jail. Earlier that year the California Supreme Court had reversed a voluntary manslaughter conviction because the defendant had been seen, against his wishes, in jail clothes by the jury, and the shackling of defendants in court had caused other reversals. Angelo did not want the jurors to see him in shackles, and if they did the Supreme Court would certainly find this prejudicial. The judge resolved the dilemma by advising Angelo that he also had the right *not* to go along on the jury-views. Angelo was told that he could go or not, but if he did, it must be in shackles. He decided not to go.

The judge and jury were transported to the jury-views in a Sheriff's Department van, escorted by motorcycle police, the detectives and attorneys following in separate cars. Each principal detective acted as a sort of master of ceremonies at the location for which he had primary investigative responsibility, with Salerno piecing together what had happened at the railroad diner, Grogan pointing out how and where Lauren Wagner had been abducted, and so on. The excursions were taken at night to convey authentic circumstances. Grogan was anxious about what the jury would think of Beulah Stofer's testimony when they saw that the shrubbery in her yard now blocked completely the view from her front window to the street. (Mrs. Stofer still maintained that this had been her vantage point, so Boren and Nash had decided not to introduce her having picked both Buono and Bianchi out in the mug runs, since identification from behind the window would have seemed impossible. She had testified simply that she had definitely seen two men.) To solve the shrubbery problem, Grogan took Mrs. Stofer's garden shears and chopped the shrubbery back down to its 1977 level. The defense objected heatedly to the sergeant's landscaping, to which he admitted in court, but the judge found no fault with it.

The most dramatic of the jury-views was the visit to the "cow patch" on Landa Street. The jurors were able to see how obscure a place it was, concluding, so the prosecution hoped, that only someone who like Angelo had lived for years in the area would know about it and could find it quickly, especially in the dark. To emphasize this point, on the way up to Landa Street, Paul Tulleners pointed out Jenny Buono's house, where Angelo had grown up, and the house on Glover Street, where Candy still lived and where Angelo had lived with her. Then at the cow patch, as the jury looked down the hill toward the trash heap in the darkness, Dudley Varney described how the bodies of Dolores Cepeda and Sonja Johnson had looked when he had found them.

As the jurors waited in the December darkness on this hillside overlooking the Elysian Valley, Dudley Varney said to them: "Please follow visually the helicopter you see above you. It will turn on its spotlight to point out certain locations to us. In each instance, I'll then tell you what location that is." One by one the helicopter flew over the fateful places, switching on its spotlight and illuminating each as Dudley Varney identified its significance. Up behind the cow patch, "That is the place on Alvarado where Kimberly Martin's body was found." Below and to the north, "That is the Golden State Freeway offramp where Jane King's body was found." Farther north, Jenny

Buono's house. Across the Elysian Valley, Lauren Wagner, Kristina Weckler. And in the center, Angelo's house, or at least where it had been.

This performance had been Boren and Nash's idea, when they had cased the cow patch during the day and noticed how many of the key locations could be seen from that spot. They hoped the illuminations would have a powerful effect on the jury. Afterward, standing in the courthouse parking lot, the jury gone home, Grogan told the prosecutors:

"That was some show! Jesus. Mikey, Roger, I tell you, Warner Brothers couldn't have done it better."

The judge said it had reminded him of a *son et lumière* display he had witnessed at Pompeii, where spotlights had also illuminated scenes of death.

I like this fucking judge, Grogan thought. Please God don't let anything happen to him.

Just then Katherine Mader, in a jocular mood as she drove out of the parking lot, made a playful swerve toward the detectives and the prosecutors. Grogan did not think it was funny.

"That bitch'll be able to buy a dozen more of those Mercedes," Grogan said, "with the taxpayers' money she's making defending that asshole."

Grogan surpassed all the detectives in his aversion to Katherine Mader, because she had made a special point of trying to undermine his credibility every time he took the stand. Once, when he had said that Angelo's accent reminded him of Brooklyn, she asked whether he had ever been to Brooklyn. Of course he had, he said, but you didn't have to go to Brooklyn to know what a Brooklyn accent was. Then she asked him what his own accent was. Boston, he replied, glowering. How, Mader wanted to know, could someone with a Boston accent living in Los Angeles identify a man born in Rochester who had lived forty years in Los Angeles as having a Brooklyn accent? Grogan said nothing, but he vowed at that moment to get back at her someday. He did not care for people who implied ridicule of his Boston accent or mocked it as though it were some sort of mental impediment.

On another occasion, Mader tried to impugn Grogan's testimony that he had observed a space between Angelo's front teeth when interviewing him. She asked Grogan to come down from the stand, go over to the defendant, and look into Angelo's mouth. Grogan did so, clenching his fists to control his anger as everyone in the courtroom saw the big detective bend down to peer at Angelo, who leaned his head back and bared his teeth at Grogan with obvious malice. There was no space. What this proved, other than that Mader was trying to make a fool of him, Grogan could not imagine. Later he found out that Angelo had had dental work done since the 1979 interview.

Angelo's teeth, or one of them, threatened to delay the trial for weeks at one point. He had complained of a toothache, and since by law a defendant must be able to concentrate his full faculties on the proceedings, undistracted by molar or other pain, a dentist was summoned, first the regular jail dentist and then a specialist, who announced that Mr. Buono needed root canal work. There would be several appointments, over a period of three to four weeks. Trial would have to be adjourned on those occasions. But someone, perhaps knowing that dentists tend to be law-and-order types, telephoned the root canal specialist anonymously and reminded him that it was costing the taxpayers about five thousand dollars a day every day that the trial was adjourned. "I understand," the dentist replied. "I hadn't thought of that." He pulled Buono's tooth that afternoon, saying how sorry he was that it could not be saved. The prosecutors were relieved, since they figured that once Buono realized how easily he could foul up the trial, he might discover a new toothache or other affliction every day. Now, with his tooth a thing of the past, he might think having the trial continue preferable to losing another tooth or perhaps something even more precious—"I wish Angelo would get a pain in his balls," Grogan said.

Angelo's lawyers were as attentive as they could be, under the circumstances, to his physical comforts. One afternoon Gerald Chaleff appeared in the judge's chambers to complain that Angelo's red silk underwear had been confiscated. Although he did not see this deprivation as constituting cruel and unusual punishment, Judge George ordered the silk underwear returned to the prisoner.

Just after the new year, 1983, Judge George announced his ruling on the defense motion to dismiss or declare a mistrial because of Salerno and Finnigan's alleged misconduct. The detectives resented the attack Chaleff and Mader had mounted against them, especially since the defense lawyers had notified the media ahead of time so as to get maximum publicity for their charges. Salerno and Finnigan did not like having their integrity questioned in the newspapers, and from that point on they tried to avoid any contact with Chaleff and Mader. On the night of the jury-view of Angeles Crest, the lawyers had asked the detectives to have dinner with them, as if Chaleff and Mader had not initiated an action potentially ruinous to the detectives' careers, for surely they would be seriously damaged if found responsible for botching the Hillside Stranglers trial. The detectives refused the invitation, Finnigan saying, "I'm not that much of a hypocrite."

The judge's ruling was sweet to Salerno and Finnigan. In charging the detectives with willful misconduct, Judge George wrote, Chaleff and Mader "made the allegation recklessly, with disregard for the truth." He castigated the lawyers for deliberately stirring up publicity for their motion, thereby endangering "the right of the prosecution—like the defense—to a fair trial free of prejudicial publicity concerning unsubstantiated charges." Although Chaleff pointed out that information about Camden had originally been given to Buono's previous attorneys, not the ones presiding at the trial, the judge ruled that it was not the prosecution's fault if the defense, acting without "due diligence," had failed to follow up on material that had been available to the defense in files since 1980, material that included Camden's stay in the Indiana mental hospital. Nor was there any evidence that Camden had been "delusional" or "psychotic," nor that he had spent, as alleged by the defense, "almost his entire adult life" in mental hospitals: forty-two days appeared to be the total amount of time in which he had been, voluntarily, institutionalized, and the detectives had been within reason in believing it to have been only two weeks.

The judge threw out the motion to quash the search warrant for Angelo's house and suppress evidence found there, and he rejected as "totally unwarranted the conclusion voiced by the defense that [the detectives] perpetrated a fraud upon the court."

When interviewed by reporters after the ruling had been issued, the judge suggested that the media ought to give as prominent coverage to the clearing of the detectives' names as had been devoted to the smearing of them. For the most part, the press and television did this, and Salerno and Finnigan were able to feel wholly vindicated. It was after this ruling that Katherine Mader complained to the judge that Salerno and Finnigan had been smirking at her and had made obscene gestures to her in court; but since she gave as the sole source of these charges a "court-watcher," an old man who came to court every day to doze and pass the time, the judge brushed off her complaint.

In April the prosecutors, having introduced over a thousand exhibits and called two hundred and fifty witnesses, were about ready to rest their case when they got an important break. Cheryl Burke, who had been in the Hollywood public library the night of Kimberly Martin's murder, had testified that Bianchi had bothered her in the parking lot that night, but she had said nothing about Buono, who had stalked her in the stacks earlier that evening, frightening her into leaving the building. A couple of weeks after testifying, she happened to be at a party where a deputy attorney general, neither Boren nor Nash, was present, and he asked her what it had been like in court. Suddenly she confessed to him that she had been terrified. Not until she had gotten up on the stand did she recognize Angelo Buono as the man who had followed her around the stacks that night. "Predatory" was her word for Angelo. But she had not said anything about this in court. She had been afraid. The deputy attorney general convinced Mrs. Burke to go to Boren and Nash, and she testified again, placing Buono with Bianchi in the library that night. Her testimony, followed by that of Catherine Lorre, made what Boren and Nash thought was a powerful end to their presentation, which had taken more than a year to get through.

Ironical political changes had taken place during that year. John Van de Kamp was elected attorney general and was therefore technically in charge of a prosecution that as district attorney he had moved to drop. He kept distant from the case, however, not communicating with Boren and Nash at all, who felt oddly that they were working against the political interests of their new boss by going after Buono and that they were operating in a peculiar sort of vacuum as autonomous prosecutors. George Deukmejian had been elected governor, and the new Los Angeles County district attorney was Robert Philibosian, who had previously worked under Deukmejian in the Attorney General's Office and had supervised Boren and Nash's work on the Buono case. Philibosian had as one of his first moves as district attorney transferred Roger Kelly to Compton, which many observers considered the Siberia of the county for a deputy D.A. Occasionally Grogan would run into Kelly and would invariably snub him.

Now it was the defense's turn. Boren and Nash wondered whether Chaleff and Mader would try to argue that Bianchi had acted alone or that he had had an accomplice other than Angelo. Angelo himself was privately feuding with his attorneys. He did not want to put on any defense at all and threatened to fire Chaleff and Mader. To Angelo it made no sense to try to counter the prosecution's arguments beyond what had already been done on cross-examination. Angelo was afraid that more damaging evidence might come out the longer the case went on, and he did not want to see his lawyers recall witnesses who had already given the jury a damning portrait of his life and character. He wanted to gamble that Boren and Nash had not yet proved his guilt beyond a reasonable doubt and leave it at that. One morning he refused to leave the holding cell in the courthouse. He had had enough, he said. Judge George had him brought into the courtroom without the jury present and talked to him, explaining that by law he had to attend and that if he insisted on staying in his cell, he would have to hear everything through a loudspeaker that would be rigged up in there.

"I ain't comfortable in court," Angelo said. "I heard enough."

"But Mr. Buono," the judge said in a voice that was at once soothing and condescending, "that big chair you sit in here in court, it's much more comfortable than the hard bench in the holding cell, now isn't it?"

Angelo relented. Chaleff and Mader opened their case by recalling Markust Camden.

Camden had been hitchhiking around the country —through Illinois, Iowa, Texas, Arizona—looking for a girlfriend he had lost. His life was one long improvisation without melody. In February he had started telephoning Mader and Chaleff regularly from pay phones at truck stops, hinting that if the defense would help him locate his girlfriend, he might just change his story. He might testify that he was unsure of his identification of Angelo Buono as the abductor of Judy Miller. He wanted one more chance with his girlfriend, he said, and he would do anything if Mader and Chaleff and their staff could help him get her back. When Mader, who was taping some of the calls, refused to make a deal, the conversations ended. But at the end of March, Mader located him back home in Indiana and told him that she wanted him to come out to testify again anyway, with no deals between them. Camden replied that he would shoot to death anyone who tried to approach him, or he would escape to Alaska. Mader told him that he would be found anywhere he went.

"What would happen if I didn't come?" Camden asked.

"We'd harass you. . . . We'd harass you forever."

"Oh, really?"

"What do you think I'd do, Markust? I've got a client who's facing the gas chamber and a lot of it is based on what you're now saying is wrong information. You think I'm just going to give up? It's not going to go away."

Camden returned to California. Chaleff called him to the stand, this time in order to try to expose his mental problems to the jury, who knew nothing of them as yet.

Chaleff did a relentless, clever job on Camden, getting him to admit nervous breakdowns and brushes with the law. But Camden stuck to his original story and identification of Buono. Under Chaleff's pressure, Camden became very angry on the stand. He felt persecuted. He felt used, abused, ridiculed. Chaleff asked why, if he had been worried about becoming a suspect back in 1977 and did not want to get involved, had he not simply kept quiet? The implication was that Salerno had somehow tricked or forced him into his story. But Camden said that he had talked then "because I didn't figure you people would take and have that much disrespect for people's private lives that you have to tear them down, Chaleff."

"But you didn't want to be involved, right?"

"I didn't think you was going to drag me through the mill. I'm talking about any of you. State of California. Roger, Salerno, the whole damn bunch of you. Includes this man right here," he said, pointing to the judge. Everyone laughed.

"So that we don't have any ambiguity or unfairness," Judge George said, "the record will reflect that I have been pointed out."

"The whole State of California," Camden added. "You all been driving me crazy."

"Was it a long drive to get there for you?" Chaleff asked.

"I'm really getting off on that. Of course I understand you have to ask questions . . . but you just, you know, just ride, ride and ride and ride. Why don't you just let it go when somebody says, 'Yeah, I seen this person'? . . . You trying to make an ass out of me up here. You trying to make me look like I'm a damned nut or something because I had a nervous breakdown." And then with a colorful idiom that summed up his defense of his story in spite of his mental problems, Camden concluded: "My dog had a cold, by

God, but she had pups! Apparently something wasn't interrupting her.''

Boren and Nash were pleased with Camden's performance. He had shown more mental toughness than they could have hoped for in standing up to Chaleff's attacks.

Chaleff also tried to impugn Catherine Lorre's testimony by suggesting that she had lied earlier by saying that she had been returning home from a class at the USC medical school when Buono and Bianchi had stopped her. The idea was that if she had lied about being a medical student, which apparently she had, then she was lying or could easily be lying about meeting Buono and Bianchi. But since her story fit perfectly with Bianchi's version of the incident, Boren and Nash did not feel that Chaleff had inflicted any serious damage on her credibility.

In a year and a half, many bizarre and shocking things had occurred in the courtroom. Much of the evidence was of an almost unendurable gruesomeness, especially the color photographs of the victim's bodies. A set of these had been glued onto a piece of plasterboard the size of a double bed which was kept, along with the model of Angelo's house, in the judge's chambers because of its size and brought out when needed. The judge turned the photographs to the wall most of the time, but often, as when a reporter would interview him and question whether the length and expense of the trial were really worthwhile, he would turn the board around and, perhaps pointing to Jane King's maggot-eaten face or the burns on Lauren Wagner's hands, let the evidence speak eloquently for itself. It was disquieting to hear the most violent and obscene words in the language bandied about in the decorous setting of the courtroom by witnesses and lawyers alike: Angelo's fondness for the word "cunt," for instance, was much emphasized. But nothing quite equaled in its combination of repulsiveness and absurdity what Michael Nash would come to call Chaleff's Great Ant Experiment. That the defense planned to show that the sticky substance found on Lauren Wagner's breast with ants crawling through it could not have been left there by the ants or by either Angelo Buono or Kenneth Bianchi. A third-man theory was in the works.

Boren, Nash, and Tulleners spent the next few evenings studying what the laboratory had discovered about the sticky substance, and they read up furiously on ants. They also discussed ant behavior with an ant expert from the County Museum of Natural History. They guessed that the defense would try to show that the sticky substance was saliva and that it had come from a blood type B secretor. Both Angelo and Kenny were type AB nonsecretors. The conclusion would be drawn that Bianchi had acted with a third, unidentified man, not with Angelo.

But the prosecution team could not see how the defense could prove that the sticky substance was in fact saliva, the premise of their probable argument. It had not been proved to be saliva, and moreover, saliva was not sticky when it dried. Was it possible that the substance had been deposited by the ants or that the ants, feeding on the breast, manufactured or synthesized the substance in the process of, say, digestion? How and what did ants eat, and were they fastidious or sloppy in their dining habits? These and other aspects of ant lore Boren, Nash, and Tulleners found themselves spending hours researching, wondering whether the case had finally driven everyone into madness.

On July 7, Chaleff began elucidating his Great Ant Experiment, equipping himself with an elaborate chart and enlarged photographs of Lauren Wagner's breast with the ants marching over it. He summoned the Berkeley insect professor to the stand, eliciting credentials: Ph.D., chairman of the department, associate dean of the Graduate Division, published ninety papers of which two were about ants, expert on the carpenter ant, had testified before the Structural Pest Control Board of the State of California at least fifteen times. The professor testified that last May, at the request of the defense, he had gone to the Lauren Wagner body site on Cliff Drive and had dug up ants. (Judge George interrupted at this point to clarify that the digging had taken place only two months earlier, five and a half years after the murder.) The species was the Argentine invader ant, the professor said. No other kinds of ants were found at the spot. He and his graduate assistant had transported the ants back to Berkeley in a container, feeding them honey to keep them alive. At the university they took a hundred of the ants, separated their abdomens, put the heads and thoraxes in one maceration tube and the abdomens in another tube, and ground them up with a macerator.

The sticky substance on Lauren Wagner's breast had been found to contain amylase, an enzyme secreted with saliva and other substances, that indicated a blood type B secretor. The macerated Argentine invader ants had contained no amylase, the professor testified. Therefore, Chaleff concluded, the ants on Lauren Wagner's breast had not deposited the amylase, and the sticky substance, presumably saliva, had been left there by someone other than Buono or Bianchi who had a different blood type.

But Roger Boren, who cross-examined the professor, already knew that the ant experiment was as scientifically flawed as it was ludicrous. To begin with, the professor had gotten *the wrong ants!* The ants on the breast in the photograph had been positively identified as fire ants, not Argentine invader ants, by the expert at the county museum. Evidently the Argentine invaders, more successful than their human cousins had been against the British in the Malvinas/Falklands campaign, had driven out the fire ants since 1977. Furthermore, all ants secreted amylase, whether the Berkeley professor had found any or not. It was likely that the fire ants had been feeding on the nipple of the breast and had drooled amylase. The sticky substance itself could just as likely have been brought there from somewhere else by the ants, who might have enjoyed an earlier meal that day.

Roger Boren asked the professor whether the ants on the breast had been coming or going. The professor replied:

"Sometimes it's very difficult to tell whether they're coming or going because they are coming and going all along the trail." There was also, he said, the problem of "deviate" ants, who may be just wandering around aimlessly. But on the whole, ants are "coming and going and there is some going and they are bumping into each other."

It wasn't easy for Boren to keep a straight face at this. He asked the professor whether ants ate human flesh. The professor said that he had "never seen anything in the literature to indicate that they eat human flesh." Carpenter ants, he said, alluding to his specialty, fed off the anuses of aphids.

As any homicide detective knew, ants certainly did feed off human flesh: they did not crawl over corpses out of mere morbid curiosity. Boren now brought in his own expert, the entomologist from the County Museum, who established that the ants experimented with were the wrong ants, that ants do eat human flesh, that they secrete amylase, and that they drool.

"When ants with salivary glands eat something, let's say a fatty substance, for example, do they eat that just as other animals . . . might eat? They chew?"

"Yes. They have mandibles and they chew just like we do."

"Would their saliva be left in the same way, say, as a cat or a human might eat?"

"Yes. In proportion to their size, they probably drool at least as much as we do."

Boren was satisfied that he had demolished the ant experiment. It had been amusing in its way, but it had been useless and, as Boren pointed out to the jury, it had cost at least ten thousand dollars in experts' fees and wasted a great deal of court time.

Grogan, although he had laughed as much as anyone at the testimony and had offered facetiously to swear that he had drooled on the body himself, since he was a type B and could be the third man, resented the entire interlude for another reason. It was a grotesque example of how the victim in a murder trial became dehumanized, an object to be dissected and impersonally discussed. He was glad the Wagners had not been there to see their daughter's breast gone over with heartless objectivity: the press reported nothing of this phase of testimony. Grogan asked Boren and Nash to be sure, when they came to their closing arguments, to remind the jury that these had been young women and girls whose lives had been taken from them. Boren and Nash said that they certainly were planning to do just that.

It may be that the failure of the ant experiment discouraged Gerald Chaleff. It was not that his effectiveness was in any way diminished nor that Angelo's defense became to any degree less competent, but to court observers, including Boren and Nash, Chaleff did not seem quite his old hurrying, vigorous self during the last phase of the defense's presentation. Perhaps he was, understandably, running short of ideas. For whatever reason, when the defense called as one of the final witnesses Veronica Compton, Chaleff remained aloof, quiet, referring to the bloody-minded playwright as "her" [Mader's] witness and participating very little in the examination. What Mader planned to get from Veronica Compton the prosecutors could not imagine. Veronica had already offered to testify for the prosecution, but Boren and Nash had refused to talk to her, not wanting anything to do with her, disbelieving that she could do anything but harm to whoever used her as a witness.

Veronica, however, was anxious to get back onstage at any price, even against the advice of her lawyer, who told her that her chances for parole would be diminished by another court appearance reviving the ghoulish events for which she had been convicted. She took the stand looking ravishing and manic and, under Mader's guidance, unfolded a tale of an improbable conspiracy between Bianchi and herself to frame Angelo Buono—at the same time admitting in an aside that Kenny had always told her that Angelo was guilty. The logic and sequence of this conspiracy were impossible to follow, and her manner, that of a starlet courting recognition on a television talk show—coquettish, then dramatic, tearful, giggly, self-caressing—was far more arresting than her conspiracy story, though just as unconvincing.

Roger Boren and Michael Nash decided that the best way to handle her would be to reveal her character to the jury: there was no way to prove or disprove the supposed plot to frame Angelo. Nash cross-examined her. He was a small, wiry, intense man in his early thirties, with dark red hair and a full beard. He kept his emotions reined in, so that his cautiously phrased questions, coolly delivered, established a contrast between himself and the wildly histrionic Veronica, who looked as though at any moment she might burst into song or leap from the stand to perform an impressionistic modern dance or another strangling. Nash with studied casualness asked Veronica about her plans to open a mortuary with the Sunset Slayer, Douglas Clark, so that the two of them could enjoy sex with the dead bodies. His tone was that of someone asking about plans to buy a country cottage.

"Of course you were just kidding around?"

"No," Veronica replied warmly, "I think at that point that was something I was seriously considering."

"[Clark] also sent you photographs of decapitated bodies which pertained to this case?"

"No, he sent me one photograph of a decapitated body, a small Polaroid shot, and a picture of a girl from the head up—I mean, from the waist up. And she appeared to have been just pulled out of one of the freezers in the coroner's department."

"Did he send you these for your own sexual fantasies or was that in relation to his case?"

"It was in relation to his case and probably because I was into that gory type of thing."

Nash established that the original purpose of her relationship with Douglas Clark was to make Kenneth Bianchi jealous—although she insisted that Clark had come to mean something special to her—and he also got Veronica to admit that she was still angry with Bianchi. After all, she had tried to strangle someone for Kenny, was serving a life sentence for him, really, and what thanks had she gotten? His letters had become "so phony and just so—he was so careful that he didn't incriminate himself about anything. And I used to get so furious because it would be like, you know, he was writing to a friend in high school that he went out with one or two times, not someone that [and here tears started in her eyes] everything he and I had been through together. [The tears abruptly dried up.] And I was angry with him.''

Her anger at Bianchi was enough to cast sufficient doubt on her story of a conspiracy to convict Angelo Buono, but Nash could not imagine that any juror would find her a credible witness anyway. Veronica, after several days on the stand, retired again from the limelight, returning to her cell in Washington, where she said she was working on a series of biographies of great women.

The defense rested on August 2, but before a break to permit both sides to prepare final arguments, there was, over strong defense objections, one more jury-view.

The defense had introduced photographs depicting a view from the third floor of the Orange Grove apartments, the building that backed onto Angelo's property. A resident living in an apartment on the third floor had testified that she, an elderly woman, had stared out of her back window *day and night*, could see everything that went on at Angelo's, and was alert even to the slamming of a car door. She had never seen any bodies being carried out, she said, nor anything else of a suspicious nature. From the defense's photographs, it did indeed appear that the apartment window offered a clear view of Angelo's driveway, where, Bianchi had said, bodies had been placed in the trunks of cars. Although the defense's investigator clearly stated before the jury that the photographs had been taken from a fire escape, not from inside the woman's apartment, the prosecution feared that the jury was getting the impression that the pictures also represented what could be seen from inside, rather than from a different viewpoint on the fire escape. The photographs were part of a defense attempt to make the jury think that Bianchi had committed the murders somewhere other than at Angelo's house. If the woman had not witnessed foul play, the jury was supposed to believe, how could there have been any?

But when members of the jury actually stared down through that apartment window onto Angelo's old property, they found that they could see nothing of the driveway, only the awning until the driveway emptied out onto Colorado, as Roger Boren demonstrated by driving a car in and out. The witness would have had to have had X-ray vision to see through the awning.

The defense's photographs, as the jury-view demonstrated, presented a far different vista from that possible to view from inside the apartment; and the woman had not stated that she had spent her evenings sitting out on the fire escape. Boren and Nash felt confident that this extra jury-view had succeeded in rendering the photographs irrelevant.

On August 23, as he prepared to adjourn the court for two weeks, the judge attended to a matter of procedure which, in view of the seriousness of the charges against Angelo, seemed superfluous. As part of a formal discussion with the attorneys on the subject of exactly what the judge should include in his instructions to the jury, the judge was required to ask defense counsel whether there were any charges against the defendant which were less serious than first-degree murder.

"It seems ludicrous to inquire," Judge George said to Chaleff, "but I will ask you whether you have a request for any lesser [charges to be] included."

"You mean," Chaleff replied, "like second-degree murder?"

The judge could not resist sarcasm:

"Manslaughter?" he suggested, and, in an allusion to the body sites, "Littering?"

"I am sure," Chaleff began, the judge's dark humor eluding him for the moment, "ah, reading the law under necessarily included, ah, littering? Littering is . . ."

At this point Roger Boren whispered to him that the judge was being facetious, and Chaleff said that, no, he was not suggesting that the defense wished to include any crimes less serious than premeditated murder.

"That seems appropriate," the judge said.

Judge George took a holiday with his family on a ranch in Montana, but the case followed him there beyond the reach of telephones. In his absence Gerald

Chaleff filed a petition with the Court of Appeal, objecting to an order by Judge George directing the defense to turn over to the prosecution some material relating to certain witnesses. On August 18 the Court of Appeal ordered all further proceedings in the Hillside Stranglers trial suspended indefinitely, in order to determine the validity of a new statute authorizing such discovery.

Foreseeing a delay of weeks or even months in what had already become the longest criminal trial in the history of California, Roger Boren feared that the jury would at last disintegrate through weariness or illness or the simple necessities of going on with their lives. Boren quickly dropped the prosecution's demand for discovery and contacted the judge in Montana, and, by shortwave radio, the judge vacated his order, clearing the way for the Court of Appeal to permit the trial to continue.

TWENTY-FOUR

It was October 5, 1983, Angelo Buono's forty-ninth birthday. The attorneys were in the midst of their closing arguments to the jury. Angelo had changed a great deal outwardly since his last birthday. His hair was now mostly gray, his skin the color of frog spawn. He had lost his swagger, did not walk humbly, to be sure, but bent, head down, anger bottled up. For the second year in a row Katherine Mader brought him a birthday cake and asked bailiff Jerry Cunningham to take it to him in his cell. Court was not in session at the moment, and the jurors were waiting in the jury room, but Roger Boren and Michael Nash were there, and Paul Tulleners.

This time Jerry Cunningham refused to deliver the birthday cake. It had been his task to escort the prisoner to and from his cell every day. He had listened to every word of testimony—over thirteen million words by now—and had grown to loathe Angelo

Buono. I am not, he thought, going to take that son of a bitch another birthday cake.

"I won't do it, Kathy," Cunningham said. "Let's call it security reasons. How do I know you haven't put a file in there?"

Katherine Mader looked disappointed. She asked if anyone else would like a piece of cake. All refused.

"Gee," Mader said, "it seems such a shame. Angelo will have to celebrate his birthday without a cake."

"Look at it this way, Kathy," Paul Tulleners said. "There are ten girls who'll never celebrate a birthday again."

In her closing defense of Angelo, Katherine Mader was passionately contemporary. "There is a core of goodness in Mr. Buono," she told the jury, "a core of humanity." He did not chase women: they came after him. He was never, like Kenneth Bianchi, rejected by women. What if he did pimp and mistreat Sabra and Becky? No one said he was perfect. He had many, many friends, male and female, again unlike Bianchi.

And as for Angelo's "sexual preferences," there was nothing particularly unusual about them. They were very human. She had read a book recently, Katherine Mader said, about the sexual preferences of famous people, and it turned out that Angelo was no different from some eminent historical personages. The author of *Alice in Wonderland*, for instance, Lewis Carroll, had liked little girls. Warren Harding had carried on with a young girl while he was President. Ernest Hemingway had fallen in love with a young girl late in life. Charlie Chaplin liked young girls, too. And as for Angelo's fondness for anal sex, Mader said, "In some countries, I think somebody told me it is Greece, anal sex is just the way that the people have sexual relations there."

Continuing with her attempt to place Angelo into a relativistic sexual context, Mader proclaimed the fashionable conviction that "something is perverse only . . . if you want it to be perverse." Bondage, for example, was big business in Los Angeles. This was an enlightened society. A lot of people in L.A. were fond of bondage. There were boutiques with whips and chains, corsets, shackles, handcuffs. "This," she reassured the jury, "is not something that is so out of the ordinary, so perverse." Why, a magazine called "*Kinky Contacts* has a mailing list of fifteen thousand in the United States."

As Gerald Chaleff would elaborate, she said, the Hillside Stranglings had been committed by one man, Kenneth Bianchi, a strong, powerful individual and a pathological liar, who had, as Veronica Compton had testified, tried to frame Mr. Buono. The prosecution's tactic had been to try to "dirty up" Mr. Buono, who "hasn't done wrong" and whom women had always loved. Because he was on trial for mass murder, he was presumed to be guilty. Mr. Buono was in the same unfair position as Erin Fleming, the woman who had cared for Groucho Marx during his last years. Erin Fleming was now trying to defend herself from false allegations that she had been cruel to Groucho and had taken Groucho's money and—

Roger Boren broke in at this point to object that Groucho Marx and Erin Fleming had nothing to do with Angelo Buono. Judge George agreed, admonishing Mrs. Mader not to cite other pending cases during her closing argument.

Before finishing, Mader attacked Salerno and Grogan again, mocking the one as "honest Frank Salerno" and "honest Sergeant Salerno" and saying of Grogan: "Of all the detectives on the case, I really trust least the memory and the capacity for observation of Detective Grogan." She brought up his Boston accent once more by way of ridiculing his identification of Buono's accent as Brooklyn, and she reminded the jury that Grogan had wrongly stated that Buono had a space between his teeth. She added that both Salerno and Grogan had been unduly harsh with Mr. Buono when arresting him in 1979, saying to him, "Get out of that car. You're under arrest," as though Mr. Buono were presumed guilty. From the start, Mr.

Buono had been a victim of police embarrassment over their inability to catch the Strangler, Kenneth Bianchi. The media had promulgated the idea of two killers after "this elderly woman," Beulah Stofer, had said she had seen two men.

As she concluded, Mader started to say how "perceptive" she knew the jury members were and how well she knew they had been getting along with one another, but Boren quickly objected, and the judge warned her that "the law clearly does prohibit anything that might be construed as currying favor or complimenting the jurors."

It was after this that Bob Grogan got his chance to get back at Katherine Mader for ridiculing him in court. The two found themselves standing next to each other in the public elevator at the courthouse one afternoon. The elevator was crowded with a cross section of courthouse types—relatives of people on trial, witnesses, clerks, lawyers, the ethnic conglomeration that is downtown Los Angeles, so various in their costumes of T-shirts, starched Mexican frocks, electric-blue water-repellent leisure jackets, the odd bespectacled Ivy League legal hack in herringbone enduring woolly sweat to proclaim his distance from the multitude—and it would be a long ride down from the thirteenth floor, with many stops along the way. Grogan, dressed in his usual light-colored suit, white shirt, and tie, wanted to say something to Mader, but his tongue was thick with resentment. He stared up at the ceiling, composing vengeful phrases, but when Mader spoke to him he glared down at her. The uppermost wisps of her dark hair reached the level of his handkerchief pocket.

"Sergeant Grogan," Mader began, "I hope you're not mad at me for attacking you during the trial. You know I—I was just doing my professional job. Will you forgive me?" She smiled up at him.

Grogan took a deep breath. "Kathy," he boomed out, startling the other passengers, drawing out the "a" in her name with all the Boston he could muster, "I wouldn't forgive you on the day I die. You are an unethical cunt." He let this sink in. "And the reason I'm calling you a cunt is because I know you like it."

No one in the elevator spoke the rest of the way down.

Michael Nash's closing arguments had preceded Mader's—the order was Nash, Mader, Chaleff, Boren, with the prosecution allowed the last word because it had the burden of proof—and nothing she had said worried Nash, though all of it annoyed him. If the jury believed that kind of argument, Nash thought, then the whole case had been a waste of time anyway. He found it difficult to summarize and outline her arguments, as he was trying to do to help Roger Boren prepare for his final argument, because she seemed to leap from point to point, back and forth and back again, with no discernible logical sequence. Nothing could have been in greater contrast to Nash's own presentation, which in form had emulated the order of a mathematical proof but with emphasis, as he had promised Grogan, on the individual qualities of the ten murdered girls as they had been in life and as they were in death, beginning with a minutely detailed description of the bodies. He had hoped to rouse the jury from whatever moral slumber the two years of trial might have induced.

Nash had, with the aid of a chart, listed twelve separate categories of evidence that were damning to Angelo Buono: these were categories that corroborated Buono's guilt quite apart from the testimony of Kenneth Bianchi. The twelve included:

1. Similarity of victims and their mode of death.

2. Geographical links to Buono—abduction and dump sites.

3. Use of police ruse and police paraphernalia.

4. Other incidents (Catherine Lorre, Jan Sims/ Excalibur incident).

5. Evidence of two killers (bodies' placement, Angeles Crest, Beulah Stofer).

6. Buono's relationship with Bianchi.

7. Buono and sexual perversion.

8. Buono's admitted use of customers' cars (white Mustang).

9. Eyewitnesses: Stofer, Burke, Camden.

10. Prior contacts with two victims: Washington, Hudspeth.

11. Fiber evidence.

12. Consciousness of guilt (destroying badge, handcuffs; lying to Grogan and Finnigan on numerous points; denying owning wallet; lies to TV reporter; jailhouse confession).

In presenting all this evidence first, without referring at all to Bianchi's accusations, Nash was following a deliberate strategy, his way of getting around the problem of Bianchi's credibility. He was trying to get the jury to see that even without Bianchi's statements, there was plenty enough evidence to convict Buono. Add to it Bianchi, and you had an overwhelming case, far more than the "slight" corroborating evidence needed by law to substantiate the testimony of an accomplice. Nash now listed fourteen revelations by Bianchi to the police in Bellingham which had turned out to be accurate and which corroborated many of the other points of evidence. He then concluded by breaking down the evidence on each murder count separately and, finally, by dismissing Veronica Compton's testimony. She would have testified either way, he said, depending on who called her as a witness.

Gerald Chaleff's argument consisted mainly of an extended attack on Bianchi's credibility, the premise being that Kenny had acted alone and would not have implicated Angelo at all except by way of bargaining for his own life. For most of nine days Chaleff presented Bianchi as the master deceiver who had fooled everyone from girlfriends to doctors and lawyers. He tried to argue that to convict Angelo the jury would have to believe Bianchi "beyond a reasonable doubt," but when Boren objected to this line of reasoning, the judge cautioned Chaleff: "beyond a reasonable doubt" applied to the case as a whole, not to Bianchi's individual testimony, which was not subject to the same standard of credibility as was the actual issue of Buono's guilt. The jury could choose which parts of Bianchi's testimony to accept and which to reject. Chaleff continued with his theme to the end, however, finishing with this admonition: "If you say to yourself, 'I am going to convict Angelo Buono,' then you also say to yourself, 'Kenneth Bianchi has fooled me, too.' "

Roger Boren in his closing argument ridiculed the idea of Bianchi as such a successful liar, pointing out that people had seen through him all his life. He was the secondary character in the murders, really, acting as Angelo's mouthpiece. Boren said that a good word to describe the accumulated evidence was "propinquity," which could mean nearness in time or place and kinship or nearness of relationship. The evidence showed a propinquity between Bianchi and Buono and a propinquity among Angelo's house, the murders, and the body sites.

In the midst of Boren's argument, which took eleven days to deliver, the judge had to admonish Katherine Mader for distracting the jury by reacting visually and audibly to Boren's statements. One male juror made it known after the trial that she had been staring at him throughout the prosecution's final arguments—"eyeballing me" was his phrase—and that he had turned her away only by, he said, staring up her dress. At the bench Judge George told her:

"I don't appreciate sighs. Will you please learn to conduct yourself professionally? I mean that, Mrs. Mader. I have had enough of that. So while we are talking about it, I have not brought it up but I was advised by the bailiff and started looking: you sat there shaking your head when you didn't like things that Mr. Boren [was saying]. I do not appreciate sighs or laughter."

Later during Boren's argument, when Mader began clipping and filing her nails in front of the jury, the judge was inclined to admonish her again but let it pass.

Roger Boren spoke of the dead as though they had been his own daughters. As it happened he did have seven children—one fewer than Angelo—and he had come to take the case acutely to heart. A large, sandy, balding man, he was weary by the end, like everyone else, but he had developed a sense of mission about getting a conviction against Angelo. A Mormon, it was not at all difficult for Boren to believe that God was on his side in this instance. Although the jury knew nothing of Boren's personal life or beliefs, he was probably the ideal kind of man to have the last word against Angelo. His argument was precise and exhaustive, but his manner carried equal weight. He never showed his anger, never raised his voice, but his tone conveyed an unobtrusive moral indignation that complemented his logic. In the end he compared the evidence to a large house made of sturdy old brick. You could chip away at the brick, he said, but through it all the house still stood. And Angelo's house, though it had been demolished under suspicious circumstances, still stood at the center of the evidence: it had been the "epicenter" of that terrible earthquake of terror that had shaken the city six years before. He concluded:

> The defense at the end of their argument said to you that you could be fooled by Kenneth Bianchi.
>
> I will say to you that in the face of all this evidence . . . both in corroboration of Kenneth Bianchi and independent of Kenneth Bianchi—if in the face of reason Angelo Buono is not convicted of murder of these ten women, then you will have been fooled by Kenneth Bianchi.
>
> You will have been fooled by him and you will

also have been fooled by Angelo Buono over there
and by his two attorneys.

The evidence supports his guilt and a finding
of guilty beyond a reasonable doubt.

Good luck and thank you.

When Judge George, after hearing arguments from the attorneys, announced to them in conference that he had decided to sequester the jury until they reached a verdict, certain hostilities, if they did not explode, surfaced. Chaleff and Mader maintained that to sequester the jury now, after they had been free to go home to their families at night for two years, would act on them as pressure for an early or even a premature verdict. But the judge said that newspapers and television stations were planning to do stories on the jurors. He could not take the risk after all this time that some reporter would try to contact a juror during deliberations: that would cause a mistrial, and to have a mistrial now was unthinkable. The *Los Angeles Times* alone had assigned six reporters to do nothing but background checks on the jurors. During the trial itself reporters had tried to do stories about various jurors and had, fortunately, been discouraged. In the last month in Los Angeles there had been two mistrials because of improper approaches to jurors. Even a chance encounter in a grocery store, the judge said, could cause a mistrial. A friend could advise a juror what to do—that would be enough.

One of Gerald Chaleff's several talents as a criminal defense lawyer was to discover, after a trial was over, just such jury misconduct or jury tampering as the judge had described. Chaleff was not, therefore, at all happy with the decision to sequester, since it effectively closed off a last avenue of defense.

"I think personally," Chaleff told the judge, "I have stated throughout the record, that at times the court has done things which I felt were unfair to the defendant. And I think at this time that the only purpose of sequestration is to put pressure on the jury to arrive at some verdict, whatever that verdict may be."

Chaleff continued in this vein. The judge interrupted him:

"I think your remarks are very much out of line. . . . I resent the implication that somehow the court is again doing something as part of some grand conspiracy and is unfair to you and your client."

"No grand conspiracy," Chaleff said.

"I resent it and I think it is inappropriate and unprofessional."

The jurors were escorted to two hotels, the twelve actual jurors to one and the four remaining alternates to another. Each day the twelve would be taken back to the jury room in the courthouse to deliberate from nine to twelve o'clock and from one-thirty to four. Bailiffs were with them twenty-four hours a day. In the evenings, after dinner at the hotel or at a restaurant chosen by the bailiffs, the jurors could watch television as a group, with a bailiff switching off the set whenever anything about the trial was broadcast. They could read newspapers and magazines, but only after a bailiff had cut out stories about the trial.

Many stories about this jury had already appeared in Los Angeles publications and in the national newsmagazines. That the jurors had managed to associate together without apparent conflict throughout what had now become the longest criminal trial in the history of the United States, perhaps in the known history of the world, was itself news. They had given themselves a party on the first and second anniversaries of the proceedings, and they celebrated one another's birthdays. They were prisoners of a peculiar sort of modern war, hostages to justice, and like prisoners of other kinds of wars they tried to make the best of their predicament. If one or another of them had a particular hardship, Judge George would adjust the trial schedule, and once he had adjourned so that one juror, the Pan American flight attendant, could run in the New York Marathon. During most weeks they served four days, going to their regular jobs on Friday, which the attorneys needed to prepare witnesses and other aspects of the case. Two of the jurors encountered resentment from their civil service bosses at the amount of time lost from work—a conflict of democratic values—and the judge had conveyed warnings that to hinder a juror from his or her duty was to risk a citation for contempt of court.

But if the jurors had indeed endured with cheerful camaraderie two years of hardship and frequent tedium, acting as an exemplary enclave of ethnic and racial harmony, their ability to come to a unanimous decision on Angelo Buono was still in doubt. Judge George wondered whether the extent of the testimony —the transcript, prepared daily by two court reporters and three typists who usually worked until after eight in the evening, had now passed fifty thousand pages— and the complexity of considering ten separate murder counts would be overwhelming to twelve citizens who, however conscientious, were of varying degrees of intelligence and education. The judge's belief in the jury system was absolute, but no one could deny that this trial would put that system to the severest test imaginable. What would happen, moreover, if during the deliberations one of the jurors fell ill or even dropped dead? By law one of the alternates would have to be brought in, with deliberations begun again from the beginning. A hung jury was always a possibility: Bob Grogan in his gloomier moments thought it a probability. To end up with no verdict after all this time and money spent—the costs to the county alone already approached two million dollars—would render the trial one of the great fiascos of legal history.

Considering all of these factors, the judge determined that he would be prepared to have the jury announce a verdict on any single count as soon as agreement could be reached on it. The verdicts, in other words, could come in piecemeal. If the jurors could achieve unanimity on just one count, they could then return to deliberate on the remaining counts. The procedure was unusual but not unique, as Judge George was careful to establish. The defense, of course, strongly objected, sensing accurately that it would be far easier for the jury to agree on one count at a time than on ten together, but the judge stood his ground, citing legal precedents.

Jury deliberations began on Friday, October 21. Saturday passed with no verdict, Sunday was a day off. No one had expected a quick verdict, but when a week had gone by without a decision on any count, Boren and Nash began to feel some apprehension, Chaleff and Mader some optimism. By the end of the week the jury began asking to reexamine certain exhibits and to have certain passages of testimony read back to them: they were not permitted to read the transcript itself, which contained far more than they were allowed to know. When the jury began asking for material relevant to later counts—Cepeda and Johnson, Lauren Wagner—it was clear that they had been unable to agree on one of the strongest counts, number two, Judy Miller. Salerno wondered whether his discovery of the fiber and of Markust Camden would go for naught. Had the defense been successful in impugning Camden? How could the jury ignore the fiber? The defense had argued that Bianchi could have used material from the Trim Shop without Angelo's knowledge, but did anyone actually believe that? Could anyone possibly accept the defense's contention that because Bianchi had killed two women on his own in Bellingham he had killed ten on his own in Los Angeles? As the prosecution had countered, the depth of the ligature marks on the Bellingham girls' necks indicated that a different, more abrupt and furious kind of strangulation had taken place up there, the victims murdered quickly without even having been undressed first. And the carelessness with which the Bellingham bodies had been disposed of, the clues Bianchi had left, the ease with which he had been caught—all these factors pointed to the absence of Buono's cold-blooded meticulousness and to the absurdity of imagining that Bianchi could have achieved the Hillside murders on his own.

Grogan, who had little faith in juries anyway, grew anguished and sullen when it became clear that the jury had failed to agree on any of the first seven counts, had passed Kristina Weckler and were now considering Lauren Wagner. If they couldn't agree on Lauren, Grogan thought, with the fibers and Beulah Stofer to go on, Angelo would walk. The Wagners, Grogan knew, had already begun discussing whether they could or would kill Angelo themselves if he was acquitted.

Inside the jury room there had been trouble from the start of deliberations.

TWENTY-FIVE

It was a matter of ego. The jury's first act was to elect a foreman. They chose Edward McKay, a black man, but the vote was not unanimous. Another male juror, not black, who for the sake of his and his descendants' pride shall herein be known as Mr. Smith, had hoped to be elected, had for some reason assumed that he would be elected foreman. When he failed in this ambition, which in relation to the magnitude of the jury's task seemed to others trivial but was anything but trivial to Mr. Smith, he grew resentful, sullen, angry, and, at length, recalcitrant. He would show the others what a mistake they had made in rejecting him.

Ironically Mr. Smith had been one juror whom the prosecutors had been delighted to see impaneled two years before. He had been eager to serve and had brought with him letters from his employer describing him as a "solid citizen" type, and his answers during juror examination seemed to mark him as a law-and-order man. But, unknown to anyone but his fellow jurors, as the trial dragged on he had grown restless and irritable and was heard, as the trial adjourned for a weekend, to boast, "Well, you won't be seeing me on Monday! I've had enough! See you suckers sometime!" Now that his fellow jurors had shown their lack of appreciation for his leadership potential, he would get back at them. He had the power to foul things up, and he would express his resentment by using that power. To hell with the others. To hell with *The People* v. *Angelo Buono*.

Such egocentricity was no more rare among jurors than among the rest of humanity. Only the previous year a juror in a child pornography trial in Los Angeles had announced at the outset of deliberations that he hated the police, would rather die than give the police a victory, and would vote for acquittal no matter what the evidence and no matter what anyone else thought. He had pulled a chair into a corner of the jury room, opened a book, and refused to participate in the discussion. In the end the jury had deadlocked hopelessly at eleven to one. More common were problems with sequestered juries. Alliances often formed that had nothing to do with the case at hand. One Los Angeles bailiff told of how a woman juror had become attached to him and refused to cast her vote until he agreed to go to bed with her. When a jury was sequestered for more than a few days, romances often sprang up during the night at the hotel, affecting rational discussion the next morning. A bailiff would be asked to supply birth-control pills. Another Los Angeles bailiff recalled a romance between jurors that caused a divorce. Three days after the verdict had been reached, the lonely husband of a smitten juror telephoned to ask how much longer this trial was going to last. He missed his wife. The bailiff had to tell him that the jurors had been sent home days ago.

Mr. Smith dug in. On count number one his attitude was relatively inconspicuous. Five of the jurors were convinced from the start that Angelo was guilty on all ten counts, but only these five voted for conviction on Yolanda Washington, which everyone agreed was the count offering the least evidence implicating Buono: here there were only Bianchi's word and testimony about Yolanda's connection to the bad trick list. When the jury passed on to consider Judy Miller, Mr. Smith got the chance to throw around the weight of his pique.

After taking into consideration the Judy Miller fiber and Markust Camden's testimony, together with the proximity of Melinda Hooper's house to the body site, the jurors voted on this count eleven to one for conviction. It was then Tuesday, October 25. They had been out only four days and they were already that close to a verdict. But now Mr. Smith was showing the others where he stood. They were in his power. They would have to sit there indefinitely because of his not-guilty vote.

Others pressed him. Discussion grew angry. Two especially articulate female jurors let Mr. Smith know what they thought of him. Foreman McKay tried to calm things down. Finally, under the pressure of being a minority of one, Mr. Smith caved in. He would vote, reluctantly, he said, for conviction. The jury was at last unanimous, and Foreman McKay prepared to fill out the verdict form and signal that a verdict was ready.

But then everything fell apart again. A female juror sympathetic to Mr. Smith announced that she felt he had been pressured into his vote. She did not think it was right for him to vote against whatever he truly believed, so, as a gesture of kindness to Mr. Smith, she was changing her vote to not guilty. No one could fathom the motive of this bizarre act of self-abnegation. Could it be that she felt indebted to Mr. Smith because he had been the only one to give her a birthday present the night before? Was this a group therapy session?

Mr. Smith, rejoicing in an ally, quickly changed his vote to not guilty. Foreman McKay, perhaps trying to mollify hurt feelings now in the hope of future agreement, changed his vote to not guilty, too. In a matter of seconds the vote had gone from twelve to nothing to nine to three. Discussion passed on to Lissa Kastin.

And on: King, Cepeda, Johnson, Weckler. The tally varied on each, but Mr. Smith, emboldened by sympathy, voted for acquittal on all. He was like a stone sitting in the middle of a stream, troubling discussion whenever it approached a level flow. The articulate women grew shrill, then agreed between themselves to temper their ire. They could recognize disturbed male egos when they saw them, and they feared pushing other males over to Mr. Smith's side. The second Sunday arrived. Bailiffs escorted jurors on a tour of an arboretum, an excursion designed to keep them from going stir-crazy.

The courtroom meanwhile was for the most part deserted. Judge George worked on other matters in his chambers, where the model of Angelo's house and the pictures of the victims still rested, trying to distract himself while the jury debated in their room two doors down the hall. On one quiet day Roger Boren and Michael Nash encountered Katherine Mader in the building. They exchanged pleasantries and speculated about when the jury would finally report. Then Mader, chattering in her usual cheerful way, made a series of revelations that startled the prosecutors. Rather in the spirit of "I know something you don't know," she told them that the defense had known about several things that would have been highly useful to the prosecution, but it was too late for them now, so she would tell them.

The defense knew where the Excalibur was, she said, stored in a garage in Glendale. And it would have been useful had the prosecution known, as the defense did, that Angelo's mother had died of vaginal cancer, specifically. Didn't they think that this provided an extra deep psychological motive for Buono to kill women? And one more thing. The hairs on Lauren Wagner's hands, found mixed in with the fibers from the carpet and chair, were not cat hairs, as everyone had thought, but rabbit fur—another link to Angelo. Too bad Boren and Nash had missed all that! If the jury had been told about one or two of these things, they might not be taking so long.

Boren and Nash could not recall in their experience a defense attorney making revelations, confessions really, such as these after a trial—certainly not while the jury was still out, with a retrial always a

400

possibility should the deliberations result in a hung jury. Oh well, Nash observed, it was not the first bizarre incident in this case. It was fitting, in its way.

Halloween again, the sixth anniversary of the discovery of Judy Miller's body. Just after lunch a buzzer sounded three times in the courtroom: the signal that the jury had reached a verdict after nine days. The judge had his clerk inform the media that the jury's decision would be announced at four o'clock. Radio and television stations began broadcasting the impending event on the half-hour. By four the courtroom had filled with reporters, the detectives, and the few spectators who could get in. Absent were any friends or relatives of Angelo Buono: none had appeared at any time during the trial, except to testify. Grogan, standing near the back with the other detectives, was experiencing what Dr. Watkins might have diagnosed as dissociative reaction: he had invited friends over to his apartment that night to watch *Monday Night Football*, and he kept inquiring aloud of no one in particular, "I'm having all these people over. What am I going to do? What'll I do with all the Chinese food I ordered?"

"Ladies and gentlemen of the jury," Judge George began the ritual, "I am informed by the bailiff that you have arrived at a verdict. I would inquire of the foreman, Mr. McKay, whether this is in fact the case."

"Yes, we have."

McKay then handed the verdict form to Jerry Cunningham, who handed it to the judge, who opened the envelope and read the verdict silently. The judge seemed to take a long time to read the few words. It was like a moment of ominous quiet in the middle of a thunderstorm. He handed the form to the clerk, and she, hands shaking, read it out:

" 'We, the jury in the above-entitled action, find the defendant Angelo Buono guilty of the murder of Lauren Wagner in violation of Section 187, Penal Code, a felony, as charged in Count Eight of the Information and we further find it to be murder in the first degree. This 31st day of October, 1983. Edward McKay, Foreman.' "

"Ladies and gentlemen of the jury, is this your verdict, so say you one, so say you all?"

The jury intoned a collective yes.

Judge George, with characteristic scrupulosity, asked the clerk to poll the jurors individually, a step usually taken only at the request of the defense or prosecution. It was an act as final as the last out in the ninth inning; after it no juror could change his or her vote. Mr. Smith's turn to be polled came more than halfway through. Head low, he mumbled an affirmative like a man whose judgment was being extracted from him with forceps, as Michael Nash noted, wondering whether Mr. Smith was ill and thinking that he would have to ask the jurors after the trial whether something had been wrong with Smith. As Nash eventually learned, after nine days Smith had caved in, the evidence on the Lauren Wagner count being greater even than his pride.

The judge told the jury to resume their deliberations on the other counts in the morning, and he advised them not to be affected by the presence of so large a number of reporters and photographers in the courtroom. He had noticed, as had Boren and Nash, that the jury had registered shock at the mass of media people who had come to record the verdict: the jurors had looked rather like prisoners who, suddenly released from darkness, felt bombarded by harsh worldly light. Grogan too had noticed the jurors' seeming surprise at their public importance. Grogan figured that at least some of them had achieved, as he said, the courage of conviction only by ignoring the social impact of a unanimous verdict. "Sometimes a horse needs blinders to win," was the way Grogan phrased it.

Grogan's first act after the verdict was to rush to telephone the Wagners, who had moved to Oregon, and the Wecklers, who had moved to Hawaii. Salerno reached Cindy Hudspeth's mother, and the other detectives telephoned most of the remaining families. Sabra Hannan, who had heard the news on Phoenix television, managed to get through to Roger Boren at his courthouse office, telling him how much she appreciated the work he and Nash had done. Because of them, she said, she could now go on with her new life. She would never forget her ordeal, but she could at least have faith in people and the courts again.

Then the detectives gathered with Boren and Nash at the Code 7 bar. The name of the bar had never seemed so appropriate: it was a play on police code, 4 being the gravest emergency, an officer in distress, 7 a fantasy number suggesting that a situation so extreme had arisen that the only possible response was drink. At the Code 7 that afternoon the mood was less celebration than purgation. Boren and Nash felt less triumphant than relieved and bemused: since Van de Kamp's election as attorney general, the prosecutors had worked the case on their own without encouragement or advice from their superiors, as though as prosecutors they had not been tied to an official state office. Attorney General Van de Kamp had not telephoned to congratulate them, nor were they optimistic about their futures under his stewardship. By the second drink, emotions cracked open and the gruffest of all, Grogan, who was especially moved because the first guilty verdict had come on Lauren Wagner, began to weep. As he had said to a *Herald-Examiner* reporter, who put the quote on the front page the next day, "The man who killed Lauren Wagner deserves to die." Grogan strode around the bar hugging people, his emotions melting everyone's reserve, tears Niagarous. He grabbed Michael Nash, roaring, "My little imp, you did it, Mikey, you and Roger, my little imp!" Then Grogan proposed a toast to Judge George:

"To the greatest judge in the state. He's the real hero. He kept it going. Thank God for Judge George."

The next morning, after a long night at his apartment during which nobody talked football, Grogan awoke thinking about the judge again. He would have to do something to honor him. He decided to arrange a high-dollar lunch at the Tower Restaurant. He would pick the judge up in a police helicopter, landing on the roof of the courthouse, and fly him over to the restaurant, which was on the top floor of a skyscraper a few blocks away. Everyone would be there, Salerno and

Finnigan, Boren and Nash, Chief Gates; and Grogan's friend the maître d' would lay on snails and veal and the best wines. The lunch would take place after the rest of the verdicts and the sentencing were all over. Lying in bed, Grogan started composing the speech he would make. But all that would be weeks away. He wanted to do something for the judge right now. A compulsion seized Grogan.

He quickly showered and dressed and drove to the liquor store. It was ten in the morning. The judge would be in his chambers. Grogan bought a bottle of chilled Dom Pérignon and two wineglasses and raced to the courthouse, hiding the sack under his suitcoat. He hurried through the empty courtroom into the hallway behind and burst into chambers, pulling out the champagne and waving it aloft:

"Goddammit, Judge George"—pronounced *Geaaawge*—"let's have a drink! I got to congratulate you."

Grogan set the glasses down on the judge's desk and began struggling with the wire on the cork, slicing his finger.

The judge leaned far back in his chair, looking as though a wild animal had just broken in through the window. His mouth fell open, but he was unable to speak as Grogan twisted at the cork with bloody fingers, let it pop and hit the ceiling, and started pouring, drops of blood falling onto the desk.

"No, no, Sergeant Grogan," he finally got out. "Please, don't do that. Think, sergeant, think! This wouldn't be right. Really, I appreciate how you feel. I know what you've been through, but please take the champagne away. My God, the jury's just down the hall!"

At first Grogan looked hurt, but then, downing both glasses, he said he just wanted to let the judge know how he felt:

"Judge, it's a resurrection of faith."

And Grogan left, finishing off the champagne in the elevator.

On Thursday, November 3, the jury returned a verdict of not guilty on the Yolanda Washington charge, but immediately afterward they asked to see the Judy Miller fiber evidence again. Gerald Chaleff expressed satisfaction to the press at the not-guilty verdict, saying that it bespoke a jury capable of making up their own minds. On Friday, Katherine Mader waited around the courtroom wearing shorts and a T-shirt with the words "I'd rather be in Rochester" printed on the front. On Saturday, the jury brought in a guilty verdict on the Judy Miller count, which made Salerno feel that his efforts had not been wasted and that his integrity had been once again vindicated, and found "special circumstances" tying the Wagner and Miller killings together as multiple murders. This meant, under a recent California law passed in response to the public's outrage that killers such as Charles Manson and Robert Kennedy's assassin, Sirhan Sirhan, were eligible for parole, that Angelo Buono must be sentenced either to death or to a minimum sentence of life in prison without possibility of parole.

On Monday morning the jury returned guilty verdicts on Dolores Cepeda and Sonja Johnson, again with special circumstances applying. Dudley Varney became very emotional at this and had to leave the courtroom: the two girls had been his special charge. On this day Angelo, his pachydermal sensitivities finally affected, refused to put on civilian clothes and appeared in court wearing jailhouse blues, his tattoos revealed. He announced that he was firing Chaleff and Mader. That afternoon he was found guilty on the Kimberly Martin count. "I am no longer speaking to Mr. Chaleff," he told the judge.

Two days later the jury brought in guilty verdicts on Kristina Weckler, Lissa Kastin, and Jane King. That left only Cindy Hudspeth, but after another two days, Foreman McKay told the judge that the jury were "hopelessly deadlocked" on this last count, eleven to one. The judge instructed the jury to resume deliberations, but on the way to the hotel a woman juror suffered chest pains and was taken to the hospital. Deliberations would be suspended until she was released, or else an alternate would have to be brought in and discussion started over on the Hudspeth count.

Media commentators noted that her sudden illness would silence any remaining criticism of the judge's decision to have each verdict reported separately. At least nine counts were already safely delivered.

This time the stubborn juror was not Mr. Smith but his former female ally, the woman who had originally changed her vote on Judy Miller out of sympathy for Mr. Smith. The question here was whether the evidence showed that two men must have been involved in the dumping of Cindy Hudspeth's body miles up the Angeles Crest Highway, and everyone except this lone woman believed that there must have been two men, one following in a second car for the return trip. She argued that Kenneth Bianchi must have taken a bicycle along and had ridden down the mountain on it. To the other jurors' protests that no mention of any bicycle had ever entered anyone's mind before this, that not even the defense had suggested that Bianchi so much as owned a bicycle, she answered that she was entitled to her own opinion.

Finally on Monday, November 14, the ill juror recovered and the holdout changed her vote to guilty on Cindy Hudspeth. In all by this time the jury had noted seventy-two special circumstances tying the murders in together, so there was no question that the most lenient sentence Angelo could get would be life without parole.

All the time that the jury had been deliberating, Gerald Chaleff had not been idle. He continued to look for every possible means to argue for a mistrial, and he made two such motions, one saying that the jury had viewed a television movie prejudicial to their opinions of Angelo and the other almost metaphysical in concept. The movie was called *Chiefs*. It was set in a small Southern town, and the plot involved a corrupt white police officer, a noble black chief, and a murderous former chief, white, who killed young boys and buried them under his front yard. How seeing this movie could possibly have prejudiced the jury against Angelo neither the bailiff, who had permitted them to watch, nor the judge could imagine. The judge dismissed this motion, commenting that Chaleff's fears about the jury's exposure to this television program certainly stood in contrast to his earlier opposition to sequestering the jury.

The other motion came when the jury asked to see the big plasterboard with all the pictures of the victims on it. Chaleff argued that while the individual photographs had each been admitted to evidence, the board to which they were glued had not been formally admitted and that therefore the jury ought not to have been permitted to look at the pictures as they appeared lined up on the board. When Chaleff suggested that as a compromise the board be cut into ten separate strips, the judge said that this sort of discussion reminded him of medieval scholastic philosophy—he was about to ask Chaleff whether he thought that the board should be sliced up with William of Ockham's razor but decided the reference was too arcane—and directed that the board remain intact.

Judge George also denied Angelo's motion to represent himself during the penalty phase of the trial, when the jury would determine whether to fix the punishment at death. Angelo failed to appreciate all that Gerald Chaleff was trying to do for him, and the judge questioned Buono whether he was planning to ask for the death penalty so the state could "help you commit suicide."

"Ain't part of my motivation," Angelo replied.

"If you had a medical problem," the judge told him in a hearing held in chambers, "the way you did with your tooth, you wouldn't have pulled your tooth out. You sought a professional dentist. And when you are in a court of law, I think it is equally absurd to try to represent yourself, especially on the question of whether you should live or die." Had the judge known of the circumstances under which Angelo's tooth had been pulled, he might have chosen a different analogy. He concluded that "even a multimillionaire" could not have had a better defense and ruled that the danger of erroneously imposing a death sentence outweighed the minor infringement of Buono's asserted right to represent himself after two years in court.

But Angelo remained defiant. On November 16 he took the stand for the first and only time, as a gesture of contempt for the court, for the law, for ten dead women and their families. Chaleff asked him whether he would like to tell the jury what punishment he felt he should receive, and Angelo replied, regaining his old cockiness:

"My morals and constitutional rights has been broken."

The meaning was elusive but ultimately clear: he was thumbing his nose at everyone. The judge asked him to speak up.

"My morals and constitutional rights has been broken," Angelo repeated. "I ain't taking any procedure in this trial."

Chaleff asked him to clarify his response.

"I stand mute," Angelo said, and when the judge asked him if he had anything further to say, he added, "I am standing mute to anything further."

It was not easy, during the penalty phase, for the defense to find character witnesses for Angelo. His daughter Grace, loyal to the end, wanted to testify for him, but Angelo, talking to her alone in the judge's chambers ("a conjugal visit," Grogan called it), convinced her to keep silent. His sister Cecilia said that her brother could never commit murder, and a man who said he had known Angelo Buono for years assured the jury that Buono "wouldn't hurt a canary bird." He had once asked Angelo to do something illegal, and Angelo had refused.

"What did you ask him to do?" Michael Nash inquired.

"I asked him to burn down a guy's house. He wouldn't do it."

The witness was excused.

In the closing arguments of the penalty phase, each attorney had the opportunity to plead for mercy or for death to Buono. Michael Nash took this chance to remind the jurors once again of the victims. He knew that although the trial had now been a way of life for the jurors for years, some of them might well by now be confused about the particular identities of the murdered women; and the penalty phase itself had concentrated so much on Angelo as an individual that the individuality of the victims might have been forgotten, as Bob Grogan had all along feared. Such indeed was what so often happened in a highly publicized murder trial, the killers becoming celebrities, their victims nonentities, remembered as alive only by their families and friends. Certainly it would have been a rare member of the public who could have named anything unique about any of the women. Casual discussions with random citizens indicated that most people believed that all of the victims had been prostitutes: it was easier to accept the crimes that way; it was less threatening.

Nash succeeded in resurrecting the victims by pointing out that none of them would be able to enjoy any of the comforts which Angelo Buono would enjoy were the jury to spare his life. Because the jury had found Angelo not guilty of killing Yolanda Washington, Nash skipped over her and began with Judy Miller. He ignored that she had been a runaway and a prostitute, citing instead her simple girlish nature:

"Do you think [she] is ever going to watch television or listen to a stereo or a radio? Angelo Buono will be able to do that."

Recalling Lissa Kastin's ambitions to be a dancer and her concern with good health, Nash reminded the jury that she would never be able to go to a gym or work out. It was the same for Cindy Hudspeth, the hardworking girl who loved to dance, had won dancing contests, and was trying to earn some money to go to college by offering dance lessons. But if he were permitted to live, "Angelo Buono can get himself into tremendous physical shape if he wants to, and we all know that the better shape we are in physically, the better we feel mentally. He can do that. These girls cannot."

Nash then turned to the youngest victims:

"Dolores Cepeda and Sonja Johnson, two children that were killed by Angelo Buono and Kenneth Bianchi, never got the chance to grow up with their schoolmates. They will never get the chance to experience any of the joys of life, many of which Angelo Buono can continue to enjoy. I suppose he can make himself useful in some way. Maybe he can do some upholstery work in prison." Nash paused to let this sink in and then added, "Who the hell knows?

"Or he can worship whatever God he chooses. Jane King, she never got to pursue the career that she wanted to, an acting career. And she never got to follow up on her freedom of religious expression that she was involved in when she died." Jane King's Scientology may have seemed a strange, even a hokey sort of religion to some, but Michael Nash was pointing out that she had been deprived by Buono of one of the basic American freedoms, along with her life.

What would Buono do in prison? Nash wondered:

"Maybe he will take up sketching. Maybe he will sit in his cell and sketch people or maybe when he gets to go outside he will sketch whatever he sees. Who knows?

"Kristina Weckler—she is never going to get a chance to draw anything again.

"Angelo Buono can get visits from his family and friends. They came to testify for him in court. They care for him, so they said. Well, they can visit him in prison. They can send him birthday cards"—at this Nash shot a glance at Katherine Mader—"and they can wish him a merry Christmas. But Lauren Wagner or any of these other girls, are they going to get birthday cards, Christmas cards? Their families year after year have to live with the fact that their loved ones were killed in a cruel and inhuman and disgusting way by that man."

Continuing with his theme of family, Nash mentioned Angelo's children. How many were there, seven, eight, nine? However many there were, Buono had taken the right to have children away from Kimberly Martin. Yes, she had been a prostitute and she had had no children. But when she had pleaded for her life, she indicated that she was thinking about children: " 'I have a child. I have a baby. Don't kill me.'

"She is not going to have a child," Nash said. "She is not going to enjoy whatever the joys of childbirth and having children can bring to one. Angelo Buono has had the opportunity to do that."

Nash finished by telling the jury that they should say to Angelo Buono that "for what you've done, you deserve and should receive the ultimate penalty, death.''

But despite Nash's eloquence and Roger Boren's more strictly legal argument that the multiplicity of the murders called for a death sentence, the jury, which had taken nineteen days to determine Angelo's guilt, took only an hour of deliberation to spare his life. They fixed the punishment at life without parole. Perhaps they thought that it would be unfair to give Buono a stiffer sentence than Bianchi, but all of the jurors denied that this had been a major consideration. When it became evident that there was a division as to the proper penalty, those in favor of a death sentence gave in, unwilling to prolong deliberations that had already pushed them to the limit of their endurance. They had been sequestered for twenty-eight days in all.

Many people, under the mistaken impression that Judge George had the power to overrule the jury and impose the death penalty, wrote to the judge pleading with him to send Buono to the gas chamber. Among these were parents and friends of the victims. A friend of Lauren Wagner's wrote the judge that it would be a cheapening of the tragedy of Lauren's brief life and death not to make Buono pay with his life. Joe Wagner told the *Times* that he worried that God in His infinite mercy might let Buono into heaven. Ninety-four percent of the respondents to a *Herald-Examiner* poll said that they thought that Buono should be put to death.

Gerald Chaleff immediately began interviewing the jurors to see whether he could find grounds to impeach the verdicts. He believed, apparently, that he had found such grounds, since he did make a motion for a new trial, alleging various categories of juror prejudice and misconduct. In his opposition to the motion, Boren called Chaleff's charges trivial, and the judge agreed. They included the allegation that one juror had had a dream that Buono had been acquitted and had found the dream unpleasant: this was supposed to show prejudice. Far more alarming to Boren and Nash than Chaleff's motion was what they learned, in the process of interviewing the jurors, about the alternates. Three of the four alternates had been adamantly opposed to any guilty verdicts and were hostile toward the jurors for having convicted Buono. Two of the alternates had become so depressed as guilty verdicts had come in that they had refused to eat. If one or more of the jurors had fallen ill during deliberations or before, and one or more of the alternates had become a juror, Angelo Buono would probably never have been convicted.

The judge had no power to increase the punishment on which the jury had decided. He was able to make known his personal feelings, however, on January 9, 1984, when it was his final task in the trial to pronounce formal sentence on Buono and to determine whether or not Kenneth Bianchi had violated his plea-bargain agreement. The judge could have dealt with the two cousins at different court sessions, but he decided to bring them together once more, to make them stand together before the bench as a symmetrical denouement before physically separating them forever.

He ordered Bianchi returned to Washington, saying that far from cooperating he had done everything in his power to sabotage the case against Buono. Whether Bianchi had gone, as the judge said, "into his nut act" out of friendship for Buono or out of fear, "I don't know and I don't care," but his performance in the case had been "laughable." When he had told the truth at all it was perhaps "out of some hope that he could wheedle his way through and claim that due to mental problems he had not violated his plea bargain." Neither Buono nor Bianchi should "ever see the outside of prison walls."

As for Angelo Buono, the judge regretted not being able to sentence him to death:

> The ultimate justification for any punishment is that it is the emphatic denunciation by the community of a crime, and there are some murders which demand the most emphatic denunciation of all, namely the death penalty.
>
> In view of the jury's mercy in this verdict . . .

412

I am, of course, without authority to impose any greater punishment.

However . . . I would not have the slightest reluctance to impose the death penalty in this case were it within my power to do so. If ever there was a case where the death penalty is appropriate, this is that case . . . Angelo Buono and Kenneth Bianchi slowly squeezed out of their victims their last breath of air and their promise of a future life. And all for what?

The momentary sadistic thrill of enjoying a brief perverted sexual satisfaction and the venting of their hatred for women.

The judge then reflected that those states in the union which permit execution now employ a variety of means:

And ironically, although these two defendants utilized almost every form of legalized execution against their victims, the defendants have escaped any form of capital punishment.

Angelo Buono and Kenneth Bianchi subjected various of their murder victims to the administration of lethal gas, electrocution, strangulation by rope, and lethal hypodermic injection. Yet the two defendants are destined to spend their lives in prison, housed, fed and clothed at taxpayer expense, better cared for than some of the destitute law-abiding members of our community.

Judge George concluded by stating that he did not believe that life imprisonment for these "evil spirits" would do either them or society any good. Looking down at the cousins as they stood before him—Angelo glaring as if he were trying to put a curse on the judge, Kenny shaking his head as if to say yet again, "Why is this happening to me?"—the judge gave his final reason for believing that only death ought to have been their punishment:

I am sure, Mr. Buono and Mr. Bianchi, that you will both probably only get your thrills reliving over and over again the torturing and murdering of your victims, being incapable, as I believe you to be, of ever feeling any remorse.

In subsequent weeks, now that he was able to talk about the trial, Judge George was often asked about the harshness of his final words to Buono and Bianchi. Had he not gone too far? Did not his saying that he would have preferred to sentence them to death represent a backward step in the progress of civilization away from violence? The judge would always reply that he failed to understand how any intelligent person could imagine that civilization had progressed away from violence, when we were living in the most violent century in the history of mankind. Tyranny of any kind, whether instigated by Adolf Hitler and Josef Stalin or Angelo Buono and Kenneth Bianchi, could be countered only by superior force and will: this would always be true, and societies which lost their will to defend themselves with appropriate force had already lost their will to peace. A society that acquiesced to its criminals had made itself into a battered wife. Something of the kind had happened in America. Those who opposed the death penalty for men like Buono and Bianchi reminded him, he said, of Neville Chamberlain, whose personal weakness had helped to demoralize all of Europe and in the name of peace had sacrificed millions of lives. Society must proclaim by its acts its respect for the lives of its citizens.

It was the same with the argument for the insanity of all or most murderers. Surely men who committed such acts as Buono and Bianchi had committed were insane? Surely no rational person could do what they had done? Surely a sane man was a good man? The judge was asked such questions dozens of times after the trial. His reply—when he made it he was invariably thinking of death camps and gulags and lynchings and child molestations and sectarian assassinations as well as of Buono and Bianchi—was always the same:

"Why should we call someone insane simply because he or she chooses not to conform to our standards of civilized behavior?''

These conversations, which usually took place at cocktail parties among people who had never been in contact with violent criminals, always depressed the judge, because he doubted that he could convince anyone by reasonable argument. The temper of the times was wrong. Having a daughter strangled to death would change their minds, but reading about such acts in the newspapers never did: it was too easy for people to abstract the crimes and put them at a distance from themselves, even when, as during the Hillside Stranglings, an entire city experienced terror.

Maybe, the judge worried, the city would even have found a way to accept the dismissal of murder charges against Angelo Buono. Could people have told themselves that freeing Buono because of a supposed lack of evidence was all for the best? After all, this was Hollywood, where happy endings always worked.

Such cynical speculations faded as the tedium, horror, and frequent absurdities of the trial receded from the judge's mind. Justice had been done. The common sense of the jurors had prevailed over legal and psychiatric sophistry, over indifference and moral muddle. The dead would not awaken, but in the end the trial had provided that elusive and necessary thing, a sense of redemption.

EPILOGUE

A story such as this has no proper ending. Not only the victims but everyone connected with the Hillside Stranglers case was permanently affected by it, most obviously the members of the victims' families. After the trial a newspaper reporter had the poor taste to send each of the victims' parents a letter asking what they thought about the verdict and the sentencing and how they were coping with their lives six years after their child's murder. Even the parent who had attempted suicide received such a letter. Judy Miller's mother, by then living alone with her two surviving children in a trailer, replied feebly and sadly; Lauren Wagner's parents, who had moved to Oregon to try to start a new life, talked openly of their grief; but most of the parents had little or nothing to say. When Kristina Weckler's parents failed to reply, the reporter found out where they were living in Hawaii and telephoned Charles Weckler in the middle of the night to try to pry a statement from him. He was furious; he slammed down the receiver and then telephoned Bob Grogan to complain of this latest indignity.

Relations between Attorney General John Van de Kamp and his prosecutors Michael Nash and Roger Boren and his special investigator Paul Tulleners remained uneasy. When an emissary from the Attorney General's Office came to them and suggested that they release a public statement saying that Angelo Buono had been convicted because of new evidence that had surfaced during the course of the trial, long after Roger Kelly and Van de Kamp's motion to drop murder charges, Boren and Nash refused. They insisted that all the important evidence, including the Lauren Wagner fibers, had been known from the beginning. And Paul Tulleners said that if he was forced to join in such a statement, he would turn in his badge.

Fortunately for Boren, Governor Deukmejian soon appointed him to a municipal judgeship. Michael Nash meanwhile found himself prosecuting the death-penalty conviction of Douglas Clark, Veronica Compton's former fiancé, on appeal. Clark began sending Nash taunting letters, asking him why he was bothering to try to resist the appeal when he knew that the California Supreme Court was likely to grant it on the basis of some technicality, ordering a new trial.

In November 1984, Michael Nash married a woman to whom he had been engaged since the start of the Buono trial: he had not thought the marriage would prosper if begun while he was obsessively involved in such depressing work. Judge Boren performed the ceremony. In February 1985 Governor Deukmejian appointed Nash to a municipal judgeship and in April elevated Boren to the superior court branch.

Gerald Chaleff, his reputation enhanced by Buono's not having received the death penalty, continued his work as a prominent criminal lawyer, but he told a reporter that he would be reluctant to accept another multiple murderer as a client. He had not been surprised, he said, that the jury had convicted Buono on nine of ten counts, because most accused multiple murderers got convicted. Katherine Mader told the same reporter that "nothing seems that interesting" after the Buono trial. She was writing a book, she said, about famous Los Angeles murder trials.

Judge Ronald George was ready for a change from the criminal law after nearly twenty years' involvement in it. He switched to hearing civil cases in 1985. Late in 1984 the California Supreme Court ordered that its hypnosis ruling was to be applied retroactively. Had Judge George not had the foresight to exclude hypnotized witnesses and the wisdom to declare that Bianchi had been faking being hypnotized, the ruling would have thrown out Buono's conviction, and he would have had to have been tried all over again. To Judge George the thought was unbearable.

Angelo Buono survived his first year in Folsom Prison. Fearing death, he refused to leave his windowless cell to exercise, sitting surrounded by heaps of the hundreds of volumes of his trial's transcript, which he attempted to read.

Kenneth Bianchi found Walla Walla Prison in Washington much to his disliking. He was kept away from other prisoners, but he legally changed his name to Anthony D'Amato ("of the beloved" in Italian) and then to Nicholas Fontana, as if that would prevent the vengeful from knowing that he was one of the Hillside Stranglers. He then began petitioning for transfer to another prison and came within an ace yet again of fooling the system. Washington officials were prepared to grant his request, and arrangements were made to transfer him to Reno, Nevada, where his adoptive mother planned to move so that she could be near him and visit him daily. His bags were already packed when Paul Tulleners got wind of this scheme and put a stop to it.

Of the principal investigators, Frank Salerno, Bill Williams, and Bob Grogan continued in homicide; Dudley Varney and Pete Finnigan retired. Grogan also launched a second career for himself in Hollywood, forming his own production company, which he called Sunny, after his boat.

It happened this way. Grogan's first case after the Stranglers was the murder of a Hollywood film executive. Grogan felt sure that the victim's son, angered by a change in his father's will, had committed the murder. The surviving executives of the movie company were about to turn over assets to the son, but Grogan tipped them off: "I wouldn't do that," Grogan told them. "You wouldn't want the kid running your outfit from jail." So grateful were the executives to the sergeant—he had saved them millions—that they wanted to do something for him. They gave him an office at the studio and offered him a trip to Europe. He now spent his free time dreaming up movie and television projects. The new trial, however, ended in a hung jury, ten to two, after six months in court.

As for the trip to Europe, Grogan chose to visit the land of his fathers. He spent a month in Ireland, much of it at a pub in Tipperary called O'Looney's that was owned by an ex-policeman, cooling down from the Stranglers and sorting out his life, which had been so messed up by his six-year obsession. When he returned, he moved out of his apartment in Glendale, finally breaking connections to the Hillside murders. He drank less. He was almost enjoying life again.

Los Angeles—Tulsa—Dublin, 1981–1985

SOURCES AND ACKNOWLEDGMENTS

During many months from 1981 through January 1984, I observed court proceedings in the trial of *The People* v. *Angelo Buono*. I was also able to examine police reports on Buono and on Kenneth Bianchi and to read the 57,079-page transcript of the trial. I studied as well the nearly two thousand exhibits, including audio tapes and videotapes and written transcripts of police, psychiatrists', and others' interviews with Buono and Bianchi and some three hundred witnesses. *Two of a Kind* derives primarily from these official public records and from my own interviews with people concerned with the case.

Judge Ronald M. George and Sergeant Bob Grogan were of great help to me. Judge George, whom I have known since 1954, when we were high school students together, and who was my roommate at Princeton for four years, would not discuss Angelo Buono's trial with me until it was finished; but his insistence that the case be tried was what first alerted and attracted me to the subject.

My regard for Sergeant Grogan should be obvious in these pages. I hope I have, as it were, done him justice. In a way I like to think that the portrait of him here is also an oblique tribute to my late grandfather, Daniel J. O'Brien, who was chief of police in San Francisco during the 1920s and who, though less profane, was as admirable a cop as Grogan. The many days and nights I spent with Grogan discussing the Hillside Stranglers will remain with me as bright spots of time along a continuum that was often gloomy.

I am grateful to Patrick MacEntee, S.C., chairman of the Bar Council of the Republic of Ireland, for sharing with me his architectonic perception of the criminal mind and his informed speculations about Buono and Bianchi. His insights, many of which I have borrowed, gave me confidence.

Frank Salerno and Pete Finnigan allowed me to accompany them on visits to Angeles Crest and other stations and provided me with persuasive documents. They were in every way courteous and helpful.

Roger Boren and Michael Nash gave me important truths, helped me to verify facts, and inspired me by their commitment to a just cause.

To Paul Tulleners I must express special gratitude. Without access to his files on the early life of Angelo Buono, I could not have known much of the story of Buono's childhood and adolescence, nor would many of the details of Buono's marriages have been known to me.

Because of the restrictions imposed by the attorney-client privilege, I could not interview Gerald Chaleff or Katherine Mader about their client. I am sure they know a great deal more than they can tell.

For ease of access to documents and for other courtesies I am grateful to Lu Gonzalez, Jerry Cunningham, Pete Martinez, Judy Leff, Christopher M. George, Art Acevedo, Frank Fuller, Charline Howell, and Christine Olson.

Writing a book such as this demands the help, practical and intangible, of family and friends.

Molly O'Brien added vivid details and encouragement, and her reaction to the Bianchi psychiatric tapes helped to fashion my treatment of that peculiar episode. She also accompanied and assisted me during the final research and composition.

Suzanne Beesley gave me emotional and intellectual assistance in countless ways. Her insights into human nature, including the author's, and her unthinking kindnesses will not be forgotten.

My University of Tulsa colleagues Donald Hayden, Gordon Taylor, and Joseph Kestner helped in numerous ways. Without the support of J. Paschal Twyman, president of the university, and Thomas F. Staley, provost, I could not have considered taking on a project that required so much time away. I must thank also Dr. Corinna del Greco Lobner, professor of Italian, for deciphering and interpreting the term *mi numi* as it appeared in garbled form in police interviews and in Bianchi's Bellingham diary; and Priscilla Diaz-Dorr, my graduate student, who enlightened me on the subject of the religion of the Numa as she discovered it in Walter Pater's *Marius the Epicurean*.

Michaela Hamilton, editorial director of NAL Books, has had much to do with the appearance of this book in its present form. She anticipated errors of proportion from the start and was meticulous in her attention to detail and nuance, without once resorting to nit-picking. She was sensitive to the author's intentions and proved herself adept at the diplomatic arts. The book has benefited immeasurably from her care, commitment, and literary sophistication.

I am fortunate in having as a literary agent a fiercely loyal friend, Erica Spellman, whose role in the writing and in attendant matters has been exemplary.

D. O'B.

DARCY O'BRIEN won the Ernest Hemingway Award for Best First Novel for *A Way of Life, Like Any Other*. He has written other fiction and nonfiction books, as well as articles for *The New York Times Magazine* and *New York*. He currently is Graduate Professor of English at the University of Tulsa.